DirectX®, RDX, RSX, and MMX™ Technology

DirectX®, RDX, RSX, AND MMX™ Technology

A Jumpstart Guide to High Performance APIs

Rohan Coelho
and
Maher Hawash

ADDISON-WESLEY DEVELOPERS PRESS
An imprint of Addison Wesley Longman, Inc.

Reading, Massachusetts • Harlow, England • Menlo Park, California
Berkeley, California • Don Mills, Ontario • Sydney
Bonn • Amsterdam • Tokyo • Mexico City

Many of the designations used by manufacturers and sellers to distinguish their products are claimed as trademarks. Where those designations appear in this book, and Addison-Wesley was aware of a trademark claim, the designations have been printed in initial capital letters or all capital letters.

Library of Congress Cataloging-in-Publication Data

Coelho, Rohan.
    DirectX®, RDX, RSX, and MMX™ technology : a jumpstart guide to high performance APIs / Rohan Coelho and Maher Hawash.
        p.   cm.
    Includes index.
    ISBN 0-201-30944-0
    1. Multimedia systems.   2. DirectX.   3. Intel Realistic display mixer.   4. RSX (CompComputer file : Digital Equipment Corporation) 5. MMX technology.   I. Hawash, Maher.   II. Title.
    QA76.575.C64   1998
    006.7'768--dc21   97-33102
                                                                            CIP

Sponsoring Editor: Mary Treseler
Project Manager: John Fuller
Cover design: Chris Norum
Text design: Vicki Hochstedler
Set in 11-point Minion by Octal Publishing

1 2 3 4 5 6 7 8 9—MA—0100999897
First printing, December 1997

Addison-Wesley books are available for bulk purchases by corporations, institutions, and other organizations. For more information please contact the Corporate, Government, and Special Sales Department at (800) 238-9682.

Find us on the World-Wide Web at:
http://www.awl.com

To my parents, Mofeed and Sameeha;
To my wife Lisa, my son Jared, and baby on its way;
To my nephew Ahmad and the rest of my family;
I dedicate this book. —Maher

To my immediate family: Dad, Mom, Gail, Carmen, and Sarah;
To my extended family, blood relatives and others;
And to several others, significant but unnamed;
Thanks for touching my life. —Rohan

Special thanks to
Emilie Lengel and Gerald Holzhammer
For believing in us.

Contents

PART III   MAKING THE MEDIA MIX   67

Preface

Why Read This Book?

There's Lots of New Stuff to Learn

In the past few years, the pace of technology growth has been exhilarating. Microsoft launched Windows 95. Intel debuted the Pentium, Pentium Pro, and MMX technology processors. Netscape burst the Internet pipe with a new class of applications and architectures. These companies and others paraded out a slew of new multimedia architectures. And you've never before felt so lost in space.

Maybe you're familiar with programming for Windows 95 and now want to deliver Windows 95 multimedia applications, and you're wondering where to start. Or maybe you've programmed multimedia for DOS/Windows 3.1, and now you're scrambling to learn Windows 95, learn the new computing environment, and then learn to deliver high-performance multimedia in this environment.

Well, several new architectures have been introduced to help you deliver high-performance multimedia under Windows 9x,[1] such as DirectDraw

---

1. Windows 9x stands for both Windows 95 and the upcoming Windows 98.

DirectSound*, Direct3D*, DirectShow*, RealMedia*, Realistic Sound Experience (3D RSX), Realistic Display Mixer (RDX), and so forth. But now you've got to learn these new architectures, and you've got this steep learning curve on your hands.

On the hardware frontier, the power of personal computers has increased at a dramatic pace—both in processor and peripheral power. The Pentium, Pentium Pro, Pentium II, and MMX technology processors, the accelerated graphics port (AGP) bus, and the various graphics hardware accelerators are recent hardware advancements that affect multimedia performance. Surely your applications would sizzle if you mastered these advancements. But mastering these advancements only increases the learning curve.

And, of course, the Internet adds yet another dimension to the puzzle. The new programming space includes Internet browsers and their plug-ins; programming languages such as Java, HTML, and VRML; Internet architectures such as ActiveX, RealMedia, and a huge list of applications such as Internet Phones and Chat Worlds. More to learn, more to wade through, more time to spend.

Lightening the Learning Burden

As multimedia developers, we constantly investigate, evaluate, or learn these new technologies. Our typical sources are technical reference manuals and sample applications. With so many recent products, we've got a huge quantity of material to wade through. When time is precious, as it invariably is, just getting started can be an overwhelming problem. Spending time getting started eats away from time allocated for finishing touches and product testing. And overall quality suffers when we've spent too much time just getting up to speed.

Wouldn't it be nice if there were a simple way to *just get started?* To grasp the bare essentials and leave the esoteric stuff for on-the-job training (those need-to-know moments)? To steer clear of performance pitfalls? Well, do we have a deal for you. We, the authors, have been involved in various aspects of multimedia development on the PC for five long years. Through our employment at Intel and through our relationships with Microsoft and other key players, we've had the privilege to influence the architectures of processors, peripherals, platforms, and software components toward the betterment of multimedia on the PC. During that time, we've done our fair share of defining, reviewing, and implementing numerous multimedia architectures, both software and hardware.

With this book, we hope to use our internal vantage point to give you a jump start to high-performance multimedia development for Windows 9x. We'd like to help you cut to the chase; focus on the bare necessities; stick to the essentials; and jump-start a variety of offerings. What's more, we're hoping to take you a step beyond getting started—to extracting performance.

We hope to provide you with a quick start to a wide spectrum of multimedia advancements for Windows 9x. We hope to answer questions like *Where do I start? What do I really need? How little can I get away with? How do I get it to run faster?*

A dose of caution: there's more than one way to get jump-started and more than one way to extract performance. We'll share our experiences with you, show you "a" way. We hope you'll come away with some tricks, of course, but more important, we hope you'll come away with a thought process—an approach.

We've tried to maintain a light flavor. We hope you'll have some fun along the way.

INTRODUCTION

Organization and Conventions

WHY READ THIS CHAPTER?

Since we're talking about the organization of the chapters, it's only appropriate to note that all chapters start with the question above: "Why Read This Chapter?" Our purpose is to present you with a summary of what we intend to cover in the chapter. We recommend that you read the segment to see if what you will get is what you want.

This chapter shows you how we arranged the book, to help you get the most benefit out of it. In the following pages, we

- describe who we wrote the book for,
- show you how we present our material,
- outline the organization of the book, providing overviews of each chapter,
- show some conventions we use to highlight information, and
- list the tools that you'll need when working with the companion CD.

I.1 About the Book

When we started to outline the material for this book, we quickly recognized that we would be covering a lot of ground. We struggled with what to present and what to ignore. We asked ourselves, "What kind of a book would we have wanted when we started doing whatever we started?"

I.1.1 Where We're Coming From

Because of our roles at Intel, we've had the good fortune to work on Windows multimedia architectures right from their infancy. In our work we applied both our architectural and our CPU optimization skills, and we used them across a wide range of multimedia avenues.

Of late, we'd been called upon to help a number of software companies with their multimedia problems. Intel funded and continues to fund these software activities, in the interest of encouraging overall PC sales by promoting new uses for the PC; and in the interest of boosting demand for newer, higher-performance PCs, by promoting CPU-intensive applications.

To address multimedia performance issues, we would typically optimize critical sections of the assembly code. However, when the performance bottlenecks are at the system level, we would have to demonstrate the use of (or even develop) appropriate Windows multimedia architectures.

And this led us to think that we could write a book to offer the same thing to a larger audience, to help others get started on a number of different multimedia architectures, to help others extract a lot of performance from the PC multimedia architecture.

I.1.2 Where We're Not Venturing

We can't claim to be *The Experts* in PC multimedia. The field is too big, and there are too many excellent software engineers out there for us to presume such a status. Nonetheless we feel we've been down some paths before and can share that experience with you, to get you started.

We didn't want to delve deeply into the gory details of any single architecture; that's what the reference documents are for. Instead, we decided it would be better to get you started with the architectures, and we're sure that your application needs will steer your further learning.

On the flip side, with the breadth of architectures we wanted to cover, we knew we would have to skip basic concepts to do the architectures any justice. So we've presumed some prerequisite knowledge and targeted the book to reasonably experienced programmers. We also narrowed our selections to focus on recent/emerging advancements so as to avoid merely putting a fresh spin on previously published information.

I.1.3   Who Should Read This Book

OK, so who did we think we could help? It was clear to us that our readers would

- already know how to program under Windows,
- understand multimedia concepts and terminology,
- be familiar with programming with C, C++, and for some sections, even assembly language (Intel Architecture), and
- appreciate, or even prefer, a hands-on learning approach (like to learn by being pointed in the right direction and then be free to find their own way around).

I.2 Chapter Organization

Armed with a clearer picture of our identity and our readers, we were able to outline our approach. On the one hand, we wanted to get our readers started quickly on the latest multimedia architectures. On the other hand, we wanted to show them how to extract high performance on Intel Architecture multimedia PCs. Ergo, *we have decided to provide simple samples!*

We have partitioned the book into six major parts. Each part focuses on a specific area of multimedia, with its chapters sequentially building on each other. We specifically tried to use the same or similar samples within each part. There are a total of twenty-three chapters in the book. We concentrated on making each chapter brief, less than thirty pages each, so that wordiness wouldn't dilute our subject matter. We deliberately chose the compact format to improve retention (make it less likely for readers to forget what was said before).

Let's take a closer look at what we cover in each of the parts/chapters.

Part I: Surveying Multimedia

Chapter 1 Overview of Media on the PC. This chapter gives just a small overview of current multimedia architectures on the PC. We give a brief pass on the Graphics Device Interface (GDI), DirectDraw, DirectSound, Direct3D, DirectShow, Realistic Display Mixer (RDX), and Realistic Sound Experience (3D RSX).

Chapter 2 Processor Architecture Overview. Here we approach media from a hardware perspective. We give a high-level architectural overview of the Pentium, Pentium Pro, the Pentium processor with MMX technology, and the Pentium II processors. We also touch on the system point of view and why it is essential to optimize for the system as well as for the processor.

Part II: Sprites, Backgrounds, and Primary Surfaces

Chapter 3 Simple Sprites in GDI. This chapter introduces the concept of transparent sprites and backgrounds under Windows. We show you how to draw backgrounds and transparent sprites using GDI.

Chapter 4 Sprites with DirectDraw Primary Surfaces. We take our sprite to the next level with a DirectDraw Primary surface. We show you how to create a Primary surface to get direct access to the display screen. We then rewrite the sprite to be drawn onto a Primary surface and compare its performance with the GDI implementation.

Chapter 5 Hardware Acceleration via DirectDraw. Here we show you how to implement our beloved sprite using hardware Bltters on graphics adapters. We then show you how to use Page Flipping hardware to minimize the cost of double-buffering incurred in the Primary surface implementation. Finally, we compare the performance gain of this implementation with the Primary surface implementation.

Chapter 6 RDX: High-Performance Mixing with a High-Level API. Realistic Display Mixer (RDX) provides a high-level mixing interface without sacrificing performance. RDX uses hardware acceleration if available; otherwise it uses assembly code tuned for various processor flavors. We show you how to implement sprites with RDX, and we compare the performance of this implementation to GDI and DirectDraw implementations.

Part III: Making the Media Mix

Chapter 7 Video under Windows. This chapter introduces current multimedia architectures under Windows, including Multimedia Command Interface (MCI), Video for Windows (VFW), QuickTime for Windows (QTW), and ActiveMovie.

Chapter 8 DirectShow Filters. We start with an overview of the DirectShow filter graph architecture and show you how to use the graph editor to manipulate filters. We then show you how to build source, transform, and rendering filters, and explain how the connection mechanism works. Next we discuss filter registration, custom interfaces, and filter property pages.

Chapter 9 DirectShow Applications. Building on the previous chapter, we show you how to use filters from an application. We show you how to build a filter graph directly using the DirectShow COM interface and the Direct-Show control interface. We then show you how to access custom interfaces and property pages.

Chapter 10 Mixing Sprites, Backgrounds, and Videos. In this chapter we show you how to use RDX to access DirectShow filters. We also explain how simple it can be to overlay a sprite on top of a video and even a video on top of another video.

Chapter 11 Streaming down the Superhighway with RealMedia. In this chapter we look at the latest architecture from RealNetworks, which is a cross-platform architecture. We'll show you how to build custom File-Format and Rendering plug-ins, which allow you to stream custom data types over the Internet. We'll also show you how to use RealMedia audio services.

Part IV: Playing and Mixing Sound with DirectSound and RSX 3D

Chapter 12 Audio Mixing with DirectSound. We start the chapter with an overview of Microsoft's DirectSound. Then we show you how to play a simple WAV file. We then teach you how to mix two sound files and how to control the format of the final output—after mixing.

Chapter 13 Realistic 3D Sound Experience: RSX 3D. RSX provides a high-level programming model optimized for the Intel Architecture. We start the chapter with an overview of Intel's RSX 3D audio, and then we show you how to play one or more WAV files with it. We then give you an overview of RSX's 3D sound model and show you how to achieve a realistic sound experience with it.

Part V: Welcome to the Third Dimension

Chapter 14 An Introduction to Direct3D. We kick off our 3D section with background on 3D on the PC and an overview of Microsoft's Direct3D. Then we discuss Direct3D's modes and its Immediate mode architecture. The main purpose of this chapter is to give you the bare minimum code needed to render a triangle in Direct3D's Immediate mode.

Chapter 15 Embellishing Our Triangle with Backgrounds, Shading, and Textures. In this chapter we add some bells and whistles to the default triangle we helped you create in the previous chapter. We work through shading options, texture mapping, and Z-Buffering, and we also render Direct3D-based backgrounds.

Chapter 16 Understanding and Enhancing Direct3D Performance. In previous chapters we focused on getting our application running. In this chapter we focus on how fast Direct3D performs. We then use the Ramp driver to increase render performance and measure our improvements.

Chapter 17 Mixing 3D with Sprites, Backgrounds, and Videos. We next look at integrating 3D with the media we worked with in previous parts (sprites, backgrounds, and videos). We walk you through displaying a 3D object in a 2D world, and we render a texture-mapped triangle with a video as a texture source.

Part VI: Processors and Performance Optimization

Chapter 18 The Pentium Family. In the first chapter of this part we give you an architectural overview of the Pentium, Pentium Pro, and MMX technology processors. But first we define some of the terms and concepts that are used throughout Part VI. We then give you the 10,000-foot view of these processors so that you will begin to see how they differ from one another. Finally, we show you how to distinguish between the different flavors of these processors.

Chapter 19 The Pentium Processor. This chapter gives you a detailed view of the internal components of the Pentium processor and shows you what's important so that each component can attain optimal performance. We then analyze the assembly sprite from Part II for performance problems and show you how to fix them.

Chapter 20 The Pentium Processor with MMX Technology. Here we introduce the MMX technology instruction set, registers, and data types. We also outline the MMX scheduling rules and show you how to use them. We rewrite the sprite sample using MMX technology instructions and analyze it for performance bottlenecks.

Chapter 21 VTune and Other Performance Optimization Tools. Since hand tuning is a tedious and time-consuming process, we introduce VTune, a tool to help you analyze your code and pinpoint performance issues with ease. We show you how to use VTune to analyze the MMX sprite sample from the previous chapter. Then we show you how to use the hot-spot system monitor and the static and dynamic analyzers. We also teach you how to use the Time Stamp Counter (TSC) and the internal Pentium event counters, and the PMonitor event counter library.

Chapter 22 The Pentium II Processor. In this chapter you'll get some exposure to the Pentium II processor, the latest processor from Intel. We list new processor features and point out optimization issues specific to this processor. We introduce you to the use of the Write Combining memory type so that you can achieve better graphics performance.

Chapter 23 Memory Optimization: Know Your Data. We dedicate this chapter to system issues. Knowing where your data comes from and where it goes to is essential for achieving overall application performance and multimedia throughput. In this chapter we discuss the L1 and L2 caches, the PCI bus, and how to organize your writes to memory in the most efficient manner.

Epilogue: The Finale. In the last pages of the book we describe what we will see in the future in terms of faster processors, tighter multimedia architectures, the Internet, advances in 3D, and multimedia.

Web Site: The Annex. Two additional chapters on the latest technologies from Microsoft, **DirectShow Capture** and **Direct3D Draw Primitives,** are available on our Web Site. Access it with the following URL:

http://www.awl.com/cseng/titles/0-201-30944-0

I.3 Conventions Used in This Book

When we started writing the book, we experimented with a few ideas of how to convey our material without being too detailed. We decided to settle on a few conventions based on feedback that we received from our reviewers. Even though these conventions might seem obvious when you read the rest of this chapter, it might still be advantageous to browse through the next couple of pages.

I.3.1   Part Map

At the beginning of each part, we have inserted a part listing that shows the highlights of each chapter in the part.

1.3.2 Chapter Prologue and Epilogue

As we mentioned before, at the beginning of each chapter, we ask and answer the question "*Why read this chapter?*" by summarizing the material covered in that chapter. At the end of each chapter we reiterate what we have covered and what you should have learned from the chapter.

1.3.3 Code Listings

Side Note: A note about the text next to it

All our code is inserted between a thick and a thin rule and appears in a different font, as shown below. We use bubbles and side comments to highlight key points in the code and to present our material compactly. Extra special information merits a gray-shaded background.

```
CCodeText::SubliminalMessage()
{
    if (YouHaveNotReadThisBook)              ◊ Side comment.
        BuyThisBook();  ◄
    else                          Bubble: Highlights information about the line pointed to.
        BuyItForSomeoneElse();

}
        Extra special bubble, merits a gray shading.
```

Notice also that if we have to repeat a portion of the code, we use the **bold** font for the newly added code.

```
DOLLAR CCodeText::SubliminalMessage()
{
    if (YouHaveNotReadThisBook)
        BuyThisBook();
    else
        BuyItForSomeoneElse();

    return SomeDollarValue;
}
```

We also use plenty of icons to emphasize a point or to point out something that's not obvious. We use a star to point out the best result from a procedure and a CD icon to alert readers to when they might want to experiment with the CD that accompanies this book. Notes, and cautions are also set apart from regular text for emphasis.

Finally, notice that the code listings in the book lack a lot of the error checking code, but the code on the companion CD has all the error checking code. We decided to do this for better clarity when we describe the material in this book, and leaving out error checking code reduces clutter.

I.3.4 Coding Style

With reference to our coding style, for the code in the companion CD,

- We decided to use C++ to implement our code since it allows us to easily build the code of one chapter on the code of a previous chapter.
- For better performance, we avoid using local class declarations within our functions. Class variables declared on the stack are allocated and initialized every time the function is called, which could result in a negative impact on performance.
- We use macros for error checking so that we can easily change error reporting schemes while still retaining source file and line information.
- We use assembly language when we discuss performance optimization issues for the processor.

I.3.5 Material on the CD

To make it easier to browse through the material on the CD, we use a web browser approach similar to what you use on the Internet. Once you insert the CD in the CD ROM drive, the *AutoPlay* feature of Windows 95 and Windows NT launches your default Internet browser[1] and displays the home page of the CD.

If the web page is not automatically displayed when you insert the CD, you can manually run the batch file *AutoRun.Bat* from the root directory of the CD. Make sure that you have a web browser installed.

I.3.6 Material on the Internet

From the homepage of the CD, you can go to our web site on Addison Wesley's web server. On that server, you'll:

- Find two more chapters of the latest technologies from Microsoft, *DirectShow Capture* and *Direct3D Draw Primitives*.

- See the latest feedback and discussions of issues related to our book.

---

1. Internet Explorer 3.01 or Netscape 3.0 or later are required.

I.4 On Our Measurements

We have designed the book with a strong performance overtone. We're constantly measuring the performance of implementation path and looking for better options. Our measurements were performed on a machine equipped with a Pentium processor with MMX technology, an S3 Trio64V+ graphics adapter with 24 MB of VRAM, and 32 MB of EDO memory.

The performance of any implementation is extremely data sensitive. A particular implementation may outweigh other options given an input data set, but change the data set or vary the output configuration and the option may not do quite as well. Over the course of this book, you will be shown comparisons of different implementation choices. We hope to give you a flavor of various costs as well. But ultimately you should use *your application,* with its own algorithms, data sets, and target configurations, as your decision-making yardstick.

I.5 Tools Used in This Book

Finally, here is a list of the tools that you'll need to build the sample code on the CD:

Tool	Version	Where to Find It
Visual C++ Compiler	5.0	Buy it
Macro Assembler	6.11d	Buy it
DirectDraw SDK	3.0	MSDN (or with compiler)
Direct3D SDK	3.0	MSDN (or with compiler)
DirectSound SDK	3.0	MSDN (or with compiler)
DirectShow SDK	2.0	DirectShow SDK
Intel VTune	2.4	Evaluation copy on CD
Realistic 3D Sound Experience	2.1	on CD and http://www.intel.com
Realistic Display Mixer	3.0	on CD and http://www.intel.com
RealMedia SDK	beta 6.0	at http://www.real.com

PART I

Surveying Multimedia

WE'D LIKE TO EXTEND AN ACKNOWLEDGEMENT TO TOM'S PANCAKE HOUSE WHERE THE FIRST SPARK OF THIS BOOK WAS LIT. DARLA, CHRISTA, DIANE AND GREG. THE SERVICE IS FRIENDLY, THE FOOD IS SUPERB, AND YOU'RE GUARANTEED TO GET SOME LIP; TO LE JOI CAFÉ WHERE HSU LI WHIPS UP SOME DELICIOUS MOCHAS; AND TO PATRICIA MOORE, ANITA, ANN BRYANT, SUSAN REICHERT, NAVEEN SACHDEV, NAJI HAMDAN, DONALD FROOM, A FEW OF THE SAINTS AT SAINT VINCENT'S HOSPITAL OF PORTLAND.

CHAPTER 1

Overview of Media on the PC

WHY READ THIS CHAPTER?

This chapter introduces the current multimedia software architectures available on the PC. In this book we're only concerned with media architectures running on Windows 98 and Windows NT. We'll give you an overview of the following architectures and show you how they relate to each other:

- GDI, DirectDraw, and RDX;
- MCI, VFW, QTW, DirectShow, and RealMedia;
- WAVE, DirectSound, and RSX; and
- Direct3D

1.1 Background

Graphics hardware on the PC has evolved from monochrome CGA graphics standards through EGA, VGA, and Super VGA to the graphics cards of today, which offer custom display formats and custom graphics acceleration hardware.

Similarly, audio hardware on the PC has evolved from the lowly PC speaker through separate 8-bit, 11-kHz Mono audio cards to today's audio chip sets; chip sets integrated right on the motherboard offering 16-bit, 44-kHz, stereo formats and possibly some audio digital signal processor features.

Multimedia software developers have had to keep pace with this evolution by writing individual software modules for each device that they wanted to support. These applications had total control over the PC from the keyboard to the monitor. This "closeness" to the hardware allowed software developers to be in total control of the overall performance of their multimedia applications. But this device dependence imposed an expensive development and maintenance burden on multimedia software developers. It also slowed the adoption of advances in graphics and audio hardware.

1.2 Graphics Device Independence

With the introduction of windowed operating systems like Microsoft Windows and IBM OS/2, software developers were given a uniform programming interface that abstracted their applications from graphics hardware. Their applications could paint the screen, within a dedicated window boundary, without directly accessing the graphics hardware. Instead, the operating system accessed the hardware through device drivers. The hardware-independent interface under Microsoft Windows is known as the Graphics Device Interface (GDI); see Figure 1-1.

GDI relieved software developers of the burden of catering to each of the various graphics adapters. It also enabled hardware graphics vendors to provide hardware acceleration (such as Block Transfers, or Bltters) and to seamlessly provide the acceleration to applications through device drivers.

Although the GDI library provided a host of 2D drawing and windowing commands, it did not provide support for multimedia applications.

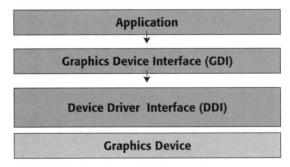

FIGURE 1-1 Graphics device independence via Microsoft Windows GDI.

1.3 Motion Video under Windows

In their first attempt at multimedia architectures, Microsoft defined the Media Control Interface (MCI) as the first multimedia interface for Windows. MCI provided a VCR-like command interface (Play, Stop, Pause, Seek, and so forth) to enable the playback of motion video, digitized audio, VCRs and audio CD players. MCI also defined an installable device interface to allow multimedia devices to be integrated into the Windows environment.

MCI, however, did not provide any means for capturing and editing motion video. So Microsoft introduced the Video for Windows (VFW) architecture, which included tools for video capture and editing and provided an architecture for capture and compression hardware, for installable codecs (compression-decompression), and for full-motion video playback (see Figure 1-2).

VFW was a significant step forward and was a launching pad for Windows multimedia applications. It spurred the development of codecs such as Intel's Indeo Video and Radius's Cinepak. The weaknesses of the initial VFW release were inadequate synchronization between audio and video tracks and poor overall graphics performance.

Around the same time, Apple ported part of its QuickTime development environment from the Macintosh to Windows, creating QuickTime for Windows (QTW). QTW supported only audio-video playback; capture, compression, and editing were supported only on the Macintosh. Yet QTW won some favor because it had better overall performance and better synchronization mechanisms than did VFW.

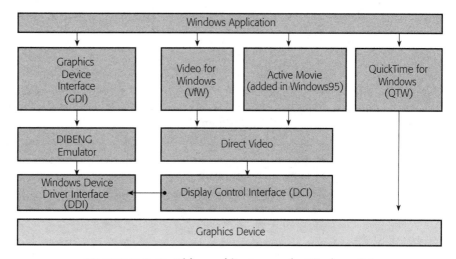

FIGURE 1-2 Video architecture under Windows 3.1.

The overhead of GDI's device-independent layer was proving too costly for graphics-intensive multimedia applications. Apple's QTW improved video performance by developing custom device drivers for various graphics devices, essentially ignoring GDI. Simultaneously, Microsoft and Intel jointly published a standard interface for graphics intensive applications—the Display Control Interface (DCI). With DCI applications could write directly to the video screen. DCI also gave users access to some video acceleration features that had not been adequately supported by GDI, namely arbitrary stretching and video-friendly YUV color formats. With DCI, full-screen, full-motion video became a reality.

At the end of 1996, Microsoft introduced the first release of ActiveMovie, targeted as a replacement for VFW. ActiveMovie addressed VFW's synchronization issues and added support for the Motion Picture Encoding Group (MPEG) class of algorithms.[1]

By the time this book is published, Microsoft will have introduced the next generation of ActiveMovie called DirectShow, which adds support for capture and compression and is integrated into the DirectX Software Development Kit (SDK). Around the same time, Apple will have released QTW Version 3.0, adding capture and compression. RealNetworks will also join the fray of multimedia architecture providers by introducing their Real Media Architecture (RMA), a multimedia streaming architecture for remote playback environments (primarily the Internet).

1.4 Multimedia Gaming under Windows 95

Although DCI accelerated motion video provided direct access to video memory, it did not offer direct access to graphics hardware for 2D operations (primarily Page Flips and Transparent Blts). Additionally, Windows lacked a DCI equivalent for audio devices. As a result of these shortcomings games developers could not achieve the levels of performance under Windows that they could under DOS.

Shortly after the release of Windows 95, Microsoft introduced the DirectX Software Development Kit (SDK), containing DirectDraw, the successor to DCI; DirectSound, which provides direct access to audio hardware devices; along with other components such as DirectInput and DirectPlay. With DirectX and Windows 95's AutoPlay features, games developers now had a device-independent platform that was more powerful than DOS. With

---

1. MPEG uses bidirectional prediction techniques for video compression.

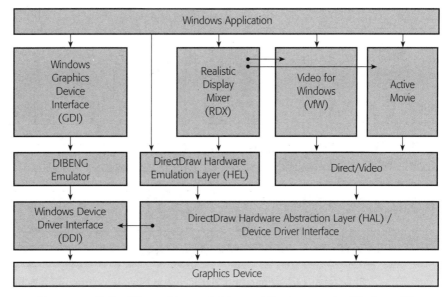

FIGURE 1-3 2D graphics and video architectures under Windows 95.

these improvements, the Windows 95 PC established itself as a powerful gaming platform. (See Figure 1-3.)

DirectDraw is a low device-level interface. With it developers can go back to working with some amount of device dependence. Intel introduced Realistic Display Mixer (RDX), a higher-level interface that abstracts a set of multimedia objects. RDX uses hardware acceleration for these objects whenever it is available. In the absence of acceleration, RDX executes assembly code, which is hand tuned for various flavors of Intel processors. As a result, the high-level interface offers high performance video and 2D while still providing device independence.

1.5 3D Video Architectures on the PC

With the release of Windows NT, Microsoft launched their own port of OpenGL to the Windows NT platform. Windows NT was targeted as a high-end workstation—similar to Silicon Graphics' and Sun Microsystems'. But OpenGL was extremely slow under Windows NT since it required a huge number of calculations to determine object geometry, lighting, and shading.

Later, other companies introduced general-purpose 3D solutions specifically tailored for the PC, including Reality Labs by Rendermorphics, BRender by

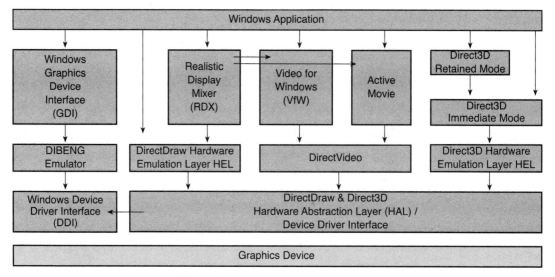

FIGURE 1-4 Video and 2D/3D graphics architecture under Windows 95.

Argonaut, RenderWare by Criterion, and 3DR by Intel. Even though these architectures were not fast enough for realistic 3D, they were fast enough to enable the development of simple 3D applications. (See Figure 1-4.)

To reduce confusion in the marketplace, Microsoft bought Reality Labs from RenderMorphics and introduced Direct3D as the single uniform solution for 3D on the PC. Some 3D games were released using Direct3D, but the general feedback has been that the performance needs to be improved and that the interface needs to be simpler, and more reliable.

By the time this book is published, Microsoft will have introduced, as part of DirectX foundation 5, the next revision of 3D for the PC, called the DrawPrimitive interface. This interface is intended to address the performance deficits and the interface complexity that was identified by previous users.

1.6 Audio Architectures on the PC

I remember writing my first program to meddle with the speaker on the PC. It was a police siren program that sent a periodic signal to the speaker and varied the frequency up and down. Boy, that was a long time ago.

Microsoft introduced the WAVE and MIDI interfaces to Windows around the same time that MCI was introduced. Both of these interfaces are still widely used today. To allow for mixing of multiple audio streams, Microsoft introduced DirectSound as part of the DirectX SDK. Since the DirectSound interface is a low-level interface, Intel introduced its own high-level audio interface, Realistic Sound Experience (RSX). RSX allows developers to easily mix multiple audio streams and control the output of these streams. RSX also models the real-world environment and provides support for a realistic 3D sound model.

WHAT HAVE YOU LEARNED?

After reading this chapter you are more familiar, perhaps, with

- GDI, DirectDraw, and RDX;
- MCI, VFW, QTW, DirectShow, and RealMedia;
- WAVE, DirectSound, and RSX; and
- Direct3D

PART I

CHAPTER 2

Processor Architecture Overview

In this book we're only concerned with Intel Architecture processors running Windows 95 and Windows NT. This chapter provides an introduction to the current multimedia hardware architectures on the PC.

We'll give you an overview of the following technologies:

- the Pentium processor and the architecture of its pipeline,
- the Pentium Pro processor and its internal architecture, and
- MMX technology and the Pentium II processor.

In the early days of multimedia, dedicated hardware was necessary to play back video, audio, and 3D. But with the giant leaps in processor and memory technologies, software-only decoders are now able to decode and render multimedia content on the PC easily. As a result, multimedia authoring and playback have become commonplace on today's PCs.

To attain such performance, developers of these software decoders had to use some of the software architectures discussed in the previous chapter, such as DirectDraw and DirectSound. In addition, they had to optimize their application for the processors that they're targeting the decoder for. In general, multimedia developers dedicate some of their development time for processor-specific optimization so that they can get the best performance out of their application.

With multimedia applications, it's not enough to just optimize for the processor; you have to optimize your application for the system that you're running on—cache, bus, and memory. When you optimize for the processor, you typically assume that the data is in the L1 cache or in a register. But this is not the case with multimedia applications, since you typically deal with a huge amount of data, and usually the data is in either the L2 cache or main memory.

In this chapter, we'll give you an overview of the current breadth of Intel processors and compare their features. We'll also touch on issues related to the system as a whole. You can find a detailed analysis of both topics in Part VI of the book.

2.1 Processor Architecture

In the following overview, we'll only be concerned with the Pentium family of processors including the original Pentium, the Pentium Pro, the Pentium II, and the Pentium processor with MMX technology. (See Figure 2-1.)

The Pentium processor is built with two integer execution units (U and V pipes), which allow the processor to execute up to two integer instructions

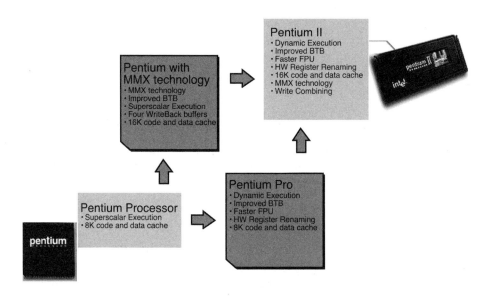

FIGURE 2-1 The Pentium processor family.

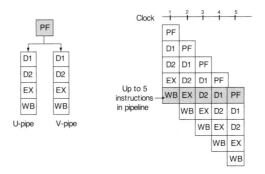

FIGURE 2-2 Pentium processor pipeline.

every clock cycle. Each execution pipeline has five distinct execution stages: Prefetch, Decode 1, Decode 2, Execute, and Writeback (see Figure 2-2). At any moment, the Pentium processor could be processing up to five instructions in each of the two pipelines. In addition, the Pentium processor includes two separate L1 instruction and data caches of 8K each, which allow the processor to access instructions and data in the same clock cycle.

Typically, applications cannot achieve an optimal instruction rate because of external data/address dependencies or unpaired instructions. Two instructions can execute simultaneously only if they adhere to the Pentium instruction pairing rules; otherwise only one instruction is executed in the U pipe. You can learn how to optimize your application and about instruction pairing rules in Part VI.

The Pentium with MMX technology processor is the first processor that provides Intel's MMX technology. MMX technology is the largest addition to the Intel Architecture since Protected mode was introduced in the Intel 386 processor. Intel added fifty-seven new MMX instructions and eight MMX registers to its Pentium processor. It also doubled the size of the L1 instruction and data caches to 16K each.

In the Pentium Pro processor, Intel moved to a twelve-stage pipeline (compared to a five-stage pipeline in the Pentium processor) with out-of-order execution. The deeper pipeline allows different processor units to operate on multiple instructions at the same time. Such deep pipelining, however, is very expensive in terms of overhead in the case of branch misprediction. To remedy that, the Pentium Pro processor includes a sophisticated branch prediction mechanism to better predict the outcome of branches before they occur.

The Pentium Pro processor has an out-of-order execution unit consisting of five parallel execution ports: two Arithmetic Logic Unit (ALU) ports, an address generation port, a Load port, and a Store port. The out-of-order nature of the execution unit allows the processor to execute future instructions while older instructions are waiting for their data or address to be resolved. You'll learn more about the benefits of out-of-order execution in Part VI.

The core of the Pentium II processor is based on the Pentium Pro processor core, with the addition of MMX technology. The Pentium II processor doubled the size of the L1 code and data caches to 16K each.

2.2 System Overview

Typically, it is not enough to just optimize your application for a certain processor. You should also be concerned with the other components in the system that can affect performance—system memory, cache, and video memory.

When you optimize for the processor, you assume that you're dealing with data that exists in the L1 cache. However, with multimedia applications, you typically deal with a huge amount of data that does not fit in the L1 cache—and sometimes not even in the L2 cache. Consequently, you should pay special attention to the access pattern of your data and optimize for a high L1 cache hit rate (see Figure 2-3).

To do that, you can use special techniques in prefetching the data to the L1 and L2 cache. You can also break down your tasks into smaller tasks that can use a smaller amount of data—and probably fit in the L1 cache. See Part VI for more details.

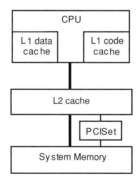

FIGURE 2-3 Memory architecture of the Pentium processor.

Finally, you should pay special attention when you write the final image to the video screen. Since you're dealing with a huge amount of data, this operation can be very time consuming. You can use DirectDraw to access the video screen directly and write your image to it, bypassing GDI's overhead. You can also off-load some operations to the graphics adapter, such as zooming and color space conversion, and in turn you will be able to do more on the CPU. With the Pentium II processor, you can use the Write Combining memory type to achieve a higher transfer rate when writing to video memory. You can learn more about these topics in Parts II and VI.

WHAT HAVE YOU LEARNED?

After getting through this chapter, you should know something about

■ the Pentium processor and its architecture
■ the Pentium Pro processor and its architecture
■ MMX technology and the Pentium II processor

PART II

Animated Graphics, Sprites, and Backgrounds

WE'D LIKE TO EXTEND AN ACKNOWLEDGEMENT TO JACK AND GLENNA RYAN, WENDY AND DAWSON YEE, PAM LUSARDI, DOUG BRUCKS, DEBBIE BURKE, SARAH NAHUM, GREG SCHWENDINGER, TERRI DEGROAT, MICHELLE CAUDILLO, JANET RASH, BLAKE AND NIKKI BENDER, BEN AND JUDY ECHOLS, JERRY ORLECK, LEORA GREGORY, CYNDI YOUNG, ROHIT AND NIDHI AGARWAL, ROGER AND SUSAN TAIT, GARY AND MARY BALDES, JUDI GOLDSTEIN, AND TOM CRONIN.

Chapter 3   **Simple Sprites in GDI**
- Define sprites and backgrounds
- Blt sprites and backgrounds with GDI
- How fast does GDI draw sprites and backgrounds?

Chapter 4   **Sprites with DirectDraw Primary Surfaces**
- Overview of Microsoft's DirectDraw
- What is a Primary surface?
- Render sprites directly to the display
- Measure C and ASM sprites drawn to the display

Chapter 5   **Hardware Acceleration via DirectDraw**
- How do you find out what the hardware can do?
- What is an OffScreen surface?
- Use hardware Bltters and Page Flippers
- Measure accelerated rendering

Chapter 6   **RDX: Animation Object Management**
- Overview of Intel's Realistic Display Mixer (RDX)
- Use RDX to render sprites and backgrounds
- Access hardware acceleration via RDX
- Measure performance of a device-independent interface

Part II consists of four chapters that cover rendering 2D graphics images under Windows9x.

■ **17** ■

The Microsoft Windows Graphics Device Interface (GDI) is a feature-rich library that provides all sorts of primitives to Block Transfer (Blt) graphics images and to draw common 2D objects (such as lines or rectangles). So why bother spending four chapters on 2D graphics? Well, because we are going to focus specifically on the sort of rendering used for composition and animation.

Although the images used for compositions are typically rectangular, the actual contents are irregularly shaped. Some of the data within the rectangle is defined as transparent and is not meant to be seen. In Chapter 3, the first chapter of this part, we will define the animation objects that we use throughout the part—specifically features that can bring potential benefits to performance.

Animation objects are composed using transparent Blt routines. In Chapter 3, we will also work through examples of rendering transparent images using GDI, and then we will measure the performance of rendering with GDI.

In Chapter 4, we examine Microsoft's DirectDraw architecture, which was designed for multimedia developers who want to render animation objects with higher performance than what is offered by GDI. In this chapter, we touch upon the first aspect of higher performance through DirectDraw—bypassing GDI and using custom routines to render directly to the display screen.

Chapter 4 will give you a good starting point for using DirectDraw, but it is by no means a complete guide. In Chapter 5, we study the second aspect of higher performance through DirectDraw—accessing hardware acceleration features. The chapter also examines mechanisms to reduce the sundry, but expensive cost of refreshing the screen.

DirectDraw is a low-level API that enables high performance at the cost of some device dependence. Intel's Realistic Display Mixer (RDX) sits on top of DirectDraw and provides high-performance animation with a higher level device-independent API. Chapter 6 will show you how to get going quickly with RDX.

Some recommendations:

- Chapter 3 contains fairly introductory material. If you are familiar with terms like *sprites* and *backgrounds* and are not interested in how to render them with GDI, you need not read this chapter.

- If you don't want to bother with the details of a low-level API like DirectDraw, then RDX in Chapter 6 is a good alternative. Chapter 6 is also a good chapter if you don't want to implement a mixing subsystem or if you want to use RDX's assembly-tuned routines as a complement to your own work.

- If you intend to work with Direct3D, you will need to know DirectDraw, and both Chapters 4 and 5 are important for you.

- If you have your own graphics objects with their own render routines, or if you enjoy high-performance assembly programming, you will *want* to know DirectDraw in enough detail that, again, you should read both Chapters 4 and 5.

CHAPTER 3

Simple Sprites in GDI

WHY READ THIS CHAPTER?

Consider this chapter as a short introduction to animation terms and concepts.

Here we define *sprites* and *backgrounds.* To visibly illustrate the concepts, we walk you through working examples of sprites and backgrounds drawn using Microsoft Windows GDI. Read the code to understand our definitions. Run the demos to visualize these definitions.

Later we use the working examples to measure just how fast we can draw sprites and backgrounds using GDI. With these measurements in hand, we'll be in a better position to assess the performance of alternate options in subsequent chapters of this part.

3.1 Graphics Device Interface (GDI) Overview

We expect that most of you (our readers) are very familiar with Microsoft's Graphics Device Interface (GDI). Still, let's not forget GDI's features while on our quest for higher performance options.

Windows GDI handles all graphic output—to the display screen as well as to other graphics output devices such as printers, plotters, and metafiles. In handling graphics output, GDI must handle the various forms of these devices (such as EGA versus VGA and laser printers versus dot-matrix printers). GDI's device drivers shield us, application developers, from many of the complexities of device-dependent issues.

With GDI's device driver model, hardware vendors can provide different levels of hardware acceleration at different price points.

GDI also acts as a sharing agent for graphics output devices. It manages multitasked output to devices through device drivers and device contexts. These management responsibilities include memory ranges, clipping regions, color palettes, and print spoolers.

As a graphics library, GDI provides a variety of objects (brushes, pens, bitmaps, pixels, text); provides attributes for these objects (fills, thickness, font, color); provides commands for manipulating objects and attributes (Create, Load, Select); and offers some other drawing functions (PolyLine, TextOut, Rectangle, BitBlt).

GDI also controls the look and feel of images on graphics devices via the definition of a standard interface for default objects (standard colors, cursors, icons, and base fonts); the definition of sizing attributes (coordinate spaces, text metrics); and the definition of control functions (coordinate mapping, font enumeration, font mapping). In short, GDI does a lot. Bypassing GDI for higher-performance options means bypassing all these capabilities. Choose your path carefully.

3.2 Animation Objects

When we mention sprites, you're probably thinking of pixies, and nymphs, and elves, and wood fairies. Toss in a few gnomes, ogres, trolls, and goblins and we'd have quite a fairy tale on our hands. But, it's time to rein in these flights of fancy.

3.2.1 Sprites

For this book, let's define *sprite* in a multimedia context. Let's use the term *sprite* to refer to regular bitmap images that are superimposed on top of other graphics images. What's more, the superimposition of sprites is not a simple block copy. Instead, sprites contain both visible and transparent pixels, and the superimposition must only render the visible pixels.

We expect—and may optimize for—

- sprites being drawn repeatedly, so that some of the time spent preparing them can be recovered during drawing;
- sprites being fairly small images so that whatever memory they require can be traded off for performance; and
- partial sprites being rarely drawn, and routines to draw partial sprites may be separate and slower than equivalent routines to draw sprites wholly.

Figure 3-1 shows a sprite that we use in our demo applications.

FIGURE 3-1 Sprite image.

The sprites we use in our demo applications are of varying sizes. You might also say that they are of odd sizes: that is, they are not square; they are not powers of two; they are not even DWORD or QWORD multiples. We chose these odd sizes deliberately, to provide you with the opportunity to study the performance impact of different sprite sizes.

3.2.2 Backgrounds

Let's also define the term *background* in a multimedia context. Let's use *background* to refer to images without transparency. Can a background be drawn on top of another? Sure it can! But we expect that images without transparency are probably going to be behind objects with transparency— hence the term *backgrounds.*

We expect that backgrounds are large images on top of which one or many sprites will be superimposed. They take up a lot of memory, and more memory cannot be used to improve performance. Also a background may be much larger than the displayed image, and moving a source rectangle around within the background is one way of creating an illusion of motion—scrolling backgrounds. Figure 3-2 depicts the background that we use in our demo applications.

FIGURE 3-2 Sample background.

Again, the background is of an odd size. We chose this size because we want to point out the special code that needs to be written to handle odd-sized backgrounds.

3.3 Transparent Blts with GDI

GDI does not contain any single function to "transparently" Blt images. Therefore our Transparent Blt algorithm uses a combination of RasterOp Bit-Blts. Our approach involves the following steps:

1. Zero out the pixels from the destination that are to be painted with "visible" sprite pixels. (To do so, we create an inverted Mask from the original source at Init-Time. And at run time, we BitBlt the mask with a SRCAND[1] RasterOp onto the destination.)

2. OR-In sprite pixels into the zeroed-out space. (RasterOps operate at the bit level, and a nonzero transparency color in the source could OR-In spurious bits into the "transparent" space. Therefore at Init-Time, we zero out the transparent pixels from the original image.)

3.4 Drawing a Sprite Using GDI

OK, now let's take a look at some sample code that implements sprites and scrolling backgrounds using GDI. Here is the base class definition for sprites, CSprite.

```
class CSprite {

public:
  dword    m_dwWidth;                            ◊ width of sprite
  dword    m_dwHeight;                           ◊ height of sprite
  byte *   m_pData;                              ◊ internal sprite data storage
  byte     m_byTransp;                           ◊ transparency pixel

  CSprite();                                     ◊ constructor -- Cannot err

  bool Init(uint nResID, byte byKey, cdc &pcWnd);◊ Init -- Can return errors
  ~CSprite();                                    ◊ destructor
  void Blt(BLTPARAMS *pDst, CPoint &point);      ◊ blt routine

};
```

> Our sample source on the JS97 CD defines and uses a BLTPARAMS structure. This structure is something like a union of various parameters needed by different Blt routines. In explaining the code we will only list the parameters the routine needs.

---

1. SRCAND is a parameter for the BitBlt function. It performs a logical AND of the source bitmap with the destination bitmap.

The Blt algorithm we use is based on an approach recommended by Microsoft on their Developer Network (MSDN) CDs. The recommended algorithm uses a three-Blt approach, but we improved the algorithm to pre-process the sprite at init-time to allow us to use a two-Blt approach.

Following are the Init and Blt routines. Note that since Windows BitmapInfo-Headers do not allow for transparency colors, we are specifying transparency as a parameter to the sprite *Init()* load function.

```
CSpriteGDI::Init(UINT nResID, BYTE byColorKey, CDC *pcdcWnd)
{
  // load bitmap from resource into a tmp bmp ready for preparation
  CDC cdcTmp;
  cdcTmp.CreateCompatibleDC(pcdcWnd);
  CBitmap cbmTmp;
  cbmTmp.LoadBitmap(nResID);
  cdcTmp.SelectObject(cbmTmp);
  BITMAP bm;
  cbmTmp.GetBitmap(&bm);
  DWORD dwWt = m_dwWidth  = bm.bmWidth;
  DWORD dwHt = m_dwHeight = bm.bmHeight;

  // get transparent color and set DC background (we use system palette)
  PALETTEENTRY peClr;
  GetSystemPaletteEntries(pcdcWnd->m_hDC, (UINT)byColorKey, 1, &peColor);
  cdcTmp.SetBkColor(PALETTERGB(peClr.peRed, peClr.peGreen, peClr.peBlue));

  // create a monochrome mask for run-time clearing of foreground pixels
  CDC cdcMask;
  cdcMask.CreateCompatibleDC(cDcWnd);
  m_pcbmMask = new CBitmap;
  m_pcbmMask->CreateBitmap(m_dwWidth, m_dwHeight, 1, 1, NULL));
  Cbitmap *pcbmOldMask = cdcMask.SelectObject(m_pcbmMask);
  cdcMask.BitBlt(0, 0, dwWt, dwHt, &cdcTmp, 0, 0, SRCCOPY);
```

> BitBlt from color-bitmap to mono-bitmap sets pixels with background=1 and foreground=0. We previously *SetBkColor* of cdcTmp to the transparency color. The result here is an inverted mask.

```
  // process src so that transparent pixels are 0
  CDC cdcSrc;
  cdcSrc.CreateCompatibleDC(pcdcWnd);
  m_pcbmSrc = new CBitmap;
  m_pcbmSrc->CreateBitmap(m_dwWidth, m_dwHeight, 1, 8, NULL);
  cdcSrc.SelectObject(m_pcbmSrc);
  cdcSrc.BitBlt(0, 0, dwWt, dwHt, &cdcMask, 0, 0, NOTSRCCOPY);
  cdcSrc.BitBlt(0, 0, dwWt, dwHt, &cdcTmp, 0, 0, SRCAND);
```

> Preprocess Source. Zero out pixels of transparent color by
> • NOTCOPYing inverted mask to result bitmap
> • and then ANDing in the actual source data

```
  return TRUE;
}
```

```
CSpriteGDI::Blt(CDC &cDc, CPoint &pt)
{
  static CDC cdcSrc, cdcMask;
  static CBitmap *pcbmOldSrc, *pcbmOldMask ;

  // setup 2 DCs with bmps prepared during sprite init
  cdcSrc.CreateCompatibleDC(&cDc);
  cdcMask.CreateCompatibleDC(&cDc);
  pcbmOldSrc = cdcSrc.SelectObject(m_pcbmSrc);
  pcbmOldMask = cdcMask.SelectObject(m_pcbmMask;

  // blt: clear away foreground pixels using mono mask (bk=1, fg=0)
  cDc.BitBlt(pt.x, pt.y, m_dwWidth, m_dwHeight, &cdcMask, 0, 0, SRCAND);
  // second blt: or preprocessed src into anded dest
  cDc.BitBlt(pt.x, pt.y, m_dwWidth, m_dwHeight, &cdcSrc,  0, 0, SRCPAINT);

  cdcMask.SelectObject(pcbmOldMask);
  cdcMask.DeleteDC();
  cdcSrc.SelectObject(pcbmOldSrc);
  cdcSrc.DeleteDC();

}
```

Release these DCs, since they are not local to this routine's scope and will not get automatically released until the application terminates.

3.5 Backgrounds

The code for backgrounds is similar to that used for sprites.

```
CBackgroundGDI::Init(UINT nResID, CDC *pcdcWnd)
{
  // load bitmap for background from resource file
  CDC cdcSrc;
  cdcSrc.CreateCompatibleDC(pcdcWnd);
  m_pcbmSrc = new CBitmap;
  m_pcbmSrc->LoadBitmap(nResID);
  Cbitmap *pcbmOldSrc = cdcSrc.SelectObject(m_pcbmSrc);
  BITMAP bm;
  m_pcbmSrc->GetBitmap(&bm);
  m_dwWidth  = bm.bmWidth;
  m_dwHeight = bm.bmHeight;
}
```

The Blt routine is straightforward, especially since, in this case, we do not have to worry about transparency. However, note that a sub-rectangle parameter can be specified to draw only a portion of a background.

```
Cbackground::Blt(CDC &cDc, CPoint &cPt, CRect &crView)
{
  // setup DC objects
  static CDC cdcSrc;
  static CBitmap *pcbmOldSrc;
  cdcSrc.CreateCompatibleDC(cDc);
  pcbmOldSrc = cdcSrc.SelectObject(m_pcbmSrc);

  // add code to error check view to within image boundary
  lWt = crView.right - crView.left;
  lHt = crView.bottom - crView.top;

  // straightforward blt
  cDc.BitBlt(cPt.x, cPt.y, lWt, lHt,
  &cdcSrc, crView.left, crView.top,  SRCCOPY);

  // release DC
  cdcSrc.SelectObject(pcbmOldSrc);
  cdcSrc.DeleteDC();


}
```

3.6 Demo Time

Run the demo that corresponds to this chapter[2]. You should see a sprite being drawn on the screen. Move the mouse around and the sprite will follow the mouse.

The sprite leaves sprite trails because on startup we have set the application to "not refresh" the background. Turn Background Refresh on and the sprite trails will disappear.

A difficulty of overlaying sprites on backgrounds directly onto the screen is that refreshing the background is followed by the transparent overlay of the sprite, which results in a noticeable flicker. For flicker-free results, the background needs to be refreshed and the sprite overlayed into a nonvisible buffer (memory DC), and then the resulting image in the nonvisible buffer must be transferred to the screen. "Compositing" in nonvisible buffers will be discussed shortly in Chapter 5. For now, treat this as an exercise for you the reader.

---

2. See the Introduction if you need instructions.

3.7 How Fast Does GDI Draw Sprites and Backgrounds?

Table 3-1 measures the speed of drawing sprites and backgrounds with GDI. These measurements were taken on our base platform described in the Introduction and will definitely vary with different configurations. We have included the application for measuring the speed of drawing sprites and its source code on our Internet site that we mentioned in the Introduction; it is called *Timing App.* Run the application on your platform and see what results you get. The source code for the timing application is also included on the CD. We have separated out the timing source code from the source for the chapter demos to simplify reading the base code.

TABLE 3-1 How Fast Does GDI Draw Sprites and Backgrounds?

Object	Time (in milliseconds)
16 sprites (width: 84; height: 63)	14.2
background (width: 734; height: 475)	8.8

WHAT HAVE YOU LEARNED?

By this time, you know what we mean by sprites and backgrounds, you've seen them work, and you also know how long it takes to mix a sprite on a background. Since this was only an introductory chapter, if you've read this far, you've got to be itching to move on to the next chapters, which introduce you to the meat of this section. Well, what are you waiting for?

CHAPTER 4

Sprites with DirectDraw Primary Surfaces

In the previous chapter, you were introduced to drawing a transparent sprite on a background using GDI. But you may not have been satisfied with the performance of sprites under GDI. This chapter will introduce you to faster sprites via the Microsoft DirectDraw interface. Read on and decide if DirectDraw works better for you.

In the previous chapter you were also introduced to graphics rendering objects (and primitives) provided by GDI. But you may have your own graphics rendering objects that are not convenient to render through GDI. In this chapter we will show you how to render your own sprites using DirectDraw. Read on and decide if our sprite example forms an appropriate foundation for rendering your objects.

By reading this chapter, you will

- get an overview of DirectDraw and what it offers,
- learn how to access the display screen and write directly to it,
- use routines to render faster sprites, and
- be exposed to some limitations of writing directly to the display screen.

4.1 Introduction to Microsoft's DirectDraw

The Graphics Device Interface (GDI) library within Microsoft Windows provides software developers with image display functions. The library abstracts graphics devices and provides a device-independent interface that developers can write to. Device independence allows developers to use a standard set of functions without having to worry about device specifics or even device capabilities.

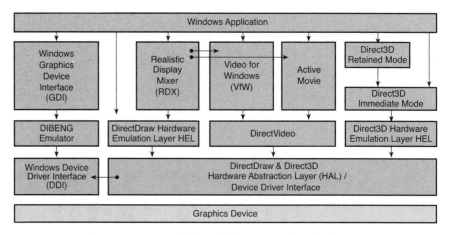

FIGURE 4-1 Display architecture under Windows 95.

Unfortunately, the overhead of GDI's device independence was too expensive for graphics intensive applications. In 1994 Intel and Microsoft jointly released the Display Control Interface (DCI) as an extension of GDI. DCI allowed direct access to graphics device memory and to device acceleration features under Windows 3.1 and Windows 95.

In 1995 Microsoft released DirectDraw for Windows 95 as a successor to DCI. Similar to DCI, DirectDraw provides direct access to graphics device memory and to device acceleration features. DirectDraw enhances device acceleration by providing access to hardware Blters and hardware palettes.

Figure 4-1 diagrams the current display architecture under Windows 95. Although Figure 4-1 shows the entire display architecture under Windows 95, in this chapter we are primarily concerned with the thick arrow that points directly from the application to the DirectDraw Hardware Emulation Layer (HEL).

Think of DirectDraw as an extension to GDI that allows you to use custom drawing routines or allows you to access custom device-specific acceleration. DirectDraw is part of Microsoft's DirectX Software Development Kit (SDK) and is the lowest level API available for display devices.

4.2 **Features of DirectDraw**

Figure 4-2 shows a graphics card laid out as a block diagram showing typical components.

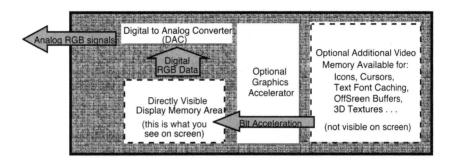

FIGURE 4-2 Block diagram of components on a typical graphics card.

All graphics cards have some video memory, so whatever you see on the screen is stored in memory on the graphics card in a place specifically reserved for that purpose. RGB data from this primary screen area is converted via a digital to analog converter (DAC) to analog signals that are sent out to the monitor. DACs support palette lookups during conversion in a palettized graphics mode.

Today's graphics cards typically have an optional graphics accelerator to support standard GDI acceleration, and they are configured with enough memory to support high-resolution (24 or 32 bits per pixel, or bpp) graphics modes. If you're operating in low-resolution graphics modes, this additional memory may be used for other purposes. DirectDraw gives you *direct access* to the graphics card to both its video memory and its acceleration hardware.

DirectDraw gives you access to the video memory through a *surface* object. Device memory exists in many forms and, therefore, there are many types of surfaces to allow you to access the various forms of device memory.

A PRIMARYSURFACE gives you direct access to the main display memory area. Anything you write to this memory area is immediately visible on the display screen. In fact you get access to the entire display screen and can write anywhere on the screen. Note that you access the screen in the user's display configuration, which can vary both in screen size (640 × 480 or 1024 × 768) and in color format (8, 16, 24, 32 bpp). Under special circumstances, DirectDraw allows you to reconfigure the display for the duration of your application.

DirectDraw's OFFSCREENSURFACE allows you to allocate and access any additional "behind-the-screen" device memory. Why is this useful? Graphics cards have acceleration features like Transparent Blts, non-RGB color formats, fast screen refreshes by Page Flipping, and even 3D graphics primitives. Offscreen surfaces are the mechanism by which you access hardware acceleration features that are not accessible through GDI. There is one caveat, however: the source and destination images for these acceleration features must live in device memory.

Beyond access to device memory and hardware acceleration, DirectDraw also supports additional features such as direct access to the primary palette, support for multiple palettes with DirectDraw *Palettes,* and support for window management with DirectDraw *Clippers.* Given that surface types and device features vary, DirectDraw supports a *capabilities* model, which can be used to query the DirectDraw driver for its capabilities before you use any specific feature.

In this chapter, we will introduce you to initializing and querying the DirectDraw driver and using DirectDraw Primary surfaces. OffScreen surfaces and device acceleration will be discussed in the next chapter.

4.3 Before You Get Overly Excited

Writing directly to *device memory* or accessing *device-specific* acceleration defeats the *device-independence* benefits of GDI. Once you access device-specific features using DirectDraw, you must respond gracefully to variations in graphics devices.

For example, memory layouts differ based on the display configuration selected by the user. Variations in configurations include pixel format (such as RGB24, RGB16, or palletized RGB8) and screen size (such as 640 × 480, 800 × 600, 1024 × 768). Memory layouts may also differ based on manufacturers' design choices. There is, for example, more than one format for the size of the color components with RGB16—5:6:5 and 5:5:5 being two popular formats. Similarly RGB24 can be either in a compact 3 bits per pixel

---

1. The emerging Advanced Graphics Port (AGP) specification will allow graphics cards to provide acceleration using system memory–based source images. DirectDraw Offscreen surfaces will continue to be the mechanism to access AGP-based graphics hardware acceleration.

format or in a DWORD-sized format with the most significant byte ignored. If you write directly to memory, you need to understand what format is currently being used and be able to write your pixels in that format.

Similarly, there is no standard set of acceleration features that all graphics devices must provide. If you use a device-specific feature, you will also need a fallback mechanism to work with devices that do not support that particular feature. DirectVideo, for example, has many code paths to use various color-conversion and stretching features.

Choosing a device-specific development option places a development burden on you. But choosing this option can give you significant performance gain.

Some graphics cards are still banked memory devices. We would need to switch to a new bank before accessing its memory. However, Microsoft now provides a mechanism (VFlatD) to disguise banked access as linear access. VFlatD traps page faults on specific memory ranges and automatically switches banks as needed. The disguise does add a noticeable performance cost.

Use the DDTEST tool that comes with the DirectX SDK to get information about your display device. Some devices, such as some S3 Trio 64 graphics cards, are incorrectly identified as banked devices. Contact the maker of your graphics card for updated DirectDraw drivers.

4.4 Instantiating a DirectDraw Object

Let's get dirty. First, let's initialize DirectDraw by instantiating, or creating an instance of, a DirectDraw object:

```
BOOL CSharedHardware::Init(HWND hWnd) {
   LPDIRECTDRAWpDDraw;
   HRESULTerr;

   // create a DirectDraw instance
   DirectDrawCreate(NULL, &pDDraw, NULL);

   // Setup to use as normal windowed app
   err = pDDraw->SetCooperativeLevel(hWnd, DDSCL_NORMAL);
   if (err == DD_OK) {
    pDDraw->Release();
    return FALSE;
   }

   // store into member variable
   m_ppDDraw = pDDraw;
   return TRUE;
}
```

DirectDrawCreate is the starting point in using DirectDraw. The DIRECTDRAW structure returned from this function provides access to the entire next level of functionality, such as *CreateSurface, EnumDisplayModes,* and so forth.

SetCooperativeLevel() sets how we plan to use DirectDraw. The settings can be

DDSCL_NORMAL	App will work as a regular Windows app.
DDSCL_EXCLUSIVE	App wants exclusive access to display area.
DDSCL_FULLSCREEN	App wants responsibility for the entire display area. GDI will be ignored.
DDSCL_ALLOWMODEX	App can deal with non-Windows modes
DDSCL_ALLOWREBOOT	Allow CTRL_ALT_DEL to work while in fullscreen exclusive mode.
DDSCL_NOWINDOWCHANGES	Don't let user change position or minimize application

PART II

4.5 Querying and Creating a Primary Surface

Now that DirectDraw has been initialized, let's get access to DirectDraw surfaces. Let's start by examining DDSURFACEDESC, a basic DirectDraw structure that describes *all* forms of surfaces in DirectDraw.

```
typedef struct _DDSURFACEDESC{
  DWORD   dwSize;
  DWORD   dwFlags;
  DWORD   dwHeight;
  DWORD   dwWidth;
  LONG    lPitch;
  union {
    DWORD   dwBackBufferCount;
    DWORD   dwMipMapCount;
    };
    union {
    DWORD           dwZBufferBitDepth;
    DWORD           dwRefreshRate;
  };
  DWORDdwAlphaBitDepth;
  DWORDdwReserved;
  LPVOID  lpSurface;
  DDCOLORKEYddckCKDestOverlay;
  DDCOLORKEYddckCKDestBlt;
  DDCOLORKEYddckCKSrcOverlay;
  DDCOLORKEYddckCKSrcBlt;
  DDPIXELFORMATddpfPixelFormat;
  DDSCAPSddsCaps;
} DDSURFACEDESC, FAR* LPDDSURFACEDESC;
```

> Not all fields of a DDSURFACEDESC structure are valid all the time. The DDColorKey fields, for example, are not needed to create a simple Primary surface. Therefore, whenever fields are used, equivalent bits in the dwFlags field indicate that the field is valid.

And now here's how to create a Primary surface:

```
CPrimarySurface::CPrimarySurface(void)
{
  // zero out the memory of the surface descriptor
  memset(&m_SurfDesc, 0, sizeof(m_SurfDesc));
  // init surface descriptor size
  m_SurfDesc.dwSize = sizeof(m_SurfDesc);
}
BOOL CPrimarySurface::Init(LPDIRECTDRAW pdDraw)
{
  // set type of surface within the surface caps structure
  m_SurfDesc.ddsCaps.dwCaps = DDSCAPS_PRIMARYSURFACE;
```

> The dwCaps field is used both to establish the type of surface requested and to set up attributes upon return. Refer to the DirectDraw documentation for more details. Some surface types to note are:
>
> | | |
> |---|---|
> | _PRIMARYSURFACE | Access to primary display area |
> | _OFFSCREENPLAIN | Access to off-screen memory |
> | _FLIP | Set up for instantaneous surface swap |
> | _SYSTEMMEMORY | Surface is in system memory. |
> | _VIDEOMEMORY | Surface is in video memory. Currently, TRUE for Primary surfaces. |
> | _VISIBLE | Writes are immediately visible. TRUE for Primary surfaces. |
> | _WRITEONLY | Data cannot be read from these surfaces. |
> | _MODEX | Setup for 320x200 or 320x240 resolutions. Typically used with SetCooperativeLevel of EXCLUSIVE, FULLSCREEN and MODEX |
>
> Other types that we will experience later include _3D, _TEXTUREMAP, _FRONTBUFFER, and _BACKBUFFER.

```
// tell driver that the caps field is valid
  m_SurfDesc.dwFlags = DDSD_CAPS;

  // call DirectDraw member  function to create primary surface
  HRESULT err;
  err = pdDraw->CreateSurface(&m_SurfDesc, &m_pSurfFns, NULL);
  if (err != DD_OK) {
    handleError(err);
    return FALSE;
  }

  return TRUE;
}
```

CreateSurface takes LPDDSURFACEDESC and (LPDIRECTDRAWSURFACE *) as parameters. DDSURFACEDESC is used to describe the surface requested/got. DIRECTDRAWSURFACE holds pointers to the member functions of the created surface.

If *CreateSurface()* was successful, DirectDraw drivers should set relevant fields in the DDSURFACEDESC structure to describe the surface that was created. In particular, dwHeight, dwWidth, and ddpfPixelFormat should be valid. To really make sure that the structure gets filled, use *IDirectDrawSurface::GetSurfaceDesc()*. However, even *GetSurfaceDesc()* will not return a valid pointer to surface memory (lpSurface). This field will only become valid after you lock the surface. More on *Lock()* shortly.

Note that we have written our libraries for an RGB8 pixel format. What happens if the Primary surface display configuration is not in RGB8 display mode? We could merely "Release" the newly created surface and flag an error. An alternate method is to check the display configuration, before creating a Primary surface:

```
bool CDirectDraw::IsDisplayModeOK(void)
{
  //initialize a surface descriptor
  ddsurfacedesc ddSurf;
  memset(&ddSurf, 0, sizeof(ddSurf));// zero out mem
  ddSurf.dwSize = sizeof(ddSurf);// set size field

  // get the primary display mode
  hresult err = m_pdDraw->GetDisplayMode(&ddSurf);

  // if call was successful, check returned descriptor
  if ((err == dd_ok) &&
     (ddSurf.ddpfPixelFormat.dwFlags == ddpf_paletteindexed8))
  return true
  else
     err = js_baddisplay;
  }

  // was error, flag and return
  handleError(err);
  return false;
}
```

EXTRA CREDIT: Explore changing the display format if it's not one you like. Look at *SetDisplayMode()* and *SetCooperativeLevel()*.

SetDisplayMode() is provided by the IDirectDraw2 interface. Our Primary surface sample code on the JS CD shows the use of the IDirectDraw2 and IDirectSurface2 interfaces. Check it out.

Let's move forward, and *write directly* to the display screen using the Primary surface that we just created.

4.6 Implementing a Simple Sprite Class

We use the same class definition for sprites as in the previous chapter. Here is a simple sprite class implementation where we control the drawing.

```
BOOL CSprite::Init(CBitmap &bitmap, BYTE byKeyColor)
{
  // get access to BITMAP to get size; alloc space for data; copy data
  BITMAP bm;
  bitmap.GetBitmap(&bm);
  m_pData = new BYTE[bm.bmWidthInBytes * bm.bmHeight];
  bitmap.GetBitmapBits(bm.bmWidthInBytes * bm.bmHeight, m_pData);
  // init member variables
  m_dwWidth = bm.bmWidth;
  m_dwHeight = bm.bmHeight;
  m_byTransp = byKeyColor;
  return TRUE;
}
```

The sprite Blt function is extremely simple. It takes in a destination pointer and pitch and draws the sprite at the specified point. The function is written in C and relies entirely on the compiler for optimization.

```
void CSprite::Blt(LPVOID lpDst, long lPitch, CPoint &point)
{
  // compute address dst and src pixels.  note pitch can be negative
  PBYTE pDst = (PBYTE)((long)lpDst + point.x + point.y * lPitch);
  PBYTE pSrc = m_pData;

  // blt the sprite on a row by row basis
  for (DWORD row = 0; row < m_dwHeight; row++) {
    for (DWORD col = 0; col < m_dwWidth;  col++, pSrc++, pDst++) {
      // test pixel for non-transp and write if so
      if (*pSrc != m_byTransp)
        *pDst = *pSrc;
    }
    // bump dst ptr forward to start of next row
    pDst += lPitch - m_dwWidth;
  }
}
```

A FASTER WAY OF DOING SPRITES

Our last sprite-based application needed a lot more performance than what we got with a per-pixel test and branch approach. We researched and developed alternate approaches in assembly. One of these approaches will be analyzed in Part VI where the optimization decisions can be discussed in greater detail. This routine is listed on the CD. We invite you to peruse the routine and adapt/adopt it if it proves suitable. See Chapter 19 for more details.

4.7 Drawing a Sprite on the DirectDraw Primary Surface

So far we've initialized DirectDraw, established that our preferred format was supported, and created a Primary surface. Now let's draw a sprite on the Primary surface—*we will be writing directly to the screen.*

```
CPrimarySurface::BltSprite(CSprite &spr, CPoint &point)
{
  // first lock surface, using "wait until lock"
  m_pSurfFns->Lock(NULL, &m_SurfDesc, DDLOCK_WAIT, NULL)
  // invoke sprite blt routine
  spr->Blt(m_SurfDesc.lpSurface, m_SurfDesc.lPitch, poin
  // release the lock
  m_pSurfFns->Unlock(NULL);
}
```

Blt writes directly to the screen.

- Graphics memory is shared by many applications. The surface must be locked to manage access to this common memory. Locking the surface returns a usable pointer in the Surface Descriptor.
- Memory in surfaces is arranged in blocks. lPitch need not equal SurfaceWidth.
- Unlock before you leave. Surface locks can lock out all GDI access.

DEBUGGING

Debugging between Lock and Unlock is tricky. Lock shuts out GDI access to the screen, so debuggers are unable to update their windows. *Single-stepping between lock and unlock in most debuggers will hang the system in Windows 95.* Debugging with NuMega's SoftIce for Windows 95 in dual monitor configuration or debugging under Windows NT 4.0 works with most debuggers.

4.8 Demo Time

At this point, you should be seeing sprites drawn directly to the display screen via DirectDraw Primary surfaces. Run the demo that corresponds to this chapter. You should see a sprite appear on the screen. Move the mouse around and the sprite will follow the mouse.

PART II

How do you know we're writing directly to the display screen? Move the mouse to the white border areas along the right or bottom edges of the clipping window. You will notice that the sprite writes data outside the clipping window. GDI would not let this happen. We have written directly to the screen without GDI.

Why can't we write anywhere on the screen? Our application tracks Mouse Move messages and draws the sprite based on mouse position. Our application stops receiving Mouse Move messages once the mouse cursor has left the main Window area. You can alter this application to write anywhere if you wish.

To be a well-behaved Windows application, your program should respect window overlaps, boundaries, and movements. You will also notice that moving the sprite leaves sprite trails. This is because the application is not set to refresh the background.

4.9 Redrawing Backgrounds on a DirectDraw Primary Surface

Here is a quick background Blt routine. Again, this version is extremely simple. It takes in a destination pointer and pitch and draws the background at the specified point. The only subtlety about Bltting backgrounds is that the rows in graphics memory are not necessarily contiguous, and therefore the Blt routine must handle a pitch.

```
void CBackground::Blt(LPBYTE lpDst, long lPitch, CPoint &point)
{
  PBYTEpDst, pSrc;
  DWORDrow, dwLeft, dwWidth, dwTop, dwRows;

  // compute address dst and src pixels.  note pitch can be negative
  pDst = (PBYTE)((long)lpDst + point.x + point.y * lPitch);

  // code removed that clamps ViewRect within background
  // dimensions; generates dwLeft, dwWidth, dwTop, dwRows
  // to define sub-region being bltted

  pSrc = m_pData + dwLeft + dwTop * m_dwWidth;

  // blt the sprite on a row by row basis
  for (row = 0; row < dwRows; row++) {
    memcpy(pDst, pSrc, dwWidth);// use simple memory copy
    pDst += lPitch;// bump dst ptr forward
    pSrc += m_dwWidth; // bump src ptr forward
  }
}
```

4.10 How Fast Can We Draw Sprites and Backgrounds?

Table 4-1 shows the speed at which sprites and backgrounds are drawn to Primary surfaces, and it presents a comparison with the GDI measurements from the previous chapter.

TABLE 4-1 How Fast Can We Draw Sprites and Backgrounds?

Method	Object		Time (in milliseconds)
CSurfacePrimary,	16 sprites	(width: 84; height: 63)	11.9
CSpriteCCode, CBackground	background	(width: 734; height: 475)	7.7
CSurfacePrimary,	16 sprites	(width: 84; height: 63)	(0.7–1.8)
CSpriteP5 CBackground	background	(width: 734; height: 475)	7.7
CSurfaceGDI	16 sprites	(width: 84; height: 63)	14.2
CSpriteGDI CBackground GDI	background	(width: 734; height: 475)	8.8

Some observations on the measurements:

■ The sprite routine written in Pentium-optimized assembly language is almost *10 times faster* than the C code version. There are two measurements noted for this routine as it is sensitive to alignment of destination writes. The faster time reflects writing sprites to DWORD-aligned start addresses.

■ We did write an assembly routine for background Blts (CBackgroundP5) that maximized DWORD-aligned writes per scan line. But we found that any performance gains detected were negligible, indicating that *memcpy* may already be similarly optimized.

4.11 Compositing Objects on a DirectDraw Primary Surface

Aaah, life would be simple if there were just one background and one sprite to worry about. We could be sipping iced teas in some tropical country; or maybe oh-nee-on soup in a Lu-wee-zee-ahna bayou. But . . .

---

2. Again, these measurements were taken on the base platform described in the Introduction and will definitely vary with different configurations. We have included the application and its source code on the Internet site. Run the application on your platform and see what results you get. We have separated out the timing code from the basic demo applications to simplify reading the base code.

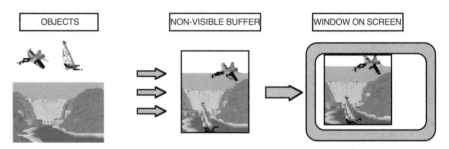

FIGURE 4-3 Compositing using a nonvisible buffer.

A difficulty of compositing sprites directly onto the Primary surface is that the compositing process is visible, so there is a noticeable flicker on the screen. You can obtain better results when you composite images on a non-visible buffer and then make this buffer visible.

The Timing Application has a menu selection for Compositing. Take a look at both the visible-buffer compositing and nonvisible-buffer compositing options. The nonvisible-buffer compositing is implemented by rendering all the graphics objects in back-to-front order in a system buffer and then Bltting this nonvisible buffer to the Primary surface as shown in Figure 4-3.

With this method we've solved a quality problem, but at the cost of a Blt. Bltting an 800 × 600 image from system memory to video memory costs about 10 milliseconds on the platform we're using (see Table 4-2). In the next chapter we will look at mechanisms to reduce the Blt cost.

TABLE 4-2 Composited Drawing to a Primary Surface

CSpriteP5 times are faster when Bltting to system memory. See details in Part VI.

CSpriteP5 84 x 63 (16)	CBackground	Refresh Screen
0.6–0.9	7.9	10.5

Note: Times in milliseconds.

WHAT HAVE YOU LEARNED?

By this time you've had an overview of DirectDraw and a taste of device dependence. You know that DirectDraw provides you with a lot more freedom than GDI does, but that there is a development burden associated with this freedom.

If you worked through the code samples, you have handled code and had direct access to the display surface using DirectDraw Primary surfaces. And if you did your extra credit work and perused the CD, you have seen Primary surface sprite demos and fast Sprite Blt code written in Pentium optimized assembly language.

And if you are still reading, you are probably ready and eager to move on to the next chapter and learn about hardware acceleration, and to later chapters where you'll read about processor optimization. Are you ready?

CHAPTER 5

Hardware Acceleration via DirectDraw

WHY READ THIS CHAPTER?
In the previous chapter you were introduced to rendering faster sprites directly to the display screen via Microsoft's DirectDraw interface. You were also introduced to the use of a second buffer to remove flicker with composited images. But making data visible by Bltting from the second buffer to the primary screen carries with it an expensive performance penalty. This section demonstrates how hardware acceleration features can reduce the cost of double-buffering.

In the previous chapter you were also introduced to rendering faster sprites directly to the display screen using custom rendering routines. In this chapter you will explore rendering sprites using hardware acceleration features.

In this chapter you will learn how to query for, set up, and use

- hardware Bltters to reduce the cost of double-buffering,
- page flipping hardware to further reduce the double-buffering cost, and
- transparency Blt hardware to reduce the cost of Bltting sprites.

5.1 Creating an Offscreen Surface

OK, roll up your sleeves. First, initialize the DirectDraw driver as in Chapter 4.

Once DirectDraw has been initialized, let's get access to an Offscreen surface. Let's create a CSurface object as usual (code follows).

```
CSurfaceOffscreen::CSurfaceOffscreen(void)
{
  // zero out the memory of the surface descriptor
  memset(&m_SurfDesc, 0, sizeof(m_SurfDesc));
  // init surface descriptor size
  m_SurfDesc.dwSize = sizeof(m_SurfDesc);
}
```

Now let's look at making some changes. In creating a Primary surface, we were getting access to the primary display surface. We took what we got— the dwWidth, the dwHeight, and the ddpfPixelFormat were all specified by the DirectDraw driver to match the user's display configuration. With Off-screen surfaces, though, we've got to specify what we want, and the driver will tell us whether or not our request can be satisfied.

DirectDraw drivers can be asked to enumerate the realm of their possibilities. If you can accept a variety of formats, you may want to use *IDirectDraw::EnumSurfaces()* to enumerate the available surfaces, and then you can choose your preference based on your personal criteria (better performance, better picture quality, or some other trade-off).

Our code only accepts RGB8, which is a very basic format and is supported by nearly all DirectDraw drivers. So we will take the easy way out and try to create an RGB8 surface and react to the errors if there are any.

Let's initialize the DDSURFACEDESC structure to our specifications and try to create an Offscreen surface.

```
BOOL CSurfaceOffscreen::Init(LPDIRECTDRAW pdDraw, CWnd *pcWnd)
{
  RECT  rWin;
  pcWnd->GetClientRect(&rWin);
  m_dwWidth = (DWORD)(rWin.right - rWin.left);
  m_dwHeight = (DWORD)(rWin.bottom - rWin.top);

  // set desired fields
  m_SurfDesc.dwHeight = m_dwHeight;
  m_SurfDesc.dwWidth = m_dwWidth;
  m_SurfDesc.ddpfPixelFormat.dwSize = sizeof(DDPIXELFORMAT);
  m_SurfDesc.ddpfPixelFormat.dwRGBBitCount = 8;
  m_SurfDesc.ddpfPixelFormat.dwFlags = DDPF_PALETTEINDEXED8 | DDPF_RGB;
  m_SurfDesc.ddsCaps.dwCaps = DDSCAPS_OFFSCREENPLAIN;
  m_SurfDesc.dwFlags =DDSD_WIDTH | DDSD_HEIGHT | DDSD_PIXELFORMAT | DDSD_CAPS;

  // try create surface
  HRESULT err;
  err = pdDraw->CreateSurface(&m_SurfDesc, &m_pSurf, NULL);
```

Need to specify the size of offscreen surface. Get the size of the client area of the application.

Specify size, type, and pixel format of surface. Note that DDPFPIXELFORMAT is a structure and therefore dwSize must be set.

Specify which fields in descriptor were set.

REQUEST SIMPLE OFFSCREEN SURFACE.

```
if (err != DD_OK) {
    handleError(err);
    return FALSE;
}
return TRUE;
}
```

Exactly how to specify the color format has never been clearly documented, and we have found that techniques that work with previous versions of DirectDraw do not work with current versions. To reach a resolution, we set our primary display format to the color format we wanted, created a primary surface, got the surface descriptor with *GetSurfaceDesc()*, and looked at how the color format was specified there.

5.2 Drawing a Sprite on the DirectDraw Offscreen Surface

We created an Offscreen surface based on our preferred format. Now let's draw a sprite on this Offscreen surface. We can use the same sprite and background Blt classes (and routines) we used in the previous chapter.

```
CSurfaceOffscreen::BltSprite(CSprite &spr, CPoint &point)
{
    m_pSurf->Lock(NULL, &m_SurfDesc, DDLOCK_WAIT, NULL);   // first lock surface
    spr->Blt(m_SurfDesc.lpSurface, m_SurfDesc.lPitch, point); // invoke blt
    m_pSurf->Unlock(NULL);                                 // release the lock
}
```

> Bltting sprites to an offscreen surface is pretty much the same as Bltting sprites to a Primary surface. Lock to get access to the surface, invoke the *SpriteBlt* routine with the newly obtained surface pointer and surface pitch, and then Unlock the surface.

When you Blt to an Offscreen surface, the results are not immediately visible. We have to Blt data from the Offscreen surface to the Primary surface to see the results.

On occasions when Offscreen surfaces are used for overlays or for texture maps, results may be immediately visible—look up the DDSCAPS_VISIBLE flag in the DirectDraw documentation on DDSCAPS.

Following is the code to transfer data to the visible surface.

```
CSurfaceOffscreen::Render(LPDIRECTDRAWSURFACE pPrimary, CWnd *pcWnd)
{
    CPOINT    ptTopLeft(0,0);
    pcWnd->ClientToScreen(&ptTopLeft);
    long    lRight  = ptTopLeft.x + m_dwWidth;
    long    lBottom = ptTopLeft.y + m_dwHeight;
    RECT rDst(ptTopLeft.x, ptTopLeft.y, lRight, lBottom);
    RECT rSrc(0, 0, m_dwWidth, m_dwHeight);

    // blt entire offscreen surface to subrect on primary surface
    err = pPrimary->Blt(&rDst, m_pSurf, &rSrc, DDBLT_WAIT, NULL);  ◄
}
```

- *IDirectDrawSurface::Blt* uses a BltFrom convention. The Blt function is invoked from the destination object; that is, the object that will get modified, *pPrimary*. This convention is consistent with the convention in MFC's *CDC::Blt*.
- The Blt operation can be further controlled by flags in the fourth parameter. There are over twenty-five controls, which include RasterOps, ColorFills, AlphaBlending, ChromaKeying, Z-Buffering, Rotation, other special effects, and more. We will use `DDBLT_KEYSRC` later in this chapter.
- Blt can be invoked asynchronously with the `DDBLT_ASYNC` flag. In Async mode, a successful return indicates no parameter errors were detected and the operation was successfully posted. See *IDirectDrawSurface::GetBltStatus* to check for completion/errors.
- We use `DDBLT_WAIT` to tell the Bltter to wait in case the Bltter hardware was already in use. The alternate option is for the Bltter to send us a `DDERR_WASSTILLDRAWING` error message if the Bltter was busy.
- Blt permits specifying a sub-rectangle of the source. By moving the sub-rectangle around you can scroll a view window within the source image. Setting Source and Dest rects to be of different sizes invokes a stretch (or shrink).

Blt can return a `DDERR_SURFACELOST` error message. Surfaces can be lost because the display card's mode was changed or because an application used an exclusive access mode. See *IDirectDrawSurface::Restore* to deal with lost surfaces.

5.3 Demo Time

At this point, you should be seeing sprites on the Primary surface. These sprites were drawn to an Offscreen surface, and the composited image was transferred to the Primary surface. Select the Primary Surface option from the sample application on the CD. You should see a sprite appear on the screen. Move the mouse around, and the sprite will follow the mouse.

How do you know we're using Offscreen surfaces? Move the mouse to the white border areas along the right or left edges. You may notice that the sprite seems to "wrap around" to the other edge. If this artifact occurs, it is because the rows of the Offscreen surface memory are packed contiguously. When we write beyond an edge, we "happen" to write into the adjacent column. This artifact may not occur if the DirectDraw driver allocated an Offscreen surface with noncontiguous rows (that is, lPitch > dwWidth).

Move the mouse to the bottom edge. You will notice that the sprite disappears *before* the mouse reaches the border. If we were to draw past the bottom border, we would write into unallocated memory and would generate a General

Protection Fault (GPF). Therefore, for this demo, we have deliberately chosen not to draw the sprite if it is going to extend past the bottom edge.

Don't search for CSurface Offscreen on our sample CD. Instead we use two variants, CSurfaceVidMem and CSurfaceSysMem, which you can search for.

5.4 How Fast Is OffScreen Surface Drawing?

Table 5-1 measures the speed of drawing sprites and backgrounds to Off-Screen surfaces[1] merely to furnish a preliminary insight. More meaningful measurements, comparisons, and discussions are upcoming in this chapter.

TABLE 5-1 Preliminary Measurements for Offscreen Surface Drawing

CSprite 84 × 63 (16)	CBackground 734 × 475	Refresh Screen 852 × 559
0.6–0.9	7.9	10.5

All times are in milliseconds.

These measurements look the same as the measurements for composited drawing to a Primary surface. So how about some acceleration? Where's the hardware?

5.5 Finding Hardware Acceleration

We used *PrimarySurface::Blt* to transfer data from the Offscreen surface to the Primary surface. Was this a hardware accelerated transfer? It's hard to say. DirectDraw has a Hardware Emulation Layer (HEL) that will emulate DirectDraw functionality in software. The purpose of the HEL is to always provide key DirectDraw features, even if the graphics hardware doesn't support them.[2]

---

1. Again, these measurements were taken on the base platform described in the Introduction and will definitely vary with different configurations.
2. Unfortunately, the DirectDraw HEL does not emulate all the features exposed by the DirectDraw interface. Therefore, you cannot rely on software emulation always being available. *DirectDraw::GetCaps* returns the capabilities of the hardware and the HEL independently.

PART II

So between the hardware and the HEL, we can't really say who did the *PrimarySurface::Blt*. Do you really need to know whether it was a hardware Blt? Yes. You may want to know for a couple of reasons.

1. Hardware Bltters are faster than software emulated Blts, and you may want to alter your application's logic to respond to the performance difference.

2. A Hardware Bltter may be available only under constraints, and you may want to constrain the environment to get hardware-accelerated performance. For example, hardware Bltting may only be available if both the source and the destination are located in video memory— therefore you may want to deliberately place objects in video memory. Similarly, the hardware might only be able to stretch in integer multiples, and you may want to disable arbitrary resizing to use hardware stretches. (Look up the DirectDraw documentation on DDCAPS, DDFXCAPS, and look for DDCAPS_CANBLTSYSMEM, DDFXCAPS_BLTSTRETCHXN, and DDFXCAPS_BLTSTRETCHYN flags for more details on these examples.)

5.6 Setting Up for Hardware Acceleration

Here's some code we can use to find out some of the hardware's capabilities.

```
CHardware::GetCaps(LPDIRECTDRAW pdDraw)
{
    DDCAPS  hwCaps = {0}, helCaps = {0};
    hwCaps.dwSize = sizeof(DDCAPS);
    helCaps.dwSize = sizeof(DDCAPS) ;
    pDDraw->GetCaps(&hwCaps, &helCaps);
    if (hwCaps.dwCaps & DDCAPS_BLT )              ◊ Can the h/w Blt?
        m_bCanBltVidMem = TRUE;
    if (hwCaps.dwCaps & DDCAPS_CANBLTSYSMEM)      ◊ Can it Blt from/to system memory?
        m_bCanBltSysMem = TRUE;
}
```

- Two DDCAPS structures are passed to *IDirectDraw::GetCaps* in which we get back descriptions of both the hardware device and the Hardware Emulation Layer.
- DDCAPS structures are huge and allow for a wide variety of features to be described. In our code we are mainly interested in DDCAPS_BLT and DDCAPS_CANBLTSYSMEM. Later in this chapter we will look for DDCAPS_COLORKEY.
- Take a look at the documentation for DDCAPS (and its contained structures) to get a feel for the breadth of hardware features that can be exposed via DirectDraw. DDCAPS_GDI, DDCAPS_VBI, and DDCAPS_ PALETTEVSYNC are features that might be useful. DDCAPS_STEREOVIEW and DDCAPS_READSCANLINE at the very least attract attention.
- DDCAPS contains within it a DDSCAPS structure that during *GetCaps* will be filled by the kinds of DirectDraw surfaces that can be created.
  Not all features may be available simultaneously. For instance, by using one feature, another may become unavailable.

Of course, a lot more information is returned in the DDSCAPS structure. We've only highlighted the capabilities we're looking for. And now, here's code to situate an Offscreen surface in video memory.

```
BOOL CSurfaceVidMem::Init(LPDIRECTDRAW pdDraw, CWnd *pcWnd)
{
    RECT  rWin;
    pcWnd->GetClientRect(&rWin);
    m_dwWidth = (DWORD)(rWin.right - rWin.left);
    m_dwHeight = (DWORD)(rWin.bottom - rWin.top);
    // check if there's enough memory for vidMem based surface
    DWORD  dwTotal, dwFree;
    DDSCAPS ddsCaps;
    ddsCaps.dwCaps = DDSCAPS_OFFSCREENPLAIN;
    pDDraw->GetAvailableVidMem(&ddsCaps, &dwTotal, &dwFree);
    DWORD dwSurfSize = m_dwWidth * m_dwHeight;
    if (dwFree < dwSurfSize) {
        handleError(DDERR_OUTOFVIDEOMEMORY);
        return FALSE;
    }

    // set desired fields
    m_SurfDesc.dwHeight = m_dwHeight;
    m_SurfDesc.dwWidth = m_dwWidth;
    m_SurfDesc.ddsCaps.dwCaps = DDSCAPS_OFFSCREENPLAIN ;
    m_SurfDesc.ddsCaps.dwCaps |= DDSCAPS_VIDEOMEMORY;
    m_SurfDesc.ddpfPixelFormat.dwSize = sizeof(DDPIXELFORMAT);
    m_SurfDesc.ddpfPixelFormat.dwRGBBitCount = 8;
    m_SurfDesc.ddpfPixelFormat.dwFlags = DDPF_PALETTEINDEXED8 | DDPF_RGB;
    m_SurfDesc.dwFlags =DDSD_WIDTH|DDSD_HEIGHT|DDSD_PIXELFORMAT|DDSD_CAPS;

    // try create surface
    HRESULT err;
    err = pdDraw->CreateSurface(&m_SurfDesc, &m_pSurf, NULL);
    if (err != DD_OK) {
        handleError(err);
        return FALSE;
    }
    return TRUE;
}
```

The *IDirectDraw* object has a function to query how much memory is available on the graphics device. Of course, you could just try to create a surface and look at the return code if the attempt failed.

Or in DDCAPS_VIDEOMEMORY flag to force surface to be created with video memory. The HEL will not allocate an emulated offscreen surface if the device failed the request.

Despite a successful negotiation of *GetAvailableVidMem,* the *CreateSurface* call can still return DDERR_OUTOFVIDEOMEMORY. This is because we calculated dwSurfSize as dwWidth*dwHeight. However, the graphics card may use an lPitch (allocated row width) larger than dwWidth and there may not be enough memory for lPitch*dwHeight.

For the times when there isn't enough memory on the video card to create a video memory surface, our code uses a CSurfaceSysMem surface. The code for this option is similar to the code we have used to situate an Offscreen surface in video memory. In this case, the DDSCAPS_SYSTEMMEMORY is used instead of the DDSCAPS_VIDEOMEMORY. Also the check for memory is not needed, since the surface will be allocated in system memory.

PART II

Following is the code that uses the hardware Bltter. Looks just like *CSurfaceOffscreen::Render*—doesn't it? Except now we know we're using the hardware Bltter, because we checked that the graphics card did indeed have a hardware Bltter, and when we created the surface we forced it to reside in video memory.

```
CSurfaceVidMem::Render(LPDIRECTDRAWSURFACE pPrimary, CWnd *pcWnd)
{
    CPOINT ptTopLeft(0,0);
    pcWnd->ClientToScreen(&ptTopLeft);
    long lRight  = ptTopLeft.x + m_dwWidth;
    long lBottom = ptTopLeft.y + m_dwHeight;
    RECT  rDst(ptTopLeft.x, ptTopLeft.y, lRight, lBottom);
    RECT rSrc(0, 0, m_dwWidth, m_dwHeight);

    // blt entire offscreen surface to subrect on primary surface
    err = pPrimary->Blt(&rDst, m_pSurf, &rSrc, DDBLT_WAIT, NULL);
}
```

5.7 How Fast Is CSurfaceVidMem Drawing?

Table 5-2 measures the speed at which objects can be drawn when using a hardware-accelerated Offscreen surface.

TABLE 5-2 Measurements for Offscreen Surface Drawing

Surface	CSprite 84 × 63 (16)	Cbackground 734 × 475	Refresh Screen 852 × 559	Post Refresh	Total
CSysMem	0.6–0.9	7.9	10.5	0.0	19.3
CVidMem	0.7–1.8	7.7	0.1	8.9	9.6/18.5

All times are in milliseconds.

Wow! Refresh Screen is a minuscule 0.1 millisecond. The total time seems halved. Wow! But what's this new column for Post Refresh? Well, when we invoke *pPrimary->Blt,* the hardware Bltter returns as soon as it has *started* the Blt. We can use the main processor, while the graphics processor does the Blt in the background. This is in effect a form of parallel processing. (Maybe one day there will be many of these little processors working in parallel. Oh wait, isn't that what's in them "soopah computahs"? Never mind.)

Parallel processing is functional as long as we don't want to use the same memory that the graphics processor is using. In other words, we would be denied access to the Primary surface while the graphics processor was still working. In this case we would have to wait until the Blt was complete. Post Refresh is a measurement of the worst-case scenario for wait time—we tried to lock the surface immediately after the Blt, and then we measured how long we had to wait.

The gist of all this is

1. We can, indeed, increase overall application speed as long as the application can work on something else while the graphics processor is Bltting in the background. This seems like a fairly workable situation.
2. We have not gained much benefit in the overall "Composite and Render" time. Time is gained *only* by parallel processing and not by reducing the length of the graphics rendering steps.

5.8 Accelerating Offscreen to Primary Transfers by Page Flips

We've used the hardware Bltter to transfer data from Offscreen surfaces to the Primary surface. On timing these data transfers, we find that despite using a hardware Bltter, the actual Blt cost is still about 9 milliseconds. Let's look at *Page Flipping hardware* in graphics devices to tap into an even faster mechanism for making background data visible.

5.8.1   What Is Graphics Page Flipping?

Consider that the display screen is being constantly refreshed at the monitor refresh rate (anywhere between 30 and 90 times per second). Pixel data to be displayed on the screen is retrieved from somewhere in graphics card memory.

What if the location of the data was specified by a pointer; that is, what if the monitor refresh hardware used an indirect reference to access pixel data. Change the value of the pointer and an entirely new image is being displayed on the screen. This in effect is Page Flipping.

TABLE 5-3 Constraints on Using Page Flipping

Page Flipping hardware, in general, is designed to get the pointer value and then de-reference the pointer to refresh the entire image.	Therefore, only the entire screen can be Page Flipped (not independent windows).
The screen area of the display can be reconfigured to different shapes. But once configured, graphics cards are designed for constant screen areas.	Therefore, all buffers used for Page Flipping must be of the same size.
With two buffers, data written into the invisible buffer is not written into the visible buffer. Data will be missing from alternate buffers unless it is written into both, and the result will be an annoying flicker.	Therefore, either the entire scene must be redrawn, or some intelligent logic must be used to make data continue to exist across buffers.
Similarly, GDI does not know that we are in Page Flip mode, and the data that GDI drew into one buffer would "vanish" when we Page Flipped. (It would reappear when we Page Flipped again, producing an apparent flicker.)	Therefore Page Flipping can only be used in "Exclusive" mode, and other applications cannot share the display while Page Flipping is in use.

5.8.2 DirectDraw Page Flipping Model

Let's say we set up two buffers. One buffer is the visible buffer and is called the *front* buffer. The second buffer is invisible and is called the *back* buffer. When the graphics card Page Flips, it makes the back buffer visible; that is, the back buffer becomes the front buffer.

Now, let's suppose we wanted to render the next image into what was previously the front buffer. Which surface do we Lock to get back a usable pointer? The code that follows in the next subsection will show that after a Page Flip, DirectDraw makes the front buffer into the back buffer and vice versa, and therefore all we need to do is to *Lock()* what was our back buffer.

5.8.3 Does the Hardware Support Page Flipping?

Let's find out whether the hardware supports Page Flipping.

```
CHardware::CanTransparentBlt()
{
    DDCAPS  hwCaps = {0}, helCaps = {0};
    hwCaps.dwSize = sizeof(DDCAPS);
    helCaps.dwSize = sizeof(DDCAPS);
    pDDraw->GetCaps(&hwCaps, &helCaps);

    BOOL bCanPageFlip = FALSE;
    if (hwCaps.ddsCaps.dwCaps & DDSCAPS_FLIP)
        bCanPageFlip = TRUE;
}
```

> DirectDraw indicates support for Page Flipping by indicating that Flip surfaces can be created.

5.8.4 Setting Up DirectDraw to Use Page Flipping

There are two ways to set up Page Flipping. The first is to have DirectDraw create a *complex* surface that automatically creates and connects multiple buffers. The second approach is to create a Primary surface, create Offscreen Surfaces, and then to *Attach* the Offscreen surfaces to the Primary Surface.

We will demonstrate the second path, because it gives us the opportunity to help you past some tough problems that you would experience if you needed to use this path.

```
BOOL CSurfaceBackBuffer::Init(LPDIRECTDRAW pDraw, CWnd *pcWnd)
{
    pDDraw->SetCooperativeLevel(pcWnd->hWnd,
                    DDSCL_EXCLUSIVE | DDSCL_FULLSCREEN);
```

First we've got to set up DirectDraw to be in FullScreen mode to do Page Flipping.
- FullScreen mode can only be setup, if we have Exclusive access to the screen.
- DirectDraw will return an error if you *SetCooperativeLevel* while you have any surfaces created. Shut down any surfaces prior to using this function.

The documentation states that *IDirectDrawSurface::Flip* can only be invoked on a buffer marked as the DDSCAPS_FRONTBUFFER surface from among a group of buffers that have been marked as DDSCAPS_FLIP. But if you tried to set the DDSCAPS_FRONTBUFFER, DirectDraw will return an error stating that DDSCAPS_FRONTBUFFER is not a settable flag, therefore this code has been commented out. We found that Flips work when you don't set these flags.

```
    // create a primary surface
    memset(&m_PrimDesc, 0, sizeof(DDSURFACEDESC));
    m_PrimDesc.dwSize = sizeof(DDSURFACEDESC);
    m_PrimDesc.ddsCaps.dwCaps = DDSCAPS_PRIMARYSURFACE;
    m_PrimDesc.dwFlags = DDSD_CAPS;
    // m_PrimDesc.ddsCaps.dwCaps |= (DDSCAPS_COMPLEX);
    // m_PrimDesc.ddsCaps.dwCaps |= (DDSCAPS_FRONTBUFFER|DDSCAPS_FLIP);
    pDDraw->CreateSurface(&m_PrimDesc, &m_PrimSurf, NULL);
```

- The back buffer must be pretty much identical to the front buffer. So tell DirectDraw to describe the primary surface and copy it over.
- Create the back buffer as a plain Offscreen surface. Force it to reside in video memory, so that graphics hardware can Flip the surface. Also, see note above on Flip flags.

```
    m_PrimSurf.GetSurfaceDesc(&m_SurfDesc);
    memcpy(&m_SurfDesc, &m_PrimDesc, sizeof(DDSURFACEDESC));
    m_SurfDesc.ddsCaps.dwCaps = DDSCAPS_OFFSCREENPLAIN|DDSCAPS_VIDEOMEMORY;
    // m_PrimDesc.ddsCaps.dwCaps |= (DDSCAPS_COMPLEX);
    // m_SurfDesc.ddsCaps.dwCaps |= (DDSCAPS_BACKBUFFER|DDSCAPS_FLIP);
    m_SurfDesc.dwFlags = DDSD_WIDTH | DDSD_HEIGHT|DDSD_PIXELFORMAT|DDSD_CAPS;
```

Attach the Offscreen surface to the Primary surface. A chain of multiple buffers can be attached.

```
    // create the offscreen surface and attach it to the primary surface
    pdDraw->CreateSurface(&m_SurfDesc, &m_pSurf, NULL);
    m_pPrimSurf->AddAttachedSurface(m_pSurf);

    return TRUE;
}
```

5.8.5 "Rendering" Flippable Surfaces

A back buffer is just like any other Offscreen surface, and the code to draw objects to CSurfaceBackBuffer is just like the code to draw objects to CSurfaceVidMem. However, the code to make the data in the back buffer visible is different. We use Flip instead of Blt to "transfer" the data to the Primary surface.

```
CSurfaceBackBuffer::Render()
{
    // Flip with WAIT-UNTIL-READY
    m_pPrimSurf.Flip(NULL, (DWORD)DDFLIP_WAIT);
}
```

5.9 How Fast Is CSurfaceBackBuffer Drawing?

Table 5-4 measures the speed of drawing objects with a hardware accelerated Offscreen surface.

TABLE 5-4 Measurements for Offscreen Surface Drawing

Surface	CSprite 84 × 63 (16)	CBackground 734 × 475	Refresh Screen 852 × 559	Post Refresh	Total
CSysMem	0.6–0.9	7.9	10.5	0.0	19.3
CVidMem	0.7–1.8	7.7	0.1	8.9	17.4/18.5
CBackBuffer	0.7–1.8	7.7	0.1	0.5–7.6	9.0–17.2

All times are in milliseconds.

The variability in the Post Refresh for back buffers is the glaring figure. *IDirectDrawSurface2::Flip()* is always synchronized with the Vertical Blank Interval[3] (VBI) of the monitor. So if you invoked *Flip()* function just before the VBI, then the *Flip()* function would be instantaneous. But if you invoked *Flip()* function just after the VBI, then you would have to wait for VBI for the flip to occur.

---

3. Vertical Blank Interval is the time interval when no monitor refresh is occurring, because the monitor's beam is returning from the end position (bottom right corner) to the start position (top left corner) after having refreshed the screen.

DirectDraw will not let you lock a back buffer surface that is waiting to be flipped. However, in contrast to the use of the Bltter, a "Wait for VBI" does not consume hardware resources, and DirectDraw will allow you to use other surfaces. So what if you had a second back buffer that you could render to, while the other one was waiting to be flipped? This is known as *triple buffering. Post Refresh cost is negligible with triple buffering*, and the only practical limit to the frame refresh rate is the refresh rate of the monitor.

EXTRA CREDIT

Implement triple buffering by extending the double-buffering sample application on the CD. Note: attached buffers are linked in a circular fashion, and the buffer attached last is the next one that will be made visible. Extend your exercise to measure the performance implications of writing into the back buffer in the wrong order. The timing application *TimingApp* has sample code for triple buffering, in case you run into problems.

5.10 Hardware Acceleration to Blt Sprites

We used hardware to Blt from Offscreen surface to Primary surface. Why not use hardware to render objects too? Sprites are transparent objects. To accelerate sprite Bltting with hardware, we must find out whether the hardware can handle data with transparency.

```
CHardware::CanTransparentBlt()
{
  DDCAPS  hwCaps = {0}, helCaps = {0};
  hwCaps.dwSize = sizeof(DDCAPS);
  helCaps.dwSize = sizeof(DDCAPS);
  pDDraw->GetCaps(&hwCaps, &helCaps);
```

DDCAPS_COLORKEY says that some form of colorkey is supported. DDCAPS_COLORKEYHWASSIST says that the color-keying is done by hardware. We would have preferred to check only for the second flag, but we found some graphics cards that only set the first flag. Graphics card vendors are not supposed to provide software emulation. You may want to test the performance of color-key implementations.

```
  BOOL bCanKey = FALSE;
  if ((hwCaps.dwCaps & DDCAPS_COLORKEY) ||
      (hwCaps.dwCaps & DDCAPS_COLORKEYHWASSIST))
      bCanKey = TRUE;
  if (bCanKey && (hwCaps.dwCKeyCaps & DDCKEYCAPS_SRCBLT))
      m_bCanTranspBlt = TRUE;
}
```

Color-keying can take many forms—there are about eighteen different flags defined in the DirectDraw documentation. The dwCKeyCaps field in the DDCAPS structure describes supported color-keying forms. Once we know that some form of color key is supported, we've got to check if it's a form we can use. For our definition of sprites, our sample application looks for DDCKEYCAPS_SRCBLT color-keying.

Once we've found that the hardware is indeed capable of Bltting sprites, we can look at code to set up sprites for hardware Bltting and to Blt the sprites.

```
BOOL CSpriteGrfx::Init(LPDIRECTDRAW pdDraw,
CBitmap &bitmap, BYTE byKeyColor)
{
  // load data from bitmap and init member variables
  BITMAP bm;
  bitmap.GetBitmap(&bm);
  pData = new BYTE[bm.bmWidth * bm.bmHeight];
  bitmap.GetBitmapBits(bm.bmWidth * bm.bmHeight, pData);
  m_dwWidth = bm.bmWidth;
  m_dwHeight = bm.bmHeight;
  m_byTransp = byKeyColor;
```

We start out just like we were creating a hardware-accelerated Offscreen surface.

```
  DWORD dwTotal, dwFree;
  DDSCAPS ddsCaps;
  ddsCaps.dwCaps = DDSCAPS_OFFSCREENPLAIN;
  pDDraw->GetAvailableVidMem(&ddsCaps, &dwTotal, &dwFree);
  DWORD dwSurfSize = m_dwHeight * m_dwWidth;
  if (dwFree < dwSurfSize) {
      handleError(DDERR_OUTOFVIDEOMEMORY);
      return FALSE;
  }
  m_SurfDesc.dwHeight = m_dwHeight;
  m_SurfDesc.dwWidth = m_dwWidth;
  m_SurfDesc.ddsCaps.dwCaps = DDSCAPS_OFFSCREENPLAIN ;
  m_SurfDesc.ddsCaps.dwCaps |= DDSCAPS_VIDEOMEMORY;
  m_SurfDesc.ddpfPixelFormat.dwSize = sizeof(DDPIXELFORMAT);
  m_SurfDesc.ddpfPixelFormat.dwFlags = DDPF_PALETTEINDEXED8;
  m_SurfDesc.dwFlags =DDSD_WIDTH|DDSD_HEIGHT|DDSD_PIXELFORMAT|DDSD_CAPS;
```

Add in specification of color key and set dwFlags to indicate that this field is valid. The Color key can be a range. Our sample only uses a single color and sets high and low to be the same.

```
  DWORD dwKey = (DWORD)byKeyColor;
  m_SurfDesc.ddckCKSrcBlt.dwColorSpaceLowValue = dwKey;
  m_SurfDesc.ddckCKSrcBlt.dwColorSpaceHighValue = dwKey;
  m_SurfDesc.dwFlags |= DDSD_CKSRCBLT;

  // try create the surface
  HRESULT err = pdDraw->CreateSurface(&m_SurfDesc,&m_pSurf,NULL);
  if (err != DD_OK) {
     handleError(err);
     return FALSE;
  }
```

Set up the sprite, by transferring data to the Offscreen surface at Init-Time. Remember to lock surface to get access and unlock surface after use.

```
m_pSurf->Lock(NULL, &m_SurfDesc, DDLOCK_WAIT, NULL);
PBYTE pDst = (PBYTE)m_SurfDesc.lpSurface;
PBYTE pSrc = m_pData;
for (DWORD dwRow = 0; dwRow < m_dwHeight; dwRow++) {
    memcpy(pDst, pSrc, m_dwWidth);
    pDst += m_SurfDesc.lPitch;
    pSrc += m_dwWidth;
}
m_pSurf->Unlock(NULL);
return TRUE;
}
```

Next we'll check out the code that Blts sprites with the hardware Bltter. It's pretty much like CSurfaceVidMem, except for the DDBLT_KEYSRC added into the Blt control flag.

```
CSpriteGrfx::Blt(LPDIRECTDRAWSURFACE pDstSurf, CPoint &ptDst)
{
    long lRight  = ptDst.x + m_dwWidth;
    long lBottom = ptDst.y + m_dwHeight;
    RECTrDst(ptDst.x, ptDst.y, lRight, lBottom);
    RECTrSrc(0, 0, m_dwWidth, m_dwHeight);

    // blt entire sprite surface to subrect on dest surface
    pDstSurf->Blt(&rDst,m_pSurf,&rSrc,DDBLT_WAIT|DDBLT_KEYSRC,NULL);
}
```

Blt sprite to destination surface. Specify that the sprite has transparency and that it is keyed on the source.

5.11 How Fast Is CSpriteGrfx (and CBackgroundGrfx) Drawing?

Table 5-5 on the next page records the speed of drawing sprites and backgrounds with and without hardware acceleration. Following the table are some observations on the measurements.

PART II

TABLE 5-5 Measurement of Hardware-Accelerated Object Drawing

CSpriteP5 84 × 63 (16)	CSpriteGrfx 84 × 63 (16)	CBackgroundP5 734 × 475	CBackgroundGrfx 734 × 475
0.7–1.8	2.4–2.7	7.9	

All times are in milliseconds.

- CSpriteGrfx is not as sensitive to unaligned writes as is CSpriteP5. But on the platform we're using the CPU-based sprite drawing routine is faster than the graphics hardware–based routine. Note that CSpriteP5's time will vary with CPU speed, while CSpriteGrfx's time probably won't.
- Non-transparency Blts run faster when you use hardware acceleration. The benefit is especially noticeable for large backgrounds. The CPU in general is faster at Transparent Blts, with the performance difference increasing with faster CPU speeds.

CPU-based rendering needs surfaces to be locked, but hardware-accelerated sprites do not—so you would need to do constant Locks and Unlocks. Lock/ Unlock costs may be comparatively large when you are rendering small sprites. Our surface-rendering code adds logic to avoid unnecessary locks and unlocks. Based on your sprite sizes, it may be worth making this effort to minimize locks and unlocks.

WHAT HAVE YOU LEARNED?

By this time, you've got a taste of accessing device features to accelerate multimedia performance under Windows. If you worked through the code samples, you would have handled code to create and accelerate offscreen buffers, set the display into full-screen mode, and performed Page Flipping. You would also have worked through code to draw sprites and backgrounds using hardware acceleration.

You should also have gotten a taste for the performance costs of various options. As a result you have some experience of how important it is to apportion device memory resources thoughtfully. Our acceleration strategy for the multimedia objects in this section would be to give triple buffering the highest priority, to give background Bltting the second highest priority, and to try to use the CPU for Transparent Blts. We hope we have sparked some ideas on what memory allocation strategy would serve your application best.

Device dependence can be burdensome. There's a lot of code to be written, debugged, profiled for performance, and optimized. In the next chapter you will learn of software libraries with higher-level APIs that work to provide high-performance multimedia without the burden of device dependence—sort of like a "GDI for Multimedia."

CHAPTER 6

RDX: High-Performance Mixing with a High-Level API

WHY READ THIS CHAPTER? In the previous chapters, you were introduced to several device-dependent paths for achieving higher-performance sprites using Microsoft DirectDraw. But for routine multimedia, wouldn't it be nice to have the multimedia equivalent of GDI—to be able to program with multimedia objects like sprites, backgrounds, and video streams without having to worry about the idiosyncrasies of device implementations?

This chapter will introduce you to Intel's Realistic Display Mixer (RDX), which offers a device-independent interface for multimedia objects. RDX has hand tuned assembly code for accomplishing high performance on unaccelerated platforms, and it accesses hardware features whenever available for further acceleration. Read on and decide whether the ease of programming makes up for having to learn a new interface. Decide whether the features and performance make up for any reduced flexibility. As you work through this chapter, you will

- get an overview of what RDX is and what it offers,
- learn how to use RDX to render fast sprites and backgrounds, and
- learn how to direct RDX's use of DirectDraw.

6.1 Introduction to Intel's RDX Animation Library

Direct access to device features, through interfaces like DCI and Direct-Draw, is one way of addressing performance problems for multimedia under Windows. The downside of direct access is device dependence. Direct access also forces the programmer to learn how a variety of graphics devices work.

Intel developed the Realistic Display Mixer (RDX) system to provide developers with a high-level interface to manage multimedia objects and multimedia devices. Since multimedia applications are performance sensitive, Intel's RDX system has been engineered to provide its high-level abstraction without sacrificing performance.

Figure 6-1 shows RDX within the context of the Windows 95 display architecture. The system can be considered as "middle-ware," providing abstractions above Microsoft's DirectDraw and Direct Video, and interacting with Video for Windows (VFW). RDX can also interface with Microsoft's Direct3D and ActiveMovie components.

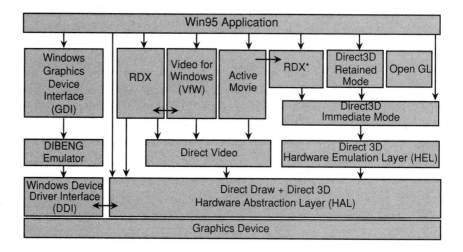

FIGURE 6-1 RDX within the Windows 95 display architecture.

6.1.1 Features of RDX

RDX is a high-performance multimedia object management system that allows developers to program at a higher level without a performance penalty. The RDX system makes extensive use of hand-tuned assembly code to obtain high performance even on unaccelerated platforms. RDX can use hardware acceleration when available and can also be upgraded with assembly code modules tuned to future processors.

Figure 6-2 shows the RDX object management system architecture. The architecture allows multimedia objects like sprites, backgrounds, video, or 3D to be mixed with one another. The system can handle even complex mixing scenarios such as video on video with differing frame rates.

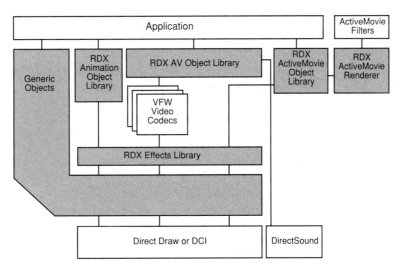

FIGURE 6-2 RDX object management system architecture.

The RDX system consists of a mixer module and some other object modules:

- The Mixer module defines generic mixable objects, object attributes, and attribute management functions. Objects that follow the rules of the mixer module can be mixed with one another without knowing about one another. The Mixer module interfaces with DirectDraw and accesses suitable hardware acceleration.
- The RDX Audio-Video (AV) module supports video tracks, audio tracks, and AV streams as mixable objects. It interfaces with the Video for Windows Audio-Video Interleaved (AVI) file format and VFW-based codecs. The AV module supports sources of transparent video such as Indeo Video Interactive.
- The RDX Animation module contains hand-tuned assembly code to support sprites, backgrounds, and tiled grids as mixable objects. The RDX Animation module also exports effects that can be applied on objects from both the Animation module and the AV module. Examples of effects include shearing and horizontal or vertical flipping.

In addition to the mixing and the predefined objects, RDX offers a fairly straightforward interface based on all objects having generic attributes. RDX uses simple function calls for various DirectDraw display modes to hide underlying device dependence.

PART II

RDX offers grouping to easily manipulate the attributes of many objects. It offers effects to transform the image data of an object at draw-time. Timers and events in RDX allow activities to be scheduled and allow the synchronizing of time-stamped material such as video streams. Collision and hot spots detect interactions between objects.

This chapter deals primarily with the Animation module and the Mixer module.

6.1.2 Before You Get Overly Excited

RDX offers high performance without the programming burden or device dependence, but the ease of use may come at the expense of reduced flexibility. For example, for practical reasons RDX will only use a subset of the features that are offered by DirectDraw and Video for Windows. Similarly, RDX will only tap into a subset of the acceleration features offered by hardware devices.

Just as when we were evaluating GDI, we must measure the strengths of RDX's device independence against the possibility of reduced flexibility. RDX does not prevent simultaneous use of DirectX, but in that case, the benefits of programming ease are defeated. And! Having to learn more than one set of APIs and debugging more than one system component are added burdens.

6.2 Using RDX

RDX is an object-based system. The object hierarchy in RDX contains generic objects, render objects, and source data objects.

- All displayable RDX objects are derived from a *generic objects* base class. The generic objects base class defines a set of generic attributes and a set of attribute management functions.
- Displayable objects derive from the base class and can be called *render objects*. Sprites, backgrounds, grids/tiles, and videotracks are examples of render objects. In addition to the inherited functions, render objects also define object-specific functions, which work only on objects of that particular kind.
- Render objects inherently do not contain image data; rather they maintain links to data objects called *source data objects* (for example, bitmaps, avFiles). A single source data object can be shared by several render objects.

The RDX system also provides support objects and support functions, which operate on groups, effects, timers, events, and so forth.

6.2.1 Generic Objects with RDX

All displayable RDX objects are derived from a *base class* and inherit a set of *generic attributes* from the base class. The system provides a set of *attribute functions*, which an application can use to set, get, and change attribute values.

Table 6-1 lists the generic attributes that are inherited by all RDX objects. Functions to manipulate these generic attributes all begin with the *obj* mnemonic. For example, the functions to modify destination are *objSetDestination, objGetDestination*, and *objAdjDestination*.

TABLE 6-1   Generic Attributes Inherited by RDX Objects

View	Application-defined subset of an object's source image area
Visibility	Toggle on/off whether an object should be rendered
Draw Order	Priority order of objects drawn on top of each other
Current Image	Index to image to be rendered from within a sequence
Destination	Surface to which the object is mapped; surface destinations can themselves be mapped to windows, memory, or other surfaces
Destination Rectangle	Application-defined subset of destination area
Position	Location of object on its destination; modifying the position also modifies the Destination Rectangle and vice versa

RDX INTERFACE CONVENTION

The object-oriented nature of RDX allows objects to be treated in similar ways, giving the system a significant degree of uniformity and consistency. Though RDX is object oriented, its interfaces are based in C.

RDX uses a noun/verb naming convention for its function calls. Every function call is prefixed by a mnemonic for the object to be operated on. The prefix is followed by a verb, and further descriptors then follow.

In keeping with the noun/verb naming convention, all RDX function calls (except *xxxCreate*) take in the object as the first parameter. All RDX function calls return a DINORVAL return value. Return values are returned using pointer indirection. The return pointers are always placed last in the parameter list.

The nature of some objects forces minor variations in the generic attribute semantics. For example, an audio track has the visibility attribute, but its meaning is undefined. Similarly, the current image attribute is ambiguous for nonsequenced objects. The exceptions are fairly minor.

6.2.2 The Programming Model

The general model for building an RDX render object can be broken into three parts:

1. Create a Source Data Object (SDO) and load its data, or reference a created SDO.
2. Create the render object itself and associate it to the SDO.
3. Set any appropriate object attributes to nondefault values.

The general model for preparing render objects for display has two parts:

1. Create a surface, or reference an already created surface. Map the surface to a window or a memory buffer. This defines where the surface will be drawn at draw time.
2. Map render objects to the surface. Each time you map an object to a surface, the system uses the object's draw order to place it in an ordered display list associated with the surface.

Now draw the surface. When you do this, the system traverses the display list, drawing each object in the list into a buffer, and then the system "transmits" the buffer to the final destination. (The system will use the appropriate DirectDraw Primary or Offscreen buffers if the final destination is a window.)

6.3 Working with RDX

6.3.1 Creating an RDX Surface

Enough reading! Time to work. Here's the code for creating an RDX surface.

```
CSurfaceRdx::Init(CWnd *pcWnd)
{
    RECT rWin;
    pcWnd->GetClientRect(&rWin);
    DWORD dwWidth = (DWORD)(rWin.right - rWin.left);
    DWORD dwHeight = (DWORD)(rWin.bottom - rWin.top);
    srfCreate(dwWidth, dwHeight, RGB_CLUT8, &m_hSurf);    ◄
```

1. Create a surface with same size as the client area. The size does not have to match since RDX will clip to destination if needed. Create the smallest surface needed—reducing size increases performance by reducing the area to be redrawn and also makes it easier to fit the surface onto graphics memory.
2. Specify the color format of the surface. Objects will be mixed in this color format. We could insert color converters, but our example is simple and is designed for everything to be set up in RGB 8-bit mode.
3. RDX returns a handle to the surface in the space we pointed to in the last parameter, M_HSURF.

```
    srfSetDestWindow(m_hSurf, pcWnd->m_hWnd);
    return TRUE;
}
```

Map the surface to the destination window. RDX will watch for window movements or size changes and will clip the image if needed.

6.3.2 An RDX Sprite Class

And here's the code for initializing an RDX-based CSprite.

```
BOOL CSpriteRDX::Init(HOBJ hSurf, UINT nResID, BYTE byKeyColor)
{
    BITMAP bm;
    bitmap.GetBitmap(&bm);
    m_dwWidth = bm.bmWidth;
    m_dwHeight = bm.bmHeight;
    m_byTransp = byKeyColor;
```

Create and set up an *hbmp* (SDO).

```
    HBMPHEADER bmpHeader;
    hbmpCreate(m_dwWidth,m_dwHeight,RGB_CLUT8,&m_hBmp);    ◊ Create RDX hbmp object.
    BYTE *pData;
    hbmpGetLockedBuffer(m_hBmp, &pData, &bmpHeader);       ◊ Get access to RDX
                                                             space.
    bitmap.GetBitmapBits(m_dwWidth*m_dwHeight, pData);     ◊ Load data into RDX
                                                             space.
    hbmpReleaseBuffer(m_hBmp);                             ◊ Release access.
    hbmpSetTransparencyColor(m_hBmp, (DWORD)byKeyColor);   ◊ Specify that bitmap is
```
transparant.

Create sprite; associate data to it; associate sprite to surface.

```
    sprCreate(&m_hSpr);
    sprSetData(m_hSpr, m_hBmp);
    objSetDestination(m_hSpr, m_hSurf);

    return TRUE;
}
```

Pass sprite handle to *Obj* function call. The generic object (*Obj*) will be manipulated from the actual object.

PART II

6.3.3   Drawing the RDX Sprite

With RDX, we don't have to actually draw the sprite. We merely adjust any relevant attributes (such as position and/or draw order) and "draw" the surface to which the sprite was connected.

```
CSurfaceRdx::BltSprite(CSprite &spr, CPoint &point)
{
    objSetPosition(m_hSpr, point);      // set location in surface
    objSetDrawOrder(m_hSpr, 1);         // smaller number means in front
}

CSurfaceRdx::Render()
{
    srfDraw(m_hSurf);
}
```

> *SrfDraw* invokes, in back-to-front order, render routines of all objects mapped to the surface. This call then transfers the resulting composited image to the destination window using the appropriate *IDirectDraw* method.

6.4 Demo Time

At this point, select the RDX option in the sample application on the CD. You should be seeing sprites on the application window. These sprites were drawn using an RDX surface and an RDX sprite.

How do you know we're using RDX? Move the mouse to the white border areas along the right or left edges. The sprite is clipped to the boundaries of the clipping window. Move the window to a different position, and now move the mouse over the clipping window. The mouse is drawn at the window's new position. The Clipper code within the RDX library is automatically handling window moves.

6.4.1   How Fast Does CSurfaceRdx Draw?

Table 6-2 shows the speed at which objects are drawn with RDX in comparison to the methods used in the previous chapter. Some observations on the measurements:

■ RDX's drawing time is as good or better than our optimized routines from the previous chapter. RDX automatically senses the MMX technology capabilities of the platform we are using. The improved performance can be attributed to more finely optimized Pentium code or to benefits from MMX technology enhancements.

TABLE 6-2 Measurements for CSurfaceRdx Drawing

Surface	CSprite 84 × 63 (16)	CBackground 734 × 475	Refresh Screen 852 × 559	Post Refresh	Total
CSysMem	0.6–0.9	7.9	10.5	0.0	19.3
CVidMem	0.7–1.8	7.7	0.1	8.9	16.7/18.5
CRdx	1.3	4.3	11.7	0.0	17.3

All times are in milliseconds.

PART II

- Independently separating sprite, background, and screen refresh time when using RDX is not straightforward, since RDX always draws the entire surface. Sprite draw times were obtained by the following equation:

$$t_{spr} = t_{surf+sprites} - t_{surf}$$

and backgrounds were measured by

$$t_{bkg} = t_{surf+bkg} - t_{surf}$$

Refresh Screen still takes the most time. So how about asking RDX to use hardware acceleration if it's available?

6.5 Hardware Acceleration with RDX

With RDX we can apply effects on objects. An effect modifies the way that data is rendered, but it does not modify the original data. For example, we could render a sprite upside down by applying a vertical flip effect on it. RDX provides a variety of effects. Some of these effects can be applied on all objects; others can be applied only to specific objects. Refer to the RDX documentation for more detail on effects.

Let's start with asking RDX to set up the application in Full Screen mode and use Page Flip hardware if it's available.

6.5.1 Full Screen Mode with RDX

Full Screen mode is an effect that can be applied to surfaces. Here is some code to apply the Full Screen effect on our CSurfaceRdx.

```
class CSurfaceRdx : public CSurface
{
    // add these two member variables into class structure
    FULL_SCREEN_PARAMS  m_fxParams;
    HFX                 m_hFx;
}

CSurfaceRdx::MakeFullScreen()
{
    fxParams.dwWidth = 640;
    fxParams.dwHeight = 480;
    fxParams.iColorType = RGB_CLUT8;


    err = objApplyEffect(m_hObj, FX_FULL_SCREEN, &fxParams, &hFx);
}
```

Effect parameters are not copied but are used by reference. Therefore, effect parameters must not be declared in local (temporary) scope; they must be declared with lasting scope.

Specify the size and ColorType of the full screen window desired. If these are different from the current display mode, RDX will change the display mode to suit the parameters.

Apply the effect on the surface using the surface handle returned during *srfCreate()*. *ObjApplyEffect()* returns a handle to the newly "created" effect. Use this handle to manage the effect or to modify its parameters.

EXTRA CREDIT: Explore inserting color conversion effects on our RGB8 surface to handle non-RGB8 display modes.

6.5.2 How Fast Does CSurfaceRdx Draw in Full Screen Mode?

Table 6-3 on the next page compares CSurfaceRDX drawing in Full Screen mode with our previous measurements.

- Notice how the Refresh Screen and the Post Refresh Screen times are negligible for CRdxFullScreen. The CRdxFullScreen surface times are as good as the CBackBuffer surface times. Remember in Section 5.8.5 that CBackBuffer was set up to use Page Flipping. RDX automatically sets the system up to use Page Flipping, as soon as we request Full Screen mode. *We don't have to do anything special to turn on Page Flipping.*

- Also, notice how the variance is low for the Post Refresh Screen times for CRdxFullScreen. The variance for CRdxFullScreen is lower than the variance for CBackBuffer. *RDX automatically sets up for triple buffering, if the graphics card can support it*

The results are in! This is a simple interface with high performance.

6.5.3 Accelerating Objects with RDX

But what about accelerating objects like sprites and backgrounds?

TABLE 6-3 CSurfaceRdx Drawing in Full Screen Mode

Surface	CSprite 84 × 63 (16)	CBackground 734 × 475	Refresh Screen 852 × 559	Post Refresh	Total
CSysMem	0.6–0.9	7.9	10.5	0.0	19.3
CVidMem	0.7–1.8	7.7	0.1	8.9	8.5/18.5
CBackBuffer	0.7–1.8	7.7	0.1	0.5–7.6	9.0–17.2
CRdx	1.3	4.3	11.7	0.0	17.3
CRdxFullScreen	1.7	7.3	0.0	0.0–4.0	9.0–13.0

All times are in milliseconds.

Well, it's really quite simple. RDX supports *sprSetFlags()* and *bkgSetFlags()* calls that turn on special features of these objects. Looking at the documentation for these calls, we find that both of these objects support a HWBLIT special feature (currently this is the only special feature supported).

Here's the code that turns on and off sprite acceleration.

```
// To HW-Blt a sprite
sprSetFlags (m_hObj, SPR_FLAG_HWBLIT) :
```

> You must describe source and destination (that is, *objSetData, objSetDestination*) before you use the HWBLIT special flag. Add this line after you have completely initialized the sprite.

```
// To turn off HW-Bltting
sprClearFlags (m_hObj, SPR_FLAG_HWBLIT);
```

Table 6-4 measures the speed of hardware-accelerated objects and shows them in comparison with other RDX objects.

TABLE 6-4 Measuring Hardware-Accelerated RDX Objects

Objects Drawn with RDX	Time for 16 sprites (84 × 63)	Time for Background 734 × 475
Software objects in system memory	0.9	4.3
Software objects in video memory	1.7	7.3
Hardware objects in video memory	2.3	Out of Video Memory

All times are in milliseconds.

Some observations based on the results:

■ RDX's software-based spriting is actually faster than hardware-accelerated sprites. So with this configuration there is no real benefit to using HWBLIT.

■ To use hardware acceleration you (or RDX) must place the source objects into video memory. Video memory is a scarce resource. After RDX set up the system for triple buffering, we did not have any memory left for our background.

■ As we mentioned in the Introduction, timings are configuration dependent, and you may see different results on different configurations. With faster CPUs the software may be even faster. With faster hardware, the graphics card could be faster.

Video memory is a scarce resource, and in general you will get the best results by setting up for triple buffering before you accelerate individual objects. In the future, AGP-based graphics cards may offer Bltting from system memory, and then the scarcity of video memory will not be an issue. Although you still might not see any performance boosts with Transparent Blts, you will most probably see performance boosts with non-Transparent Blts—that is, your backgrounds will run faster. And when that time comes, you will be armed with the knowledge of how to accelerate your backgrounds with RDX.

WHAT HAVE YOU LEARNED?

By this time, you've had an overview of RDX and gotten a taste of what it is like to use a high-level interface to manage multimedia objects. You've also gotten a feel for RDX's performance capabilities. You should have an idea of how the interface provides device independence and how to control RDX's usage of DirectDraw. In short, you should have a good starting point for using RDX and for deciding whether it will work for you.

We've come to the end of this part. Hope you had a pleasant trip.

PART III

Making the
Media Mix

WE'D LIKE TO EXTEND AN ACKNOWLEDGEMENT TO ROGER HURWITZ, TODD SCHWARTZ, TIMOTHY STRELCHUN, MARK LEAVY, BYRON GRIFFIN FROM INTEL; PAT BOYLE FROM REAL NETWORKS; DANNY MILLER, JASON WHITE AND RALPH LIPE FROM MICROSOFT CORP.; DR. MICHAEL CHWIALKOWSKI FROM THE UNIVERSITY OF TEXAS AT ARLINGTON; CHRIS EDDIE FROM XING TECHNOLOGIES, GEORGE HABER FROM COMPCORE MULTIMEDIA.

Chapter 11   **Streaming Down the Superhighway with RealMedia**

- Real-time Internet streaming
- Data flows and data management interfaces
- File-Format plug-in and rendering plug-in
- RealMedia Audio Services

In the past few years, the PC has become powerful enough to handle both the capture and the playback of motion video under Windows. In the process, Microsoft has defined a few multimedia architectures on the Windows platform, including the Multimedia Command Interface (MCI), Video for Windows (VFW), and, lately, DirectShow (a.k.a. Active-Movie). Apple, on the other hand, defined a multimedia architecture for both the Macintosh OS and Windows "QuickTime." Recently, with the explosion of the Internet, RealNetworks defined RealAudio, RealVideo, and, later, RealMedia.

In this part of the book we'll address a few of these multimedia architectures; namely, DirectShow from Microsoft, RealMedia from RealNetworks, and RDX from Intel. DirectShow is a streaming media architecture that supports multi-stream synchronization and MPEG-style video. The first release of DirectShow, known as ActiveMovie 1.0, lacked support for capture and compression. DirectShow, however, includes both capture and compression interfaces.

To understand the DirectShow architecture, it's best to first understand the filter graph model. To do that, you should first launch the graph editor application that comes with the DirectShow SDK and construct a filter graph. After doing so, you should be ready to delve into the details of the internals of filters—Chapter 8. You'll learn how to create a filter and pins and how to connect filters together. You'll also learn about how to add property pages to a filter, as well as custom interfaces.

You can then jump to Chapter 9, where you'll learn how to build filter graphs from an application using the DirectShow ActiveX control, the COM interface, or the GRF file. The ActiveX control is the easiest way to render a media file using the DirectShow filters. The ActiveX control provides all the necessary GUI interfaces to play, stop, and pause a media file. To have more control over the creation of a filter, you can use the COM interface or a GRF file to create and manipulate the filter. In this case, you have to provide the GUI interface and manage the events of the filters. Finally, in this chapter you'll learn how to expose a filter's property page and how to hook into a filter's custom interface.

Now, if you don't necessarily want to understand the internal architecture of DirectShow and its filters, or if you want to mix multiple video, audio, or animation objects together, you can use Intel's Realistic Display Mixer (RDX) to do that. RDX is a high-level interface that uses DirectShow to play and mix multiple video and audio objects.

Finally, since the Internet has been exerting a huge force on the computing environment, we thought it only appropriate to discuss one of the major architecture advancements for multimedia delivery on the Internet—the RealMedia Architecture (RMA). RMA is a modular extendible version of the RealAudio architecture. It uses a combination of a RealMedia server and client to deliver real-time multimedia content (audio, video, stock quotes, and so forth) over the Internet. With RMA you can stream any media type by adding a custom plug-in on both the server and the client sides.

To help you understand the RealMedia architecture, we will first focus on the topology of the architecture and then delve into the details of the plug-ins. To deliver custom data using RMA, you must first learn how to build File-Format and Rendering plug-ins. To play audio data on the client, you should use the RMA Audio Services, since it supports multiple platforms and performs the mixing of multiple audio streams. It also allows for pre- and post-processing of the audio streams.

PART III

CHAPTER 7

Video under Windows

WHY READ THIS CHAPTER? This chapter gives a brief introduction to motion video and discusses the supporting architectures under Windows. It is meant to give background on the topics that are discussed in the rest of Part III.

If you feel comfortable with

- motion video on the personal computer,
- multimedia architectures under Windows (MCI, VFW, QTW, and ActiveMovie), and
- the principles of video compression and decompression,

you may wish to skip this chapter.

7.1 Concepts of Motion Video

I am sure you've watched a few cartoons in your life; my all-time favorite is *Bugs Bunny*. As you know, these cartoons, as well as real movies, are made up of a series of pictures displayed at a rate fast enough that it looks like motion video to the human eye. Throughout the world there are three dominant standards for television: NTSC, PAL, and SECAM. NTSC is primarily used in North America and specifies an interlaced refresh rate of 59.94 fields per second[1] (approximately 30 frames per second, fps). Both of the European standards, PAL and SECAM, specify an interlaced refresh rate of 50 fields per second (25 fps).

---

1. Interlaced display rate specifies the rate of displaying both the odd and even fields in a frame.

MOTION VIDEO TERMS

The NTSC television standard supports an *interlaced* video format of 30 frames per second. An *interlaced video frame* is composed of two separate *field* pictures, each of which has the same width as the full picture but is half the height of the entire picture: an even and an odd field. Both fields are displayed at 60 fields per second. The even field is displayed first starting at the top line and skipping every other line on the screen. The odd field is then displayed in the locations where the even field skipped.

In addition to the interlaced display, computer monitors support a *non-interlaced* video format, which basically displays the picture one line at a time on the screen (see Figure 7-1).

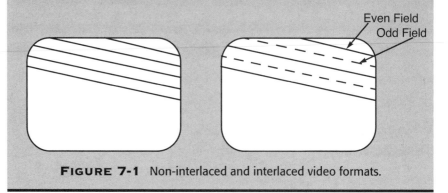

Even Field
Odd Field

FIGURE 7-1 Non-interlaced and interlaced video formats.

7.2 Capturing and Compressing Video

In the past few years, personal computers have become powerful enough to be able to play back motion video at the specified frame rates, and even faster. To play back a visual sequence on the PC, you must first digitize it with a video capture adapter and store the digitized clip on your hard disk or a CD-ROM. Typical video capture adapters can digitize an NTSC clip up to a 640 × 480 in size. If our memory serves us right, this results in a huge file if the video captured spans a few seconds or minutes. Let's calculate the amount of space required to store a video clip. To achieve the best quality, each pixel should contain a 24-bit RGB color quantity. (*RGB* stands for the red, green, and blue color format used in computers.)

Size of 1 Frame = 640 (width) × 480 (height) × 3 bytes/pixel = 900 K

To store 1 full second (30 frames) requires

Size of a 1-second clip = 900 K/frame × 30 frames/second = 27 MB

27 MB/second ! Even the fastest CD-ROM today cannot sustain such a high data rate. For example, a 10× CD-ROM can only sustain, at best, a transfer rate of 1.5 MB/second. So that the video file will be usable, we must reduce the size of the video clip before storing it on a CD-ROM.

To enable motion video on such media, the digitized video clip must go through a few compression steps:

1. You could sacrifice some of the image quality by capturing a smaller size of the image (for example, 320 × 240 or 352 × 288). As a result, the data transfer rate is reduced by 75 percent to about 6.5 MB/sec for a 24-bit color clip.

2. Depending on the type of application, you could capture the video clip in either RGB or YUV color format. Typically, the YUV color space is more suitable for applications with motion video. The YUV color space contains one luminance (black-and-white) component and two chrominance (color) components (U and V). Naturally, there is a direct relationship between the RGB color space and the YUV color space.

YUV AND RGB

The RGB color space is used to represent colors on computer graphics adapters and terminals. In true color, with 8 bits for each color, you can generate up to 2^{24} distinct colors. The YUV color space is used to represent color in motion video. The YUV format represents the same format as that of the analog television signal, where there are one luminance component (black-and-white) and two chrominance (color) components. In this case, the Y is the luminance and the U and V are the chrominance. The YUV color scheme is used for motion video simply because it is easier to separate the black-and-white component of the picture from the color components, which makes it easier to compress the video clip.

The YUV color space is a good choice for motion video because it separates the black-and-white contents of the picture from its color components. This is very useful since the human eye cannot easily detect degradation in the color of an image, but it is extremely sensitive to any loss in luminance. Hence, the color information can be easily reduced without any noticeable degradation in video quality.

PART III

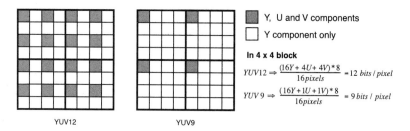

$$YUV12 \Rightarrow \frac{(16Y + 4U + 4V)*8}{16 pixels} = 12 \ bits \ / \ pixel$$

$$YUV9 \Rightarrow \frac{(16Y + 1U + 1V)*8}{16 pixels} = 9 \ bits \ / \ pixel$$

FIGURE 7-2 UV color subsampling for motion video.

Figure 7-2 shows two UV subsampling formats, YUV12 and YUV9. On average, each pixel requires 12 bits to represent in the YUV12 format, and 9 bits in the YUV9 format. To reconstruct the color information for the "white" pixels, two or more neighboring U and V components are linearly interpolated to generate the appropriate color information.

Notice that the size of the final YUV12 image (Figure 7-2) is reduced by 50 percent since it only requires 12 bits to represent each pixel rather than 24. Similarly, the size of the final YUV9 image is reduced even further by 62.5 percent because it only requires 9 bits to represent each pixel.

3. The final YUV12 or YUV9 image is compressed even further using some of the well-known compression algorithms such as MPEG or Intel's Indeo. Even though these algorithms are lossy in nature, they can reduce the size of the image dramatically while maintaining superb image quality. Such algorithms can produce motion video clips suitable for a 1X CD-ROM at 150Kps.

As you can see, using these compression techniques allows you to smoothly integrate motion video with the PC. In 1997 a new breed of CD-ROMs and processors will allow for even better multimedia experience on the PC. DVD-ROM is a new CD-ROM media that can hold up to 17 GB of data on a single platter and can sustain up to 1.5MB per second. The Pentium II processor will be capable of playing back MPEG2 video clips as large as 720×576 at 25 to 30 fps.

7.3 Windows Multimedia Architectures

Microsoft's first attempt at multimedia came through the Multimedia Command Interface (MCI). MCI is a simple VCR-like interface with useful commands such as Play, Pause, Stop, Rewind, Seek, and so forth. In fact, MCI is an integral part of Windows and is still used by a certain class of applications such as audio CD players. But as a compromise to simplicity, MCI lacks many of the basic features required for multimedia recording and editing.

In 1993 Microsoft introduced Video for Windows (VFW) as an answer to the missing features in MCI. VFW defines interfaces for recording and editing both audio and video clips. As part of the standard, VFW also defined the Audio Video Interleaved (AVI) file format, which allows for interleaving multiple video, audio, or text streams in the same file. VFW also defined an interface for installable codecs to enable installation of custom compression and conversion algorithms. (Codecs are compression/decompression drivers.)

Even though Video for Windows was a great step for multimedia under Windows, it lacks some essential features. For example, even though VFW allows for multiple streams in an AVI file, it does not provide any means of synchronizing these streams together. In addition, VFW lacks the necessary features to support certain classes of algorithms such as MPEG video[2].

Around the same time, Apple moved its QuickTime architecture from the Macintosh environment to Windows and called it QuickTime for Windows (QTW). QTW only allowed for video playback in the Windows environment and did not allow for video capture or editing. All the video production remained on the Macintosh.

Back to Microsoft. To resolve some of the deficiencies in VFW, Microsoft introduced the first release of its latest multimedia architecture, Active-Movie, at the end of 1996. ActiveMovie is targeted specifically for Windows 95 and Windows NT. The first release supports video and audio streaming and provides synchronization mechanisms between multiple streams. The first release, however, lacks capture and compression support.

As a follow-up to their commitment, Microsoft is releasing a follow-up technology, DirectShow, which is basically ActiveMovie with a name change and added support for capture and compression. We've dedicated the next three chapters to showing you how to use DirectShow.

Intel, on the other hand, released a graphics and video mixing architecture called Realistic Sound Experience (RDX). We've dedicated a chapter to showing you how easy it is to use RDX to mix multiple video and graphics objects.

Finally, RealNetworks is releasing their RealMedia Architecture, which allows for real-time streaming of video, audio, or any other media type over

---

2. VFW lacks support for future frame prediction techniques required by MPEG. Refer to the section "Overview of Video Codes" later in this chapter.

the Internet. We've dedicated one chapter to discussing the RealMedia plug-in architecture.

7.4 Overview of Video Codecs

Regardless of the multimedia architecture used, most video codecs apply similar methods to compress and decompress video. Let's have the ten-thousand-foot view of what a video codec does.

As we've mentioned earlier, video capture hardware produces an image composed of three color planes: Y, U, and V. Typically, the codec uses the same algorithm to compress each of the planes separately.

Typically, each plane is subdivided into 8×8 blocks, and each block is processed separately. The blocks are then transformed into a frequency domain using one of the well-known transformation processes (DCT, HAAR, SLANT, and so forth). The frequency domain block represents the amount of change in color from one pixel to the entire 8×8 pixel grid. Typically, video images don't change that drastically within an 8×8 block, and therefore, the high-frequency components of the frequency domain end up being mostly zeros. In fact, this is why the frequency domain is most suitable for video compression since consecutive zeros are easily represented with a small number of bits using the run length encoding (RLE) algorithm. Finally, the frequency domain block is quantized and encoded using the Huffman coding algorithm.

To decompress a frame, the exact opposite process is used. First the inverse Huffman algorithm is applied on the input bit stream generating 8×8 quantized blocks. These blocks are then dequantized using the same quantization matrix used when the frame was compressed. The Inverse frequency transformation is then applied on the dequantized block in order to produce the corresponding 8×8 Y, U, or V block. Finally, the Y, U, and V blocks are converted to RGB either by the application software or by specialized color conversion hardware on the graphics adapter (see Chapter 5, "Hardware Acceleration via DirectDraw").

The method that we've described so far is called *intra-frame* compression, and the frame is called the *I-frame* or *Key frame*. Intra-frames are compressed and decompressed independently from any other frames in the video sequence.

Inter-frames, on the other hand, can only be compressed or decompressed using data from other frames in the video sequence. Typically, at 25 or 30 fps, changes from one frame to the next are small enough that you can use the information from previous or future frames to predict the contents of the current frame. In fact, this type of a frame is called the *Predicted frame* or *P-frame*.

When compressing inter-frames, the difference between this frame and the reference frame is found first, then the difference information is transformed into the frequency domain. This technique is very useful in compressing motion video where some of the blocks end up being zero because the change between the two frames is insignificant.

The *Bi-directional frame* type is an extension of the P-frame. Here a previous and a future frame are used for reference at the same time. Typically, *B-frames*, as they're also called, produce higher compression than P- or I-frames, but they require more computational bandwidth and more memory to hold the reference frames.

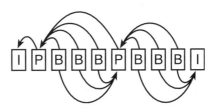

FIGURE 7-3 MPEG frame types.

WHAT HAVE YOU LEARNED?

After making your way through this chapter you probably have a good sense of

- motion video on the PC,
- multimedia architectures under Windows,
- video compression and decompression.

CHAPTER **8**

DirectShow Filters

PART III

WHY READ THIS CHAPTER? You must have heard of or even tried the latest release of Microsoft's DirectShow (formerly known as ActiveMovie), but you're not sure what it has to offer. You're ready to move your current drivers from VFW or MCI to DirectShow, but you don't know where to start.

This chapter helps you

- understand the architecture of DirectShow and filter graphs,
- build source, transform, and rendering filters,
- understand the connection mechanism between filters,
- know how to use a registry file to add a filter to the registry or do filter self-registration,
- add custom interfaces to your filter, and
- add property pages to a filter.

To help you along the way, you can use the following articles on the CD:

- debugging hints for filters,
- adding a custom file type,
- how to build and run the sample files.

8.1 DirectShow Components

Figure 8-1 shows a high-level block diagram of the current multimedia architectures under Windows 95/NT. The DirectShow components are shown inside the dotted line.

■ 79 ■

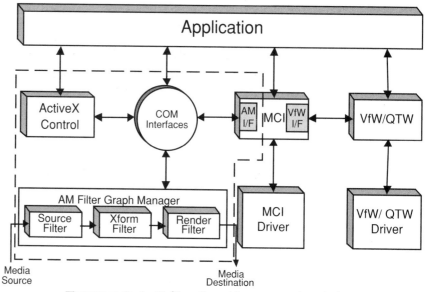

FIGURE 8-1 Multimedia architectures under Windows
(DirectShow components fall within dotted line).

As you can see, you can access the DirectShow components in one of three ways:

■ directly through the COM interface and the Filter Graph Manager (FGM),

■ using the MCI command set where the MCI layer has been updated to communicate with the DirectShow FGM, or

■ through the ActiveX control interface, which is part of the DirectShow SDK. The ActiveX interface provides a high-level interface that gives applications a simple method for controlling DirectShow and its components. It also acts as an easy plug-in for the Internet Explorer.

We'll show you how to use the COM interface and the ActiveX control to access the DirectShow filter in the next chapter.

The Filter Graph Manager and the associated filters are the crux of Direct-Show. The Filter Graph Manager provides applications with interfaces through the COM layer. (Applications cannot access the filters directly. They have to go through the FGM.) The FGM orchestrates the connection of the filters with the applications and the allocation of the shared buffers between them. It also controls the streaming of data and provides synchronization services (clock) so that filters can synchronize the delivery of multiple time-stamped data samples at the right time.

8.2 What's a Filter Graph?

Before we delve into the details of filters and filter graphs, it might be a good idea to go ahead and play with the Filter Graph Editor (FGE) applet that comes with the DirectShow SDK. The Filter Graph Editor is a tool that comes with the DirectShow SDK. Typically, applications will interact with the filter graph directly using the COM interface or the ActiveX control, discussed later.

You can use the Filter Graph Editor to build a custom filter graph and save it in a *.grf* file. The *.grf* file can then be used to construct the exact same filter graph—without using DirectShow's automatic filter graph construction methods.

We're assuming that you've installed the FGE on your PC by now—NO? What are you waiting for? Once you've installed the SDK, launch the FGE applet and select the File->RenderMediaFile option from the menu. At the prompt, select the name of the sample MPEG file that comes with the DirectShow SDK (*Blastoff.Mpg*) and press OK. You should see something similar to what is shown in Figure 8-2.

Each individual rectangle in the figure represents a *filter* that performs a specific function. The arrows between the filters indicate that the output pin of one filter is connected to the input pin on the filter to its right. Notice that the media flows in the direction indicated by the arrows. The entire

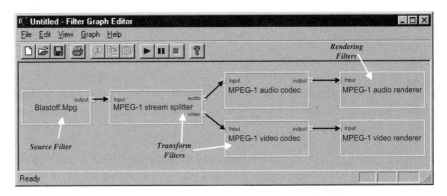

FIGURE 8-2 Filter graph for an MPEG-1 file.

mesh of connected filters is called the *filter graph*. You'll learn more about filters, pins, and the connection between them in the remainder of this chapter.

What's nice about the filter graph model is that you can easily replace one of the filters without even touching the remainder of the graph. For example, you can easily replace the source filter that reads the MPEG file from a hard disk or a CD-ROM with another source filter that reads it off the Internet or from a digital satellite link. This is a big win for developers since they only need to implement and distribute one filter rather than the entire filter graph or an entire VFW driver.

You can also insert other filters between any two filters and change the behavior of the filter graph—again, without touching any of the other filters. For example, you can insert a contrast filter in between the MPEG-1 video codec and the MPEG-1 video renderer. The contrast filter allows you to change the contrast of the video data on its way to the renderer. *Try it!*

8.3 Understanding the Mighty Filter

The filter is the basic building block of a DirectShow filter graph. A filter is basically a COM object with its own Global Unique Identifier (GUID). Typically, each filter comes with one or more input/output pins, which are used to move the data from one filter to the next. In order to connect two filters, the pins have to go through a simple process of negotiation.

At connection time, under the direction of the filter graph manager (FGM), the two pins negotiate on a media type that is common between them. Once the two pins agree on a media type, they negotiate on the allocation of the shared memory buffer used to transport the data between the two filters. Once the two pins settle their differences, they are joined in holy matrimony till death do them part.

In addition to the pins, filters may expose a set of *property pages,* which are used to display the filter-specific status or configuration. To see the property page of a filter, right-click the mouse on the filter and select Properties.

DirectShow defines three major types of filters: *source, transform,* and *rendering.* A *source filter* has no input pins and has one or more output pins. Typically a source filter is responsible for reading the raw data from a source file, network, or any other media.

A *transform filter* has one or more input pins and one or more output pins. Typically, a transform filter accepts data from an input pin or pins and converts it to another format before sending it out to the downstream filter.

A *rendering filter* has one input pin and no output pins. A rendering filter accepts data on the input pin and delivers it to its final destination (screen, audio card, file, and so forth).

8.4 An Overview of the Samples

Let's have an overview of the samples and explain what they do before we jump into the code. In this chapter, we'll show you how to create the three types of filters: source, transform, and rendering filters. To make it simple, we've chosen "simple text" as the media type to transport (see Figure 8-3).

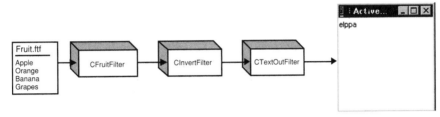

FIGURE 8-3 Overview of the sample filters covered in this chapter.

The source filter CFruitFilter[1] reads one line at a time from the text file *Fruit.ftf* and passes it to the next filter. The CInvertFilter is a transform filter that accepts a string on the input pin and delivers an inverted string to its output pin. Finally, the CTextOutFilter is a rendering filter that displays the string presented at the input pin to a text window. This is a good time to run the sample application for this chapter on the companion CD.

8.5 Creating a Source Filter

Our source filter, CFruitFilter, prompts the user for a filename, opens the selected file, and reads it one line at a time. It delivers each line to the filter connected to its output pin for further processing.

---

1. We used the name *CFruitFilter* merely because each line in the input file is a name of a piece of fruit.

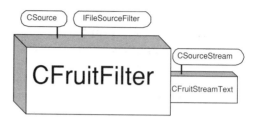

FIGURE 8-4 Source filter.

 For a better understanding of the code below, it might be useful to install the filter and see how it works before you go on. You can find detailed instructions on how to install and run this filter on the companion CD.

Notice that, before you can use any of these filters, you must first add them to the system registry. We'll show you how to do this at the end of the chapter (see "Section 8.10 Adding a Filter to the Registry").

It's actually pretty simple to create a source filter. DirectShow provides a couple of built-in classes that you can use to derive your source filter: The CSource and CSourceStream. CSource is the base class for all source filters. CSourceStream represents the output pin of a source filter. It handles moving the data from the file to the downstream filter. Notice in Figure 8-4 that our CFruitFilter also derives from the IFileSourceFilter, which is necessary to manage the filename of the input file. You'll see how this works later.

In our discussion, we'll first step through the CFruitFilter class where we'll show you how to create an instance of the filter, how to attach the source stream to it, and how to handle the IFileSourceFilter interface. We'll then step through the CFruitStreamText class, which handles the connection of the output pin, opening the input file, and transporting the data from the source file to the next filter down the stream.

8.5.1 The Source Filter Class

To create your own source filter, you need only derive a filter from the CSource base class, then override and implement a few of the base class member functions. As we've mentioned earlier, you can also derive a filter from the IFileSourceFilter to manage the input filename.

```
class CFruitFilter:
    public Csource,                  // Base source filter
    public IFileSourceFilter         // This is for accepting input file
{
```

Must be **static** since it is called before the class is created.

```
public :
    static CUnknown * WINAPI CreateInstance(LPUNKNOWN lpunk, HRESULT *phr);

private:
```

The following lines are required for iFlleSourceFilter support.

```
DECLARE_IUNKNOWN
STDMETHODIMP GetCurFile(LPOLESTR * ppszFileName,AM_MEDIA_TYPE *pmt);
STDMETHODIMP Load(LPCOLESTR pszFileName, const AM_MEDIA_TYPE *pmt);
STDMETHODIMP NonDelegatingQueryInterface(REFIID riid, void ** ppv);
```

Notice that the constructor is in the *private* section; therefore you can only create this object from within the only static function, *CreateInstance()*.

```
CFruitFilter(LPUNKNOWN lpunk, HRESULT *phr);
OLECHAR m_szFileName[_MAX_PATH];
};
```

8.5.2   Create an Instance of the Source Filter

Looking closely at the class declaration, you can see that the *CreateInstance()* function is the only public member of the class—even the constructor is private. As a result, you can only create an instance of the filter from within the *CreateInstance()* member function. In addition, notice that *CreateInstance()* must be declared as a *static* function so that it can be called even before the filter is created.

When the filter graph manager (FGM) loads a filter, it looks for the variables g_Templates[] and g_cTemplates in the executable file of the filter. The FGM uses these variables to figure out which objects exist and how to create them. For example, FGM uses the third element of the g_Templates to retrieve a pointer to the *CreateInstance()* function, which is called to create an instance of the filter. The function returns the address of the newly created instance.

```
CFactoryTemplate g_Templates[] = {
  { L"Fruit Source Filter"
  , &CLSID_FruitFilter
  , CFruitFilter::CreateInstance
  , NULL
  , NULL}
};
```

PART III

```
int g_cTemplates = sizeof(g_Templates) / sizeof(g_Templates[0]);

CUnknown * WINAPI
CFruitFilter::CreateInstance(LPUNKNOWN lpunk, HRESULT *phr)
{
    // Create and return an instance of the filter
    CUnknown *punk = new CFruitFilter(lpunk, phr);
    if (punk == NULL) {
        *phr = E_OUTOFMEMORY;
    }
    return punk;
}
```

When you create a new instance of the filter, the CFruitFilter constructor is called. The constructor creates the streams supported by the filter and adds these streams' output pins to the m_paStreams member variable. DirectShow uses this list to keep track of the streams attached to the source filter. In our case, we only create the CFruitStreamText stream and add it to the m_paStreams list.

The sample source filters in the DirectShow SDK show the following code to create each of the source streams (pins) in the source filter constructor:

```
m_paStreams    = (CSourceStream **) new CSourceStream[1];
if (m_paStreams == NULL) {
    *phr = E_OUTOFMEMORY;
        return;
}

m_paStreams[0] = new CFruitStreamText(phr, this, L"Text!");
if (m_paStreams[0] == NULL) {
    *phr = E_OUTOFMEMORY;
    return;
}
```

However, we found that the source filter was leaking memory. After tracing through the CSource and CSourceStream classes, we found that both filters are properly handling the m_paStreams array. Therefore, we don't have to assign anything to the m_paStreams variable. So the above "erroneous" code should be replaced as shown in our example below.

```
CFruitFilter::CFruitFilter(LPUNKNOWN lpunk, HRESULT *phr) :
    CSource(NAME("Fruit Source Filter"),
    lpunk, CLSID_FruitFilter)
{
    CAutoLock cAutoLock(&m_cStateLock);
```

> *NAME()* is used in debug builds for object tracing. See the DirectShow SDK for more details.

```
// The CSourceStream constructor handles the allocation and assignment
// of the m_paStreams[] array.  On return from the constructor, the
// m_paStreams[0] would have the right value.
//
new CFruitStreamText(phr, this, L"Text!");
if (m_paStreams[0] == NULL) {
    *phr = E_OUTOFMEMORY;
    return;
}
}
```

This is the name of the output pin.

Once you've created the filter and its pins, the FGE interrogates the filter for the interfaces that it wants to use. As shown in the code below, the filter responds to the *IUnKnown::NonDelegatingQueryInterface()* member function to expose its own interfaces. In our case, the source filter supports all the interfaces of the base CSource class plus the IFileSourceFilter interface.

```
STDMETHODIMP
CFruitFilter::NonDelegatingQueryInterface(REFIID riid, void ** ppv)
{
    CheckPointer(ppv,E_POINTER);

    // We support the IFileSourceFilter interface and whatever
    // the base CSource supports..
    if (riid == IID_IFileSourceFilter)
        return GetInterface((IFileSourceFilter *) this, ppv);

    return CSource::NonDelegatingQueryInterface(riid, ppv);
}
```

Now that we've indicated that we support the IFileSourceFilter interface, the FGE prompts the user for the input filename and then calls the *Load()* function using that filename and the media type associated with that file. For example, an MPEG file is of MEDIATYPE_MPEGVideo type. Typically, the *Load()* function saves the filename and media type so that the filter can supply them when the *GetCurFile()* function is called. DirectShow or another application could request the active filename and media type anytime throughout the life of the filter.

```
STDMETHODIMP
CFruitFilter::Load(LPCOLESTR pszFileName,const AM_MEDIA_TYPE *pmt)
{
    lstrcpyW(m_szFileName, pszFileName);       // This is a UNICODE name
    return NOERROR;
}
```

```
STDMETHODIMP
CFruitFilter::GetCurFile(LPOLESTR * ppszFileName,AM_MEDIA_TYPE *pmt)
{
    CheckPointer(ppszFileName, E_POINTER);

    // Allocate an instance specific buffer to hold the filename.
    *ppszFileName = (LPOLESTR)
        CoTaskMemAlloc(sizeof(WCHAR) * (1+lstrlenW(m_szFileName)));
    if (*ppszFileName != NULL) {
        lstrcpyW(*ppszFileName, m_szFileName);
    }

    // we didn't save the media type, since we always return a NULL type.
    if(pmt) {
        ZeroMemory(pmt, sizeof(*pmt));
        pmt->majortype = MEDIATYPE_NULL;
        pmt->subtype = MEDIASUBTYPE_NULL;
    }
    return S_OK;
}
```

8.5.3   The Source Stream Class

As mentioned earlier, the CFruitStreamText class represents the output pin of the source filter (see Figure 8-4 on page 84). As a descendant of CSourceStream, the CFruitStreamText handles the connection process with the downstream filter, buffer allocation, and the movement of data from the input file to the downstream filter. In addition, CFruitStreamText is responsible for processing the Start, Stop, Pause, and other commands coming from the application through the filter graph manager.

```
class CFruitStreamText: public CSourceStream
{
public:
    CFruitStreamText(HRESULT *phr, CFruitFilter *pParent, LPCWSTR pPinName);
    ~CFruitStreamText();

    HRESULT FillBuffer(IMediaSample *pms) ;              ◊ Called to fill the buffer with data.

    HRESULT GetMediaType(int iPos, CMediaType *pmt)◊ Returns all media types supported.
    HRESULT CheckMediaType(const CMediaType *pmt); ◊ Verifies if media type is acceptable.
    HRESULT SetMediaType(const CMediaType *pmt);    ◊ Accepts media type.
    HRESULT DecideBufferSize(IMemAllocator *pima,   ◊ Decides how big the buffer needs
            ALLOCATOR_PROPERTIES *pProperties);          to be for data movement.

    // Called when the stream is started and stopped
    HRESULT OnThreadCreate(void);
    HRESULT OnThreadDestroy();
};
```

8.5.4 The Connection Process

The filter graph manager starts the connection process by retrieving the output pin of one filter and trying to connect it to an input pin of another filter. In order to do that, the FGM calls upon the output pin of the source filter to connect to the input pin of the downstream filter. This is where the negotiation begins.

The output pin queries the input pin for a list of the media types that it supports—it repeatedly calls the input pin's *GetMediaType()* function to get the media type list. For each of these media types, the output pin calls its own *CheckMediaType()* function to see if it supports this media type. If the output pin can handle one of the media types, it returns S_OK, and the negotiation continues for the shared buffer; otherwise, *CheckMediaType()* returns an error.

```
HRESULT
CFruitStreamText::CheckMediaType(const CMediaType *pMediaType)
{
    CAutoLock cAutoLock(m_pFilter->pStateLock());

    if (*(pMediaType->Type()) != MEDIATYPE_Text)
        return E_INVALIDARG;
    return S_OK;
}
```

Of course, it is possible that the output pin could reject all the input pin media types. In that case, the output pin tries its preferred list of media types on the input pin. To do so, the output pin first calls its own *GetMediaType()* function to retrieve its own list of media types. Again, for each media type, the output pin calls the *CheckMediaType()* function of the input pin, of the downstream filter, to qualify that media type. In the case where the input pin rejects all the media types suggested by the output pin, the connection process is aborted and an error is returned to the application; otherwise, the negotiation continues for the shared memory buffer.

Notice that the default connection process tries the media types in the same order as *GetMediaType()* returns them. Therefore, the first media type returned by the function has the highest priority over any consequent media types. For example, if your filter supports RGB 8-, 15-, and 24-bit video but prefers the RGB24 format, then you should return the RGB24 format first.

```
HRESULT CFruitStreamText::GetMediaType(int iPosition, CMediaType *pmt)
{
    CAutoLock cAutoLock(m_pFilter->pStateLock());
    if (iPosition < 0)                                    ◊ Index must start with 0.
        return E_INVALIDARG ;

    if (iPosition > 0)                                    ◊ Only support 1 media type.
        return VFW_S_NO_MORE_ITEMS;

    pmt->SetType(&MEDIATYPE_JS97Text);                    ◊ Here it is, "Simple Text."
    return NOERROR;
}
```

Once the two pins agree on media types, the *SetMediaType()* is called to confirm that selection. Typically, the output pin saves the media type in order to use it later to calculate the size of the shared buffer. This is simply done by calling the corresponding function in the base class.

```
HRESULT CFruitStreamText::SetMediaType(const CMediaType *pMediaType)
{
    CAutoLock cAutoLock(m_pFilter->pStateLock());

    return CSourceStream::SetMediaType(pMediaType);
}
```

To allocate the shared buffer, the output pin determines the size of the shared buffer by calling its member function *DecideBufferSize()*. This function calculates the amount of memory required based on the media type and the header information of the input file (for example, the picture width and height). After determining what size the buffer should be, *DecideBufferSize()* calls the allocator function, *SetProperties()*, to verify that there is enough memory to allocate this buffer—the actual buffer is allocated later.

Typically, you don't have to worry about who allocates the buffer or when it gets allocated; you only have to assure that you calculate the size of the buffer correctly.

```
HRESULT
CFruitStreamText::DecideBufferSize(
    IMemAllocator *pAlloc,              // Allocator object
    ALLOCATOR_PROPERTIES *pProperties  // Allocator properties
    )
```

```
{
    HRESULT hr = NOERROR;
    ALLOCATOR_PROPERTIES Actual;
    CAutoLock cAutoLock(m_pFilter->pStateLock());

    // Request the allocation of one buffer of size 1024 bytes
    pProperties->cBuffers = 1;
    pProperties->cbBuffer = 1024;

    hr = pAlloc->SetProperties(pProperties,&Actual);
    if (FAILED(hr)) {
        return hr;
    }

    // Verify that the allocator is able to allocate what we requested.
    if (Actual.cbBuffer < pProperties->cbBuffer) {
        return E_FAIL;
    }

    return NOERROR;
}
```

8.5.5 Starting and Stopping

All set and ready to roll—well, at least these two filters are. To complete the filter graph, the remaining filters down the stream follow the same negotiation process to connect their output pins with the appropriate input pins. Once the remaining filters are connected, the filter graph is ready to rumba.

At this stage, an application can *start* the filter graph, causing the source stream to read data from the file and send it downstream for further processing. When the filter graph is started, DirectShow creates a new thread for each CSourceStream in the filter graph, that is, a new thread for each output pin in the source filter. For example, if you have two output pins on the source filter, the FGM creates two additional threads to handle each of these pins. This allows the two pins to pump their data independent from one another.

When the thread is first created, the FGM calls the *OnThreadCreate()* function on the output pin, to initialize the state of the source stream—in our case, we open the source file. When you *stop* the filter graph, the FGM calls the *OnThreadDestroy()* function before it destroys the thread—in our case, we close the input file.

Notice that these functions are called every time the filter is started and stopped.

```
HRESULT CFruitStreamText::OnThreadCreate()
{
    CAutoLock cAutoLockShared(&m_cSharedState);

    // Convert file name from UNICODE to single byte char..
    char szTmp[256];
    WideCharToMultiByte(CP_ACP, 0,
            ((CFruitFilter*)m_pFilter)->m_szFileName, -1,
            szTmp, sizeof(szTmp), NULL, NULL);
    m_inFile.open(szTmp);

    return NOERROR;
}

HRESULT CFruitStreamText::OnThreadDestroy()
{
    m_inFile.close();
    return NOERROR;
}
```

8.5.6 Moving the Data

As long as the filter graph is running, each of the threads repeatedly calls the *FillBuffer()* function to fill the shared buffer with raw data from the input file. *FillBuffer()* then calls the *SetActualDataLength()* function in order to set the size of valid bytes in the shared buffer. The data buffer (media sample object) is automatically delivered to the downstream filter when the *FillBuffer()* function returns successfully.

```
HRESULT CFruitStreamText::FillBuffer(IMediaSample *pms)
{
    BYTE *pData;
    long lDataLen;

    pms->GetPointer(&pData);      // Retrieve a pointer to the buffer
    lDataLen = pms->GetSize();  // How big is the buffer - should be 1024

    // Read one line at a time till end of file..
    if (m_inFile.getline(pData, lDataLen))
        pms->SetActualDataLength(strlen((char*)pData)+1);
    else {
        return S_FALSE;
    }

    return S_OK;
}
```

When the input file runs out of data, *FillBuffer()* returns an error, S_FALSE, which marks the end of the stream, and, as a result, the filter graph stops, and, finally, the threads are terminated.

8.6 Creating a Transform Filter

Now, let's see how you can create a transform filter. As you recall, a *transform filter* accepts data from its input pin, applies some transformation on the data, and then sends it out to the filter connected to its output pin (see Figure 8-5). In our sample, the transform filter, CInvertFilter, inverts a text string before sending it out to the next downstream filter.

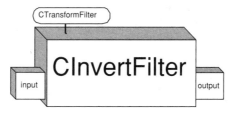

FIGURE 8-5 Transform filter.

As with the source filter, you can easily create a transform filter by deriving it from the base CTransformFilter. As shown in Figure 8-5, the CTransformFilter defines one input pin and one output pin connected to an upstream and a downstream filter respectively. Notice that you can add additional pins to the transform filter; for example, the MPEG-1 stream splitter in Figure 8-2 has one input pin and two output pins.

```
class CInvertFilter : public CTransformFilter
{
public:
    // Input Pin override functions…
    HRESULT CheckInputType(const CMediaType* mtIn);
    HRESULT CheckTransform(CMediaType* pmtIn,CMediaType* pmtOut);
    HRESULT Receive(IMediaSample *pSample);

    CInvertFilter(TCHAR *pName, LPUNKNOWN pUnk, HRESULT *pHr);
    ~CInvertFilter();

    // Necessary COM functions…
    static CUnknown * WINAPI CreateInstance(LPUNKNOWN, HRESULT *);
    STDMETHODIMP NonDelegatingQueryInterface(REFIID riid, void ** ppv);
    DECLARE_IUNKNOWN;
```

PART III

```
                     // Output pin datatype and buffer size functions
                     HRESULT GetMediaType(int iPos, CMediaType *pmt);
                     HRESULT CheckMediaType(const CMediaType *pmt);
                     HRESULT SetMediaType(const CMediaType *pmt);
                     HRESULT DecideBufferSize(IMemAllocator *pima, ALLOCATOR_PROPERTIES
                             *pProperties);
    };
```

Notice that the output pin of a transform filter overrides the same functions as the output pin of the source filter discussed in the previous section, namely *GetMediaType()*, *CheckMediaType()*, *SetMediaType()*, and *DecideBufferSize()*. Therefore, we're going to skip these functions and only discuss the new ones: *CheckInputType()*, *CheckTransform()*, and *Receive()*. Now, when the output pin of an upstream filter tries to connect to the input pin of a transform filter, the upstream filter verifies its media types against the transform filter's by calling the *CheckInputType()* function[2] of the transform filter. If the transform filter supports the media type, it returns S_OK; otherwise, it returns an error.

```
HRESULT CInvertFilter::CheckInputType(const CMediaType* pmtIn)
{
    DbgLog((LOG_TRACE, 2, TEXT("CInvertFilter::CheckInputType")));
    if ( (*pmtIn->Type() != MEDIATYPE_Text ) )
        return E_INVALIDARG;
    return S_OK;
}
```

DbgLog() is a useful debug macro. *See article on CD.*

Typically, the input pin of the transform filter is connected before its output pins. But it is possible for an input pin of a transform filter to connect to an upstream filter *after* one of the output pins has already established a connection with a downstream filter. In such a case the transform filter calls the *CheckTransform()* function to assure that the transform filter can convert the input media type to the output media type.

```
HRESULT CInvertFilter::CheckTransform(CMediaType* pmtIn,CMediaType* pmtOut)
{
    return S_OK;
}
```

---

2. Actually, the output pin of the upstream filter calls the *CheckMediaType()* of the input pin of the transform filter, which in turn calls our transform filter, which is a member of the CTransformFilter.

The transform filter is ready to run once both input and output pins are connected to their respective filters. When the filter graph is started, the upstream filter calls the *Receive()* function to deliver data to the transform filter. In our case, the transform filter inverts the string before delivering it to the downstream filter. The *Receive()* function accepts an IMediaSample as an input, which is the interface used to transport the data.

The *Receive()* function calls the *IMediaSample::GetPointer()* function to retrieve a pointer to the input buffer. It then calls the output pin's *GetDeliveryBuffer()* function in order to retrieve a pointer to the shared output buffer. The *Receive()* function inverts the input string and inserts it in the output buffer. Finally, it calls the output pin's *Deliver()* function in order to deliver the data to the downstream filter.

```
HRESULT CInvertFilter::Receive(IMediaSample *pSample)
{
    LPBYTE pData;
    HRESULT  hr;
    CAutoLock lck(&m_csReceive);

    // Get pointer to input buffer and size of valid data
    hr = pSample->GetPointer(&pData);
    int lDataLen = pSample->GetActualDataLength();

    if (FAILED(hr))
        return hr;

    // Get the output pin sample buffer
    IMediaSample *pOutSample;
    if ( FAILED(m_pOutput->GetDeliveryBuffer(&pOutSample, NULL, NULL, 0)) )
        return E_POINTER;

    LPBYTE pDst;
    if ( FAILED(pOutSample->GetPointer(&pDst)) )
        return E_POINTER;

    // Copy inverted string to output buffer
    CopyMemory(pDst, pData, lDataLen);
    strrev((LPTSTR)pDst);

    // deliver data to downstream filter
    pOutSample->SetActualDataLength(lDataLen);
    m_pOutput->Deliver(pOutSample);
    pOutSample->Release();
    return S_OK;
}
```

8.7 Creating a Rendering Filter

Finally, let's create a rendering filter. As you recall, a *rendering filter* supports one input pin and no output pins. It accepts data from an upstream filter and renders it to a dump file, the screen, an audio device, or the Internet. The rendering filter is the last stop for the data in the filter graph. In our sample renderer, the input pin accepts a text string and displays it to a text window on the screen (see Figure 8-3 on page 83).

DirectShow implements a base renderer, CBaseRenderer, which makes it easy to derive our text-rendering filter. Again, we'll discuss only the new functions that are relevant to the rendering filter: *CompleteConnect()*, *BreakConnect()*, *OnReceiveFirstSample()*, and *DoRenderSample()*.

```
class CTextOutFilter : public CBaseRenderer
{
    CTextOutWindow m_TextWindow;

public:
    HRESULT CompleteConnect(IPin *pReceivePin);
    HRESULT BreakConnect();
    void OnReceiveFirstSample(IMediaSample *pMediaSample);
    HRESULT DoRenderSample(IMediaSample *pMediaSample);

    CTextOutFilter(LPUNKNOWN pUnk,HRESULT *phr);
    ~CTextOutFilter();
    static CUnknown * WINAPI CreateInstance(LPUNKNOWN pUnk, HRESULT *phr);
    STDMETHODIMP NonDelegatingQueryInterface(REFIID, void **);
    DECLARE_IUNKNOWN
    HRESULT CheckMediaType(const CMediaType *pmt);
};
```

Notice that in the code we've also defined the member variable m_TextWindow, which handles the output window. CTextOutWindow is based on the CBaseControlWindow class, which is part of the DirectShow class library. CBaseControlWindow simplifies the creating and handling of output to the client window. We're not going to discuss the CBaseControlWindow interface in detail here; we'll just initialize the m_TextWindow variable in the constructor of the filter and respond to the query of the interface as follows:

```
CTextOutFilter::CTextOutFilter(LPUNKNOWN pUnk,HRESULT *phr) :
    CBaseRenderer(CLSID_TextRender, NAME("TextOut Filter"), pUnk, phr),
    m_TextWindow(NAME("TextOut"), GetOwner(),phr, &m_InterfaceLock, this)
{
}

STDMETHODIMP
CTextOutFilter::NonDelegatingQueryInterface(REFIID riid,void **ppv)
```

```
{
    CheckPointer(ppv,E_POINTER);
    if (riid == IID_IVideoWindow) {
        return m_TextWindow.NonDelegatingQueryInterface(riid,ppv);
    }
    return CBaseRenderer::NonDelegatingQueryInterface(riid,ppv);
}
```

As with the transform filter, the input pin of the rendering filter connects to an upstream filter when both filters agree on the media type and the shared buffer size. Consequently, the *CompleteConnect()* function of the rendering filter is called to affirm the connection between the two pins. This is the last chance for the rendering filter to reject the connection between the two pins.

When the input pin is disconnected from the upstream filter, the *BreakConnect()* function is called, which typically hides and destroys the output window.

```
HRESULT CTextOutFilter::CompleteConnect(IPin *pReceivePin)
{
    // It's a good time to create the window
    return S_OK;
}

HRESULT CTextOutFilter::BreakConnect()
{
    m_TextWindow.InactivateWindow();
    m_TextWindow.DoShowWindow(SW_HIDE);
    return S_OK;
}
```

At this stage, the rendering filter is ready to run. The filter exposes two functions to handle the rendering of the data: *OnReceiveFirstSample()* and *DoRenderSample()*. The *OnReceiveFirstSample()* function is always called to render the first sample of data. Typically, this function handles the first sample of data that arrives after the Pause or Start commands are issued to the filter graph. In motion video, it is necessary to display the last video frame when the video clip is paused.

```
void CTextOutFilter::OnReceiveFirstSample(IMediaSample *pMediaSample)
{
    if(IsStreaming() == FALSE) {
        ASSERT(pMediaSample);
        DrawText(pMediaSample);
    }
}
```

PART III

The *DoRenderSample()* function is repeatedly called when the upstream filter delivers the samples to the rendering filter. This function handles rendering the data to the screen, file, audio device, or the Internet. Typically, you only need to implement this function; you don't have to worry about the *OnReceiveFirstSample()* function.

```
HRESULT CTextOutFilter::DoRenderSample(IMediaSample *pMediaSample)
{
    ASSERT(pMediaSample);
    DrawText(pMediaSample);
    return NOERROR;
}
```

8.8 Adding Your Own Interface

Now you know how to create a source filter, a transform filter, and a rendering filter. As you can see, DirectShow defines the necessary interfaces to build a filter graph and control the state of this graph. It allows you to start, stop, and pause the filter graph. All fine and dandy, but what if you have a cool feature that's not supported by one of the DirectShow interfaces? This is when you have to add your own interface. As it turns out, adding a new interface is easily supported by the COM paradigm.

Suppose you'd like to retrieve the statistics of the stream received by CTextOutFilter. For example, you'd like to figure out how many characters and how many words the renderer handles from start to stop. To do this, you must add your own interface to CTextOutFilter.

To create a custom interface, you must first create an interface template, declare its name and methods, and assign a unique GUID for it—in this case, we'll call it the ITextStat interface. A template only *declares* the member functions of the interface; it does not *define* or *implement* the body of these functions. The function bodies must be defined in the class that derives from this interface.

> Use *GuidGen.Exe* to generate unique GUIDs.

```
DEFINE_GUID( IID_ITextStat,
0x48025244, 0x2d3a, 0x11ce, 0x87, 0x5d, 0x0, 0x60, 0x8c, 0xb7, 0x80, 0x66);

DECLARE_INTERFACE_( ITextStat, IUnknown )
{
    STDMETHOD(get_NumberOfChars) (THIS_  int *pNumChar) PURE;
    STDMETHOD(get_NumberOfWords) (THIS_  int *pNumWords) PURE;
};
```

> The deriving class must implement all pure interfaces.

Next you need to include the ITextStat interface as one of the base classes of the CTextOutFilter class.

```
class CTextOutFilter :
    public CBaseRenderer,
    public ITextStat
{
    CTextOutWindow m_TextWindow;

public:
    CTextOutFilter(LPUNKNOWN pUnk,HRESULT *phr);
    ~CTextOutFilter();
    static CUnknown * WINAPI CreateInstance(LPUNKNOWN pUnk, HRESULT *phr);
    STDMETHODIMP NonDelegatingQueryInterface(REFIID, void **);
    DECLARE_IUNKNOWN

    // These are the custom functions
    STDMETHODIMP get_NumberOfChars(int *pNumChar);
    STDMETHODIMP get_NumberOfWords(int *pNumWords);
    int m_nChars;
    int m_nWords;
};
```

In addition, you must implement all the functions of the ITextStat interface. Notice on the CD that the m_nChars and m_nWords fields are incremented in the *DoRenderSample()* function of the rendering filter (not shown here).

```
STDMETHODIMP CTextOutFilter::get_NumberOfChars(int *pChars)
{
    *pChars = m_nChars; // number of chars received so far.
    return NOERROR;
}

STDMETHODIMP CTextOutFilter::get_NumberOfWords(int *pWords)
{
    *pWords = m_nWords; // number of words received so far..
    return NOERROR;
}
```

Finally, you need to respond to the *NonDelagatingQueryInterface()* function of the filter in order to satisfy queries for the ITextStat interface.

```
STDMETHODIMP CTextOutFilter::NonDelegatingQueryInterface(REFIID riid,void **ppv)
{
    if (riid == IID_ITextStat) {
        return GetInterface((ITextStat *)this, ppv);
    else if (riid == IID_IVideoWindow) {
        return m_TextWindow.NonDelegatingQueryInterface(riid,ppv);
    }
    return CBaseRenderer::NonDelegatingQueryInterface(riid,ppv);
}
```

Well, now that we've arrived at this point, you're ready to use your custom interface in your application. You can access your custom interface by first calling the *QueryInterface()* function of the CTextOutFilter—specifying your custom GUID, IID_ITextStat, as the first parameter. *QueryInterface()* returns a pointer to the custom interface in the second parameter of the function. You can use that pointer to call the appropriate member function in the custom interface, for example, *Get_NumberOfChars()*, *Get_NumberOfWords()*.

```
ITextStat *pTextStat;
hr = pUnknown->QueryInterface(IID_ITextStat,(void **)&pTextStat);
if (FAILED(hr))
    return E_NOINTERFACE;

m_pTextStat->get_NumberOfChars(&m_Chars);
m_pTextStat->get_NumberOfWords(&m_Words);
```

8.9 Adding Property Pages to Filters

As we've mentioned earlier, a filter can expose one or more property pages that are specific to that filter. Typically, you would use a property page to display the status or configuration of your filter. You can access property pages either from the graph editor or from your application. We'll show you how to access property pages from an application in the following chapter.

To view the property pages for CTextOutFilter in the graph editor, right-click the mouse on the filter and select Properties. You should see something similar to what is shown in Figure 8-6.

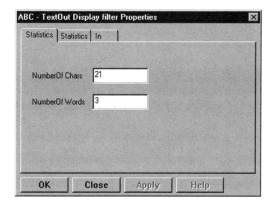

FIGURE 8-6 Property pages for CTextOutFilter.

Oooh, your fingers must be tingling at the thought of adding a property page to your own filter. It's actually pretty simple. To add one or more property pages to your filter you need to take the following steps:

1. Add the property page interface to the filter.
2. Implement the property page interface.

We break down these two steps in more detail in the following subsections.

8.9.1 Adding the Property Interface to the Filter

Actually, adding a property page is very similar to adding a custom interface. First, you must add the ISpecifyPropertyPage property interface as a base class to the CTextOutFilter declaration.

```
class CTextOutFilter :
    public CBaseRenderer,
    public ITextStat,
    public ISpecifyPropertyPages
{
    CTextOutWindow m_TextWindow;

public:
    CTextOutFilter(LPUNKNOWN pUnk,HRESULT *phr);
    ~CTextOutFilter();
    static CUnknown * WINAPI CreateInstance(LPUNKNOWN pUnk, HRESULT *phr);
    STDMETHODIMP NonDelegatingQueryInterface(REFIID, void **);
    DECLARE_IUNKNOWN

    STDMETHODIMP get_NumberOfChars(int *pNumChar);
    STDMETHODIMP get_NumberOfWords(int *pNumWords);
    int m_nChars;
    int m_nWords;
```

```
    // required for ISpecifyPropertyPages
    STDMETHODIMP GetPages(CAUUID *pPages);
};
```

You must then respond to the *NonDelegatingQueryInterface()* in order to
expose the property page interface to the application as follows:

```
STDMETHODIMP CTextOutFilter::NonDelegatingQueryInterface(REFIID riid,void
**ppv)
{
    if (riid == IID_ISpecifyPropertyPages) {
        return GetInterface((ISpecifyPropertyPages *) this, ppv);
    } else if (riid == IID_ITextStat) {
      return GetInterface((ITextStat *)this, ppv);
    } else if (riid == IID_IVideoWindow) {
        return m_TextWindow.NonDelegatingQueryInterface(riid,ppv);
    }
    return CBaseRenderer::NonDelegatingQueryInterface(riid,ppv);
}
```

Since the property page is actually a separate COM object, you must inform
DirectShow of how to create an instance of that object. To do that, you must
add the property page template to the factory template list, g_Templates[].

```
DEFINE_GUID(CLSID_TextOutPropertyPage,
0x48025243, 0x2d39, 0x11ce, 0x87, 0x5d, 0x0, 0x60, 0x8c, 0xb7, 0x80, 0x66);

CFactoryTemplate g_Templates[] = {
    { L"ABC - TextOut Display filter"
    , &CLSID_TextRender
    , CTextOutFilter::CreateInstance
    , NULL
    , &sudTextoutAx}

      { L"ABC - TextOut Property Page"
      , &CLSID_TextOutPropertyPage
      , CTextOutProperties::CreateInstance }
};
```

Finally, you must implement the *GetPages()* function of the filter. When an
application displays the property page, DirectShow calls this function to
retrieve the GUIDs of the property pages exposed by this filter. *GetPages()*
returns a list of the property pages supported by this filter. In CTextOutFilter
we're exposing the same property page twice just to show you how to support
more than one property page in a filter.

```
STDMETHODIMP CTextOutFilter::GetPages(CAUUID *pPages)
{
    pPages->cElems = 2;

    // allocate enough memory to hold their GUIDs
    pPages->pElems = (GUID *) CoTaskMemAlloc(sizeof(GUID));

    if (pPages->pElems == NULL) {
        return E_OUTOFMEMORY;
    }
    pPages->pElems[0] = CLSID_TextOutPropertyPage; // 1st property page
    pPages->pElems[1] = CLSID_TextOutPropertyPage; // 2nd property page

    return NOERROR;
}
```

8.9.2   Implementing the Property Page Interface

To implement the property page, you must first derive an interface from the base CBasePropertyPage class and implement a couple of its member functions.

PART III

```
class CTextOutProperties : public CBasePropertyPage
{
public:
    static CUnknown * WINAPI CreateInstance(LPUNKNOWN lpunk, HRESULT *phr);

private:
    CTextOutProperties(LPUNKNOWN lpunk, HRESULT *phr);
    HRESULT OnConnect(IUnknown *pUnknown);
    HRESULT OnDisconnect();
    HRESULT OnActivate();

    ITextStat *m_pTextStat;
    int m_Chars;
    int m_Words;
};
```

DirectShow then calls the *CreateInstance()* function, which creates an instance of the specified property page. Notice that the property page resource ID and name is specified when the base constructor is called.

```
CUnknown * WINAPI
CTextOutProperties::CreateInstance(LPUNKNOWN lpUnk, HRESULT *phr)
{
    return new CTextOutProperties(lpUnk, phr);
}
```

```
CTextOutProperties::CTextOutProperties(LPUNKNOWN pUnk,HRESULT *phr) :
CBasePropertyPage(NAME("TextOut Prop Page"), pUnk, IDD_PROPPAGE, IDS_NAME)
{
    ASSERT(phr);
}
```

IDD_PRPPAGE Property page resource ID.

Before the property page is displayed, DirectShow calls the *OnConnect()* function of the property page interface, using the address of the filter as a parameter. At this stage, you must retrieve any information that your property page needs from the filter. The property page retrieves the custom interface that we defined earlier, ITextStat, from CTextOutFilter in order to figure out the number of characters and words that the filter has processed already.

```
HRESULT CTextOutProperties::OnConnect(IUnknown *pUnknown)
{
    HRESULT hr;

    // get a pointer to the ITestStat interface..
    hr = pUnknown->QueryInterface(IID_ITextStat,(void **)&m_pTextStat);
    if (FAILED(hr))
        return E_NOINTERFACE;

    // get the statistics of #chars & #words from filter
    m_pTextStat->get_NumberOfChars(&m_Chars);
    m_pTextStat->get_NumberOfWords(&m_Words);
    return NOERROR;
}
```

When the property page is displayed, the *OnActivate()* function is called to update the fields of the property page.

```
HRESULT CTextOutProperties::OnActivate()
{
    TCHAR buf[50];

    wsprintf(buf,"%d", m_Chars);
    SendDlgItemMessage(m_Dlg, IDC_NumberChars, WM_SETTEXT,0, (DWORD) buf);
    wsprintf(buf,"%d", m_Words);
    SendDlgItemMessage(m_Dlg, IDC_NumberWords, WM_SETTEXT, 0, (DWORD) buf);

    return NOERROR;
}
```

Finally, when the property page is dismissed, the FGM calls the *OnDisconnect()* function in order to release any interfaces or memory.

```
HRESULT CTextOutProperties::OnDisconnect()
{
    if (m_pTextStat == NULL)
        return E_UNEXPECTED;
    m_pTextStat->Release();
    m_pTextStat = NULL;
    return NOERROR;
}
```

8.10 Adding a Filter to the Registry

DirectShow uses the system registry to hold its configuration information, filter list, and media types. When you create your own filter, you must add it to the appropriate part of the registry so that DirectShow can recognize and load your filter. Here is a list of the registry keys used by DirectShow with a brief description of each key:

\\ Hkey_Class_Root **\Filter**	DirectShow looks here for a list of filter IDs (GUIDs).
\\ Hkey_Class_Root **\CLSID**	This is where all COM objects live. Holds the settings for each GUID (for example, the filename of executable). DirectShow looks up filter GUIDs here to get information about the filter.
\\Hkey_Class_Root **\Media Type**	List of media types (for example, MPEG1Stream) and the associated source filter that can handle this media type. This is used for automatic rendering of source files. You can find more information on the CD under "Adding Custom File Types."
\\Hkey_Local_Machine **\Software\Debug**	This area holds useful debug configuration for each filter. You can find more information on the CD under "DirectShow Debugging Hints."

You can easily add the necessary entries for your filter in the registry in one of two ways. You can build a registry file with all the necessary entries and add it to the registry with the RegEdit.Exe. Or you can embed the registry information in the filter and use the RegSvr32.Exe command to add the information to the registry.

8.10.1 Using a Registry File Is Not Recommended

Windows registry editor, RegEdit.Exe, supports a command line option, -s, which allows you to specify a registry file in order to add information to the registry. Here is the registry file for CTextOutFilter:

```
; FileName: TextOut.Reg
[HKEY_CLASSES_ROOT\Filter\{CC01B761-A537-11d0-9C71-00AA0058A735}]

@="ABC - Text Display Filter"

[HKEY_CLASSES_ROOT\Clsid\{CC01B761-A537-11d0-9C71-00AA0058A735}]
@="Text Display Filter"
"Merit"=dword:00800000

[HKEY_CLASSES_ROOT\Clsid\{CC01B761-A537-11d0-9C71-00AA0058A735}\InprocServer32]
@="c:\\filter\\textout.ax"
"ThreadingModel"="Both"

[HKEY_CLASSES_ROOT\Clsid\{CC01B761-A537-11d0-9C71-00AA0058A735}\Pins]
[HKEY_CLASSES_ROOT\Clsid\{CC01B761-A537-11d0-9C71-00AA0058A735}\Pins\TextOut]
"AllowedMany"=dword:00000000
"AllowedZero"=dword:00000000
"Direction"=dword:00000000
"IsRendered"=dword:00000001

[HKEY_CLASSES_ROOT\Clsid\{CC01B761-A537-11d0-9C71-00AA0058A735}\Pins\TextOut\Types]
[HKEY_CLASSES_ROOT\Clsid\{CC01B761-A537-11d0-9C71-00AA0058A735}\Pins\TextOut\Types\
{73747874-0000-0010-8000-00AA00389B71}]
[HKEY_CLASSES_ROOT\Clsid\{CC01B761-A537-11d0-9C71-00AA0058A735}\Pins\TextOut\Types\
{73747874-0000-0010-8000-00AA00389B71}\{00000000-0000-0000-0000-000000000000}]
```

◊ Register filter GUID and name with DirectShow.

◊ Add filter GUID to CLSID section.

◊ Path and filename of filter.

◊ Supported pins and their properties.

◊ Major and minor media types that the output pin supports.

To add the information in the file to the registry, run:

```
RegEdit.Exe -s TextOut.Reg
```

The problem with this method is that the information in the registry file is static and may not reflect the current state of the filter. For example, the path to the filter is hard coded and must be manually updated if the path changes.

8.10.2 Using Filter Self-Registration Is Recommended

DirectShow supports the COM self-registration procedure, which allows a filter to automatically add its information to the registry. To use self-registration, you must embed the information in the filter and then run the RegSvr32.Exe command. This command retrieves the embedded information from the filter and adds it to the system registry.

First you must add the DirectShow setup information, *sudTextOutAx,* in the factory template *m_gTemplates[]*. The DirectShow setup information allows you to specify the filter name, the number of pins, and the supported media types for each pin.

```
const AMOVIESETUP_MEDIATYPE sudIpPinTypes ={
    &MEDIATYPE_Text,                          ◊ Major and minor media types supported
    &MEDIASUBTYPE_NULL                          by this pin.
};
                                              Pin information array. If there is more
const AMOVIESETUP_PIN sudIpPins [] = {    ◊ than one pin, just add its information here.
  { L"TextOut",                  ◊ Pin name.
    FALSE,                       ◊ Does the pin render the data it receives?
    FALSE,                       ◊ Is it an output pin?
    FALSE,                       ◊ Is filter allowed to have zero pins of this type?
    FALSE,                       ◊ Does the filter have more than one instance of this pin?
    &CLSID_NULL,                 ◊ The pin connects to the pin with this CLSID.
    NULL,                        ◊ The pin connects to the pin with this name.
    1,                           ◊ Number of supported media types.
    &sudIpPinTypes }             ◊ Address of media type list.
};

                                              Filter information that is inserted in the
const AMOVIESETUP_FILTER sudTextoutAx = { ◊ registry.
    &CLSID_PlainText,            ◊ GUID of this filter.
    L"ABC Text Display Filter",  ◊ Filter name.
    MERIT_NORMAL,                ◊ Filter merit. This is used for automatic connection
    1,                           ◊ Number of pins.
    &sudIpPins                   ◊ Address of list of pins.
};

CFactoryTemplate g_Templates[] = {
  {  L"ABC - TextOut Display filter"
    , &CLSID_PlainText
    , CTextOutFilter::CreateInstance
    , NULL
    , &sudTextoutAx }            ◊ Pointer to filter self-registration information (optional).
};
```

Finally, you must implement and export two functions: *DllRegisterServer()* and *DllUnregisterServer()*. *DllRegisterServer()* is called to add the filter information to the registry, and *DllUnregisterServer()* is called to remove that information from the registry. Both functions call the appropriate DirectShow function to do the actual registration and de-registration. Of course, you can add your own code here to add information to or remove information from the registry.

```
STDAPI DllRegisterServer()
{
    return AMovieDllRegisterServer2( TRUE );
}

STDAPI DllUnregisterServer()
{
    return AMovieDllRegisterServer2( FALSE );
}
```

You can export the functions in the Definition (DEF) file as follows:

```
EXPORTS
        DllRegisterServer
        DllUnregisterServer
```

Once you've built the filter successfully, you can register the filter by running:

```
RegSvr32.Exe TextOut.Ax
```

(*TextOut.Ax* is the filter filename), and you can unregister the filter by running:

```
RegSvr32.Exe -u TextOut.Ax
```

WHAT HAVE YOU LEARNED?

By the end of this chapter, you should

- have an understanding of the filter graph model of DirectShow;
- understand the connection between input and output pins;
- know how to create your own source, transform, and rendering filters and know the difference between them;
- be able to add custom interfaces to your filter;
- know how to add property pages to a filter; and
- understand how to either create a registry file or embed the registry information in the filter.

In the following chapter, we'll show you how to access these filters from the application point of view. After all, you wrote these filters for a reason.

CHAPTER 9

DirectShow Applications

WHY READ THIS CHAPTER?

Now that you've created your own DirectShow filters, you probably want to use them within your application. What a coincidence! This is exactly what we're covering in this chapter.

We'll show you how to access DirectShow filters using your application by one of two methods: direct low-level access using the COM interfaces, and high-level access using the DirectShow ActiveX control.

For the COM interface, we'll show you how to

- use the automatic method for building filter graphs,
- use a preprepared filter graph file (*.grf) for building filter graphs,
- use a manual method for building filter graphs,
- control the state of the filter graph (Start/Stop/Pause),
- access custom interfaces within a specific filter,
- display filter-specific property pages from within your application, and
- handle events posted by the filters and the filter graph manager.

As for the ActiveX interface, we'll show you how to

- add the DirectShow ActiveX control to your application and then access it,
- control the state of the filter graph (Start/Stop/Pause), and
- handle events posted by ActiveX control.

9.1 DirectShow Mechanisms for Working on Filter Graphs

In the previous chapter, you learned how to build your own DirectShow filters—source, transform, and rendering. You also learned how to add property pages and custom interfaces to your filters. To test your filter, you used the *Graph Editor* graphical applet, which allows you to add individual filters and connect their pins together. The applet also allows you to run the filter graph, save the filter graph into a *.grf* file for later use, and display that slick property page that you embedded in your filter.

In this chapter, you'll learn how to manipulate filters in the same manner as you did using the graph editor. As you recall from the previous chapter, DirectShow provides three ways to access the filter graph (see Figure 9-1):

■ directly through the Filter Graph Manager (FGM) COM interfaces;

■ through the DirectShow ActiveX control, which is part of the DirectShow SDK; and

■ indirectly through the MCI interface.

In this chapter, we'll only discuss the first two methods: the COM interface and the ActiveX control.

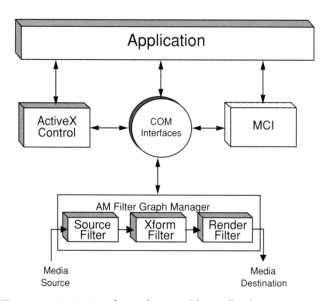

FIGURE 9-1 Interfaces that provide applications access to the DirectShow filter graph.

DirectShow provides various levels of application support. At the high level, ActiveX, you only need to embed the ActiveX control in your application, and ActiveX control will handle the rest. It opens the media file, builds the filter graph, and even provides the user interface for controlling the filter graph (Run, Stop, Pause, and so forth).

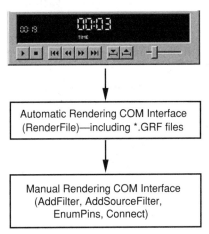

FIGURE 9-2 Various levels of DirectShow application interfaces.

For mid-level control, DirectShow offers an automatic rendering method using its COM interfaces. At this level, you can construct the entire filter graph with a simple function call, *IFilterGraph::RenderFile()*, and Direct-Show determines the appropriate filters to load and how to connect their pins. You can also use the *RenderFile()* function to re-create a preconfigured filter graph from a GRF file—GRF files can be created with the Filter Graph Editor (FGE). When you use the mid-level method, you have direct access to your custom interfaces and property pages. In addition, you can receive and handle filter graph notification events.

At the lowest level, DirectShow offers a wide range of manual rendering COM interfaces that allow you to have total control over your filters. You can manually load each filter and connect its pins together. You can use this low-level method when you want to bypass DirectShow automatic rendering techniques and assure that you are loading the correct filters.

PART III

9.2 COM: Automatic Construction of Filter Graphs

Let's start at this level, in the middle, because it offers the best of both worlds. At this level, you can construct a filter graph easily and still maintain full access to the filters and their events.

IGraphBuilder functions:
*AddFilter(),
AddSourceFilter(),
RemoveFilter(),
EnumFilters(),
FindFilterByName(),
Connect(),
Render(),
RenderFile(),
SetLogFile(), and
more*

DirectShow defines the graph builder interface, IGraphBuilder, which allows you to build filter graphs from within your application. To do this, the graph builder interface uses the settings in the system registry to determine the appropriate filters to load and connect in order to construct the filter graph.[1]

Before you create the graph builder object, you must first initialize the COM libraries with the *CoInitialize()* function. You can then call the *CoCreateInstance()* function to create an instance of the IGraphBuilder interface. The function looks up the CLSID_FilterGraph in the system registry and loads the appropriate Dynamic Link Library (DLL) associated with this class ID. It creates an instance of the IGraphBuilder object and returns it in the `m_pGraph` parameter.

```
if(FAILED(CoInitialize())                    // initialize the COM intreface
    return FALSE;

// Create a Graph Builder object
IGraphBuilder * m_pGraph;
HRESULT hr = CoCreateInstance(
    &CLSID_FilterGraph,          ◊ CLSID for DirectShow graph builder (Quartz.Dll)
    NULL ,                       ◊ Created standalone—not aggregated
    CLSCTX_INPROC_SERVER,        ◊ Created within the same process space of the app
    &IID_IGraphBuilder,          ◊ GUID of requested interface
    &m_pGraph);                  ◊ Holds a pointer to IGraphBuilder interface on
                                   return
```

Once you've obtained an instance of the filter graph builder, you can call its *RenderFile()* function to create the entire filter graph. This function accepts the input filename as a parameter.

```
if (FAILED(hr) || FAILED( m_pGraph->RenderFile(wPath, NULL) ))
    return FALSE;
```

1. You can find out more about the system registry setting on the CD under *"Adding Your Own Custom File Format."*

The *RenderFile()* function first determines which source filter to load based on the contents of the input file. Notice that DirectShow does not use the file extension (**.mpg, *.avi*, and so forth) to determine the type of media in the file; rather, it searches the input file for certain byte values residing at certain byte locations, and, based on what it finds, it determines what type of media the file represents. The source filter that handles that type of file typically knows those byte locations and their values. For more information, refer to "Adding Your Own Custom File Format" on the CD.

BUILDING A LIST OF FIGURES

The following code segment illustrates how to retrieve the list of filters in the system registry. You can use the IAMCollection interface and the *IMediaControl::get_RegFilterCollection()* to enumerate the filters in the system registry as follows:

```
BOOL CRegFiltersDlg::OnInitDialog()
{
    IAMCollection *pMCollection;
    char szTmp[256];
    LONG lCount;

    // Get the collection of filters from the registry and find
    // how many filters is there..
    m_pMC->get_RegFilterCollection((IDispatch**)&pMCollection);
    pMCollection->get_Count(&lCount);

    IRegFilterInfo *pInfo;
    BSTR pTmp;

    // For each filter, add its name the list box…
    for (int i=0; i<lCount; i++) {
            pMCollection->Item(i, (IUnknown**)(&pInfo));
            pInfo->get_Name(&pTmp);
            WideCharToMultiByte(CP_ACP, 0, pTmp, -1, szTmp,
              sizeof(szTmp), NULL, NULL);
            m_FilterList.AddString(szTmp);
            pInfo->Release();
    }
    pMCollection->Release();
    return TRUE;
}
```

You can get a similar list of loaded filters in the filter graph. All you have to do is replace the *get_RegFilterCollection()* with the *get_FilterCollection()* and the IRegFilterInfo with the IFilterInfo.

Once *RenderFile()* determines and loads the source filter, it enumerates the filter pins and determines the media types that they support. For each of the media types, the graph builder searches the system registry for a filter that accepts that media type as an input. If such a filter is found, *Render-File()* loads that filter and connects its pin to the output pin of the source filter. From there on, the same process is repeated for each output pin until the entire filter graph is assembled.

IMediaControl functions:
Run(),
Pause(),
Stop(),
StopWhenReady(),
GetState(),
RenderFile(),
AddSourceFilter(),
get_FilterCollection(),
and more

Now that the filter graph is built, you can start, pause, or stop the filter graph at will. To do that, you must first obtain a pointer to the media control interface, IMediaControl, of the filter graph. You can simply call the *IGraph-Builder::QueryInterface()* function to retrieve a pointer to the media control interface using `IID_IMEDIACONTROL` as a parameter. The *QueryInterface()* function returns the media control interface in the second parameter, &m_pMC, which you can use to call the appropriate function to run, stop, or pause the filter graph.

```
// Obtain the interface to our filter graph
    if(FAILED(m_pGraph->QueryInterface(IID_IMediaControl,(void**) &m_pMC)))
    return FALSE;

    hr = m_pMC->Run();
    hr = m_pMC->Stop();
    hr = m_pMC->Pause();

    m_pMC->Release();
```

Make sure to Release the interface when you're done with it.

Notice that the Stop command exposed by the media control interface stops the video clip at the last key frame, or intra-frame.[2] However, you could choose to modify the behavior of the Stop command so that after the video stopped the video clip would always rewind to the beginning of the sequence.

IMediaPosition functions:
get_Duration(),
get_CurrentPosition(),
put_CurrentPosition(),
get_StopTime(),
put_StopTime(),
get_PrerollTime(),
set_PreRollTime(),
get_Rate(),
put_Rate(), and
more

To do that, you must first acquire a pointer to the media position interface, IMediaPosition, which manages the position of the stream. As with the media control, you must first call the *IGraphBuilder::QueryInterface()* to retrieve a pointer to the media position interface. You can then use that pointer to call the *IMediaPosition::put_CurrentPosition()* function and set the position of the stream to zero.

---

2. A key or intra-frame is a frame that can be decoded independent of any other frame in the sequence.

```
hr = m_pMC->Pause();          // Ask the filter graph to pause

// Rewind the stream to the beginning when the user issues the STOP
// command or when the EC_COMPLETE event is received.
IMediaPosition * pMP;
hr = m_pGraph->QueryInterface(IID_IMediaPosition, (void**) &pMP);

if (SUCCEEDED(hr)) {
    pMP->put_CurrentPosition(0);
    pMP->Release();
}

// wait for pause to complete
OAFilterState state;
m_pMC->GetState(INFINITE, &state);

// now really do the stop
m_pMC->Stop();
```

> *IMediaControl::Pause()* is asynchronous and returns immediately before it completely pauses the clip. The *GetState()* function blocks until the filter is completely paused.

9.3 COM: Manual Construction of Filter Graphs

That was surprisingly easy! So why would you want to create a filter graph manually anyway? We're sure you have your own reason for doing this, but it usually boils down to this: you don't want to rely on the setting of the registry, and you want to guarantee that your filter is always loaded. After all, you spent your heart and soul writing it.

9.3.1 Adding Filters to the Filter Graph

DirectShow defines two methods for adding filters to the filter graph: one for adding source filters and the other for adding transform and rendering filters. To add a source filter, you can call either the *IMediaControl::AddSourceFilter()* function or the *IGraphBuilder::AddSourceFilter()* function. To add a transform or rendering filter, you can call either the *IGraphBuilder::AddFilter()* function or the *IRegFilterInfor::Filter()* function.

For simplicity's sake, we'll use CFruitFilter and the CTextOut filter from the example of Chapter 8 to demonstrate how to construct a filter graph manually. First we'll show you how to add the CFruitFilter source filter and then how to add the CTextOut rendering filter. We'll then enumerate their pins and connect the two filters together.

9.3.2 Adding Source Filters

The DirectShow SDK only describes how to use the *AddSourceFilter()* function to add a source filter to a filter graph. But this function behaves in a similar manner to the *RenderFile()* function in that it uses the system registry to determine the source filter associated with an input file. Unlike the *RenderFile()* function, the *AddSourceFilter()* only loads the source filter; it does not build the entire graph. As a result, you have full control when it comes to loading the remaining filters in the graph. (Pssst ... Do you really want to have full control over loading your source filter? Read on below.)

OK, here is how you would use the *IFilterGraph::AddSourceFilter()* function to add a source filter to the filter graph. It's pretty simple!

```
// Load the source file associated with the Fruit.FTF file
WCHAR wFileName[] = L"Fruit.FTF";
m_pGraph->AddSourceFilter(wFileName, wFileName, &pSrcFilter);
```

> The *Fruit.ftf* file has the string FRUIT TEXT at the beginning of the file (the *ftf* file extension stands for "fruit text file"). The registry associates any file starting with that string with CFruitFilter. See "Adding Your Custom File Types" on the CD.

What actually happens when you call the *AddSourceFilter()* function? DirectShow associates the specified filename with a source filter through the mapping specified in the registry. In this case, any file that starts with "FRUIT TEXT" is associated with CFruitFilter. In turn, the *AddSourceFilter()* function loads CFruitFilter into the filter graph. DirectShow then queries the filter for the IFileSourceFilter interface. The IFileSourceFilter interface is used to pass the filename and media type information to/from the filter. If the interface exists, DirectShow calls the *IFileSourceFilter::Load()* function, using the input filename and media type as parameters.

You could ask the question, "Well, can I mimic this behavior if I don't want to rely on the registry mapping to load my source filter?" The answer is, "Yes you can."

To do this, you must first find your source filter in the registry and then add it to the filter graph (see our *LoadFilter()* function below). To find the source filter in the registry, you must call the *IMediaControl::get_RegFilterCollection()* function to enumerate all the DirectShow filters in the registry. The function returns an IAMCollection interface, which you can use to retrieve information about each of the filters, IRegFilterInfo. You can then use the *IRegFilterInfo::get_Name()* function to retrieve the filter name and match it against the name of your filter.

Once you have found your source filter, you can call the *IRegFilterInfo::Filter()* function to load the filter into the filter graph. Notice that the *Filter()* function returns a pointer to an IFilterInfo interface rather than the filter itself; you should call the *IFilterInfo::get_Filter()* function to retrieve a pointer to the newly added filter.

```
HRESULT
CCustomFilterGraph::LoadFilter (
    WCHAR *pszName,             // Filter Name to match against registry
    IBaseFilter **pFilter)      // on return holds a pointer to added filter
{
    BSTR pTmp;
    LONG lCount;
    HRESULT hr;
    IAMCollection *pMCollection=NULL;
    IRegFilterInfo *pRegInfo=NULL;
    IFilterInfo *pFilterInfo=NULL;

    // Get a list of all registered DirectShow filters
    m_pMC->get_RegFilterCollection((IDispatch**)&pMCollection);
    pMCollection->get_Count(&lCount);

    // For each filter, find out if its name matches the name of our filter
    for (int i=0; i<lCount; i++) {
        RetOnErr( pMCollection->Item(i, (IUnknown**)(&pRegInfo)) );
        pRegInfo->get_Name(&pTmp);

        // Once found, add filter to the graph and get a pointer to it.
        if (lstrcmpW(pszName, pTmp) == 0) {
            pRegInfo->Filter((IDispatch**)&pFilterInfo);
            pFilterInfo->get_Filter((IUnknown**)pFilter);
            break;
        }

        pRegInfo->Release();
        pRegInfo=NULL;
    }

    pMCollection->Release();
    pRegInfo->Release();
    return hr;
}
```

So far we've loaded the source filter without using the automatic mapping of the registry. To mimic the exact behavior of the *AddSourceFilter()* function, you need to query the source filter for its IFileSourceFilter interface. If you find it, you must call the *Load()* function of that interface, using the input filename as a parameter. That's it!

PART III

```
LoadFilter (L"ABC - Fruit Source Filter", &pFilter);

hr = pFilter->QueryInterface(IID_IFileSourceFilter,(void**)&pFSFilter);
if (SUCCEEDED(hr)  {
    pFSFilter->Load(wPath, NULL);
    pFSFilter->Release();
}
```

9.3.3 Adding Transform and Rendering Filters

That wasn't too complex, was it? Let's keep going. To add a transform or a rendering filter, you only have to call the same *LoadFilter()* function with the filter name as a parameter. And, Voilà!

```
// Load the Rendering Filter.
LoadFilter (L"ABC - Text Display Filter", &pRenderFilter);
```

9.3.4 Connecting the Two Pins

Once the two filters are loaded, you need to connect the output pin of CFruitFilter with the input pin of the CTextOut filter. Well, first you need to find the pins before you can connect them together.

Once you have a pointer to a filter, you can enumerate a list of its pins by calling the member function *IBaseFilter::EnumPins()*, which returns an IEnumPins object. You can then call the *IEnumPins::Next()* function to retrieve a pointer to the pin interface, IPin. Once you have a pointer to the pin, you can get the pin name by calling the *IPin::QueryPinInfo()* function, which returns the pin name in a PIN_INFO structure.

```
HRESULT CCustomFilterGraph::FindPin(
    IBaseFilter *pFilter,      // Filter to search for pins
    WCHAR *pszName,            // Name of pin
    IPin **ppPin)              // returns the IPin interface
{
    IEnumPins *pEnumPins=NULL;
    IPin *pPin=NULL;
    PIN_INFO PinInfo;
    HRESULT hr;
    ULONG nFetched;

    // Get an enumerated list of the pins in this filter
    pFilter->EnumPins(&pEnumPins);
```

> Notice that the *IBaseFilter::FindPin()* method exposed by the filter does not find the pin based on the actual pin name. This function works in conjunction with the *QueryId()* function to implement graph persistency (Save/Restore). Refer to the SDK for more information about persistence.

```
while (SUCCEEDED( hr = pEnumPins->Next(1, &pPin, &nFetched)) ) {
    pPin->QueryPinInfo(&PinInfo);

    // Silly, but we have to release this since QueryPinInfo() adds
    // a reference to the filter..
    if (PinInfo.pFilter)
        PinInfo.pFilter->Release();

    // Return the IPin interface when you find a match..
    if (lstrcmpW(PinInfo.achName, pszName) == 0) {
        *ppPin = pPin;
        break;
    }
    pPin->Release();
}

pEnumPins->Release();
return hr;
}
```

You can call our *FindPin()* function to find the output pin of the source filter, Text!, and the input pin of the rendering filter, In, as follows:

```
FindPin(pSrcFilter, L"Text!", &pTextPin);
FindPin(pRenderFilter, L"In", &pRenderPin);
```

Finally, you can call the *IGraphBuilder::Connect()* function to connect the
two pins together. Then the media type negotiation starts. Once that phase
is done, you will have the complete filter graph.

```
m_pGraph->Connect(pTextPin, pDisplayPin);
```

9.4 COM: Accessing Custom Interfaces

In the previous chapter you learned how to add the custom interface IText-
Stat to CTextOutFilter. As you recall, the ITextStat interface exposes two
functions that return the number of characters and the number of words
processed by the CTextOutFilter. You also learned how to access this custom
interface and retrieve this data from the property page of the filter.

Now, suppose that you want to find out the same information from within
your application so you could log it to a file or display it in some other format, in a chart, for example. Actually, the process is a bit similar to what we

did in the previous chapter except that you must first obtain a pointer to the CTextOutFilter and then get a pointer to the custom interface.

Assuming that you've already loaded the filter in the filter graph, you can call the *IFilterGraph::FindFilterByName()* function to get a pointer to the filter. The function accepts the filter name as a parameter and returns a pointer to the filter.

```
#include <initguid.h>                              ◊ Must have this here for proper COM
                                                     initialization.
#include "..\\Filters\\Frender\ITextStat.h"  ◊ ITextStat custom interface definition.
void CActiveFilterDlg::OnItextstat()
{
    HRESULT hr;
    IBaseFilter *pFilter;
    IFilterGraph *pFGraph;

    // First, find the filter in the filter graph..
    m_pMC->QueryInterface(IID_IFilterGraph, (void**)&pFGraph);
    hr = pFGraph->FindFilterByName(L"ABC - Text Display Filter", &pFilter);
    pFGraph->Release();

    if (FAILED(hr))
        return;
```

Once you have a pointer to the filter, you can call the *IBaseFilter::Query-Interface()* function to get a pointer to the custom interface. Now you can call the appropriate functions exposed by the custom interface, *get_NumberOfChars()* and *get_NumberOfWords()*, to retrieve the number of characters and words processed by the CTextOutFilter.

```
    // Get a reference to the custom ITextStat interface..
    ITextStat *pTextStat;
    int nChars, nWords;
    hr = pFilter->QueryInterface(IID_ITextStat, (void**)&pTextStat);

    if (SUCCEEDED(hr)) {
        // Call the declared interface methods..
        pTextStat->get_NumberOfChars(&nChars);
        pTextStat->get_NumberOfWords(&nWords);
        wsprintf (szTmp, "NumWords: %d, NumChars: %d", nWords, nChars);
        AfxMessageBox(szTmp);
        pTextStat->Release();
    }

    pFilter->Release();
}
```

9.5 COM: Showing Filter Property Pages

Typically, filters display their status and configuration information in their own property pages. In the previous chapter, you learned how to add a property page to the CTextOutFilter and used the graph editor to display it. Let's see how you would display property pages from within your own application.

As when you worked with the custom interface, you must first retrieve a pointer to the TextOut filter. You must then call the *IBaseFilter::QueryInterface()* function to retrieve a reference to the property page interface, ISpecifyPropertyPages. If the filter exposes a property page, you can then call the *ISpecifyPropertyPages::GetPages()* function to obtain a list of the property pages exposed by the filter. This function actually returns the CLSIDs of the property pages. Finally, you can call the standard COM function *OleCreatePropertyFrame()* to display the property pages.

```
void CActiveFilterDlg::OnPropertypage()
{
    HRESULT hr;
    IBaseFilter *pFilter;

    // Find the TextOut filter
    IFilterGraph *pFGraph;
    m_pMC->QueryInterface(IID_IFilterGraph, (void**)&pFGraph);
    hr = pFGraph->FindFilterByName(L"ABC - Text Display Filter", &pFilter);
    pFGraph->Release();

    // Get a reference to the ISpecifyPropertyPage interface from the
    // filter.  It will fail if the filter does not contain any prop pages
    ISpecifyPropertyPages *pPropertyPage;
    CAUUID Pages;

    hr = pFilter->QueryInterface(IID_ISpecifyPropertyPages,
              (void**)&pPropertyPage);

    // Now get the property page information and
    // call the OLE function to display the prop page...
    if (SUCCEEDED(hr) ) {
        pPropertyPage->GetPages(&Pages);
        OleCreatePropertyFrame(
            m_hWnd,                         ◊ Handle of parent window
            0 ,                             ◊ X position of Window
            0,                              ◊ Y position of Window
            L"Hello",                       ◊ Title of property sheet dialog box
            1,                              ◊ Number of objects in next parameter
            (LPUNKNOWN *)&pFilter,          ◊ Object that holds the prop sheet
            Pages.cElems,                   ◊ Number of property pages
            Pages.pElems,                   ◊ Pointer to their CLSIDs (or GUIDs)
            NULL,                           ◊ local identifier (ignore)
            0,                              ◊ reserved
            NULL                            ◊ reserved
            );
```

```
        CoTaskMemFree(Pages.pElems);
        pPropertyPage->Release();
    }

    pFilter->Release();
}
```

Free this pointer to avoid memory leaks.

Notice that the *GetPages()* function allocates a task specific memory to hold the list of property pages. Make sure to free that memory to avoid memory leaks.

9.6 Creating Events under DirectShow

Filters and the Filter Graph Manager (FGM) send messages, also known as events, to alert the application of special conditions. For example, there are events that inform the application when an error occurs, when the end of a stream is reached, or when the video size has changed.

DirectShow uses the Win32 *CreateEvent()* function to create a manual-reset event, which is used for signaling the application. On one side, the filter sets the Win32 event when it needs to post a message, and it inserts the message in an internal queue. On the other side, the application waits for the event to be signaled, retrieves the message from the internal queue, and resets the Win32 event.

From an application, you can call the *IMediaEvent::GetEventHandle()* function to retrieve a handle to the Win32 event. You can then call the *WaitForSingleObject()* or *MsgWaitForMultipleObjects()* function to wait for that event to be signaled. The latter function returns when a Windows message is posted to the application message queue or when the Win32 event is signaled. Refer to the sample applications on the DirectShow SDK to learn how to use this function for event handling.

In our example, we choose to use the *WaitForSingleObject()* function running in a separate thread. We choose to do so because we are using a dialog box as the main window and could not hook into the message pump. Also this implementation turned out to be a bit simpler.

```
// This is called when the thread is running
int CFilterGraph::Run()
{
    // get hold of the event notification handle so we can wait for
    // completion
    IMediaEvent *pME;
    HANDLE hGraphNotifyEvent;
    HRESULT hr = m_pGraph->QueryInterface(IID_IMediaEvent, (void **) &pME);
```

```
    if (FAILED(hr))
        return FALSE;

    hr = pME->GetEventHandle((OAEVENT*) &hGraphNotifyEvent);
    pME->Release();

    if (FAILED(hr))
        return FALSE;

    DWORD result;

    while (TRUE) {
        // Block until an event arrives from the filter graph
        result = WaitForSingleObject (hGraphNotifyEvent, INFINITE);
        OnGraphNotify();
    }

    return FALSE;
}
```

The *WaitForSingleObject()* function returns only when the Win32 event is set, so there is an infinite timeout. At that point, you can call *IMediaEvent:: GetEvent()* to retrieve the pending DirectShow event from the internal queue. This function returns the event code sent by the filter or the filter graph manager and resets the Win32 event. Notice that you must call the *IMediaEvent:: FreeEventParams()* function in order to free any memory allocated when the *GetEvent()* was called.

```
void CFilterGraph::OnGraphNotify()
{
    IMediaEvent *pME;
    long lEventCode, lParm1, lParm2;

    // Get a reference to the IMediaEvent interface
    HRESULT hr = m_pGraph->QueryInterface(IID_IMediaEvent, (void **)&pME);

    // Now, get the event and handle it accordingly.
    if( SUCCEEDED(hr)){
        if( SUCCEEDED(pME->GetEvent(&lEventCode, &lParm1, &lParm2, 0)) ) {
            switch (lEventCode) {
                case EC_COMPLETE:
                    Stop();
                    break;
                case EC_USERABORT:
                case EC_ERRORABORT:
                    Stop();
            }
        }
        // frees memory used for GetEvent()
        pME->FreeEventParams(lEventCode, lParm1, lParm2);
        pME->Release();
    }
}
```

PART III

9.7 ActiveX: A Simple Way to Control DirectShow

The DirectShow SDK includes an ActiveX control, which communicates directly with the DirectShow COM interface discussed above. It is a high-level interface that includes its own user interface for controlling the media stream. We'll show you how to disable this user interface if you so desire.

Notice that with the ActiveX control you have less control over the filter graph. For example, you cannot access any of your custom filter interfaces or display the filter property pages as you can with the COM interface.

9.7.1 Playing a File Using the ActiveX Interface

Let's see how you can load and play a file with the ActiveX control interface using the Microsoft Visual C++ development environment. We're assuming that you're using Microsoft Foundation Classes (MFC) to implement a dialog-based application.

Similar to any OLE/COM component, you can insert the DirectShow Control Object into your project from the Microsoft Visual C++ compiler. The compiler creates a new MFC class, which serves as a wrapper to the ActiveX control. The default class name is CActiveMovie.

At this stage you can either use the *Create()* member function of the class to create an instance of the DirectShow control, or you can embed it in a dialog box. In the interests of simplicity, let's see how we can do this within a dialog box. You should be able to figure out the *Create()* function easily.

Notice that when you add an ActiveX control to your project, you automatically add a new icon for that control in the control toolbar (Figure 9-3). Now you can add the DirectShow ActiveX control in the same fashion as you would add a push button or an edit box.

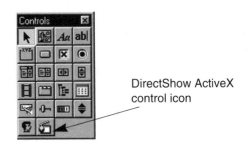

DirectShow ActiveX
control icon

FIGURE 9-3 Visual C++ dialog editor template.

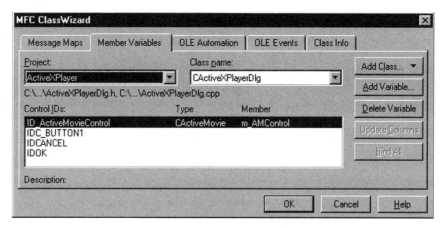

FIGURE 9-4 Associate the DirectShow control with a member variable.

To access this control from your application, you must first associate the newly added control with a member variable in the dialog box class. To do so, launch the class wizard (available on the Microsoft compiler) and add a variable for the ActiveX control ID as shown in Figure 9-4. Note that we used the name *m_AMControl.*

Now you're ready to play the file. To play a file, you need only call the *CDirectShow::SetFileName()* and pass the filename as a parameter. In turn, the ActiveX control communicates directly with the DirectShow COM interface and uses the automatic method to build the entire filter graph.

```
void CActiveXPlayerDlg::OnOpenFile()
{
    // Prompt the user for a file name..
    static char cszFilter[] =
    "Multimedia Files|*.mpg; *.avi; *.mov; *.FTF | All Files (*.*)|*.*||";

    CFileDialog cFile(TRUE, NULL, NULL,
            OFN_HIDEREADONLY | OFN_OVERWRITEPROMPT, cszFilter);

    if (cFile.DoModal() == IDOK) {
        CString str = cFile.GetPathName();
        m_AMControl.SetFileName(str);   // Set ActiveX control filename...
    }
}
```

> You can add your own file extensions here; *.ftf* is the Fruit text file extension.

Whenever the ActiveX control is used, it displays the standard user interface shown in Figure 9-5. You can use this interface to Start/Stop/Pause or navigate through the movie.

PART III

FIGURE 9-5   ActiveMovie ActiveX control interface.

9.7.2   Controlling the ActiveX Control from Your Application

Suppose that the supplied user interface does not match your application look and feel, or you just don't like it. Luckily, with the ActiveX control you can disable the user interface and instead control the movie from within your own application.

Figure 9-6 shows the default user interface of the ActiveX control with the controls grouped according to their functionality. You can enable/disable or show/hide each of these groups separately.

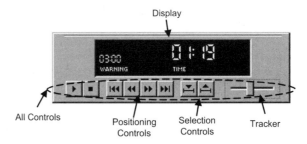

FIGURE 9-6   ActiveX control default user interface components.

You can use the *SetShowControls()* function to either show or hide all the controls. The setting of the master control takes precedence over the individual group settings described below. For example, if you call this function with FALSE as a parameter, none of the individual controls will be shown regardless of their individual settings.

```
m_AMControl.SetShowControls(TRUE);      ◊ Controls are shown per group setting.
m_AMControl.SetShowControls(FALSE);     ◊ All controls are hidden regardless of group setting.
```

Assuming that the master control is enabled, you can use the *SetShowPositionControls()* function to show/hide the positioning buttons and the *SetEnablePositionControls()* function to enable/disable the same buttons.

```
m_AMControl.SetShowPositionControls(TRUE);
m_AMControl.SetShowPositionControls(FALSE);
m_AMControl.SetEnablePositionControls(TRUE);
m_AMControl.SetEnablePositionControls(FALSE);
```

Similar functions are used to show/hide and enable/disable the selection controls, the tracker bar, display, and the context menu.

```
// Show/Hide functions
m_AMControl.SetShowSelectionControls(TRUE or FALSE);
m_AMControl.SetShowTracker (TRUE or FALSE);
m_AMControl.SetShowDisplay(TRUE or FALSE);

// Enable/Disable functions
m_AMControl.SetEnableSelectionControls(TRUE or FALSE);
m_AMControl.SetEnableTracker(TRUE or FALSE);
m_AMControl.SetEnableContextMenu(TRUE or FALSE);
```

In addition to controlling which part of the user interface to show, you can also control the running state of the movie. For example, you can call the *Run()*, *Stop()*, and *Pause()* functions to perform the specified operation.

```
m_AMControl.Run();
m_AMControl.Stop();
m_AMControl.Pause();
```

PART III

9.8 ActiveX: Handling Events

The ActiveX control provides an abstracted list of events to handle. These events do not map directly to the events generated by the filter or the filter graph manager, but they are important events at such a high-level interface. For example, you receive events when the state of the movie changes or when the position of the movie changes.

To handle such events, you can use the Microsoft Visual C++ class wizard to add a handler for each event. Notice that you have to select the Direct-Show ActiveX control ID that you specified in the resource editor in order to display its events. Figure 9-7 shows how to add a handler for the *StateChange* event.

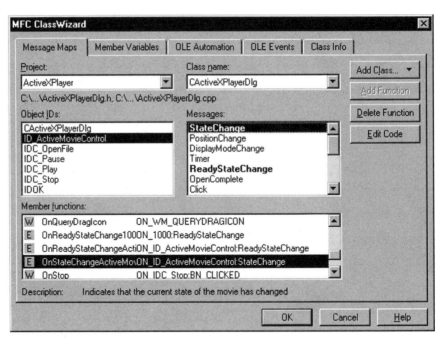

FIGURE 9-7 Handling DirectShow ActiveX control events using the Microsoft Visual C++ class wizard.

WHAT HAVE YOU LEARNED?

By the end of the chapter, you should have learned how to build DirectShow filter graphs from within your application in one of three ways: with the ActiveX controls, the automatic COM interface, or the manual COM interface.

You should also know how to access your filter's custom interface and its property pages. You should be able to handle filter events and control the running state of the DirectShow filter.

Lastly, you should be able to enumerate all the registered DirectShow filters, loaded filters, and pins in a filter.

CHAPTER 10

Mixing Sprites, Backgrounds, and Videos

WHY READ THIS CHAPTER?

It was certainly nice to play a video clip with DirectShow, but wouldn't it be even better if you could use video as part of your game or application? Surely, video is not the only thing moving on the screen; you probably have some moving sprites, backgrounds, and animation bouncing around the screen at the same time.

In this chapter we'll show you how to

- mix multiple objects together and how to place them relative to each other—in the front, middle, or the back of the viewing area, and
- use RDX to mix video, backgrounds, and sprites.

10.1 Introduction to Mixing

You've seen how mixing works throughout Part II when we showed you how to superimpose a static sprite on top of a static background using GDI, DirectDraw, and RDX. That was nice, but it can get boring fast.

Typically, multimedia applications have multiple sprites, backgrounds, animation, and video clips moving around on the screen all at the same time— sometimes with music playing in the background. For example, you could play a video clip with animation moving in the front and a moving background.

PART III

10.1.1   Mixing Sprites with Video

First let's review how we draw a static sprite on top of a static background. As you recall, some of the pixels in the sprite are transparent and should not be drawn on top of the background. For optimal performance, we typically mix the two objects in system memory and then write the mixed result to the screen.

As you can see in Figure 10-1, you can first copy the background to the mixing buffer, then overlay the sprite on top of it. Actually, you can overlay many sprites on top of the background at this stage. Finally, you can write the mixed result to video memory to make it visible on the screen. Notice that you only have to update the display whenever the sprite or the background moves around the screen.

With motion video, you display so many frames per second (fps) to give the illusion of motion. Now, if you treat every frame in the video as if it were a static background, you can apply the same technique we just discussed, mixing sprites with a background, for mixing sprites over video. In this case, however, you need to update the display screen whenever the sprite or the video moves on the screen *and* whenever a new video frame is displayed.

10.1.2   Mixing Animation with Video

Suppose you want to mix an animation sequence on top of video—an animation clip is a sequence of sprites with transparent pixels, which gives the effect of a moving picture. Similar to motion video, animation clips are displayed at a specific rate measured in frames per second. To mix an animation on top of a video, you can use the same concept as when you mix a sprite over video.

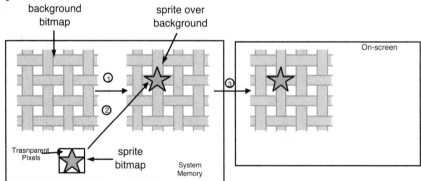

FIGURE 10-1 Mixing a static sprite with a static background.

At any given moment, you only need to deal with one sprite from the animation and one frame from the video. This is exactly the case when we displayed a sprite over a static background. In this case, however, you need to update the display whenever a new frame is displayed from either the animation or the video *and* whenever the animation or the video hops around the screen.

Of course, you can apply this same technique for mixing a video on top of another video. The same technique is used on TV shows and in the movies when there is a scene inside a car and the back window shows some video clip giving the illusion that the car is moving. To do that, you typically film the car in front of a blue background—blue is your transparency color. Then you mix this video clip, with the blue background, with another video clip exactly the same way you mixed animation over video.

10.2 Mixing with RDX

In Part II you've learned how to use RDX for mixing static sprites on top of static backgrounds. Here we'll show you how to use RDX to mix a static sprite over video. You can use the same technique to superimpose video over video or animation over video.

Before we go into that, let's first review some of the techniques RDX uses to perform object mixing. RDX uses a *draw order* to decide which object should be rendered first on the screen. For example, if you want to give the illusion that a background is "behind" a sprite, you would assign the background a higher draw order number than the sprite. RDX in turn paints the background first, then overlays the sprite on top of it (Figure 10-2).

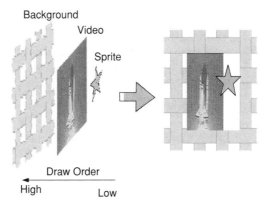

FIGURE 10-2 RDX draw order. Higher order objects are displayed behind lower order objects.

10.2.1 Playing Video with the RDX DirectShow Interface

First let's show you how to play a video clip using RDX. RDX supports multiple architectures for video playback, such as DirectShow and VFW. Since we've been discussing DirectShow, we will show you how to play a video clip using that interface. In this example, we'll use an MPEG file as the video clip.

To display an MPEG file, we first ask RDX to create a filter graph object and associate the MPEG file with it. RDX in turn creates a DirectShow filter graph for the input file and returns a handle to an RDX video object that represents that file.

```
fgCreate(&m_hAM);
fgAssociateFile(m_hAM, "blastoff.mpg");
fgGetVideoObject(m_hAM, 0, &m_hVid);
```

> Create a DirectShow filter graph "fg" object and set the MPEG file as the source. If successful, get a pointer to the RDX video object for later use.

Now you can instruct DirectShow to place the final output to the RDX surface, *hSurf* (refer to Chapter 6 to learn how to create an RDX surface). You can then set the draw order for the video such that it would be drawn behind the sprite. As an example, we use 100 for the sprite and 150 for the video clip. Finally, we declare that this object is visible.

```
objSetDestination (m_hAM, hSurf);
objSetDrawOrder (m_hAM, 150);
objSetVisibility(m_hAM, TRUE);
```

When DirectShow renders the MPEG file, it writes the final image not to the screen but to the RDX surface, which is typically in system memory or offscreen video memory. To display each frame to the screen, you must call the *srfDraw()* function, which copies the contents of the RDX surface to the appropriate location on the screen.

Alternatively, you can request that RDX automatically call the *srfDraw()* function to render each frame to the screen. To do that, you can use RDX's timers and events to schedule a draw event every frame. A *timer* is an object that counts user-defined time periods. An *event* is an object that defines an activity that you want to perform on an episodic or periodic basis.

To create a timer, you must call the *TimerCreate()* function with a handle to the video object and the timer sampling rate. You can then activate the timer with the *TimerStart()* function. Even though the timer is generating so many ticks per second, the timer tick does not generate any callback or event. So what use is this timer anyway ?

```
fgGetVidInfo(m_hAM, m_hVid, FG_INFO_SAMPLERATE, &dwFPS);
timerCreate((WORD)dwFPS, (HTIMER *)phTimer);
timerStart(*phTimer);
m_hTimer = *phTimer;
```

CAUTION: Make sure to stop *phTimer* before you destroy the RDX objects. Use *TimerStop()* or *TimerDestroy()*.

To make it worthwhile, you must associate the timer with a draw event—a draw event informs RDX to call the *srfDraw()* function. When the timer ticks, it sends RDX a draw event advising it that it is time to render the frame. To create a draw event, you must call the *eventCreate()* function with EVENT_DRAW as a parameter. You must then associate the event with the timer that will raise that event.

```
if (bAutoDraw) {
    eventCreate(m_hObj, EVENT_DRAW, 0, 0, &m_hDrawEvent);
    eventSchedule(m_hTimer, m_hDrawEvent, 1, RELATIVE_TIME, 1, 0xffff);
}
```

The third paramater, wPeriod, in *eventSchedule* allows you to specify the number of timer ticks per event period, for example, if the timer generates 30 ticks/sec and the event wPeriod is 3, then an event is generated every 3 timer ticks.

Note

Even though DirectShow decodes the video clip according to its frame rate, the number of frames rendered to the screen depends on the timer's sampling rate and the event's period.

Now that you have everything set up, you can call the *fgPlay()* function to put the DirectShow filter graph in run state.

```
objPrepare(m_hAM);
fgPlay(m_hAM, PLAYMODE_REPEAT, 0, 0);
```

At this stage, DirectShow decodes every frame into an RDX surface, the timer generates a draw event on every decoded frame, and RDX calls the *srfDraw()* function to copy the image from the RDX surface to the screen.

Why don't you fire up the sample application on the CD and select the option for this chapter from the menu. You should see a video clip playing on the screen.

10.2.2   Mixing a Sprite on Top of Video

Now that you have the video playing, let's see how we can overlay a sprite on top of it. As in Chapter 6, you must first load the sprite bitmap into memory and create an RDX sprite object. Once the sprite object is created, you can associate it with the RDX surface, *hSurf.*

```
bitmap bm;
bitmap.GetBitmap(&bm);
m_dwWidth = bm.bmWidth;
m_dwHeight = bm.bmHeight;
m_byTransp = byKeyColor;
```
┌──┐
│ Create and set up an hbmp (Source Data Object).   │
└──┘
```
HBMPHEADER bmpHeader;
hbmpCreate(m_dwWidth,m_dwHeight,RGB_CLUT8,&m_hBmp);
BYTE *pData;
hbmpGetLockedBuffer(m_hBmp, &pData, &bmpHeader);
bitmap.GetBitmapBits(m_dwWidth*m_dwHeight, pData);
hbmpReleaseBuffer(m_hBmp);
hbmpSetTransparencyColor(m_hBmp, (DWORD)byKeyColor);
```
┌──┐
│ Create sprite; associate data to it; associate sprite to surface. │
└──┘
```
sprCreate(&m_hSpr);
sprSetData(m_hSpr, m_hBmp);
objSetDestination(m_hSpr, m_hSurf);
```

Finally, you need to set the draw order and visibility of the sprite. Notice that we set the draw order to be lower than that of the video clip so that the sprite is drawn in front of the video clip.

```
objSetDrawOrder(m_hSpr, 100);
objSetVisibility(m_hSpr, TRUE);
```

MIXING WITH RDX ■ 137

10.2.3 Mixing Video on Video

As we've mentioned earlier, you should be able to mix an animation or a video on top of another video. Let's see how you can overlay a video clip with a transparency color on top of another video.

You can actually use the same code from section 10.2.1 to start the video clip in the foreground—with a couple of modifications. First, you must inform RDX about the transparent color of the video. To do that, you must call the *fgvidSetTransparencyColor()* function.

```
fgvidSetTransparencyColor(m_hAM2, (DWORD)byKeyColor);
```

As with the sprite, you should set the draw order of the video clip to be in front of the background video clip. Notice that in our example we positioned this video clip between the background video (150) clip and the sprite (100).

```
objSetDrawOrder (m_hAM2, 120);
```

At this stage, you'll have two video clips playing, one on top of another with a sprite in front of both of them. Notice that since the two video clips could have different frame rates, you need to use the higher frame rate when you create the timer for the draw event. This way, you're drawing at the rate of the faster video clip.

WHAT HAVE YOU LEARNED?

By now you should be familiar with mixing different objects on top of each other. In this chapter you learned

- about mixing sprites, video, and animation together,
- about draw order and how to position objects relative to each other,
- about RDX timers and events and how to create them,
- how to use RDX to mix a sprite on top of video, and
- how to mix video or animation on top of another video.

PART III

Streaming Down the Superhighway with RealMedia

WHY READ THIS CHAPTER?

The Internet! You must have heard of it by now. Yes, and while cruising the Net, you must have been struck by all of these RealAudio icons *"To Listen, Click Here*  *."* RealAudio has become THE audio streaming solution on the Internet.

With its success, RealNetworks released a similar technology for video on the Internet—RealVideo. In 1997 the company is building on its success with streaming on the Internet and is releasing a new streaming architecture, which allows for installable media types to be streamed on the Internet. This technology is called RealMedia.

In this chapter, you will

- get an overview of RealMedia and learn about its plug-in model,
- be introduced to the concept of a RealMedia plug-in and how to build File-Format and Rendering plug-ins,
- learn about Audio Services and how to use them within a plug-in, and
- learn about metafiles and how to use them.

In the past few years, the number of people connected to the Internet has grown astronomically. Similar to television, radio, and newspaper, the Internet has become the information medium of choice for millions of people. The Internet, however, offers an additional quality that does not exist in any of the earlier mediums: interactivity. Televisions and radios allow you to select between a preset number of local or cable channels; the Internet, on the other hand, opens the gate to millions of information servers, games, and music archives throughout the world.

RealNetworks (RN) seized the opportunity and established itself as THE Internet audio streaming technology on the Internet. Its RealAudio technology is specifically designed for real-time audio streaming on the Internet. With real-time audio streaming, you don't have to download an audio file first and then play it back; rather, you play the data as you retrieve it from the Internet server. Building on their success with RealAudio, RN introduced a similar streaming technology for video called RealVideo, and then RealMedia.

RealMedia is a real-time streaming technology specifically designed for the Internet. RealMedia includes both the RealVideo and RealAudio technologies as part of its core. With the plug-in mechanism that it provides, you can stream and synchronize the playback of any data type, in real time, over the Internet. For example, you can stream a new file format like MPEG, text, animation, MIDI, financial data, weather information, industrial information, or VRML.[1]

In our effort to present only technologies of the future, we wrote this chapter while the RealMedia SDK was still in its late beta cycle. Therefore some of the APIs might have changed slightly by the time this book is published. Nonetheless, the material in this chapter should be relevant and reflect the RealMedia architecture accurately. Use this chapter for the concept, but use the RealMedia SDK for the actual API definitions.

11.1 Overview of RealMedia

RealMedia is an open, cross-platform technology for streaming multimedia presentations over the Internet—or networks in general. (See Figure 11-1.) It uses the Real Time Streaming Protocol (RTSP) for communicating over the Internet[2] and the Real Time Session Language (RTSL) to define presentations. What does all of this mean?

---

1. VRML: Virtual Reality Modeling Language.
2. RTSP supports multicasting, unicasting, and RTP protocols.

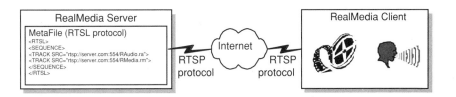

FIGURE 11-1 The roles of the RTSP protocol and RTSL session language.

RealMedia uses the RTSP protocol to transport data across networks—both the Internet and Intranets.[1] RTSP defines an application interface for controlling the delivery of real-time data. It allows for delivery of multiple streams simultaneously, such as video and audio and time-stamped data packets. For a reliable delivery, the RealMedia client uses the RTSP protocol to acknowledge the server when a packet is received; otherwise, the client resends another request for the packet or decides to throw it away. This decision depends on the quality setting of the application.

RTSL is a presentation language that is similar in form to the HyperText Markup Language (HTML). HTML is used to create Web documents on the Internet. RTSL allows you to define a presentation sequence that consists of multiple audio, video, and other data streams. With RTSL, the RealMedia server and client can negotiate the type of content delivered based on the information in the RTSL file (a.k.a. a metafile) and the settings of the player. For example, in the metafile, you can specify different media files (audio, video) depending on the bandwidth of the Internet pipe (28.8K, ISDN, and so forth) and on the language (English, French, and so forth). For a 28.8K pipe you can deliver a file with low quality and a low rate of data; for ISDN, you can deliver a better quality file with a higher rate of data. (See the RTSL definition in the RealMedia SDK for more details.)

We won't go into all the details of RTSP and RTSL in this book. Since RealMedia handles all the communication between the client and the server internally, you never have to deal directly with the RTSP protocol. However, as a content developer (someone who designs metafiles), you will need to learn more about the RTSL protocol and how to use it. Refer to RealMedia SDK for more details.

11.2 The RealMedia Plug-in Architecture

RealMedia is a simple plug-in architecture for adding custom data types. Figure 11-2 shows three RealMedia plug-in interfaces: *File-System, File-Format,* and *Rendering* plug-ins.

FIGURE 11-2 RealMedia plug-in architecture.

The *File-System* plug-in is only responsible for reading "raw" data from a source. The source could be a prerecorded audio/video file, a satellite feed, or a database server. This plug-in is typically loaded by the RealMedia server. The File-System plug-in does not know, or care, how the data will be parsed; it only knows how to read, write, and seek through a file. Since the RealMedia binaries come with a slew of File-System plug-ins, you typically don't have to implement a File-System plug-in to stream custom data types.

Supported Datatypes	
Text	Text
AVI	Audio/video
MOV	QuickTime
WAV	Audio
SND	Audio
AIFF	Audio
AU	Audio

The *File-Format* plug-in is responsible for parsing the data, splitting it into multiple streams, and breaking it into smaller packets for delivery over the Internet. This plug-in is typically loaded by the RealMedia server. The File-Format plug-in does not know how to read the data from the source, and it does not know how to send the data over the Internet. Currently, Real-Media supports AVI, WAV, AU, SND, AIFF, RealAudio, RealVideo, RealMedia, and RealText file formats.

The *Rendering* plug-in understands the contents of the data and knows how to render it to its final destination—screen, audio device, and so forth. This plug-in is typically loaded by the RealMedia player or client.

> **Note**
>
> In Figure 11-2, we show that the File-System and File-Format plug-ins are loaded by the RealMedia server. If you're playing a RealMedia file on a local machine, the RealMedia player loads the File-System, File-Format, and the Rendering plug-ins on the same PC.

Notice that none of the plug-ins we've discussed so far deal with data delivery over the Internet. They only worry about reading the data, breaking it into smaller packets, and rendering the final result. The RealMedia server and client handle all the necessary communication over the Internet. Real-Media allows for streaming any data type and synchronizing the playback of multiple data types.

So what do you really need to do to stream your own custom data type? Typically, you only need to implement a File-Format plug-in and a Rendering plug-in, since they both have to understand the new data type. The File-System plug-in, on the other hand, is only required if you have to read data from a source not supported by the RealMedia binaries, for example, from a database server.

In this chapter, you'll learn how to build a File-Format and a Rendering plug-in. You'll also learn about RealMedia metafiles and how to use them to configure the Web server.

Let's go over some of the basic RealMedia concepts and interfaces. First we'll describe the data flow model between the server and client. Then we'll glance over some of the basic RealMedia interfaces that are used in the sample code in this chapter.

11.3 Data Flows: Server to Client

For the purposes of this discussion, we're assuming that you know how to use a Web browser such as Internet Explorer or Netscape Navigator. When you select a hot link in the browser, it takes you to a new Web page or downloads a file to your local drive. If the hot link points to an audio or a video file, the browser first downloads the file to your local machine and then launches the media player to play it. Web browsers allow you to associate any file extension with an application that will be launched when such a file is downloaded. For example, *.doc is associated with launching *WinWord*.

To perform realtime streaming, RealMedia adds another step to this process. Instead of pointing the hot link to the RealMedia file on the server, you point it to a *metafile*. Metafiles hold configuration information that allows the client (RealPlayer) to communicate directly with the server. They also hold the list of media files to play when the metafile hot link is selected. We'll discuss metafiles in more detail later in this chapter.

So what really happens when you select a metafile hot link? Since the metafile file extension *.rts* is associated with the RealMedia player, the player is launched when the metafile hot link is activated. The player parses the metafile to find the streams that it should request from the RealMedia server. Notice that once the metafile is downloaded, the player makes the connection directly to the RealMedia server and bypasses both the Web browser and the Web server.

On the server side, the server loads the appropriate plug-ins and starts delivering data packets to the player (Figure 11-2). The RealMedia server loads a File-System plug-in to read the raw data from a file. It then loads the appropriate File-Format plug-in based on the file extension of the media file. The File-Format plug-in parses the media file and determines the MIME type of each stream in the file.[3] The server sends the MIME type of each stream to the client, over the Internet, and the RealMedia client, in turn, loads the appropriate Rendering plug-in for that MIME type.

Once the plug-ins are loaded, the RealMedia server requests a data packet from the File-Format plug-in. The File-System plug-in reads the raw data from the file, the File-Format plug-in parses it and breaks it into smaller packets. The RealMedia server sends the packet over the Internet to the client where it is rendered by the Rendering plug-in.

In a nutshell, File-Format plug-ins make the packets, Rendering plug-ins receive the packets and play them, and the RealMedia engine handles all the underlying communication and timing of shuttling the packets from the server to the player.

11.4 Data Management Objects

RealMedia defines a set of data objects to transport the data from the server to the client. These objects include dynamic memory allocation, indexed lists, and data packet objects.

Although all the RealMedia objects are COM interfaces, they are not specific to the Windows environment. Even though COM was defined for Windows, the COM architecture does not require Windows.

11.4.1 IRMABuffer: Dynamic Memory Allocation Object

The IRMA[4] Buffer object allows you to allocate a memory buffer at runtime. Typically, the buffer is used to transport data over the Internet. To allocate a memory buffer in RealMedia, you need to create an instance of the IRMA-Buffer object, set the size of the buffer, and then request a pointer to it. And you thought *malloc()* was hard to use!

---

3. A MIME type specifies the type of data in the message. MIME, or Multipurpose Internet Mail Extension, allows for transporting mail messages with binary data and many parts such as attachments and such.
4. IRMA: Interface RealMedia Architecture.

To create an instance of the IRMABuffer object, you need to call the *IRMA-CommonClassFactory::CreateInstance()* function using `CLSID_IRMABUFFER` as a parameter. You'll soon learn how to request a pointer to an IRMACommonClassFactory object. To set the size of the buffer, you must call the *IRMABuffer::SetSize()* member function; the actual memory allocation happens here. If successful, you can then call the *IRMABuffer::GetBuffer()* function to obtain a pointer to the data buffer. When you're done with the buffer, you should release the object to avoid any memory leaks.

```
m_pClassFactory->CreateInstance(CLSID_IRMABuffer,(void**)&pTitle);
pTitle->SetSize(INFO_SIZE+1);
pTitleData= (char*)pTitle->GetBuffer();
strncpy(pTitleData,pBufferData,INFO_SIZE);
pTitle->Release();
```

IRMABuffer functions:
Get()
Set()
SetSize()
GetSize()
GetBuffer()

11.4.2   IRMAValues: Indexed List Object

The IRMAValues object allows you to build an indexed list at runtime and send it off to other plug-ins over the Internet. The index is an ASCII string that specifies some special property. The value is either an IRMABuffer object or an unsigned long. For instance, you could use the IRMAValues object to build the following indexed list.

Index	"Title"	"Author"	"Copyright"	"Count"
Value	"Carrots"	"Bugs Bunny"	"BigEars Inc"	3

As with the IRMABuffer object, you must first create an instance of the IRMAValues object with the *IRMACommonClassFactory::CreateInstance()* function. You can then call the member function *SetPropertyULONG32()* or *SetPropertyBuffer()* to add an unsigned long or an IRMABuffer object to the list, respectively. Notice that the string index, for example, "title," is specified in the first parameter.

```
m_pClassFactory->CreateInstance(CLSID_IRMAValues, (void**)&pHeader))
pHeader->SetPropertyBuffer ("Title", pTitle);
pHeader->SetPropertyULONG32("StreamCount", 1);

pHeader->GetPropertyBuffer("Title", pTitle);
pTitleData = pTitle->GetBuffer();
pTitle->Release();
pHeader->Release();
```

IRMAValues functions:
SetPropertyULONG32 ()
GetPropertyULONG32()
GetFirstPropertyULONG32()
GetNextPropertyULONG32()
SetPropertyBuffer()
GetPropertyBuffer()
GetFirstPropertyBuffer()
GetNextPropertyBuffer()

To retrieve an item from the list, you can call the *GetPropertyBuffer()* or the *GetPropertyULONG32()* function for an IRMABuffer object or an unsigned long, respectively. In addition, you can enumerate the entire indexed list with the *GetFirstXyz()* and *GetNextXyz()* member functions. Refer to the Include file in the RealMedia SDK for prototypes of these functions.

The following rules describe when to use the *AddRef()* and *Release()* functions with RealMedia objects:

■ If an object is passed to your code as a parameter of a function call, you must use *AddRef()* to reference the object. When your code is finished with the object, you must use *Release()* to release the object.

```
Void Function (IRMAObject  "pObject) (
    pObject->AddRef();
    ...Use Object Here...
    PObject->Release();
```

■ For objects returned by functions, use *AddRef()* to reference the object inside the function. You must use *Release()* to release the object when you're done with it. The following functions use the *AddRef()* function to increment the reference count of the objects before returning them:

RMACreateInstance

IRMAFileSystem::CreateFile

IRMACommonClassFactory::CreateInstance

IUnknown::QueryInterface

IRMAFileSystem::CreateDir

■ If your code creates an object using the C++ new operator, your code must use the *AddRef()* function to reference the object. When your code is finished with the object, it must use *Release()* to release the object.

11.4.3   IRMAPacket: Packet Transport Object

The IRMAPacket *object* is used to transport data packets from the File-Format plug-in on the server side to the Rendering Plug-in on the client side.

Again, you must first call the *IRMACommonClassFactory::CreateInstance()* function to create an instance of the IRMAPacket object. You can then call the *Set()* member function to specify the IRMABuffer object that holds the data of each packet. With the *Set()* function you can also set a time stamp for the packet and a priority flag indicating the importance of the packet—Can it be dropped or not?

```
m_pClassFactory->CreateInstance(CLSID_IRMAPacket,(void**)&pPacket))
pPacket->Set(pBuffer,m_ulCurrentTime,0,0,PN_RELIABLE_NORMAL);
pPacket->Release();
```

11.5 RealMedia Asynchronous Interfaces

File-Format plug-ins are responsible for parsing the data and splitting it into multiple streams. They're also responsible for breaking the data in each stream into smaller packets before sending it over the Internet.

In addition to the IRMAPlugin interface, File-Format plug-ins implement both the **IRMAFileFormatObject** and **IRMAFileResponse** interfaces. The IRMAFileFormatObject interface defines the functionality of the DLL as a File Format plug-in. The RealMedia server uses this interface to retrieve header information from the source file and the header for each stream. It also uses this interface to request data packets to send out over the Internet.

IRMAFileResponse is a callback interface used to notify the plug-in when an asynchronous operation is complete. As you recall, the File-Format plug-in uses the services of the File-System plug-in to read raw data from the input source. Since all the File-System plug-in's operations are asynchronous, the File-Format plug-in exposes the IRMAFileResponse interface in order to receive notification when these operations are complete.

RealMedia defines nonblocking interfaces for the File-Format and the File-System plug-ins. These asynchronous interfaces allow the server to process requests from the clients while the plug-ins are busy preparing data packets from the input source.

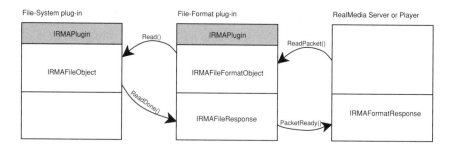

FIGURE 11-3 RealMedia asynchronous interfaces.

Suppose that the RealMedia server wants to get a data packet to transmit over the Internet. The server calls the File-Format plug-in function *IRMA-FileFormatObject::GetPacket()* to obtain a data packet. The *GetPacket()* function, in turn, calls the File-System function *IRMAFileObject::Read()* to read a block of raw data from the input source. Now, since both the IRMA-FileFormatObject and the IRMAFileObject interfaces are asynchronous, both the *Read()* and the *GetPacket()* functions return before the packet is created. At this stage, the server could process previous packets in the queue.

When the raw data is read from the input source, the File-System plug-in calls the File-Format plug-in function *IRMAFileResponse::ReadDone()* to notify it that the raw data read is done. The File-Format plug-in, in turn, calls the server back at the *IRMAFormatResponse::PacketReady()* function to notify it that the packet is ready to send.

11.6 Common Requirements for All Plug-ins

Although we're only dealing with Windows 95 in this book, it's worth mentioning that RealMedia is a cross-platform architecture. Nonetheless, writing a File-Format or a Rendering plug-in should require little or no operating system services. The File-System plug-in, on the other hand, is platform dependent since it requires direct access to the input devices—file, satellite, and so forth.

To create RealMedia plug-in, you must keep the following in mind:

- The plug-in you create must export the C-style function *RMACreate-Instance()*, which is used to create an instance of the plug-in. This function must be exported externally in the DEF file.
- The plug-in must implement the base IRMAPlugin interface. RealMedia applications use this interface to retrieve information about the plug-in.

■ Each plug-in must implement at least one additional plug-in object that defines the functionality of the plug-in. For example, Rendering plug-ins implement the IRMARenderer object, and File-Format plug-ins implement the IRMAFileFormatObject.

When a RealMedia application loads a plug-in, it calls the *RMACreate-Instance()* function, which creates an instance of that plug-in and then returns a pointer to it.

```
STDAPI RMACreateInstance(IUnknown** ppIUnknown)
{
    *ppIUnknown = (IUnknown*)(IRMAPlugin*)new CExampleFileFormat();
    if (*ppIUnknown) {
        (*ppIUnknown)->AddRef();
        return S_OK;
    }
    return E_OUTOFMEMORY;
}
```

> Make sure to Export this function in the DEF file.

Once the plug-in is created, RealMedia calls the *IRMAPlugin::InitPlugin()* function to initialize it. This function accepts only one parameter, PCONTEXT, which allows you to retrieve a pointer to the common class factory. Remember, this is the IRMACommonClassFactory object we used to create the buffers earlier in the chapter.

```
STDMETHODIMP CExampleFileFormat::InitPlugin(IUnknown* pContext)
{
    m_pContext = pContext;
    m_pContext->AddRef();
    m_pContext->QueryInterface(IID_IRMACommonClassFactory
            (void**)&m_pClassFactory);
    return S_OK;
}
```

> **IRMAPlugin** functions:
> *InitPlugin()*
> *GetPlugininfo()*

> IRMACommonClassFactory provides a *CreateInstance()* function, which serves the same purpose as the COM *CoCreateInstance()* function.

The *IRMAPlugin::GetPluginInfo()* function is then called to retrieve filter-specific configuration information. The BLOADMULTIPLE parameter specifies whether multiple instances of this plug-in could be created at the same time—this must always be *true* for a File-Format plug-in. The other three parameters are self-explanatory.

PART III

```
#define PCCHAR const char*
PCCHAR CExampleFileFormat::zm_pDescription    = "Example File Format Plugin";
PCCHAR CExampleFileFormat::zm_pCopyright      = "Your Company, All rights
reserved";
PCCHAR CExampleFileFormat::zm_pMoreInfoURL    = "http://www.yourcompany.com";

STDMETHODIMP CExampleFileFormat::GetPluginInfo (
    REF(BOOL)          bLoadMultiple,
    REF(const char*)   pDescription,
    REF(const char*)   pCopyright,
    REF(const char*)   pMoreInfoURL
    )
{
    bLoadMultiple = TRUE;
    pDescription  = zm_pDescription;
    pCopyright    = zm_pCopyright;
    pMoreInfoURL  = zm_pMoreInfoURL;
    return S_OK;
}
```

REF(): parameters are passed by reference.

All plug-ins go through the same initialization up to this point. Other initialization is done based on the type of plug-in you're writing. Let's start with the File-Format plug-in and then move on to the Rendering plug-in.

11.7 Building a File-Format Plug-in

11.7.1 Initializing the File-Format Plug-in

Once the IRMAPlugin interface is initialized, the File-Format plug-in function *GetFileFormatInfo()* is called. This function returns a list of the supported MIME types along with the default file extensions of the supported input files. *This is it!* This is where you declare that this plug-in can support the list of file extensions.

```
#define PCCHAR const char*
PCCHAR CExampleFileFormat::zm_pFileMimeTypes[]   = {"application/x-yourfileformat", NULL};
PCCHAR CExampleFileFormat::zm_pFileExtensions[]  = {"eff", NULL};
PCCHAR CExampleFileFormat::zm_pFileOpenNames[]   = {"Example File Format (*.eff)", NULL};
```

To support multiple streams and file formats, add the second, third, and so forth, stream information here. Make sure to terminate the list with NULL.

```
STDMETHODIMP CExampleFileFormat::GetFileFormatInfo (
    REF(const char**) pFileMimeTypes,
    REF(const char**) pFileExtensions,
    REF(const char**) pFileOpenNames
    )
{
    pFileMimeTypes   = zm_pFileMimeTypes;
    pFileExtensions  = zm_pFileExtensions;
    pFileOpenNames   = zm_pFileOpenNames;
    return S_OK;
}
```

> **IRMAFileFormat-Object functions:**
> *GetFileFormatInfo()*
> *InitFileFormat()*
> *GetFileHeader()*
> *GetStreamHeader()*
> *GetPacket()*
> *Seek()*
> *Close()*

When the server receives a URL to load, it calls the *InitFileFormat()* function with that URL and two other object pointers: IRMAFileObject and IRMAFormatResponse. As we mentioned earlier, IRMAFileObject is an asynchronous interface used for reading, writing, or seeking a file. *IRMAFormatResponse* is used to notify the RealMedia server when an operation is complete.

In order for IRMAFileObject to notify us when an operation is complete, it needs to obtain a pointer to the File-Format plug-in's IRMAFileResponse interface. To do so, we must pass the pointer to "this" plug-in to the IRMAFileObject interface. IRMAFileObject, in turn, calls our *QueryInterface()* function to retrieve a pointer to the IRMAFileResponse interface.

```
STDMETHODIMP CExampleFileFormat::InitFileFormat(
    const char* pURL,
    IRMAFormatResponse* pFormatResponse,
    IRMAFileObject*  pFileObject
    )
{
```

Copy the URL to a member variable. Make sure to allocate enough space.

```
    if (m_pURL) {
        delete m_pURL;
        m_pURL = NULL;
    }
    if (pURL) {
        m_pURL = new char[strlen(pURL)+1];
        if (!m_pURL) return E_OUTOFMEMORY;
            strcpy(m_pURL,pURL);
    }
```

Save the File Object to read/seek data from the input source; save the File Response to notify the server when the operation is complete. We *AddRef()* these objects to keep them around for later use.

```
    m_pFFResponse = pFormatResponse;
    m_pFileObject = pFileObject;

    if (m_pFFResponse)    m_pFFResponse->AddRef();
    if (m_pFileObject)    m_pFileObject->AddRef();
```

> Due to the asynchronous nature of the File Object, we use the variable m_state, to build a simple state machine to determine when an operations completes. Also, notice that we pass the file object a pointer to *this* plug-in so it could retrieve our callback interface, IRMAFileResponse.

```
    m_state = InitPending;
    m_pFileObject->Init(m_pURL, PN_FILE_READ | PN_FILE_BINARY, this);
    return S_OK;
}
```

Notice that you must expose the IRMAFileResponse interface by responding to the Global Unique Identifier (GUID), IID_IRMAFileResponse, in the *QueryInterface()* function.

```
STDMETHODIMP CExampleFileFormat::QueryInterface(REFIID riid, void** ppvObj)
{
    if (IsEqualIID(riid, IID_IRMAFileResponse)) {
        AddRef();
        *ppvObj = (IRMAFileResponse*)this;
        return S_OK;
    }

    *ppvObj = NULL;
    return E_NOINTERFACE;
}
```

Now, since the *IRMAFileObject::Init()* function is asynchronous, it returns before it initializes the object. Once the initialization is complete, IRMA-FileObject calls the callback function *IRMAFileResponse::InitDone()* with the status of the operation. In turn, the *InitDone()* function calls the server's notification function *IRMAFormatResponse::InitDone()* to inform it that the File-Format plug-in initialization is complete. Remember that both the IRMAFileObject and IRMAFileFormatObject interfaces are asynchronous in nature.

```
STDMETHODIMP CExampleFileFormat::InitDone(PN_STATUS status)
{
    if (m_state != InitPending)
        return E_UNEXPECTED;

    m_state = Ready;
    m_pFFResponse->InitDone(status);
    return S_OK;
}
```

Pay special attention to the *m_state* member variable; we've used it to build a simple state machine to handle the asynchroneity of the IRMAFileObject interface.

11.7.2 File and Stream Headers

Once the plug-in is initialized and the file is ready for reading, the Real-Media server calls the *GetFileHeader()* function to retrieve the media file header. In this example, we seek to zero since the file header is located at the beginning of the file.

```
STDMETHODIMP CExampleFileFormat::GetFileHeader()
{
    if (m_state != Ready)
        return E_UNEXPECTED;

    m_state = GetFileHeaderSeekPending;
    m_pFileObject->Seek(0,FALSE);
    return S_OK;
}
```

Since the *Seek()* function is an asynchronous function, you have to wait for the *SeekDone()* callback before you can start reading from the file. When the seek is done, you can call the *IRMAFileObject::Read()* function to read the header from the file.

```
STDMETHODIMP CExampleFileFormat::SeekDone(PN_STATUS status)
{
    if (m_state == GetFileHeaderSeekPending) {
        m_state = GetFileHeaderReadPending;
        m_pFileObject->Read(FILE_HEADER_SIZE);
    }
}
```

Again, since the *Read()* function is an asynchronous function, the function *ReadDone()* will be called when the data is read. The *ReadDone()* function receives a status flag indicating the outcome of the read. If successful, the raw data is returned in the IRMABuffer object. You can then extract the data from the buffer and call the *IRMAFormatResponse::FileHeaderReady()* function to notify the server that the file header is ready.

PART III

```
STDMETHODIMP
CExampleFileFormat::ReadDone(PN_STATUS status, IRMABuffer* pBuffer)
{
    if (m_state == GetFileHeaderReadPending) {
        m_state = Ready;

        IRMAValues* pHeader;
        IRMABuffer* pTitle = NULL, *pAuthor = NULL;
        char        *pTitleData, *pAuthorData, *pBufferData;
```

> Create an indexed list to hold the header, IRMAValues, and two buffers to hold the header data, pTitle & pAuthor. Set the buffer size appropriately and get a pointer to the buffer.

```
        m_pClassFactory->CreateInstance(CLSID_IRMAValues, (void**)&pHeader);
        m_pClassFactory->CreateInstance(CLSID_IRMABuffer,(void**)&pTitle);
        m_pClassFactory->CreateInstance(CLSID_IRMABuffer,(void**)&pAuthor);

        pTitle->SetSize(INFO_SIZE+1);
        pAuthor->SetSize(INFO_SIZE+1);

        pTitleData  = (char*)pTitle->GetBuffer();
        pAuthorData = (char*)pAuthor->GetBuffer();
        pBufferData = (char*)pBuffer->GetBuffer();

        strncpy(pTitleData,pBufferData,INFO_SIZE);
        pTitleData[INFO_SIZE] = '\0';

        strncpy(pAuthorData,pBufferData+INFO_SIZE,INFO_SIZE);
        pAuthorData[INFO_SIZE] = '\0';
```

> Set the indexed list properties and inform the server that the file header is ready. Make sure to release whatever you've created to avoid memory leakage.

```
        pHeader->SetPropertyBuffer ("Title",      pTitle);
        pHeader->SetPropertyBuffer ("Author",     pAuthor);
        pHeader->SetPropertyULONG32("StreamCount",  1);
```
Speicify the number of streams in the file here.
```
        m_pFFResponse->FileHeaderReady(status, pHeader);

        pHeader->Release();
        pTitle->Release();
        pAuthor->Release();
    }
}
```

Notice that we specified the number of streams in the input file in the StreamCount index. For each stream, the server calls the *GetStream-Header()* function to retrieve the specific header for the stream. As when we were working with the file header, you would look for the stream header—asynchronously—and read the data at that location.

```
STDMETHODIMP CExampleFileFormat::GetStreamHeader(UINT16 unStreamNumber)
{
    // Seek to the stream header
    if (m_state == Ready) {
        m_state = GetStreamHeaderSeekPending;
        m_pFileObject->Seek(FILE_HEADER_OFFSET+FILE_HEADER_SIZE,FALSE);
    }
}

STDMETHODIMP CExampleFileFormat::SeekDone(PN_STATUS status)
{
    // read the stream header
    if (m_state == GetStreamHeaderSeekPending){
        m_state = GetStreamHeaderReadPending;
        m_pFileObject->Read(STREAM_HEADER_SIZE);
    }
}
```

When the read is done, the *ReadDone()* function is called with the data in the IRMABuffer object. As with the file header, you can retrieve the data from the buffer and pass it on as an indexed list.

```
STDMETHODIMP
CExampleFileFormat::ReadDone(PN_STATUS status, IRMABuffer* pBuffer)
{
    if (m_state == GetStreamHeaderReadPending) {
        m_state = Ready;

        IRMAValues* pHeader;
        m_pClassFactory->CreateInstance(CLSID_IRMAValues,(void**)&pHeader);
```

This is where you specify the output type of the stream; this MIME type also specifies what kind of rendering plug-in must be loaded to render this stream.

```
        IRMABuffer*    pMimeType = NULL;
        char    szMimeType[] = "application/x-yourRenderFormat";
        m_pClassFactory->CreateInstance(CLSID_IRMABuffer,(void**)&pMimeType;
        pMimeType->Set((const UCHAR*)szMimeType,strlen(szMimeType)+1);
```

This is the stream header information. It includes the data buffer, pBuffer, bit rate, packet size information, timing, and stream type.

```
        pHeader->SetPropertyBuffer ("OpaqueData",     pBuffer);
        pHeader->SetPropertyULONG32("StreamNumber",   0);
        pHeader->SetPropertyULONG32("MaxBitRate",     MAX_BITRATE);
        pHeader->SetPropertyULONG32("AvgBitRate",     AVG_BITRATE);
        pHeader->SetPropertyULONG32("MaxPacketSize",  MAX_PACKETSIZE);
        pHeader->SetPropertyULONG32("AvgPacketSize",  AVG_PACKETSIZE);
        pHeader->SetPropertyULONG32("StartTime",      0);
        pHeader->SetPropertyULONG32("Preroll",        0);
        pHeader->SetPropertyULONG32("Duration",       2000);
        pHeader->SetPropertyBuffer ("StreamName",     NULL);
        pHeader->SetPropertyBuffer ("MimeType",       pMimeType);
        pHeader->SetPropertyULONG32("PopupWindow",     1);
```

> Notify the server that the stream header is ready and release memory objects.

```
        m_pFFResponse->StreamHeaderReady(status, pHeader);
        pHeader->Release();
        pMimeType->Release();

    }
}
```

11.7.3   Let the Streaming Begin!

At this stage the File-Format plug-in is ready to generate data packets for delivery over the Internet. The server calls the *GetPacket()* function to read one data packet. The File-Format plug-in requests a read of the data, and when ready, inserts it into an IRMAPacket object along with the time stamp. It also informs the server that the packet is ready through the *IRMAFormat-Response::PacketReady()* function.

```
STDMETHODIMP CExampleFileFormat::GetPacket(UINT16 unStreamNumber)
{
    if (m_state == Ready) {
        m_state = GetPacketReadPending;
        m_pFileObject->Read(PACKET_SIZE);
    }
}
```

PN_RELIABLE_:	specifies the priority level of the packet.
REQUIRED	must be sent or the entire stream will be aborted; for example, renderer initialization information.
HIGH	must arrive or there will be serious problems in the presentation; for example, *Key Frames*.
NORMAL	normal priority; for example, *Audio packets*.
LOW	lower priority; for example, *Images*.
VERY_LOW	can be sent only if there is enough resources available (Server load, network bandwidth, etc).

```
STDMETHODIMP
CExampleFileFormat::ReadDone(PN_STATUS      status, IRMABuffer *pBuffer)
{
```

> If the read failed, notify the server that we reached end of stream.

```
    if (status != PN_STATUS_OK) {
        m_ulCurrentTime = 0;
        m_pFFResponse->StreamDone(0);
    }

    if (m_state == GetPacketReadPending) {
        m_state = Ready;
        IRMAPacket* pPacket;
```

> Create an IRMAPacket and attach the packet data to it along with the priority level and the time stamp. Then increment the time stamp. *(Continued next page)*

Create an IRMAPacket and attach the packet data to it along with the priority level and the time stamp. Then increment the time stamp.

```
        m_ulCurrentTime += TIME_PER_PACKET;
        m_pFFResponse->PacketReady(status, pPacket);
        pPacket->Release();
    }
}
```

The server calls the *GetPacket()* function repeatedly until the end of file or stream is reached.

11.8 Building a Rendering Plug-in

Rendering plug-ins are responsible for decoding the data, if compressed, and sending it to its final destination—screen, audio device, and so forth. Rendering plug-ins run on the client side and accept data from the Internet in small packets—IRMAPackets.

After the base plug-in interface IRMAPlugin is initialized, the client application calls the *GetRendererInfo()* function to retrieve a list of the supported MIME types. In order to render a stream, the MIME stream type must match one of the supported renderer MIME types (see the File-Format plug-in function *GetStreamHeader()* to learn how to set the MIME type of a stream).

In addition to the MIME types, the *GetRendererInfo()* function returns the rendering refresh rate. This specifies how often you want to render the final data to its destination—screen, audio device, and so forth.

```
PCCHAR CExampleRenderer::zm_pStreamMimeTypes[] = {"application/x-yourRenderFormat",
NULL};

STDMETHODIMP CExampleRenderer::GetRendererInfo(
    REF(const char**)  pStreamMimeTypes,
    REF(UINT32)        unInitialGranularity
    )
{
    pStreamMimeTypes = zm_pStreamMimeTypes;
    unInitialGranularity = 100;
    return S_OK;
}
```

Causes the *OnTimeSync()* function to be called every 100 milliseconds.

The *StartStream()* function is then called to initialize the stream. The function receives a pointer to the stream, IRMAStream, and a pointer to the player, IRMAPlayer. IRMAStream allows you to retrieve information about the stream such as the stream number, type, and input source file. It also allows you to set the quality of the playback, request additional buffered packets, and adjust the refresh granularity. IRMAPlayer gives access to player-related information. It also allows you to start, stop, and seek the stream.

```
STDMETHODIMP
CExampleRenderer::StartStream(
    IRMAStream* pStream,
    IRMAPlayer*    pPlayer
    )
{
    m_pStream  = pStream;
    m_pPlayer  = pPlayer;

    if (m_pStream ) m_pStream->AddRef();
    if (m_pPlayer ) m_pPlayer->AddRef();

    return S_OK;
}
```

> **IRMAStream functions:**
> *GetSource()*
> *GetStreamNumber()*
> *GetStreamType()*
> *ReportQualityOfService()*
> *ReportRebufferStatus()*
> *SetGranularity()*
>
> **IRMAPlayer functions:**
> *GetClientEngine()*
> *IsDone()*
> *GetCurrentPlayTime()*
> *OpenURL()*
> *Begin(), Stop(), Pause()*
> *Seek()*

The *OnHeader()* function receives the indexed list prepared earlier by the *OnStreamHeader()* function of the File-Format plug-in. You can use the *GetPropertyBuffer()* and *GetPropertyULONG32()* functions to retrieve the information from the indexed list.

```
STDMETHODIMP CExampleRenderer::OnHeader(IRMAValues* pHeader)
{
    // Keep this for later use...
    m_pHeader = pHeader;
    m_pHeader->AddRef();

    // Get the packet data buffer.  Of course you can get more packet info.
    IRMABuffer *pBuffer;
    pHeader->GetPropertyBuffer ("OpaqueData", pBuffer);
    LPBYTE pBuf = pBuffer->GetBuffer();

    return S_OK;
}
```

Once the stream is initialized, the Rendering plug-in receives data packets through the *OnPacket()* function. You can choose to render the data in the packet or wait for the next refresh timer tick—in *OnTimeSynch()* discussed later. In our case, we just save a reference to the packet.

```
STDMETHODIMP CExampleRenderer::OnPacket(IRMAPacket* pPacket)
{
    // Release the last packet if we had one...
    if (m_pLastPacket)
      m_pLastPacket->Release();

    // Keep this one for later use...
    m_pLastPacket = pPacket;

    if (m_pLastPacket)
        m_pLastPacket->AddRef();

    return S_OK;
}
```

When the user starts playing for the first time or resumes playing after a pause, the *OnBegin()* function is called with the stream's time stamp for the next packet.

```
STDMETHODIMP CExampleRenderer::OnBegin(ULONG32 ulTime)
{
    return S_OK;
}
```

To maintain a smooth playback, the RealMedia engine pre-loads extra packets just in case the network gets congested. The RealMedia engine requests additional buffers when the stream starts playing, when the position of the stream is changed (when you seek forward/backwards), or when the number of reserved packets becomes very low. Of course, this action requires CPU cycles both on the server and the client. The client can relinquish CPU cycles by dropping frames or reducing the quality of the final output. This is exactly why the renderer function *OnBuffering()* is called—so that the renderer can adjust the amount of CPU cycles it uses accordingly.

```
STDMETHODIMP
CExampleRenderer::OnBuffering(ULONG32 ulFlags, UINT16 unPercentComplete)
{
    return S_OK;
}
```

When the user pauses playback, the *OnPause()* function is called. This function is typically used to display a static video frame when the movie is paused.

```
STDMETHODIMP CExampleRenderer::OnPause(ULONG32 ulTime)
{
    return S_OK;
}
```

When the user decides to seek forward or backward into the stream, the *OnPreSeek()*, *OnPostSeek()* functions are called. Both pass the time stamp of the packet before and after the seek.

```
STDMETHODIMP
CExampleRenderer::OnPreSeek(ULONG32 ulOldTime, ULONG32 ulNewTime)
{
    return S_OK;
}

STDMETHODIMP
CExampleRenderer::OnPostSeek(ULONG32 ulOldTime, ULONG32 ulNewTime)
{
    return S_OK;
}
```

The *OnTimeSync()* function is periodically called according to the granularity set in the *GetRendererInfo()* function. Notice that when the player is handling multiple streams, the refresh rate is the same for all streams, and it is equal to the lowest granularity rate of all the streams. The *OnTimeSync()* function is called to update the screen or send data to the audio device.

```
STDMETHODIMP CExampleRenderer::OnTimeSync(ULONG32 ulTime)
{
    // Here's a good time to actually render the data!
    m_ulLastTime = ulTime;

    // Redraw the window.  DamageRect() is similar to the Win32
InvalidateRect()
    CPNxRect    rect(0,0,400,100);
    m_pWindow->DamageRect(rect);

    return S_OK;
}
```

The *UseWindow()* function is called to inform the renderer that it should use a particular window to draw its data, for example, the browser's window. Since RealMedia supports multiple platforms, you should use the platform-independent window interface IRMASimpleWindow. This interface provides platform-independent functions to perform common operations on a window. To get access to the window handler routine, you need to subclass the window and hook into its windows procedure. To simplify cross-platform development, you can use the class PNxSubclassing-Window, which handles platform-independent window subclassing and painting to the window (you can find the definition of this class in RealMedia's sample directory).

In our case, we only set the size of the window and make it visible.

```
STDMETHODIMP CExampleRenderer::UseWindow(IRMASimpleWindow* pWindow)
{
    HRESULT hRes = PNxSubclassingWindow::UseWindow(pWindow);

    // Set the size and visibility of the window
    if (hRes == S_OK) {
        CPNxSize size(400,100);
        hRes = pWindow->SetSize(size);
        pWindow->SetVisibility(TRUE);
    }
    return hRes;
}
```

The window procedure handler of the PNxSubclassingWindow calls the member function *Draw()* to do the painting on the screen. You must override this function to render the output to the window. Since our packets are simple text, we use the *TextOut()* function to display the text in the window.

```
void CExampleRenderer::Draw()
{
    IRMABuffer*pBuffer = NULL;

    if (m_pLastPacket) {
        pBuffer = m_pLastPacket->GetBuffer();
        ::TextOut(m_hDC,0,0,pBuffer->GetBuffer(),pBuffer->GetSize());
    }
}
```

Finally, when the player closes the file, you must release the subclassing window, which in turn destroys the window.

```
STDMETHODIMP CExampleRenderer::ReleaseWindow(IRMASimpleWindow* pWindow)
{
    return PNxSubclassingWindow::ReleaseWindow(pWindow);
}
```

11.9 RealMedia Audio Services

As part of the goal of platform independence, RealMedia defines a hardware-independent interface that provides the necessary methods to deliver audio data to the audio device and to control that device's components—volume, sample bit rate, mono versus stereo, and so forth. This interface is called the *Audio Services* interface.

In addition to hardware independence, the Audio Services interface provides audio mixing capabilities so that multiple audio streams can be mixed together before they're sent out to the audio hardware. It also allows Rendering plug-ins to process the output data of each stream before mixing and to process the final audio data after mixing (see "Touching the Audio Data Before and After Mixing").

Notice that RealMedia comes with a few built-in renderers that can handle RealAudio, WAVE, AU, AIFF, and SND audio file formats. So, you wonder, "Why should I care about Audio Services?" Typically, if you're only dealing with RealAudio or any of the audio formats we have mentioned previously, you don't have to worry about Audio Services. But if you need to handle a new audio format, MPEG audio for example, you will need to use the Audio Services interface to write your data to the audio device.

"Well, why not use DirectSound or RSX?" For one, the Audio Services interface is easy to use. Although DirectSound and RSX provide mixing capabilities, RealMedia's Audio Services interface does its own mixing to maintain platform independence. As a result, if you use RSX or Direct-Sound, your audio stream will not be mixed with other RealMedia audio streams. Moreover, since the Audio Services interface is platform independent, you can easily provide versions of your custom plug-ins on multiple platforms.[5]

---

5. DirectSound and RSX are audio technologies from Microsoft and Intel. They are discussed in a later section.

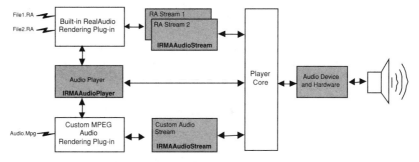

FIGURE 11-4 The RealMedia Audio Services interface in highlighted blocks.

In Figure 11-4, you can see two Rendering plug-ins: the built-in RealAudio Rendering plug-in, which handles RealAudio streams, and a custom MPEG audio Rendering plug-in, which could handle MPEG audio streams. Notice that the Audio Services are shown in the highlighted blocks. The Audio Services consist of one audio player, one audio device, and "multiple" audio streams—one for each active audio stream.

The audio player exposes the IRMAAudioPlayer interface, which allows you to create an audio stream, IRMAAudioStream. The audio stream interface allows you to write the data to the audio device. When you're playing multiple audio streams, the Audio Services mixes them together, including sample rate conversion, and sends the mixed result to the audio device. Finally, the audio device object writes the data to the audio hardware. This is where the platform independence happens.

11.9.1 Playing a Simple Pulse Coded Modulation (PCM) Audio File

Now, let's see how you can use the Audio Services to play an audio file from your custom Rendering plug-in. In this example, we'll only show you how to play a PCM file locally. PCM is the audio format that is typically sent to the audio device. We'll play the audio file whenever the mouse is clicked within the client window. This is a good time to run the demo corresponding to this chapter on the CD.

For the sake of simplicity (or our laziness) let's build on the Rendering plug-in that we've discussed earlier in this chapter. In addition to the text stream, we'll play an audio file, *frog.pcm*, whenever the user clicks the mouse in the client window. You'll know what we're talking about if you've run the demo.

We start by reading the entire PCM file into memory; it is small enough in this case. Since we'll always use the same PCM file, we might as well read it up front in *InitPlugin()*. We allocate an IRMABuffer big enough to hold the entire file and then read the file into it. You learned how to allocate buffers earlier in the chapter.

```
STDMETHODIMP CExampleRenderer::InitPlugin(IUnknown* pContext)
{
    m_pContext = pContext;
    m_pContext->AddRef();
    pContext->QueryInterface(IID_IRMACommonClassFactory, &pClassFactory);

    ULONG32 actual = 0;
    IRMACommonClassFactory* pClassFactory = NULL;

    // allocate an IRMABuffer big enough to hold the entire PCM file
    pClassFactory->CreateInstance(CLSID_IRMABuffer,(void**)&m_pBuffer);
    m_pBuffer->SetSize(LENGTH);

    // Read the file into the buffer and re-adjust its size to the length
    // of the file
    m_pFile = ::fopen(PcmFileName, "rb");
    actual = ::fread(m_pBuffer->GetBuffer(), 1, LENGTH, m_pFile);
    m_pBuffer->SetSize(actual);

    pClassFactory->Release();
    ::fclose(m_pFile);
}
```

You should then create the audio stream when you receive the header information of the stream. If the stream were coming over the Internet, the header would tell you about the stream's properties. Before you can create an audio stream, you must first retrieve a pointer to the audio player interface IRMA-AudioPlayer. To do that, you must call the *IRMAPlayer::QueryInterface()* function to get that pointer. Now, you can call the *IRMAAudioPlayer:: CreateAudioStream()* function to create the audio stream. If it is successful, you must call the *IRMAAudioStream::Init()* function to initialize the audio stream, specifying mono/stereo, the sampling rate, and the maximum sample size.

```
STDMETHODIMP CExampleRenderer::OnHeader(IRMAValues* pHeader)
{
    // Keep this for later use...
    m_pHeader = pHeader;
    m_pHeader->AddRef();
```

```
// NOTE: we got a pointer to m_pPlayer in the StartStream() function
// Get a reference to the IRMAAudioPlayer interface
m_pPlayer->QueryInterface(IID_IRMAAudioPlayer, &m_pAudioPlayer ))

// Now create an audio stream and initialize it…
RMAAudioFormat AudioFmt;

m_pAudioPlayer->CreateAudioStream(&m_pAudioStream);
AudioFmt.uChannels = 1;
AudioFmt.uBitsPerSample = 16;
AudioFmt.ulSamplesPerSec = 22050;
AudioFmt.uMaxBlockSize  = (UINT16)LENGTH;
m_pAudioStream->Init( &AudioFmt, pHeader);
}
```

The *OnMouseClick()* function will be called whenever the mouse is clicked within the client window. It's time to play the file. Since the audio data is in PCM format, we can just write it to the audio device. To do that, we must call the *IRMAAudioStream::Write()* function to send the data to the audio device. Remember: we're actually handing the data over to RealMedia Audio Services, not to the audio hardware. Behind your back, the Audio Services mixes the data with other streams before it sends it out to the audio device object, which sends it out to the audio hardware.

Notice that we set the `ulAudioTime` to a value returned by *GetInstant-Time()*. This allows us to play the file instantaneously, so we don't have to wait for it. If you'd rather have the sample be delayed before it is played, just set the time to a relative number in milliseconds. Refer to the RealMedia SDK for more details about instant time and midstream playback.

```
STDMETHODIMP CExampleRenderer::OnMouseClick()
{
    RMAAudioData AudioData;

    // Fill the AudioData structure with a pointer to the data and
    // when it should be played…  In our case, instantaneously.
    AudioData.pData = m_pBuffer;
    AudioData.ulAudioTime = m_pAudioPlayer->GetInstantTime();
    m_pAudioStream->Write(&AudioData);
}
```

11.9.2 Pump Up the Volume

With RealMedia you can also adjust the audio volume at three data points: the output of individual streams, the output of the mixed streams, and the audio device hardware. As you can see in Figure 11-5, each individual

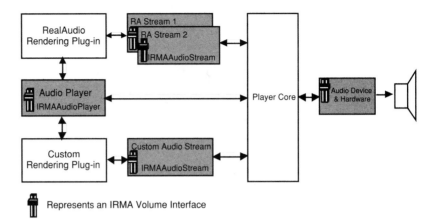

FIGURE 11-5 Volume control for indiviual streams, mixed streams, and audio hardware.

stream has its own volume control. The audio player controls the audio level of the mixed stream, and the audio device object controls the volume of the audio device.

To adjust the volume of an individual stream, you must first call the *IRMAAudioStream::GetStreamVolume()* function, which returns a pointer to a volume interface, IRMAVolume. You can call the *IRMAVolume:: SetVolume()* and *GetVolume()* functions to set/get the volume of individual audio streams. A volume setting of 100 means 100 percent of the input signal; values less than 100 reduce the volume, and values greater than 100 increase the volume.

IRMAVolume functions:
Init()
SetVolume(),
GetVolume()
GetLevel()
SetMute()
GetMute()
AddAdviseSink()
RemoveAdviseSink()

```
STDMETHODIMP CExampleRenderer::OnStreamVolume()
{
    IRMAVolume *pVolume = m_pAudioStream ->GetStreamVolume();
    pVolume->SetVolume(90);      // Decrease the volume
    pVoluem->GetVolume(110);     // Increase the volume
    pVolume->Release();
}
```

Similarly, you can adjust the audio level after the streams have been mixed. You must first call the *IRMAAudioPlayer::GetAudioVolume()* function to retrieve a pointer to the IRMAVolume interface. Again, you can call the *IRMAVolume::SetVolume()* and *GetVolume()* functions to set/get the volume of individual audio streams. A volume setting of 100 means 100 percent of the input signal; values less than 100 reduce the volume, and values greater than 100 increase the volume.

```
STDMETHODIMP CExampleRenderer::OnMixedOutputVolume()
{
    IRMAVolume *pVolume = m_pAudioPlayer->GetAudioVolume();
    pVolume->SetVolume(90);     // Decrease the volume
    pVoluem->GetVolume(110);    // Increase the volume
    pVolume->Release();
}
```

The audio device volume is also controlled by an IRMAVolume object, yet here the volume values have a slightly different meaning. In this case, a volume setting of 0 means no sound, and a volume setting of 100 is the maximum volume for the audio hardware.

```
STDMETHODIMP CExampleRenderer::OnAudioDeviceVolume()
{
    IRMAVolume *pVolume = m_pAudioPlayer->GetDeviceVolume();
    pVolume->SetVolume(90);     // Decrease the volume
    pVoluem->GetVolume(110);    // Increase the volume
    pVolume->Release();
}
```

PART III

TOUCHING THE AUDIO DATA BEFORE AND AFTER MIXING

RealMedia Audio Services allows you to access the data of individual streams before mixing and after mixing. You can use this mechanism to view or modify the data before sending it off to the audio hardware. For example, you can use the data to show an audio waveform of the data of each individual stream or the data of the mixed stream. You can even choose to modify the data before sending it to the audio hardware. For example, you can use Intel's RSX to add 3D effects to the audio data (see section 13.5 "Mixing Many WAV Files" for more details on 3D audio).

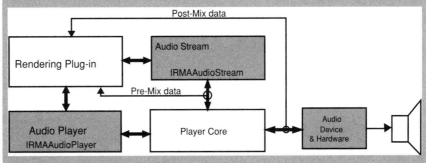

FIGURE 11-6 Using the Rendering plug-in to view or modify audio data before and after mixing.

As you can see in Figure 11-6, a plug-in can interact with the Audio Services to retrieve the audio data of each stream before mixing and after mixing. A plug-in can optionally modify the data before sending it back to Audio Services. For more detail and samples on this topic, refer to the RealMedia SDK.

WHAT HAVE YOU LEARNED?

In this chapter you've learned about the RealMedia technology for real-time streaming of data over the Internet. The data is not limited to audio and video. RealMedia is easily adaptable to stream any custom data type.

At this stage, you should

- be familiar with the concept of RealMedia plug-ins and the different types of plug-ins (File-System, File-Format, and Rendering),
- be familiar with the plug-in interfaces,
- be able to build File-Format and Rendering plug-ins,
- understand the Audio Services interface and how to use it to play additional local audio streams, and
- know how to use Audio Services to adjust the volume of individual streams, mixed streams, and the audio device.

PART IV

Playing and Mixing Sound with DirectSound and RSX 3D

WE'D LIKE TO EXTEND AN ACKNOWLEDGEMENT TO JANICE CLEARY, KEVIN O'CONNELL, MICHELLE MCNEIL, RACHEL TILLMAN, CAROL BARRETT, CHRIS ROTVIK, AND TIM ROPER.

Chapter 12 **Audio Mixing with DirectSound**
- Overview of Microsoft's DirectSound
- Play and mix WAV files with DirectSound
- Control final output format and final volume

Chapter 13 **Realistic 3D Sound Experience: RSX 3D**
- Overview of Intel's RSX 3D
- Play and mix audio files with RSX 3D
- Use RSX 3D for real-time 3D sound experience
- Apply reverberation and Doppler effects

Part IV contains quick chapters on two audio architectures for Windows 9x: Microsoft's DirectSound and Intel's 3D Realistic Sound Experience (3D RSX).

Microsoft's DirectSound was designed to address two key performance problems that arose with high-performance multimedia applications running under Windows 95: First, the per-channel overhead for mixing audio channels can be high. Second, there is a noticeable lag between when you request a sound to be played and when it is actually delivered through the speakers. In Chapter 12, we introduce you to Microsoft's Direct-Sound architecture and show you how to program with it. We show you how to mix and play WAV files and how to control output volume and formats.

Intel's 3D RSX is an architecture that lets listeners perceive sound in all directions, not only to the front and sides, but also above, below, and to the rear. 3D RSX uses just two speakers (or a set of headphones) to produce a surround sound experience. The system creates sounds based on simulations of how the human brain hears sounds and is based on a Head Related Transfer Function (HRTF) technology. In Chapter 13, we will give you an overview of 3D RSX, show you how to play audio files with it, and how to add special effects to your sounds, such as reverberation or Doppler effects.

CHAPTER 12

Audio Mixing
with DirectSound

**WHY READ
THIS CHAPTER?**

Microsoft's DirectSound was designed to address two key performance problems with standard audio for high-performance multimedia applications running on Windows 95: First, the CPU usage for mixing audio channels is high. Second, there is a noticeable lag between when you request a sound to be played and when it is actually delivered through the speakers.

If you've been facing either of these performance problems with your multimedia application and would like to understand DirectSound's solutions, or if you expect the audio component of your application to be demanding and instinctively know that you will need a high-performance audio solution, read on.

By the time you have worked through this chapter, you will

- have a good idea of how DirectSound works and what it offers,
- understand how DirectSound reduces audio latency under Windows 95,
- have learned how to play a WAV file and mix WAV files using DirectSound, and
- have learned how to control output volume and formats through DirectSound.

12.1 Overview of Audio under Windows 95

The standard Microsoft multimedia library (previously called *mmsystem.lib* and now called *winmm.lib*) provides developers with a wide range of functions for interacting with audio devices and performing audio functions. These functions range from high-level interfaces for basic audio tasks to low-level interfaces that provide more control of task and audio devices.

The *PlaySound()* function, for example, is a simple high-level way to play audio files or to play audio sounds from the system registry. The MCIWnd class, on the other hand, supplied as part of Video for Windows (*VFW.h*), provides multimedia extensions for Windows. The audio services in MCIWnd provide input, output, and recording control of a variety of devices including CD audio, WAV audio, MIDI, and audio-video devices.

Table 12-1 lists the categories of audio services provided in the standard Windows multimedia library.

TABLE 12-1 Range of Audio Services Available in Standard Windows Multimedia Library

Prefix	Service
wave	Works with sounds in the PCM waveform audio format. In addition to playing audio sounds, *wave* functions provide for audio input, for audio record, and for waveform audio device control.
midi	Plays and records Musical Instrument Digital Interface (MIDI) sound representations. The MidiMapper (with channel maps, patch maps, and key maps) provides a device-independent interface for playing MIDI files.
mixer	Provides runtime mixing of multiple MIDI or multiple WAV audio streams within a single application.
mci	Media Control Interface controls a variety of multimedia devices including audio devices such as CD Audio, WAV audio, MIDI, and audio-video.
acm	The Audio Compression Manager is an extension of the basic multimedia system that enables runtime audio compression, decompression, and filter services.

12.2 DirectSound Features

There are two performance problems with the audio services in *winmm.lib:*

■ The performance overhead of mixing audio streams is high. On baseline 90 MHz Pentium platforms, mixing eight audio sounds consumes at least 40 percent of the CPU, leaving very little capacity for even more performance intensive tasks such as running graphics. The overhead increases when audio formats differ and format conversion is necessary.

■ The latency between when an application plays a sound and when the sound is delivered through the speakers can be between 100 to 150 milliseconds. Consider comparing an audio sound to a graphics event like crashing into a wall. With a latency of 100 milliseconds and a frame rate of 30 frames per second, at least 3 frames have gone by before the sound is heard. The graphics actually seen would probably have no bearing on the sound. For adequate synchronization, the audio sound must be heard before the next frame is drawn (less than 33 milliseconds at 30 fps).

In Microsoft's words: "The overriding design goal in DirectX is speed." The Microsoft DirectSound audio library provides high-performance, low-overhead, low-latency audio mixing. DirectSound accesses hardware acceleration whenever possible. In addition, the DirectSound architecture gives Windows applications direct access to the sound device.

In addition to solving performance problems, the DirectSound component of the DirectX SDK adds a notable feature: It can mix audio streams from multiple applications. You can design your DirectSound-based application to allow mixing sounds from other DirectSound applications. With this feature, for example, a DirectSound-based Internet-audio-phone can share audio output with your DirectSound application.

12.3 DirectSound Architecture

Figure 12-1 shows how DirectSound fits into the Windows 95 audio framework. As part of the DirectSound architecture, Microsoft defined extensions to the standard Windows 95 audio device driver. The extended interface is known as the DirectSound Hardware Abstraction Layer (HAL) interface. DirectSound provides its enhanced performance and features via

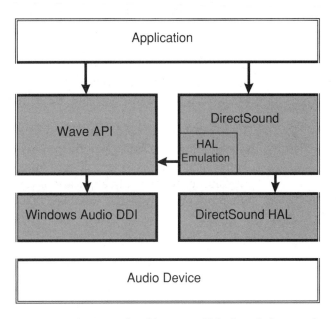

FIGURE 12-1 DirectSound architecture within the Windows 95 framework.

PART IV

the DirectSound HAL. The DirectSound path and the WAV audio path are two mutually exclusive paths to the audio hardware. They cannot be used simultaneously.

If a DirectSound driver is not available, DirectSound will use the standard Windows 95 audio device driver. In this case, DirectSound provides neither low-latency audio nor device access; but it can still provide low-overhead mixing.

To us application developers, DirectSound provides DIRECTSOUND objects as representatives of audio cards in the system. We access all further Direct-Sound functionality through these DIRECTSOUND objects. Our applications can only instantiate one DirectSound object per device. But multiple applications can each instantiate their own DirectSound objects, and the application in focus will have principal control of the audio output. (*Direct-SoundCreate()* and *DirectSoundEnumerate()* are the only two functions that can be called without having instantiated a DIRECTSOUND object.)

To create and play sounds, DirectSound provides two types of DIRECTSOUND-BUFFER objects: secondary and primary. Secondary DIRECTSOUNDBUFFER objects represent individual sounds or sound streams. DirectSound mixes individual secondary buffers into the primary DIRECTSOUNDBUFFER, and this mixed data is sent to the audio device.

Secondary buffers can be either hardware or software. Hardware buffers are created and used if the audio device supports hardware mixing. Hardware mixing reduces system overhead cost. In the absence of hardware mixing, system buffers and software mixing are used with some CPU overhead required for the mixing. Data in secondary buffers can be of varying audio formats. All data is converted to the format of the primary buffer during mixing.

The primary buffer holds data that is being played by the audio device and is invariably in the hardware. The most common model used for accessing the primary buffer is to set a desired output format or to control total output volume. Additionally, applications can write directly to the primary buffer, but by doing so they disable all DirectSound mixing.[1]

---

1. We suggest that you avoid writing directly to the primary buffers. The size of audio buffers is dictated by DirectSound device drivers. Buffers must be filled on time, as gaps in audio buffers are heard as annoying audio clicks. Timer and thread management becomes fairly complex with small buffers, and on the other hand, latency is high with large buffers.

Through an esoteric but not atypical way of using primary buffers you can reduce latency when you are playing individual short sounds. It works as follows. Null data in the primary buffer is played in LOOP_MODE, which forces data to be sent to the audio device constantly. When sound in a secondary buffer is played, data is merely mixed into the already playing buffer, and there is no initialization latency delay.

12.4 Playing a WAV File Using DirectSound

12.4.1 Initializing DirectSound

First, we need to initialize DirectSound. The starting point for using Direct-Sound is the *DirectSoundCreate()* function call. We get access to all Direct-Sound functions through the DIRECTSOUND object that *DirectSoundCreate()* instantiates.

Right after initializing the DIRECTSOUND object, we've got to establish how we plan on using DirectSound by using *IDirectSound::SetCooperativeLevel()*. DirectSound has four cooperative levels: DSSCL_NORMAL, DSSCL_PRIORITY, DSSCL_EXCLUSIVE, and DSSCL_WRITEPRIMARY.

The DSSCL_NORMAL cooperative level is sufficient for our current example of simply playing a WAV file with DirectSound. DSSCL_NORMAL sets up our use of DirectSound for smooth audio sharing with other applications; note that the final output format is automatically fixed to 8-bit, 22-kHz STEREO format, and no format conversions are required when the focus switches.

Here's the code to initialize access to the audio device through Direct-Sound:

```
BOOL CSharedHardware::Init(HWND hWnd) {
    LPDIRECTSOUND    pDSound;
    HRESULT          err;

    // create a DirectSound instance
    DirectSoundCreate(NULL, &pDSound, NULL);
```

> *DirectSoundCreate()* is the starting point in using DirectSound. The DIRECTSOUND structure returned from this function provides access to the next level of functionality, such as *CreateSoundBuffer*, *GetCaps*, and so forth.

PART IV

```
                              // Setup to use as normal windowed app
                              err = pDSound->SetCooperativeLevel(hWnd, DSSCL_NORMAL);
                              if (err != DD_OK) {
                                  pDSound->Release();
                                  return FALSE;
                              }

                              // store away
                              m_pDSound = pDSound;
                              // return success code
                              return TRUE;
                              }
```

SetCooperativeLevel() sets how we plan to use DirectSound. DirectSound permits four different levels of usage:

DSSCL_NORMAL	Most cooperative, smoothest resource sharing with other applications. However, output format is fixed to 8-bit, 22-KHz, mono.
DSSCL_PRIORITY	At this priority level, the application can change the output format.
DDSCL_EXCLUSIVE	At this level, sounds from other apps are not heard when this app has the input focus. Output format can be set.
DDSCL_WRITEPRIMARY	Application gets direct access to the primary output buffers. However, secondary buffers cannot be played and application must do its own mixing.

12.4.2 DirectSound Structures

To play sounds using DirectSound, we need to set up the sound in a Direct-Sound format. DirectSound's DSBUFFERDESC structure defines the format for sound buffers. The actual format of the sound data is defined using the standard WAVEFORMATEX structure from *mmreg.h*. Let's take a look at these structures.

```
typedef struct _dsbufferdesc{
    DWORD           dwSize;
    DWORD           dwFlags;
    DWORD           dwBufferBytes;
    DWORD           dwReserved;
    LPWAVEFORMATEX  lpwfxFormat;
} DSBUFFERDESC, *LPDSBUFFERDESC;

typedef struct {
    WORD   wFormatTag;
    WORD   nChannels;
    DWORD  nSamplesPerSec;
    DWORD  nAvgBytesPerSec;
    WORD   nBlockAlign;
    WORD   wBitsPerSample;
    WORD   cbSize;
} WAVEFORMATEX;
```

- dwBufferBytes should indicate the size of the sound buffer. The application sets this field for secondary buffers, and DirectSound sets this field for primary buffers.
- Actual sound format is defined using the standard WAVEFORMATEX structure defined in mmreg.h. We've included the definition here for quick reference.

The dwFlags field is used both to establish type of sound buffer being created as well as to describe attributes upon return. Refer to the DirectSound documentation for more details. Some interesting flags are

_DSBCAPS_PRIMARYBUFFER	Request a primary buffer. If this flag is not set, a Secondary buffer will be created.
_DSBCAPS_STATIC	Sound will be used repeatedly. Designate as good candidate for hardware acceleration.
_DSBCAPS_LOCHARDWARE	Forces the buffer to be in hardware memory.
_DSBCAPS_LOCSOFTWARE	Forces the buffer to be in system memory.

Some additional flags to control special effects that we leave for extra credit exploration are _DSBCAPS_CTRLALL, _DSBCAPS_CTRLDEFAULT, _DSBCAPS_CTRLFREQUENCY, _DSBCAPS_CTRLPAN and _DSBCAPS_CTRLVOLUME. We will use _DSBCAPS_CTRLVOLUME later in this chapter.

12.4.3 Creating Sound Buffers

We've successfully initialized DirectSound. Let's create a simple secondary DIRECTSOUNDBUFFER.

```
BOOL CSound::Init(LPDIRECTSOUND pDSound, LPSTR lpszFileName)
{
```

> We wrote a simple WavFile Load routine based on standard *mmio* calls in the *winmm* multimedia library. Upon return, this function will load WAVEFORMATEX, bufferSize, and bufferData into member variables.

```
    HRESULT err
    // first try load wave file into memory
    if (!LoadWavFile(lpszFileName)) return FALSE;

    // Create a device sound buffer
    m_dsDesc.dwFlags = DSBCAPS_STICKYFOCUS;
    m_dsDesc.dwBufferBytes = m_dwSizeData;
    m_dsDesc.lpwfxFormat = m_pWavFmt;
    pDSound->CreateSoundBuffer(&m_dsDesc, &m_pBufferFns, NULL);  ◄
```

- *CreateSoundBuffer()* takes LPDSBUFFERDESC and (LPDIRECTSOUNDBUFFER *) as parameters. We describe the surface that we're requesting in LPDSBUFFERDESC. If the Create is successful LPDIRECTSOUNDBUFFER points to the member functions of the created Sound Buffer.
- The only flag we specified was DSBCAPS_STICKYFOCUS, which will let our sounds be played even if we're not the application with the input focus. However, if we lose focus to another DirectSound application, we will lose our audio output.
- DSBCAPS_GLOBALFOCUS in DirectX allows our sounds to continue playing even if we lose focus to another DirectSound application. However, cooperative levels of DDSCL_EXCLUSIVE will override even the DSBCAPS_GLOBALFOCUS setting.
- WaveFormat and BufferLength are set to the values returned by the *LoadWavFile()* routine.

```
        ///////// transfer data from memory to dsBuffer.
        // first lock the entire buffer.
        LPVOID pBlk1, pBlk2;                 // dsound maintains split-buffers
        DWORD dwSize1, dwSize2;              // size of each buffer
        m_pBufferFns->Lock(0,m_dwSizeData,&pBlk1,&dwSize1,&pBlk2,&dwSize2,0);
        // write data into possibly 2 buffers that DirectSound returns
        CopyMemory(pBlk1, m_pSrcData, dwSize1);
        if (dwSize2 > 0)  ◄
            CopyMemory(pBlk2, m_pSrcData+dwSize1, dwSize2);
        // unlock both buffers and return
        m_pBufferFns->Unlock(pBlk1, dwSize1, pBlk2, dwSize2);
        return TRUE;
}
```

> DirectSound sees sound buffers with a circular reference pattern. Circular views enables "infinite" streaming buffers: as the front of the buffer is being consumed, the rear of the buffer can be refilled. Circular views also make it easy to implement looped sounds for "static" fixed size buffers. *Locks(), Unlocks(),* and data access with circular views use two buffer access descriptors, where a buffer access descriptor is a (pointer, size) combination.

12.4.4 Playing the Sound

Now that we've created our sound buffer, playing the sound is as simple as invoking the *IDirectSoundBuffer::Play()* member function.

```
BOOL CSound::Play()
{
    m_pBufferFns->Play(0, 0, DSBPLAY_LOOPING);
    return TRUE;
}
```

DirectSound requires the first two parameters to *IDirectSoundBuffer::Play()* to be 0. The third parameter allows for flags to control the Play mode. Currently the only flag defined is DSBPLAY_LOOPING; therefore, DirectSound permits sounds to be either PlayedOnce or Played-Forever. Playing a secondary buffer will mix the data from the sound buffer into the primary buffer. *IDirectSoundBuffer::Stop()* can be used to stop sound buffers that are playing.

12.4.5 Demo Time

Run the demo that corresponds to this chapter. Since we have set the sound to be played in LOOP_MODE, you should hear the sound play continuously. Try switching to another application such as the Calculator. You should still hear the sound even though our application has lost the input focus. This is the result of creating the buffer with the DSBCAPS_STICKYFOCUS flag. Try invoking a second instance of our sound application. You will hear only one sound being played.

EXTRA CREDIT

Recompile the application after having set the secondary buffers to be created with the DSBCAPS_GLOBALFOCUS flag. Invoke multiple instances of the application. You should hear multiple sound streams being mixed together.

12.4.6 Mixing Two WAV Files

Mixing two WAV files is as simple as creating another secondary buffer and playing it. DirectSound will automatically mix playing sounds together.

It seems ridiculous to show this code, but we'll do it anyway. Run the demo that corresponds to this chapter and create a second sound to invoke audio mixing.

```
BOOL OnNewSound(LPSTR lpszFileName)
{
    // create new sound
    CSound *pNewSound = new CSound;
    if (!pNewSound->Init(lpszFileName)) return FALSE;

    // start the sound playing
    pNewSound->Play(DSBPLAY_LOOPING);

    // and store handle in list
    gSounds[gnSounds] = pNewSound;
    gnSounds++;
}
```

12.5 Controlling the Primary Sound Buffer

So far we've played a WAV file with DirectSound using the system's default audio format. What if we want to change this output format to work with sound samples of higher (or even lower) quality? To change the output format, or to change the total output volume, we would need to control the primary sound buffer.

12.5.1 Initializing to Get Control of the Output Format

While initializing DirectSound, we need to set the CooperativeLevel to allow us to change output format privileges:

```
BOOL CSharedHardware::Init(HWND hWnd)
{
    LPDIRECTSOUND    pDSound;
    HRESULT          err;
    // create a DirectSound instance
    DirectSoundCreate(NULL, &pDSound, NULL);

    // Setup to use as priority app
    err = pDSound->SetCooperativeLevel(hWnd, DSSCL_PRIORITY);
    if (err != DD_OK) {
        pDSound->Release();
        return FALSE;
    }
    m_pDSound = pDSound;
    return TRUE;
}
```

SetCooperativeLevel() to DSSCL_PRIORITY. At this priority level, the application can change the output format.

12.5.2 Creating a Primary DirectSound Buffer

Now let's create a primary DirectSoundBuffer object so that we can get access to the *IDirectSoundBuffer::SetFormat()* function.

```
BOOL CSoundPrimary::Init(LPDIRECTSOUND pDSound)
{
    // Create a primary sound buffer
    m_dsDesc.dwFlags = DSBCAPS_PRIMAR\BUFFER | DSBCAPS_CTRLVOLUME;
    m_dsDesc.dwBufferBytes = 0;
    m_dsDesc.lpwfxFormat = NULL;
    pDSound->CreateSoundBuffer(&m_dsDesc, &m_pBufferFns, NULL);
```

- Set flags to DSBCAPS_PRIMARYBUFFER to request access to the primary buffer. Also set DSBCAPS_CTRLVOLUME flag to allow volume control to be queried and set.
- We cannot specify the size of the primary sound buffer and must set the size to 0.
- Similarly, we cannot specify output format during creation, but can change it using the *SetFormat()* function call; therefore set the waveformat pointer to NULL.

```
    // find out the format of the primary buffer
    DWORD dwSizeToAlloc;
    m_pBufferFns->GetFormat(NULL, 0, &dwSizeToAlloc);
    m_pFmt = (WAVEFORMATEX *)(new BYTE[dwSizeToAlloc]);
    m_pBufferFns->GetFormat(&m_pFmt, dwSizeToAlloc, NULL);
}
```

IDirectSoundBuffer::GetFormat() must be called twice. Once with a NULL pointer to find out the size of the buffer to allocate and then with a valid pointer to the buffer just allocated.

Now that we have created a primary DirectSoundBuffer object, we have control over the output format and the total output volume. (Note that the DSBCAPS_CTRLVOLUME must be set to allow the volume control to be modified.) Here is sample code that changes the volume and the output format of the primary buffer.

```
// change the format of the primary buffer
m_pFmt->nSamplesPerSec *= 2;
m_pFmt->nAvgBytesPerSec = m_pFmt->nSamplesPerSec * m_pFmt->nBlockAlign;
pBufferFns->SetFormat(m_pFmt);
```

For a valid WAVE-FORMAT specification, AverageBytesPerSec must be a product of the SamplesPerSec and the BlockAlignment.

```
// get & set total audio volume
long lVolume;
err = m_pBufferFns->GetVolume(&lVolume);
lVolume = 2 * lVolume;
err = m_pBufferFns->SetVolume(lVolume);
```

DirectSound does not currently support making sounds louder. The volume returned will be the current attenuation level of total volume. Doubling this already negative value will cause the sound volume to be greatly reduced. If the DSBCAPS_CTRLVOLUME flag was not set, both these calls would have returned a DSERR_CONTROLUNAVAIL error indicating that volume control was not set up during buffer creation.

12.5.3 Demo Time

Run the demo that corresponds to this chapter. Check the primary Direct-SoundBuffer option to enable the format and volume controls. Play around with the volume and sample rate controls. In particular, try reducing the sample rate of the output format and see if you can detect a quality degradation. Switch to another application with DirectSound audio *RSXDemoApp* and see if the format/volume changes persist.

WHAT HAVE YOU LEARNED?

By this time, you've had an overview of DirectSound and what it does for you. If you worked through the code samples, you have

- played a WAV file using DirectSound,
- mixed two WAV files using DirectSound, and
- controlled the final output format and volume while your application was in focus.

In the next audio chapter you will be introduced to 3D sounds and special effects using Intel's RSX 3D.

CHAPTER 13

Realistic 3D Sound Experience: RSX 3D

WHY READ THIS CHAPTER?

Now that you've looked at DirectSound, you might be wondering if there is a simple way of playing just a generic sound file without taxing application performance. Intel's Realistic 3D Sound Experience (RSX 3D) library helps you do just that. It also gives you a 3D sound model that mimics the real world environment.

To get the most out of this chapter, we recommend that you run the audio demos on the companion CD while you are reading this chapter or beforehand.

In this chapter you will

- get an overview of RSX 3D features,
- see how simple it is to play and mix two or more audio files,
- learn how to use the RSX 3D sound model to achieve a realistic sound experience, and
- learn how to add reverberation and Doppler effects to your application.

Microsoft's DirectSound provides direct access to audio devices under Windows and allows developers to implement low latency audio applications. Even though DirectSound provides some level of abstraction from the hardware, developers must still handle the intricacies of various devices.

Intel's Realistic 3D Sound Experience (RSX 3D) library provides a simple high-level interface for rendering audio under Windows. It implements an abstraction layer above the DirectSound and WAV APIs without sacrificing

PART IV

audio performance. In addition, RSX 3D introduces a new 3D environment that models the sound's physical properties, making for an immersive experience.

In this chapter, we'll first show you how easy it is to play one or more WAV files using RSX 3D. We'll then give you an overview of the RSX 3D environment and show you how to provide realistic 3D sound in your application. Finally, we'll glance over RSX 3D support for streaming audio data.

13.1 RSX 3D Features

RSX 3D is a high-performance audio library that provides developers with a simple interface for rendering audio without taxing application performance. Depending on the configuration of your system, RSX 3D uses either the DirectSound or WAV API to access the audio device. Depending on the power of you processor, RSX 3D automatically scales the output to sound better on high-end processors.

RSX 3D's simple interface allows developers to play audio files from either local drives, networked drives, or even across the Internet. The files themselves can be of different formats (WAV or MIDI) and different sample rates.

One of RSX 3D's most exciting features is its new 3D audio environment, which models real 3D graphics environments. RSX 3D can position sounds anywhere in 3D space. The sound may be above your head, below your feet, behind you, in front of you, and so forth.

Say, for example, you are standing in a hallway and a door slams shut to your right. The sound will reach your right ear earlier than it will reach your left ear (this phenomenon is called Interaural Time Delay, ITD). The sound will also be louder in your right ear than in your left ear (this is known as Interaural Intensity Difference, IID). With these cues your brain is able to correctly locate the sound as originating from your right and not from your left. RSX 3D uses these and other cues to produce realistic sounds as objects move around a scene.[1] RSX 3D also supports modifying sounds for special effects including Doppler, reverberation, and pitch calculations. In

---

1. ITDs and IIDs are combined with other cues to form Head Related Transfer Functions (HRTFs). Clinical probe microphones are inserted into the ears of volunteers to record HRTF measurements. RSX 3D uses HRTF technology and HRTF measurements to simulate 3D sound on PCs.

this chapter, we will work through examples of using RSX 3D's sound positioning capabilities and its special effects capabilities.

13.2 Creating an RSX 3D Object

The RSX 3D audio library uses Microsoft's Component Object Model (COM) interface to export its features. In order to use any COM module and the COM functions you must initialize the COM libraries at start-up time. You can initialize the COM libraries by calling the *CoInitialize()* function. In addition, you need to release any COM objects used by your application and then call *CoUninitialize()* when your application terminates.

To use RSX 3D, you must first create an RSX 3D object within your application process space. You can use *CoCreateInstance()* to create this object, specifying CLSID_RSX20 in the Class ID field. RSX 3D only supports this in-process creation model where RSX objects are created within the application memory context.

```
// Initialize the COM libraries..  ◄─────────
m_coResult = CoInitialize(NULL);
if (FAILED(m_coResult)) {
    AfxMessageBox("Failed to load COM libraries");
    return -1;
}

// Create the RSX20 object and get an IUnknown pointer to the object
HRESULT hr = CoCreateInstance(
    CLSID_RSX20,              ◊ GUID for RSX20. Defined in rsx.h.
    NULL,                     ◊ Create object within processes (only supported mode).
    CLSCTX_INPROC_SERVER,     ◊ Only need to create object and don't care about its methods.
    IID_IUnknown,             ◊ Holds the IUnknown instance of the object.
    (void ** ) &m_lpUnk);

// Make sure that everything is fine..
// If the application fails here, just get out..
//
if( (FAILED(hr)) || (!m_lpUnk) ) {
    AfxMessageBox("Failed to Create RSX Object.\n"
        "CoCreateInstance Failed - Please run RSX Setup\n");
    PostMessage(WM_CLOSE);
    return -1;
}
```

> When using COM, make sure to
> ▪ define INITGUID before include files,
> ▪ link in *OLE32.LIB*, and
> ▪ turn off automatic use of precompiled headers.

PART IV

13.3 Play one WAV file

Once you have created the RSX 3D object, it is a very simple process to play any WAV or MIDI audio file. But before we go into the details, let's first introduce the environment that RSX 3D uses to describe its objects.

To play an audio file with RSX 3D, you need to create only two objects: an *emitter* and a *listener.* I tend to think of an emitter as a jukebox, and a listener as my own ears—just like in the real world. In RSX 3D a *cached emitter* is an object that handles reading and decompressing an audio file, and a *direct listener* is an object that handles sample rate conversion and mixing and writing the output data to the audio device.

So let's create the direct listener first. As with any good COM object, you must use the *CoCreateInstance()* function to create the listener object and pass the CLSID_RSXDIRECTLISTENER for the Class ID parameter. Once the object is created, you call the *Initialize()* function to initialize the listener. In all of the initialize calls, notice that you must also pass in an IUnknown pointer to the main RSX object. Also notice that you can only have one listener active within an application and that you can call the initialize function only once throughout the life of a listener.

```
HRESULT CRsxSampleView::CreateDirectListener()
{

    // First, we need to create an instance of the listener object
    HRESULT hr = CoCreateInstance(
        CLSID_RSXDIRECTLISTENER,      ◊ GUID for Direct Listener object. Defined in rsx.h
        NULL,
        CLSCTX_INPROC_SERVER,         ◊ Create object within process context.
        IID_IRSXDirectListener,       ◊ Direct Listener Interface identifier
        (void ** ) &m_lpDL);          ◊ Holds the listener instance


    // If all is fine, you must initialize
    // the Direct Listener interface
    // before you do anything else.
    if(SUCCEEDED(hr) && m_lpDL) {
        RSXDIRECTLISTENERDESC rsxDL ;
        ZeroMemory(&rsxDL, sizeof(rsxDL);

        rsxDL.cbSize = sizeof(rsxDL);
        rsxDL.hMainWnd = m_hWnd;
        rsxDL.dwUser = 0;
        rsxDL.lpwf = NULL;
```

hMainWnd: DirectSound requires a window handle. You can set the Registry Key Device Type to DIRECTSOUND.

lpwf: Points to WAVEFORMATEX structure which specifies the format of output data. If NULL, RSX uses the default format in the RSX configuration, or in the Registry.

Follow the Registry Settings link in the RSX online help for more details.

```
        hr = m_lpDL->Initialize(&rsxDL, m_lpUnk);
    }
    return hr;
}
```

Similarly, you call the *CoCreateInstance()* function to create the cached emitter with `CLSID_RSXCACHEDEMITTER` in the Class ID field. Before you can call any other method within the emitter, you need to initialize the object by calling the *Initialize()* function.

Notice that, for a cached emitter, you can specify an audio file that exists on a local drive, network drive, or even on a URL, a Web site, or an FTP site. (Note: To use URL-based emitters, Microsoft's Internet Explorer 3.0 or later must be installed and configured on your computer.)

```
HRESULT CRsxSampleView::CreateCachedEmitter(
    LPCTSTR pszFile,
    IRSXCachedEmitter** lppCE)
{
    HRESULT hr = CoCreateInstance(
            CLSID_RSXCACHEDEMITTER,
            NULL,
            CLSCTX_INPROC_SERVER,
            IID_IRSXCachedEmitter,
            (void ** )lppCE);

    if(SUCCEEDED(hr) && *lppCE) {
        RSXCACHEDEMITTERDESC rsxCE;
        ZeroMemory(&rsxCE, sizeof(rsxCE));

        rsxCE.cbSize = sizeof(rsxCE);
        rsxCE.dwFlags = RSXEMITTERDESC_NODOPPLER |
                        RSXEMITTERDESC_NOREVERB |
                        RSXEMITTERDESC_NOATTENUATE |
                        RSXEMITTERDESC_NOSPATIIALIZE;
        rsxCE.dwUser = 0;
        strcpy(rsxCE.szFilename, pszFile);
        hr = (*lppCE)->Initialize(&rsxCE, m_lpUnk);
    }
    return hr;
}
```

dwFlags: You can combine any of the following:

_NODOPPLER:	Disable Doppler effect
_NOATTENUATE:	Disable distance attenuation
_NOSPATIALIZE:	Disable spatial calculations
_NOREVERB:	Disable sound reverberation

szFileName: Path to the audio file:

c:\media\audio.wav	On local or network drive
SomeDll.Dll 108	Resource 108 inside DLL
http://www.xyz.com/media.wav	on Web site

13.4 Play One WAV File

Once the emitter is initialized, you can call the *ControlMedia()* function with `RSX_PLAY` in order to play the file. *All set? So play it, maestro!* Put on your headphones, or crank up your speakers, and enjoy.

```
void CRsxSampleView::OnPlayOneFile()
{
    CreateDirectListener();
    CreateCachedEmitter("file1.wav", &m_lpCE);
    m_lpCE->ControlMedia(RSX_PLAY, 0, 0.0f);

}
```

> **fInitialStartTime:** starting position in seconds.

> **nLoops:** Number of loops to play. 0: infinite

13.5 Mixing Many WAV Files

That was simple, wasn't it? Now let's see what it takes to mix two different audio files together. In real life you only need to put another jukebox in the same room, and you would hear both of them together. Well, the process is very similar in RSX 3D. If you add another emitter to the set, then you'll have two audio files playing at the same time. RSX 3D takes care of mixing them for you and delivering the mixed output to the listener object. That's all it takes!

```
void CRsxSampleView::OnPlayMixtwoaudiofiles()
{
    CreateDirectListener();                        ◊ Only one listener.
    CreateCachedEmitter("file1.wav", &m_lpCE);     ◊ Sound source 1.
    CreateCachedEmitter("file2.wav", &m_lpCE2);    ◊ Sound source 2.
    m_lpCE->ControlMedia(RSX_PLAY, 0, 0.0f);       ◊ Play source 1.
    m_lpCE2->ControlMedia(RSX_PLAY, 0, 0.0f);      ◊ Play source 2.
}
```

13.6 RSX Goes 3D—True 3D Sound

Well, let's pause and think about the model that RSX 3D uses to represent its objects. Recall that RSX 3D mimics the real-world environment, using a sound emitter and a listener to represent its objects. Why not take this a bit further and add positional attributes to these objects (emitter and listener)? That's exactly what RSX 3D does (see Figure 13-1).

Similar to 3D graphics objects, RSX 3D objects can possess positional 3D attributes based on x,y,z coordinates. RSX 3D uses the relative 3D position between the listener and emitter(s) to calculate the audio volume for the left and right speaker channels. For example, if you position the emitter

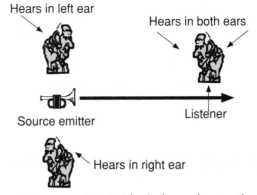

FIGURE 13-1 Physical sound properties.

exactly to the left of the listener, you would hear the sound predominantly from the left speaker channel and in your left ear—just like in real life.

Before we delve into the tiny details, let's look at the model that RSX 3D uses for the emitter. As you know, sound travels the farthest in the direction in which it is pointing, less to the sides, and even less in the opposite direction. You also know that sound volume decreases as you move away from the sound source.

The RSX 3D sound emitter mimics real-world conditions. As you can see in Figure 13-2, RSX 3D defines two ellipses for the emitter, one inside the other. The inner ellipse represents the ambient region where the sound retains maximum intensity and contains no directional information. The outer ellipse defines the region where the sound intensity decreases logarithmically as you move away from the emitter. The emitter does not contribute any of its audio outside the outer ellipse.

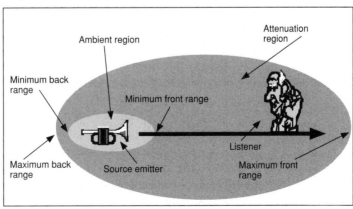

FIGURE 13-2 RSX elliptical sound model.

PART IV

You define the ellipses by the distance of the front and back ranges from the emitter. Different emitters on the scene could have different sound characteristics; for example, louder emitters would have larger ellipses.

As the relative position of the emitter and the listener changes, the sound characteristics change to mimic the real-world situation. The picture in Figure 3-2 shows 2D ellipses; in RSX 3D the ellipses are actually 3D ellipsoids.

13.7 Setting Up 3D Sound with RSX 3D

Now let's see how we can use RSX 3D to define the 3D position of the objects, emitter and listener, and allow it to deliver a *realistic 3D sound experience*. If you go back to where we created the emitter, you'll notice that we disabled the special effects such as sound attenuation, Doppler effect, and so forth. At that point, we only wanted to play some generic audio file. Now we need these cool effects, so let's go back in and enable them. The boldface line in the following block of code enables all 3D sound effects.

```
HRESULT CRsxSampleView::CreateCachedEmitter(
    LPCTSTR pszFile,
    IRSXCachedEmitter** lppCE)
{
    HRESULT hr = CoCreateInstance( CLSID_RSXCACHEDEMITTER, NULL, CLSCTX_INPROC_SERVER, IID_IRSXCachedEmitter,lppCE);
    if(SUCCEEDED(hr) && *lppCE) {
        RSXCACHEDEMITTERDESC rsxCE;
        ZeroMemory(&rsxCE, sizeof(rsxCE));
        rsxCE.cbSize = sizeof(rsxCE);

        rsxCE.dwFlags =    0;

        rsxCE.dwUser = 0;
        strcpy(rsxCE.szFilename, pszFile);
        hr = (*lppCE)->Initialize(&rsxCE, m_lpUnk);
    }

    return hr;
}
```

We can now specify the model that describes the behavior of the emitter.

The inner ellipse is specified by the `fMinFront` and `fMinBack` parameters, and the outer ellipse is specified by the `fMaxFront` and `fMaxBack` parameters as shown in Figure 13-2. Finally, you specify the maximum intensity of the ambient region and then call the *SetModel()* function to register the model with RSX 3D.

```
void CRsxSampleView::SetEmitterPosition(IRSXCachedEmitter* lpCE, int x, int y, int z)
{
    // Now we should set the emitter model
    RSXVECTOR3D v3d;
    RSXEMITTERMODEL rsxEModel;
    rsxEModel.cbSize = sizeof(RSXEMITTERMODEL);
    rsxEModel.fMinFront = 100.0f;
    rsxEModel.fMinBack = 100.0f;
    rsxEModel.fMaxFront = 800.0f;
    rsxEModel.fMaxBack = 200.0f;
    rsxEModel.fIntensity = 1.0f;
    lpCE->SetModel(&rsxEModel);
```

Finally, we need to position the emitter in the 3D scene and specify where in space it is pointing. You can call the *SetPosition()* function to set the *x,y,z* coordinates of the emitter and call the *SetOrientation()* function to define the direction in which the emitter is pointing.

```
// Place the emitter at the origin
v3d.x = (float)x;
v3d.y = (float)y;
v3d.z = (float)z;
lpCE->SetPosition(&v3d);

// Point the emitter along the Z axis -
// into the computer screen.
v3d.x = 0.0f;
v3d.y = 0.0f;
v3d.z = 1.0f;
lpCE->SetOrientation(&v3d);
}
```

Orientation
Vector

Position
(x,y,z)

Similarly, let's position the direct listener object in terms of the 3D world coordinates. The direct listener has three properties: its *x,y,z* position in the 3D world, the direction in which the listener is facing, and the up direction of the listener. Notice that the up vector is always perpendicular to the orientation vector. You can use the *SetPosition()* member function to set the *x,y,z* position of the listener. You can use the *SetOrientation()* function to set both the orientation and up vectors.

PART IV

```
HRESULT CRsxSampleView::SetListenerPosition(int x, int y, int z)

{
    RSXVECTOR3D v3d;
    RSXVECTOR3D v3dOrient;
    RSXVECTOR3D v3dUpOrient;

    // Set the DirectListener's position
    v3d.x = (float)x;
    v3d.y = (float)y;
    v3d.z = (float)z;
    m_lpDL->SetPosition(&v3d);

    // Listener orientation settings
    // This vector is the direction the listener is facing
    v3dOrient.x = 0.0f;
    v3dOrient.y = 0.0f;
    v3dOrient.z = 1.0f;

    // "up" vector - This vector points to which direction is up for the
    // listener - it can not be parallel to the listener orientation vector
    v3dUpOrient.x = 0.0f;
    v3dUpOrient.y = 1.0f;
    v3dUpOrient.z = 0.0f;

    // Set the orientation of the listener
    m_lpDL->SetOrientation(&v3dOrient, &v3dUpOrient);
    return 0;
}
```

By now you've positioned the listener and emitter as if they were objects in the real world. RSX 3D uses this information to calculate the correct intensity for the left and right speakers in order to deliver a more realistic listening experience. As you move the listener and emitter objects around (by changing their position or orientation), RSX 3D automatically recalculates the correct output for both speakers.

From a 3D graphics programmer's point of view, you only need to attach an RSX 3D sound object to your current 3D graphics objects and just move it around as part of the 3D graphics object. In turn RSX 3D figures out the audio output based on the position of this object.

13.8 Adding Special Sound Effects with RSX 3D

13.8.1 The Doppler Effect

Just in case the Doppler phenomenon is new to you, the Doppler effect is the apparent change in a sound when there is relative motion between the emitter and the listener. For example, as an airplane travels toward a listener, sound waves are compressed, effectively increasing the pitch. As the airplane travels away from the listener, the sound waves are rarefied, correspondingly decreasing the pitch. In both cases, the listener "hears" sound at a different pitch than what the emitter produced.

To enable the Doppler effect with RSX 3D, you only need to assure that the RSXEMITTERDESC_NODOPPLER flag is *not* set when you initialize the emitter.

13.8.2 The Reverberation Effect

Just in case reverberation is new to you, reverberation is the "slight echo" effect heard when sounds are generated in enclosed areas (from small chambers to wide canyons). Sound waves travel directly from the sound source to our ears. But in enclosed areas these waves also bounce off the surrounding walls and return to our ears many times. Reverberation is the collective effect of these indirect sound waves.

To enable the reverberation effect with RSX 3D, make sure that the RSXEMITTERDESC_NOREVERB flag is not set when you initialize the emitter. You then use the *SetReverb()* function to set the reverberation model parameters.

RSX 3D uses two parameters to define reverberation: decay time and intensity. The *decay time* models reverberation decay (in seconds), and the intensity models sound absorption.

```
// Must first get a pointer to an IID_RSX2 object to use the
// SetReverb() function.
HRESULT hr = m_lpUnk->QueryInterface(IID_IRSX2, (void**)&m_lpRSX);
if (FAILED(hr) || !m_lpRSX) {
    AfxMessageBox("Error getting IRSX2 interface\n");
    return 0;
}

// Now set the reverb model
RSXREVERBMODEL rsxRvb;
rszRvb.cbSize = sizeof(rsxRvb);
rsxRvb.bUseReverb = TRUE;
rsxRvb.fDecayTime = 1.5f;
rsxRvb.fIntensity = 0.1f;

m_lpRSX->SetReverb(&rsxRvb);
m_lpRSX->Release();
```

Common reverberation parameters:

Room Type	Decay	Intensity
ROOM	0.5	0.2
CHAMBER	1.0	0.2
STAGE	1.5	0.2
HALL	2.0	0.2
PLATE	2.5	0.2

PART IV

13.9 Audio Streaming in RSX 3D

RSX 3D supports two more objects for audio streaming—streaming emitter and streaming listener—where the application can examine or modify the output of the emitter on its way to the listener. *Streaming emitters* are great if you dynamically generate audio input (instead of reading a file), or if you want to stream audio from a network or want to add additional effects to the data before handing it to RSX 3D. Streaming listeners are useful for mixing RSX 3D output with other audio output or writing the data to a file instead of to the audio device.

Audio streaming with RSX 3D also provides for callback mechanisms and multiple stream synchronization.

Since the streaming sound model is exactly the same as we've used for 3D sounds earlier, we prefer that you refer to the RSX 3D documentation for more details.

WHAT HAVE YOU LEARNED?

This is a good time to run the RSX 3D samples for this chapter on the CD to get the most out of this chapter.

In this chapter, you learned how easy it is to play and mix multiple audio files with RSX 3D. You were then introduced to the RSX 3D audio environment, where you learned how to set up the position and orientation of the audio objects and how to change their sound characteristics with the Doppler effect, attenuation, and reverberation. Finally, we briefly looked at the streaming objects supported by RSX 3D.

PART V

Welcome to the
Third Dimension

WE'D LIKE TO EXTEND AN ACKNOWLEDGEMENT TO JACKIE COLLUM, SUSAN DULIS-RINNE, SALLY BROWN (NOT RELATED TO CHARLIE BROWN), JEANNETTE MADDOX, MONICA PARDY, CHARING RIOLO WITHOUT WHOM THE WORLD WOULD NOT GO AROUND.

Chapter 14   **An Introduction to Direct3D**
- Understand Direct3D's target
- Look at Direct3D architecture and modes
- Use Direct3D to draw a simple triangle with default states

Chapter 15   **Embellishing Our Triangle with Backgrounds, Shading, and Textures**
- Add bells and whistles to the simple triangle including shading, texture mapping and Z-Buffering
- Repaint the background with Direct3D

Chapter 16   **Understanding and Enhancing Direct3D Performance**
- Measure performance of the simple triangle samples
- Use Ramp model driver to get better performance
- Measure improvements

Chapter 17   **Mixing 3D with Sprites, Backgrounds, and Videos**
- Mix 3D objects on top of 2D background
- Mix 3D objects on top of 2D sprites and video
- Use video as a texture map source

Part V deals with 3D graphics for Windows 95. We'll start in Chapter 14 with a short contextual background to 3D on the PC. That should fill you in on how 3D evolved on the PC. Then we'll dive into an overview of Microsoft's Direct3D architecture.

PART V

Next we will get you started with Direct3D programming. There is a lot to be learned before you can see results with Direct3D, so Chapter 14 has simple ambitions—to show you how to render a single triangle with Direct3D.

Once you have learned how to render the simplest triangle, you will be in a position to understand how to enable various features in Direct3D. Chapter 15 shows you how to access features such as coloring, shading, texture mapping, Z-Buffering, and repainting backgrounds. Chapters 14 and 15 show you how to get your code running; they do not worry about performance.

In Chapter 16, we return to our performance-oriented angle of rendering. First we measure the performance of the code from the previous chapters. Then we focus on the high-performance rendering path in Direct3D—the Ramp model. The Ramp model offers a significant performance boost, but the model is not straightforward. That is why we deliberately delayed introducing this performance option until after we described the basics of Direct3D rendering.

Once you know how to render high-performance 3D triangles, how about mixing in 2D graphics and video, that is, mixing in the output from the previous parts of the book? We have dedicated Chapter 17 to mixing. In keeping with the previous parts, we use the list management features of RDX to mix sprites and video objects. All the Direct3D code in Chapters 14 through 17 is based on the Direct3D ExecuteBuffer model that was released as part of Microsoft's DirectX 3.0 SDK. The ExecuteBuffer API model is hard to debug, so Microsoft is releasing a new API model (the DrawPrimitive API model), with Version 5.0 of DirectX. Version 5.0 will be released in 1998 along with Windows 98.

Why didn't we use the upcoming API? The DrawPrimitive API was still under development when we wrote the book. We decided to present you with the latest information possible. We have also "printed" this chapter in electronic form on our companion CD. This CD-based chapter will show you how to get going quickly with DrawPrimitives. The performance of DrawPrimitives will continue to improve, and we recommend that you perform your own measurements of the released version.

CHAPTER 14

An Introduction to Direct3D

WHY READ THIS CHAPTER?

We'll start this chapter with a short contextual background on 3D on the PC, and then we'll jump to an overview of Microsoft's Direct3D. Next we'll get to the main purpose of this chapter: giving you the bare bones minimum information to render a triangle using Direct3D.

By the time you have worked through this chapter, you will

- understand the problem space that Direct3D is targeted at,
- get a glimpse of the architecture of Direct3D and its different modes, and
- see how Direct3D works with DirectDraw,
- learn how to get access to 3D functionality and 3D devices,
- learn how to connect DirectDraw's surfaces and palettes to equivalent Direct3D objects, and
- learn how to use execute buffers and viewports to render a triangle using Direct3D.

14.1 Some Background on 3D on the PC

Standards for 3D (such as OpenGL and PHIGS[1]) were developed on workstations and provide powerful capabilities for 3D application developers. But these rich 3D libraries on the PC offered unacceptably poor performance when they were implemented. Developers using 3D on the PC relied

---

1. PHIGS stands for Programmer's Hierarchical Interactive Graphics Systems.

PART V

heavily on high-end graphics accelerators to deliver acceptable applications. These expensive 3D graphics solutions were targeted to serious users (Computer-Aided Design, CAD, for example). As a result, 3D on a PC was out of reach for the casual user.

Then enterprising game software developers invented creative techniques for reducing the computational cost of 3D (primarily by constraining the 3D models). These approximated 3D solutions still provided a compelling illusion of 3D and triggered a wave of excitement for the PC as a platform capable of delivering 3D.

Prominent vendors introduced general-purpose 3D solutions tailored specifically for the PC, including Reality Labs by Rendermorphics, BRender by Argonaut, RenderWare by Criterion, and 3DR by Intel. These general-purpose 3D libraries were not as fast as in-house solutions tailored for application-specific needs, but they were fast enough to work with undemanding 3D applications. They were also designed to use hardware accelerators when available.

Encouraged by the emergence of 3D libraries and applications, graphics vendors started building low-cost 3D hardware accelerators. Unfortunately the multitude of software solutions did not offer graphics vendors a stable target to deliver cost-reduced accelerators. Similarly, because of the numerous variations in hardware acceleration features, developers had to customize their products to each individual accelerator.

In an attempt to move toward a ubiquitous 3D solution, Microsoft started work on Direct3D, intended as an interface to 3D hardware devices. Since the feature sets of the hardware offerings differed, Microsoft realized the need for software emulation to provide developers with a minimum baseline of functionality. In 1995 Microsoft bought Rendermorphics to integrate Reality Labs into their universal 3D solution. In working toward a universal 3D solution, Microsoft aimed at providing hardware vendors with a single driver model at which they could target their accelerators.

The initial response to Microsoft's software emulator was a consistent demand for more performance. Microsoft responded by providing Direct3D with two modes—Retained mode and Immediate mode—offering different feature and performance capabilities. In addition, Microsoft provided two different implementations of the software emulation pipeline—RGB and Mono. The various combinations of modes and drivers offer a variety of API abstractions, feature sets, and quality and performance levels.

So 3D on the PC has become a reality, although it is still in its fledgling state; whereas video, audio, and 2D have had a few years and several iterations to mature. Therefore we will continue to see evolutions in performance, quality, functionality, and API abstractions in future offerings for 3D. Nonetheless, Microsoft's Direct3D has established itself as the foundation for further iterations.

14.2 Introduction to Direct3D

Figure 14-1 shows the current display architecture available under Windows 95. In this chapter we are concerned with the interfaces within the ellipse outlining the Direct3D boxes.

Direct3D is part of Microsoft's DirectX SDK. To application developers, Direct3D provides APIs and services for 3D manipulations. To hardware vendors Direct3D provides a single driver model to enable hardware acceleration. Most significantly, Direct3D guarantees 3D functionality to software developers with a software-based emulation layer. Hardware vendors can accelerate those features that they feel fit their price/performance budget.

Direct3D is closely integrated with DirectDraw. Direct3D makes extensive use of the DirectDraw surface model to access hardware acceleration features such as Bltters and Page Flippers. This integration with DirectDraw makes it possible for Direct3D to use advanced features such as video textures and 2D overlays.

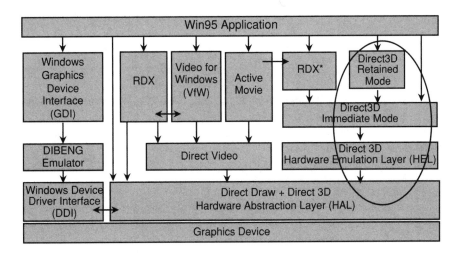

FIGURE 14-1 Display architecture under Windows 95.

Direct3D offers 3D features with two distinctively different flavors: Retained mode and Immediate mode.

■ *Retained mode* offers high-level abstraction of 3D objects and manipulations. It has a sophisticated geometry engine that allows entire scenes to be manipulated with high-level API calls. But the functionality comes at a performance cost.

■ *Immediate mode* offers a very thin layer of software functionality with high performance. It also offers direct access to hardware acceleration features. But Immediate mode does not have a geometry engine, and object transformations must be computed by the application itself.

The two Direct3D modes offer different levels of API abstractions. In addition, multiple implementations of Direct3D drivers can be installed on a system to offer different combinations of features, levels of performance, and quality.

The DirectX SDK ships with two implementations: RGB and Mono. The RGB driver offers truer color quality at a performance cost. The Mono driver makes color approximations and delivers higher performance at a cost in quality. In addition, hardware vendors make available additional Direct3D drivers to offer acceleration features.

14.2.1 A Taste of Direct3D's Retained Mode

Direct3D's Retained mode API is designed for managing entire 3D scenes. In this mode you can load predefined 3D objects from files and manipulate these objects without having to explicitly perform any matrix computations. When you integrate Retained mode with Direct3D authoring tools, you can generate entire 3D applications with minimal explicit programming effort.

Retained mode provides object abstractions and methods on these objects to free you from creating and managing the details of internal object databases. Some of the objects available through the Direct3D Retained mode API are listed in Table 14-1.

Although you can manipulate entire scenes, the Retained mode does not as yet offer compelling performance. So our use of Direct3D will focus on Direct3D's Immediate mode.

TABLE 14-1   Objects Abstracted by Direct3D's Retained Mode Interface

Object	Description
Direct3DRMDevice	Renderer destination
Direct3DRMFace	Represents a single polygon
Direct3DRMMesh	Grouping of polygonal faces and vertices
Direct3DRMMeshBuilder	Build vertices and faces into a mesh
Direct3DRMFrame	Positions objects within a scene
Direct3DRMLight	Five options of lights to illuminate objects in a scene
Direct3DRMMaterial	Properties describing how faces reflect light
Direct3DRMShadow	Define shadows on objects
Direct3DRMTexture	Rectangular image to be rendered onto polygons
Direct3DRMViewport	Define how a 3D scene is rendered into a 2D window
Direct3DRMPickedArray	Choose an object corresponding to a 2D point
Direct3DRMVisual	Placeholder for anything that can be rendered in a scene
Direct3DRMAnimation	Series of transformations that can be applied to a scene
Direct3DRMAnimationSet	Allows animation objects to be grouped together

14.2.2   Direct3D's Immediate Mode

Direct3D's Immediate mode is targeted for developers of high-performance 3D applications for the Microsoft Windows operating system. In designing this mode, Microsoft expected that developers using Immediate mode would be experienced in high-performance programming issues as well as 3D graphics.

Table 14-2 lists the objects (and methods) offered by the Direct3D Immediate mode API. Immediate mode offers direct access to the rendering pipeline. At its essence, Immediate mode is a device-independent way for applications to access low-level hardware acceleration. Direct3D's Retained mode is built on top of Immediate mode.

Low-level hardware accelerators are typically designed to accelerate the pixel-rendering stage, and they rely on the host CPU to compute geometry or lighting factors. But several factors from the geometry and lighting stages can affect rendering results, and some graphics accelerators offer advanced capabilities to render these influences. The Immediate mode pipeline contains objects such as *viewports, materials,* and *lights* to enable even lighting and geometry stages to be accelerated.

PART V

TABLE 14-2 Objects Offered via the Direct3D Immediate Mode Interface

Object Type	Description
Device	Hardware device (equivalent to DirectDraw surface)
ExecuteBuffer	List of vertex data and render instructions
Texture	DirectDraw surface containing a texture map image
Light	Light sources
Matrix	Four-by-four homogeneous transformation matrix
Material	Coloring options, such as color and texture
Viewport	Screen region to draw to

14.2.3 Before You Get Overly Excited

As we mentioned before, today's PCs are not yet capable of manipulating entire scenes at compelling performance levels. Hence, you'll have to approximate the complexity of your 3D models so that you can obtain an illusion of 3D at a low performance cost. Following are some examples of approximations:

- Using only rectangular walls within a building reduces geometry calculations to entire wall faces, even though you may want to subdivide the wall for better textural and rendering quality.

- Similarly, maintaining simple angles of intersection (30°, 45°, 60°, and 90°) among the walls can reduce the cost of computing lighting values and marking hidden surfaces.

- Using multiple versions of textures ("pre-lit") to simulate various lighting shades can eliminate the cost of rendering using other more costly lighting options.

Approximations like these are very application specific. The gains are only obtained when the application handles its own geometry and lighting calculations, so Direct3D's Immediate mode was designed to be used by this type of application. If you want high-performance 3D results using Direct3D's Immediate mode, you will need to have (or develop) your own geometry and lighting modules in your application.

Given that many users of Direct3D's Immediate mode are capable of developing their own geometry and lighting modules, the API and objects of the Immediate mode interface have been designed for developers with an advanced knowledge of 3D. If you are new to 3D, we strongly recommend that you read up on material about 3D geometry and lighting before attempting to develop any significant applications using Direct3D's Immediate mode.

14.3 Inside Direct3D

Before starting to use Direct3D, let's look at how Direct3D interacts with DirectDraw and sneak a peek inside Direct3D's architecture.

14.3.1 Direct3D and DirectDraw

Direct3D is very closely connected with DirectDraw. So much so that Direct3D is almost an extension of DirectDraw. This close connection is deliberate, because it lets you incorporate cool features such as texture mapping with video rendered into DirectDraw surfaces, or to overlay 3D scenes on 2D compositions.

There are four points of connection between Direct3D and DirectDraw involve interface objects and buffers.

- *IDirect3D.* The primary interface to Direct3D, IDirect3D is derived by creating an IDirectDraw object and querying (via *QueryInterface*) for a IID_IDirect3D interface.

- *IDirect3DDevice.* This interface gives you access to low-level Direct3D rendering functions. IDirect3DDevice is similar to using IDirectDrawSurface in DirectDraw to access low-level 2D functions. An IDirect3DDevice is "created" by creating an IDirectDrawSurface and querying for a 3D device GUID. The 3D device will render pixels to the 2D surface. In addition, you can use all standard DirectDraw functions on the 2D surface.

- *IDirect3DTexture.* This interface manages textures in Direct3D. IDirect3DTexture, like IDirect3DDevice, is an extension of IDirectDrawSurface and is "created" by creating a IDirectDrawSurface and querying for an IID_IDirect3DTexture interface. The 3D device will use the surface as a source texture during texture-mapped rendering. In addition, you can access all normal DirectDraw surface functions on the 2D surface.

- *Z-Buffers.* In Direct3D Z-Buffers are DirectDraw surfaces created with a DDSCAPS_ZBUFFER flag. The Z-Buffer therefore is easily visible by all modules. With Z-Buffers you can use normal 2D functions for carrying out simple operations on the Z-Buffer (such as clear).

14.3.2 Direct3D Rendering Engine

Figure 14-2 looks inside the Rendering engine of Direct3D. The *rendering engine* consists of three modules: the Transform module, the Lighting module, and the Raster module.

- The *Transform module* converts input vertices from model coordinates to render coordinates via a transform matrix created from world, view, and projection matrices. The Transform module also culls objects to fit within a specified viewport.

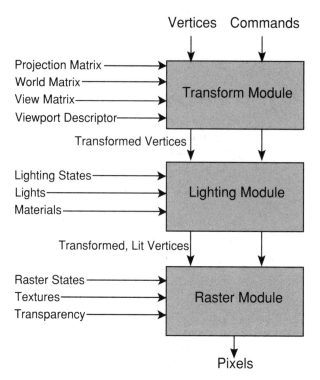

FIGURE 14-2 Direct3D Rendering engine.

- The *Lighting module* supports ambient, point, spotlight, or directional light sources and adds color information to the vertices provided by the Transform module.

- Based on raster options, such as wire-frame, solid-fill, or texture-map, the *Raster module* renders pixels conforming to the vertices and color values passed on.

All three modules are replaceable. Direct3D comes with one transformation module but with a choice of two lighting and two rasterization modules (RGB or mono). Graphics hardware vendors can provide additional replacement modules that support their 3D accelerators.

14.4 Revving Up Direct3D

Roll up your sleeves, it's coding time again. Yeeha! Over the course of working with Direct3D we will come across the objects listed in Table 14-3. We will describe each one as we get to it.

TABLE 14-3 Direct3D Objects Used in This Chapter

Object	Description
IDirect3D	Primary interface to Direct3D
IDirect3DDevice	3D device (equivalent to DirectDraw surface)
IDirect3DViewport	Screen region to draw to
IDirect3DExecuteBuffer	List of vertex data and render instructions

14.4.1 The Starting Point: IDirect3D Object

IDirect3D, as we mentioned above, is the primary interface for Direct3D. Objects such as lights, materials, and viewports are created using the IDirect3D interface. IDirect3D also has functions to enumerate (or find) 3D devices, since there can be multiple Direct3D device modules installed on a system.

Let's initialize DirectDraw and get access to Direct3D:

```
BOOL CSharedHardware::Init(HWND hWnd) {
    LPDIRECT3D    pD3D;

    // create a DirectDraw instance
    DirectDrawCreate(NULL, &m_pDDraw, NULL);

    // "create" D3D object
    m_pDDraw->QueryInterface(IID_IDirect3D, (void *)&pD3D);

    // remember to set DDraw cooperative level
    m_pDDraw->SetCooperativeLevel(hWnd, DDSCL_NORMAL);

    // assign into member variable and return
    m_pD3D = pD3D;
    return TRUE;
}
```

> Invoking *IUnknown::QueryInterface()* on the IDirectDraw object with the predefined GUID *IID_IDirect3D* returns a pointer to an IDirect3D object in the second parameter.

QueryInterface() does not create a new object; instead it provides a second interface to the DirectDraw object and increments its reference count. You must call both *IDirectDraw::Release()* and *IDirect3D::Release()* to fully release the object. If you only release the IDirect3D interface and then query for it again, the original IDirect3D state might be restored.

14.4.2 Enumerating IDirect3DDevices

We have access to the first level of Direct3D. You would think that the next step would be to ask for access to an IDirect3DDevice. But wait! To ask for access to a new interface, we've got to know the new interface's GUID. So how do we get the GUID of an IDirect3DDevice?

Direct3D was built to allow multiple 3D devices to be installed in a system. We could get the GUID from our vendor of choice and hard code it into our application. An alternate approach would be to use *IDirect3D::EnumDevices* to search among installed devices and pick a device of our choosing.

```
extern "C" static HRESULT WINAPI enumDeviceFunc(
    LPGUID lpGuid, LPSTR lpDeviceDescription, LPSTR lpDeviceName,
    LPD3DDEVICEDESC lpHWDesc, LPD3DDEVICEDESC lpHELDesc, LPVOID lpCookie
);
```

IDirect3D::EnumDevices will call a callback function of this form for each driver installed in the system. Note that "C" calling convention is used. The parameters passed to the callback function are

LPGUID lpGuid	Pointer to the GUID for this driver
LPSTR lpDeviceDescription	String describing the driver. (For example: "Microsoft Direct3D Mono (Ramp) Software Emulation")
LPSTR lpDeviceName	String name of the driver. (For example: "Ramp Emulation")
LPD3DDEVICEDESC lpHWDesc	If this descriptor is valid, then driver is hardware based.
LPD3DDEVICEDESC lpHELDesc	If this descriptor is valid, then driver is software emulation.
LPVOID lpCookie	LPVOID sized data passed on from the main application.

```
BOOL CSharedHardware::InitDirect3D(DWORD dwCookie)
{
    // enum drivers and pick one
    // Ask D3D to call our "C" callback
    m_pD3D->EnumDevices(enumDeviceFunc, (LPVOID)dwCookie);

    // return
    return TRUE;
}
```

Invoke *IDirect3D::EnumDevices()* with the address of our callback function.
dwCookie, an LPVOID sized object, can be anything we want. It will be passed on unchanged to our callback function.

IDirect3D::EnumDevices will call our callback function once for each driver installed in the system, giving us the driver's GUID, a couple of text strings identifying the driver, and two D3DDEVICEDESC descriptors to tell us about the capabilities of each driver.

Only one of the two D3DDEVICEDESC descriptors is valid. Browsing through Direct3D's sample code, we found that the prescribed method of checking the validity of a D3DDEVICEDESC descriptor is to check whether the dcmColor-Model field is set to a valid value (currently it can be either D3DCOLOR_MONO or D3DCOLOR_RGB).

We get information for a single 3D device on each call of our callback. If this device matches our selection criterion, we can tell Direct3D to stop calling us by returning D3DENUMRET_CANCEL. Otherwise, our callback is supposed to return D3DENUMRET_OK—and Direct3D will continue to call us for any remaining un-enumerated choices.

We designed our callback function to choose the first driver that matched an input criterion. Our input criterion can be:

USE_HARDWARE	Reject any software emulation drivers. Specifying both USE_HARDWARE and USE_SOFTWARE is illegal; neither is ok, the first one will be chosen.*
USE_SOFTWARE	Reject any hardware drivers. Specifying both USE_HARDWARE and USE_SOFTWARE is illegal; neither is ok, the first one will be chosen.*
USE_RGB	Use the higher-quality RGB model. Specifying both USE_RGB and USE_RAMP is illegal; neither is ok, the first one will be chosen.*
USE_RAMP	Use the lower-quality, higher-performance Mono/Ramp model. Specifying both USE_RGB and USE_RAMP is illegal; neither is ok, the first one will be chosen.*
USE_ANY	Use the first 3D driver enumerated by Direct3D

* If you don't specify a choice, then the choice will be made on a first-come basis. If you specify a choice, then your choice will be honored.

Here is the code for our callback function:

```
extern "C" static HRESULT WINAPI enumDeviceFunc(
    LPGUID lpGuid, LPSTR lpDeviceDescription, LPSTR lpDeviceName,
    LPD3DDEVICEDESC lpHWDesc, LPD3DDEVICEDESC lpHELDesc, LPVOID lpCookie
)
{
    DWORD dwFlags = (DWORD)lpCookie;
    CSharedHardware *pGrfx  = gpAppWide->m_pGrfxCard;
```

Pick the valid driver from the two device descriptors.

```
    LPD3DDEVICEDESC pChoice = lpHWDesc;
    if (!pChoice->dcmColorModel)
        pChoice = lpHELDesc;
```

The method to check whether a D3DDEVICEDESC is valid—as approved in Direct3D sample code—is to check dcmColorModel for a valid value.

PART V

Check our option flags for hardware/software force.

```
if (dwFlags & USE_HARDWARE) {
    if (!lpHWDesc->dcmColorModel)
        return D3DENUMRET_OK;
    pChoice = lpHWDesc;
    }
    if (dwFlags & USE_SOFTWARE) {
        if (!lpHELDesc->dcmColorModel)
            return D3DENUMRET_OK;
        pChoice = lpHELDesc;
    }
```

Returning D3DENUMRET_OK gets us the next driver.

Our application only works in 8 bpp mode. Check supported Render modes for this format. Devices may support multiple output formats. Direct3D uses a packed format to specify all the formats that a device can support. DDBD_x bit flags define the output formats that can be returned.

```
if (!pChoice->dwDeviceRenderBitDepth & DDBD_8)
    return D3DENUMRET_OK;
```

Check our option flags for RGB/Mono color model force.

```
if ((dwFlags & USE_RGB) &&
    (pChoice->dcmColorModel != D3DCOLOR_RGB))
    return D3DENUMRET_OK;
if ((dwFlags & USE_RAMP) &&
    (pChoice->dcmColorModel != D3DCOLOR_MONO))
    return D3DENUMRET_OK;
```

Got what we wanted. Copy the GUID and set some descriptive flags.

```
m_bFound3Ddriver = TRUE;
memcpy((void *)&pGrfx->m_3dGuid, lpGuid, sizeof(GUID));
if (pChoice == lpHWDesc) pGrfx->m_bIsHardware3d = TRUE;
return (D3DENUMRET_CANCEL);
}
```

Returning D3DENUMRET_CANCEL tells D3D to stop enumerating.

When control returns from Direct3D to the original function that invoked *IDirect3D::EnumDevices,* our callback function would have copied a GUID for a Direct3D device that matched our specification (if there was one). We can now use this GUID to query for a IDirect3Ddevice object.

14.4.3 Creating an IDirect3DDevice

Now we're really getting down! An IDirect3DDevice interface provides low-level access to Direct3D rendering functions. IDirect3DDevice is not an object in its own right; it is an extension to an IDirectDrawSurface object. To get an IDirect3DDevice object, we've got to first create an IDirectDrawSurface and then "extend" the surface by querying for 3D capabilities.

To extend an IDirectDrawSurface into an IDirect3DDevice, the surface needs to have been created using DDSCAPS_3DDEVICE set in the surface caps (*ddsCaps.dwCaps*) field.

Let's create a suitable IDirectDrawSurface. We don't want to see the flicker that results from compositing directly onto the display screen, so we're using an Offscreen surface (although tests showed that we could successfully extend the Primary surface for 3D). The code for creating an IDirectDrawSurface is pretty much the same as the code we used in Chapter 5, except for the addition of the DDSCAPS_3DDEVICE flag:

```
CSurfaceSysMem::Init(CWnd *pcWnd, LPDIRECTDRAW2 pDDraw)
{
    // get size of client to create similar off.screen window
    RECT    rWin;
    pcWnd->GetClientRect(&rWin);
    m_dwWidth = (dword)(rWin.right - rWin.left);
    m_dwHeight = (dword)(rWin.bottom - rWin.top);

    // init surface descriptor and create offscreen surf
    m_SurfDesc.dwHeight = m_dwHeight & (~0x03);
    m_SurfDesc.dwWidth = m_dwWidth & (~0x03);

    // specify desired 8bpp color format
    m_SurfDesc.ddpfPixelFormat.dwSize = sizeof(DDPIXELFORMAT);
    m_SurfDesc.ddpfPixelFormat.dwRGBBitCount = 8;
    m_SurfDesc.ddpfPixelFormat.dwFlags = DDPF_PALETTEINDEXED8 | DDPF_RGB;

    // ask for offScreenSurface, in system memory, with 3d capabilities
    m_SurfDesc.ddsCaps.dwCaps = DDSCAPS_OFFSCREENPLAIN;
    m_SurfDesc.ddsCaps.dwCaps |= DDSCAPS_SYSTEMMEMORY;
    m_SurfDesc.ddsCaps.dwCaps |= DDSCAPS_3DDEVICE;    ◄──   Add the DDSCAPS_3DDEVICE flag to tell DirectDraw
                                                            that we will extend this surface for 3D.
    // specify which fields in SurfDesc are valid
    m_SurfDesc.dwFlags = DDSD_CAPS | DDSD_WIDTH | DDSD_HEIGHT | DDSD_PIXELFORMAT;

    // create the surface
    pDDraw->CreateSurface(&m_SurfDesc, &m_pSurfFns, NULL);
    return TRUE;
}
```

Even though we've created a suitable DirectDraw surface, we are not yet ready to extend it for 3D. When using Direct3D to write into a palletized surface, we must attach a palette to the surface before extending the surface for 3D.

14.4.4 Preparing a DirectDraw Palette

Following is the code for creating a palette using DirectDraw's Palette functions. We've initialized the new palette to the system palette and attached it to both the Primary and the Offscreen surfaces.

The Direct3D RGB driver operates in a high-quality RGB color model. It must then reduce the colors in the scene to appropriate palette entries. Direct3D needs to be able to select these palette entries. So we've "prepared" the palette for Direct3D by setting flags that tell Direct3D which values it can modify.

```
BOOL CSharedHardware::InitPalette(void)
{
    // Get the current system palette.
    PALETTEENTRY ppeSysPal[256];
    HDC hdc = GetDC(NULL);
    GetSystemPaletteEntries(hdc, 0, (1 << 8), ppeSysPal);
    ReleaseDC(NULL, hdc);
```

Allow D3D to change middle entries. For windowed case, preserve top ten and bottom ten colors. In Full Screen mode we could allow all but the top and bottom color to be changed.

```
    int i;
    for (i = 0; i < 10; i++)
        ppeSysPal[i].peFlags = D3DPAL_READONLY;
    for (i = 10; i < 246; i++)
        ppeSysPal[i].peFlags = D3DPAL_FREE | PC_RESERVED ;
    for (i = 246; i < 256; i++)
        ppeSysPal[i].peFlags = D3DPAL_READONLY;

    // create palette and init with above values
    m_pDDraw->CreatePalette(DDPCAPS_8BIT | DDPCAPS_INITIALIZE,
                            ppeSysPal, &m_pPalette, NULL);
    return TRUE;
}
```

Create a DirectDraw palette. A pointer to an IDirectDrawPalette object is returned in the third parameter.

```
BOOL CSharedHardware::SetPalette(LPDIRECTDRAWSURFACE2 pSurfFns)
{
    // set created palette on specified surface
    pSurfFns->SetPalette(m_pPalette);
    return TRUE;
}
```

14.4.5 Extending the Surface for 3D

Now we're ready to extend the DirectDraw surface and get an IDirect3DDevice object:

```
BOOL CSurface3d::Init(CWnd *pcWnd, LPDIRECTDRAWSURFACE2 p2dFns)
{
    p2dFns->QueryInterface(gpAppWide->m_pGrfxCard->m_3dGuid, &m_p3dFns);
```

> We're invoking *IUnknown::QueryInterface()* on the IDirectDrawSurface object with the GUID that we chose earlier in our *EnumDevices* callback function. We get back a pointer to the IDirect3DDevice object in the second parameter.

> Get the 2D surface descriptors and copy some info about 2D surface.

```
    DDSURFACEDESC ddsdTmp;
    memset(&ddsdTmp, 0, sizeof(DDSURFACEDESC));
    ddsdTmp.dwSize = sizeof(DDSURFACEDESC);
    err = p2dFns->GetSurfaceDesc(&ddsdTmp);          // get surface descriptor
    m_dwWidth = ddsdTmp.dwWidth;                     // get width of 2d surface
    m_dwHeight = ddsdTmp.dwHeight;                   // get height of 2d surface
    if (ddsdTmp.ddsCaps.dwCaps & DDSCAPS_VIDEOMEMORY) m_bIsVidMem = TRUE;
    m_p2dFns = p2dFns;                               // remember 2d surface fns

    return TRUE;
}
```

Voilà! Pardon my French, but I am happy to announce that the IDirectDrawSurface has now been extended to allow for 3D capabilities. Also allow me to point out again that *QueryInterface()* does not create a new object. Instead, it provides a second interface in addition to the original IDirectDrawSurface object and increments its reference count. You must call both *IDirectDrawSurface::Release()* and *IDirect3DDevice::Release()* to fully release the object.

Note that only this surface has been "extended" for 3D capabilities. As such we could say that this surface is a "3D surface." If you browse our code for this chapter on the CD, you will notice that we use *Surface3D* to refer to IDirect3DDevice, because as we said before, it's only this surface that has been 3D enabled.

Just as with 2D surfaces, 3DDevices are described by a descriptor, D3DDEVICEDESC. You can use *IDirect3DDevice::GetCaps* to get the descriptor of the device. In this chapter we are mainly concerned with getting a triangle rendered through Direct3D without adding any bells and whistles—yet. So we don't really need to look at the device capabilities and the D3DDEVICEDESC structure at this point. We'll leave that for our later chapter on accelerating Direct3D, Chapter 15.

PART V

14.4.6 Mapping from a 3D Model to the 2D Surface Using Viewports

We've got our 3D surface (3DDevice), and pretty soon we'll want to render some 3D objects. 3D objects are represented with 3D coordinates in a 3D model. We will have to tell Direct3D how to project 3D objects onto a 2D screen. Direct3D provides an IDirect3DViewport object to control this mapping.

A *viewport* defines a visible 3D volume and the projection of this 3D volume onto a 2D screen area. For perspective viewing, the visible 3D volume is a portion of a pyramid between a front clipping plane and a back clipping plane. For orthographic viewing, the visible 3D volume is cuboid.

For perspective projection, the viewing position is at the tip of the pyramid as in Figure 14-3. The z-axis runs from the tip of the pyramid to the center of the pyramid's base. The front clipping plane is at a distance P, the back clipping plane is at a distance Q from the front clipping plane. The height of the front clipping plane is $2H$, and it defines the field of view.

With Direct3D's Retained mode, you could use *IDirect3DRMViewport ::SetFront()*, *::SetBack()*, and *::SetField()* functions to set the values of P, Q, and H, respectively. But with Direct3D's Immediate mode you've got to compute equivalent values for P, Q, and H and fill these values into a D3DVIEWPORT structure.

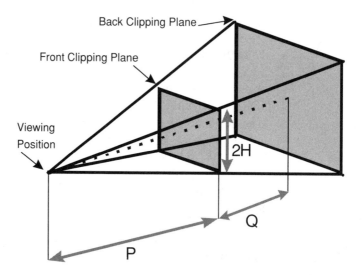

FIGURE 14-3 Using a viewport for perspective projection.

Let's take a look at the D3DVIEWPORT structure:

```
typedef struct _D3DVIEWPORT {
    DWORD       dwSize;
    DWORD       dwX;
    DWORD       dwY;
    DWORD       dwWidth;
    DWORD       dwHeight;
    D3DVALUE    dvScaleX;
    D3DVALUE    dvScaleY;
    D3DVALUE    dvMaxX;
    D3DVALUE    dvMaxY;
    D3DVALUE    dvMinZ;
    D3DVALUE    dvMaxZ;
} D3DVIEWPORT, *LPD3DVIEWPORT;
```

Coordinates of the top-left corner of the viewport and dimensions of the viewport. These are defined relative to the top left of the device.

Scale parameters can be used to maximize the window area occupied by the 3D scene. For example, Direct3D suggests that the scale parameters be set such that the larger dimension (width or height) of the front plane fills the window.

dvMaxX, dvMaxY, dvMinZ, and dvMaxZ describe the maximum and minimum homogeneous coordinates of *x*, *y*, and *z*. Use these coordinates to describe the viewing volume.

We create an IDirect3DViewport object by using *IDirect3D::CreateViewport()*, and we set the viewport's parameters using *IDirect3DViewport::SetViewport()*. Once we've created an IDirect3DViewport object we've got to associate it to our 3D surface using *IDirect3DDevice::AddViewport()*. Here's the code for doing that:

```
BOOL CSurface3d::InitViewport(lpdirect3d pD3D)
{
    pD3D->CreateViewport(&m_p3dViewport, null) ;      ◊ Use IDirect3D to create the viewport.
    m_p3dFns->AddViewport(m_p3dViewport);             ◊ Once created, attach the viewport to 3D surface.

    // Setup viewport to be equivalent to window
    D3DVIEWPORT viewData;
    memset(&viewData, 0, sizeof(D3DVIEWPORT));
    viewData.dwSize = sizeof(D3DVIEWPORT);
    viewData.dwX = 0;
    viewData.dwY = 0;
    viewData.dwWidth = m_dwWidth;
    viewData.dwHeight = m_dwHeight;
    viewData.dvScaleX = (float)1.0;
    viewData.dvScaleY = (float)1.0 ;
    viewData.dvMaxX = (float)viewData.dwWidth;
    viewData.dvMaxY = (float)viewData.dwHeight;
    m_p3dViewport->SetViewport(&viewData);
```

Our purpose in this chapter is merely to render a triangle. So we've set up the simplest possible viewport, where the viewport is the same size as the drawing window, and there's no scaling and projection.

```
    return true;
}
```

PART V

Based on our viewport parameters, the driver builds a transformation matrix to convert incoming vertices from a 3D model space to a projected 2D space.

Direct3D lets us create multiple viewports. We tell Direct3D which viewport to use only when we're rendering an object. In this way we could, if we wanted, mix objects rendered with different perspectives onto the same surface.

14.4.7 Talking to 3D Devices Through Execute Buffers

Okay, we've got our 3D device called Surface3D on the CD, and we've described our viewport. Now let's render some triangles, which brings up our next step—talking to the 3D device.

We send instructions to 3D devices in lists called *Execute Buffers*. Figure 14-4 is a picture of an Execute Buffer. Data items sent to 3D devices via Execute Buffers are usually either triangle vertices or render operations.

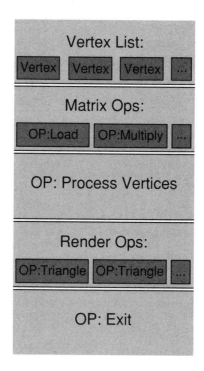

FIGURE 14-4 Sample Execute Buffer.

A vertex is typically sent using a `D3DVERTEX` structure. A vertex processed by the Transform module and Lighting modules is converted into a `D3DTLVERTEX` structure, which occupies the same data space as a `D3DVERTEX` structure. This process allows transformation and lighting to be performed in place. To make in-place transformation and lighting convenient, 3D devices expect vertices to precede all operations.

3D devices can be commanded to perform operations using a set of *opcodes* defined by Direct3D. We will examine the opcodes in more detail shortly (in 14.4.8). In general, there are opcodes to load data (such as matrices or textures) into device memory; opcodes to set state values in the Transformation, Lighting, or Render modules; and opcodes to process data.

IDirect3DDevice has a *CreateExecuteBuffer()* method to create an Execute Buffer object. The IDirect3DExecuteBuffer object returned is only an interface object and does not yet provide the actual buffer space into which you can insert commands.

When we're asking an IDirect3DDevice object to create an Execute Buffer, we've got to describe the buffer we'd like created. Here's the `D3DEXECUTEBUFFERDESC` structure used to describe our needs:

```
typedef struct _D3DExecuteBufferDesc {
    DWORD   dwSize;
    DWORD   dwFlags ;
    DWORD   dwCaps;
    DWORD   dwBufferSize;
    LPVOID  lpData;
} D3DEXECUTEBUFFERDESC;
```

Hardware devices prefer their data (including vertices) to reside in video memory. Software emulators, on the other hand, prefer that their data reside in system memory. Specify the memory type in the dwCaps field based on the 3D device created. SystemMemory is the default if the field is left unspecified. The field can be

D3DDEBCAPS_SYSTEMMEMORY	The Execute Buffer data must reside in system memory.
D3DDEBCAPS_VIDEOMEMORY	The Execute Buffer data must reside in video memory.
D3DDEBCAPS_MEM	A logical OR of D3DDEBCAPS_SYSTEMMEMORY and D3DDEBCAPS_VIDEOMEMORY.

In the same lines as the DirectDraw convention, not all fields in descriptor structures are valid. dwFlags specifies which fields in the descriptor have been set. For D3DEXECUTEBUFFERDESC the flags are

D3DDEB_BUFSIZE	The dwBufferSize member is valid.
D3DDEB_CAPS	The dwCaps member is valid. [See above].
D3DDEB_LPDATA	The lpData member is valid. The 3D device returns a pointer to Execute Buffer data space in this field. Could be used to provide the driver with a pre-initialized buffer, but this doesn't always work.

Here's code that demonstrates the creation of an Execute Buffer:

```
// compute size of execute buffer needed to render one triangle
size_t sztEx = 0;
sztEx = sizeof(D3DTLVERTEX) * 3;
sztEx += sizeof(D3DINSTRUCTION)*3;
sztEx += sizeof(D3DPROCESSVERTICES);
sztEx += sizeof(D3DTRIANGLE) * 1;
```

We need to tell the device how large a buffer we will need. For our example we are requesting enough buffer space to contain commands to render one triangle. Don't worry about the actual sizes and instructions in the Execute Buffer—we'll be looking at this shortly.

```
// Describe ExecuteBuffer to be created
D3DEXECUTEBUFFERDESC debDesc;
memset(&debDesc, 0, sizeof(debDesc));
debDesc.dwSize = sizeof(debDesc);
debDesc.dwFlags = D3DDEB_BUFSIZE;
debDesc.dwBufferSize = sztEx; ◄
```

Some 3D devices limit the size of the Execute Buffer that can be created. *CreateExecuteBuffer()* may fail if you request too large a buffer. You can find out the allowed limit by using *GetCaps()*.

```
// Create ExecuteBuffer
m_p3dFns->CreateExecuteBuffer(&debDesc, & m_pExBufFns, NULL) ;
```

Create the Execute Buffer according to description passed in first parameter. An interface object pointer (LPDIRECT3DEXECUTEBUFFER) is returned in the second parameter.

As we mentioned before, the IDirect3DExecuteBuffer object we just created is only an interface object and does not yet provide buffer space for inserting commands. We get access to usable buffer space by using the *IDirect3DExecuteBuffer::Lock* function. The lock returns a buffer pointer into which we can enter our commands. Once we finish entering our commands, we must use the *::Unlock()* function to unlock the buffer. Here's a quick example:

Copy the triangle into the Execute Buffer space. Assume that the commands were in a preset buffer. Don't worry about the actual instructions—we'll examine these in detail shortly.

```
m_pExBufFns->Lock(&m_ExDesc);        // lock buffer
PVOID pTmp = m_ExDesc.lpData;        // get returned ptr
memcpy(pTmp, pSomeBuffer, sztEx);    // copy data over
m_pExBufFns->Unlock();               // unlock buffer
```

After entering the commands, we tell the 3D device that we've given it new instructions by invoking *::SetExecuteData()*. At this point we're also describing to the 3D device the makeup of our Execute Buffer—where the vertices start, how many vertices there are, where the instructions start and end.

This information is provided to the 3D device using a D3DEXECUTEDATA structure. The structure is simple, and its use is demonstrated in the following code:

```
// describe make-up of recently copied execute buffer
D3DEXECUTEDATA ExecData;
memset(&ExecData, 0, sizeof(D3DEXECUTEDATA));
ExecData.dwSize = sizeof(D3DEXECUTEDATA);
ExecData.dwVertexOffset = 0;
ExecData.dwVertexCount = 3;
ExecData.dwInstructionOffset = sizeof(D3DTLVERTEX) * 3;
ExecData.dwInstructionLength = sizSomeBuffer - (sizeof(D3DTLVERTEX)*3);
pExecCmds->SetExecuteData(&ExecData);
```

After transferring an Execute Buffer to the 3D device using the Lock/Copy/Unlock sequence, we need to describe the makeup of the recently copied Execute Buffer, using *SetExecuteData()* and a D3DEXECUTEDATA structure. Here are the fields in the structure:

dwVertexOffset	Where do vertices start within the Execute Buffer?
dwVertexCount	Number of vertices in vertex list.
dwInstructionOffset	Where do instructions start within the Execute Buffer?
dwInstructionLength	Where do vertices end? This need not be the end of the buffer.
dsStatus	D3DSTATUS structure used to return the screen extents needed after vertex transformations.

OK, we've waited long enough. Let's see what operations we can perform with Direct3D.

14.4.8 Execute Operations

Operands are passed to the 3D device using a _D3DINSTRUCTION structure:

```
typedef struct _D3DINSTRUCTION {
    BYTE bOpcode;
    BYTE bSize;
    WORD wCount;
} D3DINSTRUCTION, *LPD3DINSTRUCTION;
```

The first field in the _D3DINSTRUCTION structure is the opcode. Opcodes available in Direct3D are listed in Table 14-4. With the exception of D3DOP_EXIT and D3DOP_NOP, all operations are followed by an operand. Operands are specified with a structure format unique to the operation. D3DOP_POINT, for example uses a D3DPOINT structure. The sizes of operand structures vary, and they must be entered in the bSize field. The sizes are used to advance pointers while parsing instructions in an instruction stream.

PART V

TABLE 14-4 Direct3D Execute Opcodes

Opcode	Purpose
D3DOP_TEXTURELOAD	Causes device to load a texture into device data space
D3DOP_MATRIXLOAD	Causes device to load a texture into device data space
D3DOP_MATRIXMULTIPLY	Causes matrix to multiply via the rendering pipeline
D3DOP_STATETRANSFORM	Sets value of specified transformation module state variable
D3DOP_STATELIGHT	Sets value of specified lighting module state variable
D3DOP_STATERENDER	Sets value of specified render module state variable
D3DOP_POINT	Renders a point via the renderer
D3DOP_SPAN	Spans a list of points with the same y value
D3DOP_LINE	Renders a line via the renderer
D3DOP_TRIANGLE	Renders a triangle via the renderer
D3DOP_PROCESSVERTICES	Causes vertices to be transformed, lit, and copied to device space
D3DOP_BRANCHFORWARD	Enables a branching mechanism within an Execute Buffer
D3DOP_NOP	Used for optimization to align data on QWORD boundaries
D3DOP_EXIT	Signals that the end of the list has been reached
D3DOP_SETSTATUS	Resets the status of the Execute Buffer

In a typical usage scenario, operations are quite often repeated with different parameters. For example, let's look at rendering multiple triangles. The wCount field in the _D3DINSTRUCTION structure allows the repetition to be optimized and specifies that the operation will be followed by wCount operands.

14.4.9 Operations Used to Render a Simple Triangle

Let's set up an Execute Buffer to render a simple triangle. For a simple triangle we will need three vertices in the vertex list. We will also need at least three operations. Two of the operations—D3DOP_TRIANGLE and D3DOP_EXIT—are straightforward. The third, D3DOP_PROCESSVERTICES, is needed to tell the 3D driver that we will provide vertices that don't need transformation or lighting. Both the D3DOP_TRIANGLE and D3DOP_PROCESSVERTICES operations are followed by operand structures.

Figure 14-5 shows a picture of the Execute Buffer we need to render our simple triangle. Now let's create this Execute Buffer. Our code will build the instruction stream in system memory. We will then create an Execute Buffer and copy the system memory buffer into the Execute Buffer using the code that we showed in 14.4.5.

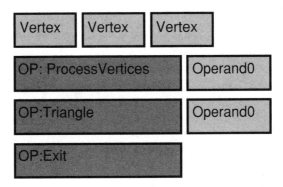

FIGURE 14-5 An Execute Buffer to render our simple triangle.

Here's the code that computes the size of the Execute Buffer needed and then allocates a system memory, or sysmem, buffer of this size:

```
// Create an execute buffer in system memory to render 1 triangle
size_t sztEx = 0;
sztEx = sizeof(D3DTLVERTEX) * 3;     // 3 vertices for a triangle
sztEx += sizeof(D3DINSTRUCTION)*3;   // processVerts, tri, exit
sztEx += sizeof(D3DPROCESSVERTICES); // 1 processVerts operand
sztEx += sizeof(D3DTRIANGLE) * 1;    // 1 triangle operand
m_pSysExBuffer = new BYTE [sztEx];   // setup exec buffer in sysmem first
```

Let's insert three vertices into our sysmem buffer.

We've picked a triangle of an arbitrary size and decided to color it green. In addition, to keep our example simple, we will instruct the driver not to transform or light the vertices. Our code provides pre-lit vertices in screen coordinates using a D3DTLVERTEX structure (instead of a standard D3DVERTEX structure):

PART V

```
// get ready to insert vertices
D3DTLVERTEX *pVerts = (D3DTLVERTEX *)m_pSysExBuffer;

    // V 0
    pVerts[0].dvSX = D3DVAL(10.0)
    pVerts[0].dvSY = D3DVAL(10.0)
    pVerts[0].dvSZ = D3DVAL(0.1);
    pVerts[0].dvRHW = D3DVAL(1.0);
    pVerts[0].dcColor = RGBA_MAKE(128, 255, 128, 0);
pVerts[0].dcSpecular = 0;
pVerts[0].dvTU = 0;
pVerts[0].dvTV = 0;
```

In a D3DTLVERTEX structure, dvSX, dvSY and dvSZ specify screen coordinates of the vertex. Note that the fields are in floating point.

dvRHW is the reciprocal of homogeneous w. You can compute this value as 1 divided by the distance from origin to vertex along the *z*-axis.

dcColor sets the color of a vertex. With flat shading, all pixels in a triangle are set to the first vertex color, and the other two colors are ignored. With Gouraud shading, pixel colors are interpolated from the three vertex colors.

```
    // V 1
    pVerts[1].dvSX = D3DVAL(300.0);
    pVerts[1].dvSY = D3DVAL(50.0);
    pVerts[1].dvSZ = D3DVAL(0.1);
    pVerts[1].dvRHW = D3DVAL(1.0);
    pVerts[1].dcColor = RGBA_MAKE(128, 255, 128, 0);
pVerts[1].dcSpecular = 0;
pVerts[1].dvTU = 0;
pVerts[1].dvTV = 0;
```

dcSpecular sets the reflectiveness of the material. You can use this field to add a metallic look to objects. We will experiment with it in Chapter 15.

```
    // V 2
    pVerts[2].dvSX = D3DVAL(150.0);
    pVerts[2].dvSY = D3DVAL(180.0);
    pVerts[2].dvSZ = D3DVAL(0.1);
    pVerts[2].dvRHW = D3DVAL(1.0);
    pVerts[2].dcColor = RGBA_MAKE(128, 255, 128, 0);
pVerts[2].dcSpecular = 0;
pVerts[2].dvTU = 0;
pVerts[2].dvTV = 0;
```

dvTU and dvTV are used to map a vertex into texture coordinates. Here again, we will use these fields in Chapter 15.

Now let's enter our three operations after the vertices. The Direct3D SDK has a helper file (*d3dmacs.h*) with macros for inserting operations into an Execute Buffer. These macros do a decent job, and we have used them in our examples. We recommend that you take some time to look at these Direct3D macros.

```
pInsStart = m_pSysExBuffer + 3*sizeof(D3DTLVERTEX);      ◊ Remember where instructions start.
    pTmp = (PVOID pIns);                                  ◊ Convert to void pointer for d3d macros.
```

The OP_XXX macros below take both a count and a void pointer as parameters. Once used, the macros increment the void pointer to point to the next valid location. Count is used to set the wCount field of the D3DINSTRUCTION as explained earlier. Remember to follow each opcode with the correct number of operands. Also note that macros for more complex opcodes require other parameters in addition.

```
    // make sure vertices are copied to device memory
→OP_PROCESS_VERTICES(1, pTmp);
    →  PROCESSVERTICES_DATA(D3DPROCESSVERTICES_COPY, 0, 3, pTmp);
```

The first parameter passed to OP_PROCESS_VERTICES indicates how the vertices should be processed. Four important options are

D3DPROCESSVERTICES_COPY	Vertices should simply be copied—they have been transformed and lit.
D3DPROCESSVERTICES_TRANSFORM	Vertices should be transformed.
D3DPROCESSVERTICES_TRANSFORMLIGHT	Vertices should be transformed and lit.
D3DPROCESSVERTICES_NOCOLOR	Vertices should not be colored.

ProcessVertices needs to know where to start and the number of vertices to process. The start vertex is specified by its index position.

```
    // render triangle
    OP_TRIANGLE_LIST(1, pTmp);
        ((LPD3DTRIANGLE)pTmp)->v1 = 0;
        ((LPD3DTRIANGLE)pTmp)->v2 = 1;          Vertices of a triangle are specified as a
        ((LPD3DTRIANGLE)pTmp)->v3 = 2;          Word-sized index into the vertex list.
    →  ((LPD3DTRIANGLE)pTmp)->wFlags = 0;
    pTmp = ((char*)pTmp) + sizeof(D3DTRIANGLE);
```

In addition to the vertices, triangle opcodes take a wFlags parameter that can be used to control how edges are drawn in wire-frame, strip, and fan modes. This is an advanced topic and is left as an extra credit exercise.

```
    // exit operation
    OP_EXIT(pTmp);                  ◊ Terminate Execute Buffer list with OPEXIT.
    pInsEnd = (char*)pTmp;          ◊ Remember where instructions end.
```

The following code is the same as what we listed in 14.4.5 to create an Execute Buffer and copy over an instruction from a system memory buffer. We've copied it here for your convenience:

```
// Describe ExecuteBuffer to be created
D3DEXECUTEBUFFERDESC debDesc;
memset(&debDesc, 0, sizeof(debDesc));
debDesc.dwSize = sizeof(debDesc);
debDesc.dwFlags = D3DDEB_BUFSIZE;
debDesc.dwBufferSize = sztEx;

// Create ExecuteBuffer and copy system buffer over
m_p3dFns->CreateExecuteBuffer(&debDesc, &m_pExBufFns, NULL);
m_pExBufFns->Lock(&m_ExDesc);                    // lock buffer
pTmp = m_ExDesc.lpData;                          // get returned ptr
memcpy(pTmp, m_pSysExBuffer, sztEx);             // copy data over
m_pExBufFns->Unlock();                           // unlock buffer
```

```
// describe make-up of recently copied execute buffer
D3DEXECUTEDATA ExecData;
memset(&ExecData, 0, sizeof(D3DEXECUTEDATA));
ExecData.dwSize = sizeof(D3DEXECUTEDATA);
ExecData.dwVertexOffset = 0;
ExecData.dwVertexCount = 3;
ExecData.dwInstructionOffset = pInsStart - m_pSysExBuffer;
ExecData.dwInstructionLength = pInsEnd - pInsStart;
m_pExBufFns->SetExecuteData(&ExecData);
```

Whew! We're done setting up. Now we are ready to run.

14.4.10 Executing the Execute Buffers

3D graphics accelerators are often integrally linked to the system's standard graphics card. Hardware resources can be shared between 2D and 3D drivers. The device drivers may like to "context-swap," if you will, between the 2D and 3D tasks. To enable this context-swapping, Direct3D requires that the *IDirect3DDevice::Execute()* function be bracketed by *IDirect3DDevice::BeginScene()* and *IDirect3DDevice::EndScene()* calls.

Let's execute!

```
// "execute" the execute buffer
m_p3dFns->BeginScene();
m_p3dFns->Execute(pExecCmds, m_p3dViewport, D3DEXECUTE_UNCLIPPED);
m_p3dFns->EndScene();
```

> *IDirect3DDevice::Execute()* takes three parameters: an IDirect3DExecuteBuffer object, an IDirect3DExecuteBuffer object, and a DWORD with modifier flags. With the *Execute* function being defined as a member of the IDirect3DDevice object, you can create multiple Execute Buffers to represent multiple objects and render objects selectively within a scene.
>
> Similarly, since the viewport must be specified with each *Execute()* call, you could use a single Execute Buffer with different viewports to get different views of the object; alternatively, you could also render objects with differing viewing positions within a single scene.
>
> The only modifier flags supported on *Execute()* are D3DEXECUTE_CLIPPED or D3DEXECUTE_UNCLIPPED. If you know that all objects in the Execute Buffer will fit within the 2D screen coordinates, you can improve performance by setting the flags to D3DEXECUTE_UNCLIPPED.

Be careful when executing Execute Buffers: They are hard to debug. If your application crashes while executing a set of instructions, all you know is that there was an error. The best that you can hope for is that the error didn't lock your machine into an unrecoverable state. Save often! Set yourself up for trial-and-error debugging. Start with small Execute Buffers and increase the size and complexity in small steps.

14.4.11   Seeing Results from 3D Devices

At this point, our Execute Buffer should render a triangle—we debugged it, so we know it is error-free. The 3D device will render the triangle into the 2D surface that it was "extended from." To actually see the triangle, we've got to make the 2D surface visible. This step requires standard DirectDraw programming that we learned in Part II. Here's the code to do it:

```
BOOL CSurface3d::UpdateScreen(LPDIRECTDRAWSURFACE2 pPrimary)
{
    // offset dst rect for client area position on primary surface
    long lRight = m_ptZeroZero.x + m_dwWidth;
    long lBottom = m_ptZeroZero.y + m_dwHeight;
    RECT rDst = {m_ptZeroZero.x, m_ptZeroZero.y, lRight, lBottom};
    RECT rSrc = {0, 0, m_dwWidth, m_dwHeight};

    // Blt with WAIT-UNTIL-BLITTER IS READY and no effects
    pPrimary->Blt(&rDst, m_p2dFns, &rSrc, DDBLT_WAIT, NULL);
    return TRUE;
}
```

Oh! Just one more thing, our display is in an RGB palette mode, and we'll need to realize the colors used to render our 3D object. If you remember the code way back in Section 14.4.3—we were forced to create a palette and attach it to the 2D surface before Direct3D would allow us to successfully create a 3D device. We even arranged the palette to permit the 3D device to modify palette colors. But this palette is attached to our Offscreen surface and does not automatically get realized.

Here's the code that realizes the palette by invoking *SetPalette()* on the Primary surface:

```
void CView::OnActivateView(…)
{
    // reset palette on primary surface
    LPDIRECTDRAWSURFACE2 pPrimary = gpAppWide->m_pGrfxCard->m_pSurfFns;
    LPDIRECTDRAWPALETTE  pPalette = gpAppWide->m_pGrfxCard->m_pPalette;
    if (pPrimary && pPalette) pPrimary->SetPalette(pPalette);
}
```

14.5 Demo Time

 Try running the demo for this chapter on the CD. You should see a triangle appear on the screen. Move the mouse around and the triangle will follow the mouse. You have now worked through enough code to have an idea of how to get a triangle rendered using Direct3D's Immediate mode. Congratulations!

WHAT HAVE YOU LEARNED?

We spent some time filling you in on the background of 3D on the PC, primarily to demonstrate that the field is still in its infancy: The evolution has begun, the pace will be furious, the best is yet to come, and Direct3D is the foundation for the evolution. Within this foundation, we saw the two 3D modes that Direct3D offers: Retained mode for high-level abstraction, and Immediate mode for high performance.

If you worked through the code samples, you have

- handled code to get access to Direct3D functionality and 3D devices,
- linked Direct3D devices to DirectDraw surfaces and DirectDraw,
- set up a simple viewport to map a 3D world to 2D screen coordinates, and
- finally, you have created an Execute Buffer to render a triangle with a 3D device to a 2D surface (using the viewport and palette).

And now you're prepared . . . prepared for the next chapter on how to extend our simple triangle with texture mapping.

CHAPTER 15

Embellishing Our Triangle with Backgrounds, Shading, and Textures

WHY READ THIS CHAPTER?

In the previous chapter, we walked you through the bare minimum code needed to render a triangle with Direct3D. Our triangle from that chapter was solid filled, with a flat shaded color. What's more, we didn't redraw the background, and moving the triangle around left "triangle trails." Let's add some bells and whistles to our simple triangle.

In this chapter, you will

- learn how to use Direct3D to repaint the background and get rid of the "triangle trails" (we could have used a 2D background from Part II—but you'll need to understand how to use 3D backgrounds when you add lighting to your 3D scenes);
- play around with shading options and vary the coloring of triangles;
- load and use a texture to render the triangle with texture mapping; and
- understand the benefits of Z-Buffering and learn how to use Z-Buffering while rendering triangles.

15.1 Continuing Our Look into Direct3D

Over the course of this chapter, we will come across the Direct3D objects listed below in Table 15-1. We will describe the objects and the structures they use as we get to them.

Structures in Direct3D often contain unions of two naming conventions. Let's take, for example, the D3DTRIANGLE structure that we used as an operand in the last chapter. (See code on the next page.)

TABLE 15-1 Direct3D Objects Used in This Chapter

Object	Description
IDirect3DMaterial	Coloring options, such as color and texture
IDirect3DTexture	DirectDraw surface containing a texture map image

```
typedef struct _D3DTRIANGLE {
    union {
        WORD v1;
        WORD wV1;
    };
    union {
        WORD v2;
        WORD wV2;
    };
    union {
        WORD v3;
        WORD wV3;
    };
    WORD    wFlags;
} D3DTRIANGLE
```

Notice that each vertex in the structure is a union of two Word fields with different names for both Hungarian and non-Hungarian naming conventions. To simplify our discussions of structures, we will only show the Hungarian version and drop the unions.

The simplified D3DTRIANGLE structure would therefore be:

```
typedef struct _D3DTRIANGLE {
    WORD wV1;
    WORD wV2;
    WORD wV3;
    WORD wFlags;
} D3DTRIANGLE
```

15.2 Repainting the Background Using Direct3D

Let's continue where we left off in the previous chapter: Backgrounds weren't redrawn, and moving our triangle around left "triangle trails." Let's use Direct3D to repaint the background and get rid of the "triangle trails."

Why use Direct3D and why not use a 2D background from Part II? At some later stage you may want to add a spotlight into your 3D model. Moving the spotlight around might cause it to shine past 3D objects and onto some backdrop. Direct3D needs to know about this background to be able to illuminate it correctly. We'll use Direct3D to redraw this background.

Unlike triangles, backgrounds in Direct3D are not individual objects. Instead they are controlled as a method of an IDirect3DViewport object. The *IDirect3DViewport::SetBackground()* method takes a *material handle* as a parameter. So let's learn about materials.

15.2.1   Looking at Direct3D Materials

Even though lighting is computed by the Lighting module, some rendering methods are influenced by lighting factors. Lighting options in the Rendering module are controlled by the D3DOP_STATELIGHT opcode. Light state options that can be changed with this opcode are Fog, Ambient, and Material (defined as D3DLIGHTSTATETYPE).

In the Rendering module, Fog and Ambient controls apply globally to all objects. The material control, on the other hand, controls lighting properties of specific objects. Lighting controls are specified using a D3DMATERIAL structure. Let's look at the simplified version of this structure:

```
typedef struct _D3DMATERIAL {
        DWORD            dwSize;
        D3DCOLORVALUE    dcvDiffuse;
        D3DCOLORVALUE    dcvAmbient ;      Four different color components.
        D3DCOLORVALUE    dcvSpecular;
        D3DCOLORVALUE    dcvEmissive;
        D3DVALUE         dvPower ;      ◊ Specify sharpness of specular reflections.
        D3DTEXTUREHANDLE hTexture;      ◊ Combine a texture with specified coloring.
        DWORD            dwRampSize;    ◊ Shading gradient of colors in Ramp/Mono model.
} D3DMATERIAL, *LPD3DMATERIAL;
```

The D3DMATERIAL structure provides dcvDiffuse, dcvAmbient, dcvEmissive, and dcvSpecular/dvPower to control four different color components of rendered objects. The D3DTLVERTEX structure also has dcColor and dcSpecular fields to control colors of rendered objects. The dual controls are combined during rendering. We will look at controlling colors later in this chapter.

Other fields in the D3DMATERIAL structure are: hTexture, through which we apply texture maps to a rendered object (discussed later in this chapter);

and dwRampSize, used by the Ramp/Mono driver to control fineness of shading in its approximated color model (to be seen in Chapter 16).

The D3DMATERIAL structure uses D3DCOLORVALUE type to define colors as opposed to the D3DCOLOR type used by D3DTLVERTEX structures. RGB values in D3DCOLORVALUE are floating point fields within a structure (normally ranging from 0.0 to 1.0); RGB values in D3DCOLOR are byte-sized values packed into a DWORD (ranging from 0 to 255).

15.2.2 Creating a Direct3D Background

Again, since backgrounds in Direct3D are not individually rendered objects, we cannot set the color of backgrounds with D3DTLVERTEX.dcColor (as we did for triangles). Instead, we set the color of backgrounds with the color fields of a D3DMATERIAL structure. (Given that materials can also contain a texture, we can render an image as a background using textures—but we're getting ahead of ourselves! We will get to texture mapping shortly.)

The field of interest presently is D3DMATERIAL.dcvDiffuse. It is diffuse reflections of light that give objects their basic color; such as a blue ball or a red box. With Direct3D materials we use *dcvDiffuse* to set the basic color of the material.

Let's use Direct3D to implement a CBackground3d class with a single color. We start by first creating and setting up a material and then associating the material with our viewport.

In Direct3D, materials are managed through an *IDirect3DMaterial* interface object. Here is the code to create an IDirect3DMaterial object and to set its properties with a D3DMATERIAL structure and the *IDirect3DMaterial::Set-Material()* method:

```
BOOL CBackground3d::Init(LPDIRECT3D pD3D)
{
    // create a material for the background
    pD3D->CreateMaterial(&m_pMaterialFns, NULL);

    // init material descriptor
    memset(&m_MaterialDesc, 0, sizeof(m_MaterialDesc));
    m_MaterialDesc.dwSize = sizeof(m_MaterialDesc);

    // set diffuse coloring ("pinkish color")
    m_MaterialDesc.dcvDiffuse.dvR = D3DVALUE(0.85);
    m_MaterialDesc.dcvDiffuse.dvG = D3DVALUE(0.15) ;
    m_MaterialDesc.dcvDiffuse.dvB = D3DVALUE(0.50);
    m_MaterialDesc.dcvDiffuse.dvA = D3DVALUE(0.0);
```

IDirect3D::CreateMaterial() returns an IDirect3DMaterial interface object.

Set color of background by setting the dcvDiffuse component of material.

```
    // set material with above description
    m_pMaterialFns->SetMaterial(&m_MaterialDesc);
    return TRUE;
}
```

IDirect3DMaterial::SetMaterial() actually sets material properties.

And now we will set up our background with this material:

```
BOOL CBackground3d::Attach(LPDIRECT3DDEVICE p3dSurfFns, LPDIRECT3DVIEWPORT pView)
{
    // need material handle
    m_pMaterialFns->GetHandle(p3dSurfFns, &m_hMaterial);

    // set background of viewport
    pView->SetBackground(m_hMaterial);
    return TRUE;
}
```

For hardware acceleration devices, source data might have to reside in video memory. Video memory is limited, and Direct3D occasionally uses "handles" for memory allocation. The *GetHandle()* method loads an object onto the specified device and returns a handle to the loaded object.

15.2.3 Bltting a Direct3D Background

We have set up our viewport to have a background. Viewport backgrounds are not automatically drawn. The *IDirect3DViewport::Clear()* method is used to control the drawing of backgrounds. By using *Clear()*, we can control when the background gets redrawn. In addition, *Clear()* uses an array of rectangles to specify how much of the background gets redrawn, helping us reduce the cost of repainting backgrounds with appropriate "dirty rectangle" logic.

Here's our code to Blt backgrounds. We have not implemented any "dirty rectangle" logic. But in keeping with the CBackground class from Part II, we can specify a sub-rectangle to the Blt method to implement moving backgrounds.

```
BOOL CBackground3d::Blt(LPDIRECT3DVIEWPORT pView, POINT *pptDst, RECT *prSrc)
{
    // draw specified sub-rect of background at specified pt
    DWORD dwWidth = prSrc->right - prSrc->left;
    DWORD dwHeight = prSrc->bottom - prSrc->top;

    //create a d3dRect to clear background (needs to be clipped)
    D3DRECT     drDst;
    drDst.x1 = pptDst->x;
    drDst.y1 = pptDst->y;
```

IDirect3DViewport::Clear() expects an array of D3DRECTs.

PART V

```
        drDst.x2 = drDst.x1 + dwWidth ;
        drDst.y2 = drDst.y1 + dwHeight;
        #define nRECTS 1

        // clear viewport to "draw" background
        pView->Clear(nRECTS, &drDst, D3DCLEAR_TARGET);
        return TRUE;
}
```

The first two parameters specify an array of rectangles to control "how much" gets cleared by *IDirect3DViewport::Clear()*. The third parameter to *IDirect3DViewport::Clear()* specifies flags to control "what" gets cleared—options are the rendering target or the Z-Buffer or both.

We are now all set to have the 3DDevice clear our background. As we mentioned in the previous chapter, 3DDevices may batch rendering operations and the actual clear (redraw) is only guaranteed to have been completed on return from the *IDirect3DDevice::EndScene()* call.

 Try running the demo for this chapter on the CD. Voilà! No more triangle trails!

15.3 Controlling Shading Options

In the last chapter, we worked through the bare minimum code needed to render a triangle. We pretty much left the Rendering module in its default state. The Immediate mode Rendering module in Direct3D offers a lot of rendering options. Let's take a look at how to control these options and then play around with some of them.

15.3.1 Looking at Some Render States and Their Default Values

With Direct3D Immediate mode's `D3DOP_STATERENDER` opcode we can control various states of the Rendering module. Some of the straightforward Render states are listed in Table 15-2.

TABLE 15-2 Direct3D Render State Types

D3DRENDERSTATETYPE	Description
D3DRENDERSTATE_FILLMODE	Fill triangle, draw edges, draw vertices
D3DRENDERSTATE_SHADEMODE	Flat, Gouraud, (future: Phong)
D3DRENDERSTATE_TEXTUREHANDLE	Set mode to texture mapping and specify texture
D3DRENDERSTATE_DITHERENABLE	Enable/disable dithered coloring
D3DRENDERSTATE_SPECULARENABLE	Enable/disable specular highlights
D3DRENDERSTATE_ZENABLE	Enable/disable Z-Buffering

Now let's look at the default state of these render states and examine their impact on our simple triangle render example:

_FILLMODE	The default value is D3DFILL_SOLID, which is what we want for our simple triangle.
_SHADEMODE	The default is D3DSHADE_GOURAUD. The implication is that the colors of the vertices would have been interpolated across the intervening space. But if you look at the code, you'll see that we set all the vertices to the same color and got a flat-shaded effect.
_TEXTUREHANDLE	The default is NUL—which is how we turn off texture mapping and render shaded triangles. Note that there is no equivalent SHADEMODE setting to turn off shading.
_DITHERENABLE	The default is FALSE. If we'd opted for differing colors at the triangle vertices, we might have ended up with a banded picture on our low-resolution 8 bpp screen. Dithering improves the picture quality of Gouraud interpolation but reduces rendering performance.
_SPECULARENABLE	The default is TRUE. But we deliberately disabled specular highlights by setting dcSpecular of all vertices to 0.
_ZENABLE	The default is FALSE, which means that triangles will be rendered sequentially. Z-Buffering does not really affect our single triangle example. But if we rendered multiple triangles without Z-Buffering, we would have to order the triangles from back to front.

There are too many states to list here (three Transform states; seven Lighting states; and about seventy-two Render states including thirty-two stipple patterns). We strongly recommend that you look through the Direct3D documentation and familiarize yourself with the various states and their *default values*.

15.3.2 Coloring a Pixel in Direct3D

Direct3D drivers combine vertex components (such as color, specularity, and alpha blending) and render effects (such as fog, dither, anti-alias) to compute the final value of a pixel. Vertex components are specified at each vertex, and values at intervening pixels are computed from vertex components based on a shade mode. *Shade modes* currently permitted are flat and Gouraud. No interpolation is done with flat shading, and the component values at the first vertex of a triangle are applied across the entire triangle. With Gouraud shading, component values from the three triangle vertices are linearly interpolated to get the values at intervening pixels. Phong

PART V

shading, where all lighting is reevaluated for each pixel of a triangle, is not currently supported, but it has been defined for possible future support.

Based on the shade mode, an intervening pixel's color is computed from the RGB color values specified at the triangle's vertices. The meaning of the color values and the result of the interpolation varies with the color model used (RGB or Ramp). We'll examine this factor in more detail shortly.

A shaded pixel is further modified by adding its *specular* component. Specularity is specified as an RGB color value at each vertex. The specularity of intervening pixels is computed using the shade mode in effect. Once again, the approach to computing specularity and its result varies with the color model used. We'll look at this in more detail too.

When alpha blending is enabled the *alpha* component of a color is also interpolated according to the shade mode. However, pixel values are not affected by alpha interpolation if blending is implemented by stippling. Alternatively, pixel values are effected by alpha interpolation, if alpha blending is implemented by texture blending. (Note: When alpha components are not supported in a given mode, the alpha value of colors is implicitly 255. This is the maximum possible alpha; that is, alpha is at full intensity.)

When *texture mapping* is enabled, the source "texel" value also contributes to the pixel's value. As we mentioned earlier, shading cannot be turned off; therefore, the texel value is only a partial contributor. This contribution is "blended" with the value of the color and the specular components. Blending is controlled by D3DRENDERSTATE_TEXTUREMAPBLEND. The default value is D3DTBLEND_MODULATE, where RGB values of the texture are multiplied with the computed RGB values. (Alpha values in the texture supersede computed alpha values.)

One of the values that we can set D3DRENDERSTATE_TEXTUREMAPBLEND to is D3DTBLEND_COPY. In Copy mode, the renderer ignores color computations and simply copies texels to the screen; therefore, textures must have the same pixel format and the same palette as the primary surface. Copy mode effectively turns off shading and typically offers a significant performance boost. This is often a good technique to attain higher performance with pre-lit textured scenes.

15.3.3   Shading with the RGB Color Model

Direct3D offers two different color models: RGB and Ramp (Mono). The two models treat pixel coloring differently, offering varying quality versus performance options. Let's take a quick look at how shading is treated by the RGB color models.

The *RGB model* operates in true color space using 24 bits to combine red, green, and blue light. With Gouraud shading in the RGB color model, each of the red, blue, and green components is individually interpolated and then recombined to produce the shaded pixel. Specular values are similarly computed. The alpha component is independently interpolated to allow the driver to choose the interpolation technique that matches the implemented alpha blending approach.

We can use the 24-bit RGB driver to render to 8-, 16-, 24-, and 32-bit displays. However, banding artifacts are sometimes apparent when the RGB driver has to render a scene down to less than 24 bits. Turning on dithered rendering helps us reduce the apparent effects of banding artifacts.

15.3.4   Shading with the Ramp Color Model

Our code samples from both the previous chapter and the current one use the RGB color model. Programming with the Ramp model requires a little more explanation, and we will look at it in Chapter 16. But while we're on the subject of pixel coloring and shading models, why don't we take a quick look at how pixels are colored by the Ramp model.

The *Ramp model* operates through lookup tables. Colors have no real meaning. In fact, the Ramp driver uses only the blue component of an RGB color specification. When interpolating between two vertices, the Ramp driver interpolates this blue component with no regard to the actual color. The driver then accesses "a lookup table" to interpret the final result.

The Ramp driver builds lookup tables from material definitions. For materials with no specularity, the driver builds a "color ramp" ranging from the ambient color to the maximum diffuse color. For materials with specularity, the driver builds a two-stage color ramp; the first stage ranges from the ambient color to the maximum diffuse color, and the second stage ranges from maximum diffuse color light to the maximum specular color. For materials with textures, the Ramp driver builds a color ramp for each color in the texture.

We can control the size of the ramp with the dwRampSize field in the material definition. In a palletized display mode, each ramp entry equates to a palette entry. Increasing ramp sizes will increase shading resolution, but this method will consume valuable palette space. After all free palette entries are used up, the Direct3D system will find colors that most closely match the intended colors. Huge ramps or a large variety of colors can also cause poor caching and therefore degrade rendering performance.

15.3.5 Changing Default Render States

Let's play around with shading and changing render states. First, we will revisit our simple triangle and change vertex colors to see the effect of Gouraud shading.

```
// modify colors of vertices
D3DTLVERTEX *pVerts = (D3DTLVERTEX *)m_pSysExBuffer;
pVerts[0].dcColor = RGBA_MAKE(128, 255, 128, 0);
pVerts[1].dcColor = RGBA_MAKE(128, 0, 128, 0);
pVerts[2].dcColor = RGBA_MAKE(0, 255, 128, 0);
```

> dcColor sets the color of each vertex. With Gouraud shading, pixel colors are interpolated from the three vertex colors. With flat shading, all pixels in a triangle are set to the first vertex color, and the other two colors are ignored.

Now run the demo for this chapter and check the Gouraud shading option. You should see the colors varying throughout our triangle. Do you see what we mean by banding artifacts?

Next we enable dithering, that is, set D3DRENDERSTATE_DITHERENABLE to TRUE. We change render states by using the D3DOP_STATERENDER operation. A single D3DOP_STATERENDER instruction controls one state variable and is followed by the state to be changed and its new value. (Use D3DOP_STATETRANSFORM to change transform states and D3DOP_STATELIGHT to change lighting states.)

Here's code that adds the D3DOP_STATERENDER instruction into our previous execute buffer:

> Compute size of Execute Buffer needed for triangle and state change.

```
sztEx = sizeof(D3DTLVERTEX) * 3;       // 3 vertices for a triangle
sztEx += sizeof(D3DINSTRUCTION) * 4;   // state, processVerts, tri, exit
sztEx += sizeof(D3DSTATE) * 1;         // 1 texture render state
sztEx += sizeof(D3DPROCESSVERTICES);   // 1 process vertice operand
sztEx += sizeof(D3DTRIANGLE) * 1;      // 1 triangle operand
m_pSysExBuffer = new BYTE [sztEx];     // setup ex buffer in sysmem first
memset(m_pSysExBuffer, 0, sztEx);      // zero out sys mem buffer
```

> Modify operations from last chapter to add render state operation.

```
LPBYTE lpInsStart = m_pSysExBuffer + sizeof(D3DTLVERTEX)*3;
LPVOID lpTmp = (LPVOID)lpInsStart;
OP_STATE_RENDER(1, lpTmp);
    STATE_DATA(D3DRENDERSTATE_DITHERENABLE, TRUE, lpTmp);
OP_PROCESS_VERTICES(1, lpTmp);
    PROCESSVERTICES_DATA(D3DPROCESSVERTICES_COPY, 0, 3, lpTmp);
OP_TRIANGLE_LIST(1, lpTmp);
    ((LPD3DTRIANGLE)lpTmp)->v1 = 0;
    ((LPD3DTRIANGLE)lpTmp)->v2 = 1;
    ((LPD3DTRIANGLE)lpTmp)->v3 = 2;
    ((LPD3DTRIANGLE)lpTmp)->wFlags = 0;
    lpTmp = ((char*)lpTmp) + sizeof(D3DTRIANGLE);
OP_EXIT(lpTmp);
LPBYTE lpInsEnd = (LPBYTE)lpTmp;
```

> Insert D3DOP_STATERENDER using the OP_STATE_RENDER macro from *d3dmacs.h*

Run the demo for this chapter and toggle the Dither option. How's the quality? We'll measure performance in Chapter 16.

Well, now you know how to change render states. Why don't you try some out for yourself?

Try setting D3DRENDERSTATE_SHADEMODE to D3DSHADE_FLAT and see how only the first vertex color is used. Other options we're sure you can handle are D3DRENDERSTATE_ANTIALIAS and D3DRENDERSTATE_FILLMODE. Have at it!

15.4 Texture Mapping with Direct3D

OK! How about we whip up a batch of some texture mapping?

15.4.1 Creating a Texture Map

To start out, texture maps, like IDirect3DDevices, are "converted" Direct-Draw surfaces. So to create an IDirect3DTexture object, we first create an IDirectDrawSurface and then use *QueryInterface* to retrieve an IID_IDirect3DTexture interface.

PART V

Pixel format allowed for texture surfaces varies based on the Direct3D driver being used. With the RGB HEL driver, we can create textures of various bit depths (including 1-, 2-, 4-, 8-, 16-, 24-, and 32-bit textures) and various formats (such as DDPF_RGB, DDPF_PALETTEINDEXED8). Check the Direct3D documentation for a complete list of formats supported for texture maps.

With the Mono/Ramp HEL driver, textures must either be palletized textures or be textures of the same format as those of the primary display surface. Hardware acceleration devices can also support a variety of formats for texture maps. Surfaces must be enumerated to find out the supported formats.

We will work with the Ramp HEL driver in Section 18.3. For now let's continue using the RGB HEL driver with 8 bpp surfaces. Here's code that demonstrates how to create a surface suitable for texture mapping. The code then "converts" the surface to create an IDirect3DTexture object, and finally it loads a bitmap image into the texture.

```
BOOL CTriangleTex::Init(LPDIRECTDRAW2 pDDraw, LPDIRECTDRAWPALETTE pPalette, UINT nRes)
{
```

> Standard GDI code to load bitmap data from resource.

```
CBitmap     cBmp;
cBmp.LoadBitmap(nRes);
BITMAP bm;
cBmp.GetBitmap(&bm);
pData = new BYTE[bm.bmHeight * bm.bmWidth];
cBmp.GetBitmapBits(bm.bmWidth * bm.bmHeight, pData);
```

> Setup to create a structure suitable for texture maps.

```
m_SurfDesc.dwHeight = roundUpPowerOfTwo(bm.bmHeight);
m_SurfDesc.dwWidth =  roundUpPowerOfTwo(bm.bmWidth);
m_SurfDesc.ddpfPixelFormat.dwRGBBitCount = 8;
m_SurfDesc.ddpfPixelFormat.dwFlags = DDPF_PALETTEINDEXED8 | DDPF_RGB;
m_SurfDesc.ddpfPixelFormat.dwSize = sizeof(DDPIXELFORMAT);
m_SurfDesc.ddsCaps.dwCaps = DDSCAPS_TEXTURE;      ← Specify that this surface will be used for texture mapping.
m_SurfDesc.dwFlags = DDSD_WIDTH | DDSD_HEIGHT;
m_SurfDesc.dwFlags |= DDSD_CAPS | DDSD_PIXELFORMAT;
```

Standard DirectDraw code to create a surface and load an image into the surface's data space.

```
LPDIRECTDRAWSURFACE      pDD1Surf;
pDDraw->CreateSurface(&m_SurfDesc, &pDD1Surf, NULL);
pDD1Surf->Lock(NULL, &m_SurfDesc, DDLOCK_WAIT, NULL);
PBYTE pDst = (PBYTE)m_SurfDesc.lpSurface;
PBYTE pSrc = pData;
for (DWORD dwRow = 0; dwRow < m_dwHeight; dwRow++) {
    memset(pDst, 0, m_SurfDesc.lPitch);
    memcpy(pDst, pSrc, m_dwWidth);
    pDst += m_SurfDesc.lPitch;
    pSrc += bm.bmWidth;
}
pDD1Surf->Unlock(NULL);
pDD1Surf->SetPalette(pPalette);

// Convert to TextureObject and get its handle
pDD1Surf->QueryInterface(IID_IDirect3DTexture, &m_pSurfFns);
pDD1Surf->Release();
m_pSurfFns->GetHandle(p3dFns, &m_hTexture);

// free temporary memory, return
delete pData;
return TRUE;
}
```

Our texture map surface has a DDPF_PALETTEINDEXED8 pixel format. Direct3D requires us to set the palette before getting an IDirect3DTexture interface. Our application has been designed to use the same palette on all objects.

QueryInterface on the IDirectDrawSurface gives us an IDirect3DTexture interface to the same object. We now have two separate interfaces to the same object. Both interfaces must be released for the object to be completely freed. In this simple example, we will not use any DirectDraw functionality on the texture surface; therefore, we have used a local variable for temporary access to the IDirectDrawSurface, and we are releasing the interface before we exit. In later examples we will use DirectDraw functionality on the texture surface and then even the IDirectDrawSurface will be part of the CSpriteTex object.

The Height and Width of texture map surfaces used for texture mapping *must* be a power of two. *CreateSurface()* will successfully create a surface with non-"power-of-two" dimensions. But later at *Execute()* time, the rendering engine will crash, and there will be no indication of the nature of the error.

IDirect3DTexture::GetHandle() loads a texture into device memory and returns a handle to the object. To provide more control of device memory use, *IDirect3DTexture* has *Load()* and *Unload()* methods. These methods will work only with surfaces created with the DDSCAPS_ALLOCONLOAD flag set in the ddsCaps.dwCaps field of the surface descriptor.

EXTRA CREDIT

If you're looking for an extra credit opportunity, read the Direct3D documentation on texture compression and write code to compress a texture. Here's a hint: DDSCAPS_ALLOCONLOAD and *Load()*. Go on! You can do it!

PART V

15.4.2   Setting Up Triangle Vertices for Texture Mapping

So far we've created and loaded a texture. Now using code that we've mostly seen in the previous chapter, let's set up an Execute Buffer to render a texture-mapped triangle:

```
BOOL CTriangleTex::Init(LPDIRECTDRAW2 pDDraw, LPDIRECT3DDEVICE p3dFns, UINT nResID)
{
```

> Compute size of Execute Buffer needed to render simple texture-mapped triangle.

```
sztEx = sizeof(D3DTLVERTEX) * 3;      // 3 vertices for a triangle
sztEx += sizeof(D3DINSTRUCTION) * 4;  // state, processVerts, tri, exit
sztEx += sizeof(D3DSTATE) * 1;        // 1 texture render state
sztEx += sizeof(D3DPROCESSVERTICES);  // 1 process vertice operand
sztEx += sizeof(D3DTRIANGLE) * 1;     // 1 triangle operand
m_pSysExBuffer = new BYTE [sztEx];    // setup ex buffer in sysmem first
memset(m_pSysExBuffer, 0, sztEx);     // zero out sys mem buffer
```

> Set up vertex info for texture-mapped triangle.

```
D3DTLVERTEX *pVerts = (D3DTLVERTEX *)m_pSysExBuffer;
// V 0
pVerts[0].dvSX = D3DVAL(0.0);
pVerts[0].dvSY = D3DVAL(0.0);
pVerts[0].dvSZ = D3DVAL(0.1);
pVerts[0].dvRHW = D3DVAL(1.0);
pVerts[0].dcColor = RGBA_MAKE(255, 255, 255, 255) ;
pVerts[0].dvTU = D3DVAL(0.0);
pVerts[0].dvTV = D3DVAL(0.0);
// V 1
pVerts[1].dvSX = pVerts[0].sx + D3DVAL(300.0);
pVerts[1].dvSY = pVerts[0].sy + D3DVAL(100.0);
pVerts[1].dvSZ = D3DVAL(0.1);
pVerts[1].dvRHW = D3DVAL(1.0);
pVerts[1].dcColor = RGBA_MAKE(255, 255, 255, 255);
pVerts[1].dvTU = D3DVAL(1.0);
pVerts[1].dvTV = D3DVAL(1.0);
// V 2
pVerts[2].dvSXsx = pVerts[0].sx + D3DVAL(150.0);
pVerts[2].dvSYsy = pVerts[0].sy + D3DVAL(180.0);
pVerts[2].dvSZsz = D3DVAL(0.1);
pVerts[2].dvRHrhw = D3DVAL(1.0);
pVerts[2].dcColor = RGBA_MAKE(255, 255, 255, 255);
pVerts[2].dvTU = D3DVAL(0.0);
pVerts[2].dvTV = D3DVAL(1.0);
```

> For now, set color value to white. We will explain this later in the chapter.

> Specify in floating point values how each triangle vertex maps to the texture. Texture itself ranges from 0.0 (top, left) to 1.0 (right, bottom).

The difference in setting up the vertices is the setting of texture coordinates in the dvTU and dvTV fields of the D3DTLVERTEX structure. For each vertex, we need to specify how it maps to the texture. All textures, no matter their size, are defined to range from 0.0 to 1.0. Values for dvTU and dvTV need not lie within the "0.0 to 1.0" range. We can specify any legal floating point value, either negative or positive.

How the rendering engine reacts to texture addresses outside the "0.0 to 1.0" range depends on the D3DRENDERSTATE_TEXTUREADDRESS state variable. Valid values are D3DTADDRESS_WRAP, D3DTADDRESS_MIRROR, and D3DTADDRESS_CLAMP. The default state is D3DTADDRESS_WRAP. Refer to the Direct3D documentation for a deeper understanding of each state.

15.4.3 Setting Up Render Operations for Texture Mapping

Now we will set up the operations to render our texture-mapped triangle. The code for this procedure again is pretty much the same as that from the previous chapter. The significant difference is that we've now got to tell the rendering engine to use texture mapping while rendering, and we need to tell it which texture to use.

Looking through the various render states, we come across the D3DRENDERSTATE_TEXTUREHANDLE state type. The TEXTUREHANDLE state type with a D3DOP_STATERENDER opcode tells the rendering engine to use texture mapping, and the operand specifies which texture to use:

Modify operations from the last chapter to render texture-mapped triangle.

```
LPBYTE lpInsStart = m_pSysExBuffer + sizeof(D3DTLVERTEX)*3;
LPVOID lpTmp = (LPVOID)lpInsStart;
OP_STATE_RENDER(1, lpTmp);
    STATE_DATA(D3DRENDERSTATE_TEXTUREHANDLE, m_hTexture, lpTmp);
OP_PROCESS_VERTICES(1, lpTmp);
    PROCESSVERTICES_DATA(D3DPROCESSVERTICES_COPY, 0, 3, lpTmp);
OP_TRIANGLE_LIST(1, lpTmp);
    ((LPD3DTRIANGLE)lpTmp)->v1 = 0;
    ((LPD3DTRIANGLE)lpTmp)->v2 = 1;
    ((LPD3DTRIANGLE)lpTmp)->v3 = 2;
    ((LPD3DTRIANGLE)lpTmp)->wFlags = 0;
    lpTmp = ((char*)lpTmp) + sizeof(D3DTRIANGLE);
op_exit(lpTmp);
lpbyte lpInsEnd = (LPBYTE)lpTmp;
```

Tell the rendering engine to render all of the following triangles using texture mapping with the texture specified in the parameter. Once again, our code sets up Execute Buffer operations with the macros in *d3dmacs.h*.

Finally let's create our Execute Buffer, copy our instruction stream into device data space, and then describe our buffer to the 3D device. This code is identical to code we've seen before:

Same code as in the last chapter to set up an Execute Buffer on a 3D device.

```
m_ExDesc.dwFlags = D3DDEB_BUFSIZE;
m_ExDesc.dwBufferSize = m_sztEx;
p3dFns->CreateExecuteBuffer(&m_ExDesc, &m_pExBufFns, NULL);

// copy triangle into execute buffer space
m_pExBufFns->Lock(&m_ExDesc);
lpTmp = (LPBYTE)m_ExDesc.lpData;
memcpy(lpTmp, m_pSysExBuffer, lpInsEnd-m_pSysExBuffer);
m_pExBufFns->Unlock();

// describe execute buffer to 3ddevice
m_ExData.dwVertexOffset = 0;
m_ExData.dwVertexCount = 3;
m_ExData.dwInstructionOffset = lpInsStart - m_pSysExBuffer;
m_ExData.dwInstructionLength = lpInsEnd - lpInsStart;
m_pExBufFns->SetExecuteData(&m_ExData);

return TRUE;
}
```

Run the demo for this chapter and check the Texture Mapping option. You should see a texture-mapped triangle chasing the mouse around.

15.4.4   Handling "Lit" Texture Maps

We'd like to get back to something that we brought up earlier but left for later. Remember when we were setting up vertices for texture mapping (in 15.4.2), we set the dcColor field of all the vertices to WHITE and said that we would explain it later.

We mentioned earlier that

- the texel contribution is "blended" with the computed pixel value;
- blending is controlled by D3DRENDERSTATE_TEXTUREMAPBLEND; and
- the default blending state is D3DTBLEND_MODULATE.

D3DTBLEND_MODULATE *multiplies* source texels by computed values. Colors within the Rendering module are treated as values from 0 to 1. Multiplying values in these ranges will produce smaller results (unless either value is 1). Therefore modulation reduces the brightness of color components unless one of the source components is 1. The simplest way to ensure that the colors of a texture do not change during texture mapping is to set dcColor to WHITE (255, 255, 255) and to set dcSpecular to BLACK (0, 0, 0).

An alternate way to ensure that the colors of a texture do not change during texture mapping is to change the RENDERSTATE_TEXTUREMAPBLEND render state to D3DTBLEND_COPY. In Copy mode, the renderer ignores color computations and simply copies texels to the screen. But the textures must have the same pixel format as the Primary surface, and they also must also use the same palette. Our simple triangle application has been set up this way.

You should find changing render states to be pretty trivial by now. Here's the code that we insert into our Execute Buffer to use Copy mode:

```
// Don't forget to increase the size of execute buffer needed
// change render state to use Copy mode
OP_STATE_RENDER(1, lpTmp);
    STATE_DATA(D3DRENDERSTATE_TEXTUREMAPBLEND, D3DTBLEND_COPY, lpTmp);
```

Run the demo for this chapter and turn on the Copy mode option. Toggling Gouraud shading should have no effect. Turn Copy mode off then toggle Gouraud shading. Notice how the texture map colors have become duller?

One last point before we move on from texture mapping. Since a texture is also a DirectDraw surface, we can render into the texture using DirectDraw surface functions, such as *Lock()* and *Unlock()*, and then texture map this data onto a 3D object.

15.5 Z-Buffering with Direct3D

15.5.1 Why Bother with Z-Buffering?

Take a look at the two triangles in Figure 15-1. Let's assume we have an Execute Buffer that has triangle 1 inserted first and triangle 2 inserted second. Without Z-Buffering, the triangles are rendered in the order that they are encountered. Triangle 2 will be drawn after triangle 1, and therefore it will be drawn on top of triangle 1 as shown in the figure.

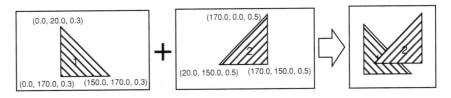

FIGURE 15-1 Triangles rendered from back to front regardless of Z-values.

PART V

Now let's take a look at the Z-values of the triangles. All the Z-values in triangle 1 are 0.3, and all the Z-values in triangle 2 are 0.5. But viewport coordinates are defined to go from 0.0 in front to 1.0 in the back, so by this definition triangle 1 should have been drawn in front of triangle 2. Instead, the renderer ignored the Z-values to render the triangles. (Without Z-Buffering, Z-values are only used to correct perspective while texture mapping.)

Without Z-Buffering, it is our responsibility to sort the triangles and insert them in the correct order. The compute expense to re-sort triangles may be very expensive for some application scenarios. (For instance, for 3D models with many overlapping objects and complete freedom of movement. In these scenarios it may be preferable to use Z-Buffering, so that the triangles will be rendered according to their Z-values and regardless of the sort order.)

Let's take a look at a second example as shown in Figure 15-2.

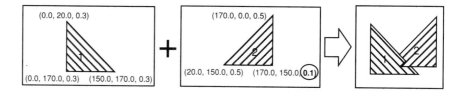

FIGURE 15-2 Intersecting triangles rendered with Z-Buffering.

The ellipse highlights the Z-value of the second vertex in triangle 2. We've changed this Z-value from the previous value of 0.5 to a new value of 0.1. This vertex is now *in front* of the vertices of triangle 1. As a result, triangle 2 now partially overlaps triangle 1.

Once again, without Z-Buffering the renderer ignores Z-values, and it will render the triangles without any overlap. *Without Z-Buffering, it is our responsibility to split up intersecting triangles.* With complex models, we may want to opt for Z-Buffering, because the renderer will test the Z-value of each pixel that it draws, and intersecting triangles will be correctly rendered.

15.5.2 Setting Up for Z-Buffering

Let's look at the code needed to set up and use Z-Buffering. Z-Buffers in Direct3D are merely another form of DirectDraw surfaces. Unlike with 3D devices and texture maps, there is no functionality applicable directly to Z-Buffers, so there is no need to create a new interface object.

So creating a Z-Buffer is as simple as creating a DirectDraw surface. The only point worth mentioning is that we don't get to choose the Z-Buffer pixel depth—this choice is made by the 3D driver. Well, how do we find out about the 3D device's choice? There are two ways: use *IDirect3DDevice::GetCaps()* or remember it from section 14.4.2, when we enumerated device drivers.

In the code for this chapter, we've inserted our Z-Buffer analysis into our device enumeration callback. Here's the snippet of code that was inserted:

Examine the chosen LPD3DDEVICEDESC structure for Z-Buffering support.

```
pGrfx->m_bCanZbuf = FALSE;
if (pChoice->dwDeviceZBufferBitDepth != 0) {
    pGrfx->m_bCanZbuf = TRUE;
    // bit depth is in DDBD format
    DWORD ddbd = pChoice->dwDeviceZBufferBitDepth;
    // convert to bpp format
    pGrfx->m_dwZBufferBPP = cvtToBPP(ddbd);
}
```

Test for Z-Buffering support by looking at the dwDeviceZBufferBitDepth field.

Even though dwDeviceZBufferBitDepth is specified using the packed DDBD format, the documentation for D3DDEVICEDESC states that this field can only be *one of* these formats: DDBD_8, DDBD_16, DDBD_24, or DDBD_32. Packed DDBD format are #defines that need to be converted to get pixel depth.

Now that we know that our device can Z-Buffer (and we know the depth of its Z-Buffer), we can go on to create a Z-Buffer using straightforward DirectDraw code:

```
BOOL CSurface3d::InitZbuffer(LPDIRECTDRAW2 pDDraw, DWORD dwZBufferBPP)
{
```

Setup descriptor for Z-Buffer (a special form of DirectDraw surface).

```
//use same width and height as 3d surface; use specified bpp
m_ZSurfDesc.dwHeight = m_dwHeight;
m_ZSurfDesc.dwWidth = m_dwWidth;
m_ZSurfDesc.dwZBufferBitDepth = dwZBufferBPP;
// set caps flag
m_ZSurfDesc.ddsCaps.dwCaps = DDSCAPS_ZBUFFER;
DWORD dwMem = (m_bIsVidMem) ? DDSCAPS_VIDEOMEMORY : DDSCAPS_SYSTEMMEMORY;
m_ZSurfDesc.ddsCaps.dwCaps |= dwMem;
// set which fields in structure were valid
m_ZSurfDesc.dwFlags = DDSD_WIDTH | DDSD_HEIGHT;
m_ZSurfDesc.dwFlags |= DDSD_CAPS | DDSD_ZBUFFERBITDEPTH;
```

Request Z-Buffer.

Put Z-Buffer in same memory as 3D surface.

```
        // Create Z-buffer using DirectDraw create surface
        pDDraw->CreateSurface(&m_ZSurfDesc, &m_pZSurfFns, NULL);
        return TRUE;
}
```

Create the Z-Buffer!

We've created our Z-Buffer, but as of yet it's floating around freely, single and unattached. We've got to marry it to our 3D surface. It so happens that we cannot attach the Z-Buffer directly to the 3D surface. Instead we've got to use a matchmaker—the 2D surface that was "converted" to the 3D surface.

```
BOOL CSurface3d::AttachZbuffer(LPDIRECTDRAWSURFACE p2dFns)
{
    // Attach the Z-buffer to the 2dSurface so D3D will find it
    p2dFns->AddAttachedSurface(m_pZSurfFns);
    // set internal state and return
    m_bIsZEnabled = TRUE;
    return TRUE;
}
```

One more task: we've got to tell the renderer to use Z-Buffering. As usual, we communicate with the renderer through an Execute Buffer. Here are the state variables that we've got to toggle to let the renderer know about Z-Buffering:

Turn on Z-Buffering by setting the D3DRENDERSTATE_ZENABLE to TRUE.

```
    // Don't forget to increase the size of execute buffer needed
    OP_STATE_RENDER(1, lpTmp);
        STATE_DATA(D3DRENDERSTATE_ZENABLE, m_bIsZEnabled, lpBuffer);
        STATE_DATA(D3DRENDERSTATE_ZWRITEENABLE, m_bIsZEnabled, lpBuffer);
        STATE_DATA(D3DRENDERSTATE_ZFUNC, D3DCMP_LESSEQUAL, lpBuffer);
```

Although their default values are adequate for our purposes, you may also want to look at the states of the additional two Z-Buffering control states:

D3DRENDERSTATE_ZWRITEENABLE	Default is TRUE. If set to FALSE, the renderer will continue to examine the Z-Buffer while rendering (as specified by _ZENABLE); but it will not update the Z-Buffer with new z-values.
D3DRENDERSTATE_ZFUNC	Default is D3DCMP_LESSEQUAL. With the z-comparison function, you can change the way the renderer interprets z-distance. For instance, you can reverse z-ordering by setting the state to D3DCMP_GREATEREQUAL.

Refer to Direct3D documentation for more information.

Run the demo for this chapter; check both the Z-Buffer option and the intersecting triangles option. Play around with toggling Z-Buffering on and off and see how the intersecting portion of the triangle 2 is and isn't rendered. You should also notice that the render order of the triangles changes as you switch between Z-Buffered and non-Z-Buffered rendering.

It's time to conclude this chapter. We proclaim you to be proficient with Direct3D—that is, as long as you actually worked with the code!

WHAT HAVE YOU LEARNED?

Wow! Our triangle has come a long way, baby! We started the chapter with a plain old triangle with a single color that left triangle trails. Here's what we have accomplished since then:

- The first thing we covered was removing those annoying triangle trails through Direct3D backgrounds. Along the way we learned about and worked with Direct3D materials.
- Next we looked at how Direct3D dealt with coloring and shading triangles. Then we played around with vertex colors to see how Gouraud shading looked.
- Gouraud shading produced banding artifacts, so we learned about render states and improved the quality of Gouraud shading by changing a render state to turn on dithering.
- With ever increasing confidence in navigating through Direct3D, we tackled texture mapping—"converting" a DirectDraw surface to a texture object, and rendering triangles with our texture map.
- Finally, we tried our hand at some true 3D rendering—turning on Z-Buffering and even rendering intersecting triangles correctly.

We have come a long way from where we started. We're sure you're pretty handy with Direct3D programming by now. Let's turn our attention to performance in the next chapter.

CHAPTER 16

Understanding and Enhancing Direct3D Performance

WHY READ THIS CHAPTER?

Previous chapters showed rendering a simple triangle with Direct3D, adding various shading options, and then adding texture mapping to the triangle. But we were mainly concerned with getting the basic application running, so we didn't really pay much attention to how fast it ran. In this chapter we'll take our measuring microscope out and measure the performance of our previous examples. Then we'll look at ways to accelerate these samples.

By working through this chapter you will

- get a feel for the performance of various rendering options with the RGB model driver,
- learn how to use the Ramp model driver to get better performance, and
- measure the results of rendering using the Ramp model driver.

16.1 How Fast Does Our Triangle Run?

We've been drawing triangles with various options through Direct3D. So far we've focused on getting things to work and on exploring possibilities. But for serious multimedia application development, we've also got to focus on performance.

Direct3D's Immediate mode API is a very low level API. But it was designed this way to offer high performance. In which case, why measure performance? Shouldn't the fact that we're using Immediate mode be sufficient? Sadly, no. Not all performance paths are equal (some are more equal than others).

PART V

■ 247 ■

Let's measure the performance of our triangle on Direct3D and then look at performance enhancement opportunities. But first a word about our measurements:

- All measurements were taken on our base platform described in Section 2.5. Results will definitely vary on different platforms or even on the same platform with different display configurations.

- We have included the timing application and its source code on the CD. Use it to profile your platform and see how it performs.

- We have separated the timing source code from the source for the basic demos, to simplify reading the base code and to give you a performance tool to measure various configurations.

16.1.1 Stages of Rendering Our Triangle

Let's start by looking at what it takes to render a scene. We have broken the scene rendering into the following stages:

- *Init.* This stage occurs once while the entire application is being initialized. We put all our one-time initialization activities into this stage. This stage is typically not time critical, and we do not measure this stage.

- *Prepare Scene.* This stage occurs at the start of every scene render. We invoke *IDirect3DDevice::BeginScene()* in this stage. If we used Z-Buffers, we would typically clear them in this stage (prior to objects being rendered).

- *Draw background.* If a background was created, then we would invoke the *Background::Blt()* function in this stage, which translates to *IDirect3DViewport::Clear(...target...)* in Direct3D. We are not measuring a background for our base case triangle.

- *Edit Execute Buffer.* Typically, objects in a 3D scene are moving around. (If we were only going to draw a stationary object, then we might as well Blt a bitmap.) This is the stage when we edit the Execute Buffer. We then need to transfer the edited data to the Direct3D driver, using the hopefully familiar Lock, Copy, and Unlock sequence.

- *Set Execute Buffer.* In the code from the previous chapters, we saw that after transferring Execute Buffer data, we described the makeup of the new Execute Buffer to the Direct3D device.

- *Execute.* Here's where we get the device to execute our Execute Buffer (or Buffers, if we had many).

- *End Scene.* This stage occurs at the end of every stage render. First we invoke *IDirect3DDevice::EndScene()*. Next we set our palette and refresh the window with the newly rendered scene.

16.1.2 Measuring the Rendering Stages of Our Triangle

Table 16-1 measures the time taken in the various rendering stages to render our triangle. We are using the Direct3D RGB color model driver with no hardware acceleration. (The default Rendering state is Gouraud shaded, solid fills with specularity enabled, and dithering disabled.)

TABLE 16-1 Timing Render Stages for Our Base Triangle

	Time (milliseconds)	
Stage	**625 × 128**	**16 × 5000**
Prepare scene	0.0	0.0
Edit Execute Buffer	10.9	0.4
Set Execute Buffer	3.3	0.1
Execute	75.1	60.6
End scene	7.5	7.5
TOTAL	96.6	68.5

We measured two scenes: The first scene had 625 small triangles. For this initial test, we invoked Blt for every triangle. All the triangles were of the same shape—with reference vertices of (0,0), (16, 16), and (0,16)—for a size of 128 pixels per triangle and 80,000 pixels per scene. We chose this configuration based on experience as representative of medium complexity 3D applications.

The second scene had 16 large triangles. Again, we used triangles of the same shape and invoked Blt for each one. Reference vertices were (0,0), (100, 100), and (0,100)—for triangles of 5,000 pixels each and 80,000 pixels per scene. We measured this configuration to demonstrate the impact that polygon size can have on render performance.

We varied the positions of the triangles in each scene to study the effect of alignment. The tabulated values are the averaged results.

Following are some observations on the results:

■ Large triangles rendered significantly faster than small triangles. Even though the total pixels in both scenes were the same, the render time for the second scene was much faster than the first scene. This indicates that you would increase performance by using, wherever possible, larger triangles instead of a bunch of smaller triangles.

- The cost of invoking *BeginScene()* and *EndScene()* in this example is imperceptible.

- Editing the Execute Buffer to reposition vertices consumes a significant amount of time in scene 1. (The cost is not noticeable in scene 2, since there aren't too many triangles in that scene.)

16.1.3 Trimming Some Fat from the Rendering Stages

Let's make changes to our Render stages to see if there's some easy performance pickin's to be had:

- *Set Execute Buffer (1).* If our only changes to an Execute Buffer are data related, and we do not change the makeup of the Execute Buffer, then do we really need to "redescribe" the Execute Buffer to the Direct3D device? The Direct3D documentation does not specify what's correct behavior. We ran tests and found that we *do not* need to "redescribe" if only the data changes. (In fact, as long as the four fields of the D3DEXECUTEDATA structure do not change, then we can even change instruction opcodes and operands without "re-describing" the Execute Buffer.)*

- *Set Execute Buffer (2).* If we only wanted to change a couple of vertices, do we really have to recopy the entire buffer to the Direct3D device? In other words, can we see our previous data with the pointer returned by *Lock()*? We ran tests and found that *yes, indeed,* we do get access to our previous data, and we can edit in place if we wish. *

- *End Scene.* Our initial code reset the palette on every scene render. Again, we ran some tests and found that the Direct3D RGB color model driver does not change the palette from frame to frame. We rewrote our code to set up the palette only when our application gets focus and removed this work from the End Scene stage.*

- *Execute.* Our initial code invoked *Blt()* on each triangle. We were executing an Execute Buffer with only one triangle. We rewrote this code to execute all our triangles (625 or 16) via single Execute Buffers (using only one buffer per list of triangles).*

* You may wish to reverify the results and rerun these tests with any hardware accelerator drivers you choose to use.

Table 16-2 lists new measurements based on the edited code:

TABLE 16-2 Trimming Some Fat from the Render Stages

Stage	Original (milliseconds)		Long Buffer (milliseconds)		Edit in Place (milliseconds)	
	625 × 128	16 × 5000	625 × 128	16 × 5000	625 × 128	16 × 5000
Prepare scene	0.0	0.0	0.0	0.0	0.0	0.0
Edit Execute Buffer	10.9	0.4	1.1*	0.0*	10.4	0.3
Set Execute Buffer	3.3	0.1	0.0	0.0	0.0	0.0
Execute	75.1	60.6	72.4	60.7	75.4	60.7
End scene	7.5	7.5	7.1	7.1	7.1	7.1
TOTAL	96.7	68.6	*	*	92.9	68.1

*We used pre-initialized Execute Buffers, while testing Long Execute Buffers, and we have listed only the time taken to copy the buffers to the 3D device space. For a fair apples-to-apples comparison, you would need to add the time taken to edit the vertex positions in the pre-initialized Execute Buffers.

Following are some conclusions based on our code rearrangement:

- Not "redescribing" the Execute Buffer and using Long Execute Buffers saved 16 milliseconds in scene 1. While the savings are low relative to the Execute cost, we will find that the savings are significant when we find faster Execute methods (as we will see later in this chapter).

- None of the changes produced any significant tangible benefit for scene 2, which indicates that overhead in Direct3D has been minimized, and it would only become significant over a large number of invocations.

- Not setting the palette only saved 0.3 milliseconds. This is a useful measurement to remember, since you can retain the code to constantly change palettes in case a Direct3D driver does change palettes frequently.

16.2 Measuring Shading Options

Over the course of the previous two chapters, we have rendered our triangle with a variety of options, including Gouraud shading, flat shading, dithering, texture mapping, and Z-Buffering. Let's look at how these options affect our render performance.

16.2.1 Measuring the Performance of Shading Options in Our Triangle

Table 16-3 measures the time taken to draw triangles with various shading options. We are using the Direct3D RGB color model driver with no hardware acceleration. We are only measuring one of the two scenes from the previous tests—the scene with sixteen triangles of 5,000 pixels each. Once again, we drew the triangles at various alignments and have tabulated averaged results. The timings listed are only those taken to render the sprites. Redrawing backgrounds and refreshing the screen are additional costs.

TABLE 16-3 Timing Sixteen Triangles with the Direct3D RGB Color Model Driver

Rendering Option	Time	Megapixels/Second
Gouraud	55.3 milliseconds	1.45
Gouraud (with constant colors)	55.3 milliseconds	1.45
Flat shaded	55.3 milliseconds	1.45
Gouraud and dither	55.3 milliseconds	1.45

Two glaring observations leap out at us:

■ Flat shading *does not perform better* than Gouraud shading. You would expect that not computing shaded colors would result in better performance. But it doesn't.

■ Enabling dithering *does not reduce* rendering performance. This is a rare occasion—you can add an improvement at no performance cost.

Since varying shading options didn't make any difference whatsoever to rendering performance, we decided to see whether this constant performance persisted after we added some specular highlights.

Table 16-4 compares the performance of the shading options with and without specular highlights. We found that adding specular highlights cost us a 9 percent performance penalty.

TABLE 16-4 Measuring the Impact of Adding Specular Highlights

Rendering Option	Without Specular Highlights	With Specular Highlights
Gouraud	55.3 milliseconds	60.3 milliseconds
Gouraud (with constant colors)	55.3 milliseconds	60.3 milliseconds
Flat shaded	55.3 milliseconds	60.2 milliseconds
Gouraud and dither	55.3 milliseconds	60.0 milliseconds

Note that all these measurements were taken with the RGB color model driver rendering to an 8 bpp palletized target surface. Since shading options and specular highlighting modify individual RGB components, you can bet that performance on 16-, 24-, and 32-bpp targets will be very different.

EXTRA CREDIT

Our performance application for this chapter will only work with 8 bpp palletized targets. To motivate you to work with the source code, we've left supporting other target modes as an extra credit exercise. Go on! It's fairly simple.

16.2.2 Measuring the Performance of Texture-Mapping in Our Triangle

Next we move on to measuring texture-mapped triangles. Remember from our discussion of rendering options in Section 15.3.3 that

- texture mapping can be disabled, but shading cannot;
- the default texture mapping mode combines texels with shading values; and
- texture mapping needs to be set to Copy mode to turn shading off.

Table 16-5 tabulates measurements of rendering our triangles with a texture map of 64×32 pixels. For good measure, we've included the impact of adding specular highlights to our texture-mapped triangles.

TABLE 16-5 Texture-Mapped Triangle with and without Specular Highlights

Rendering Option	Without Specular Highlights		With Specular Highlights	
	(milliseconds)	(megapixels/ second)	(milliseconds)	(megapixels/ second)
Texture and Gouraud	62.5	1.28	68.2	1.18
Texture and Flat Shaded	62.5	1.28	67.9	1.18
Texture and Gouraud and Dither	62.7	1.28	67.9	1.18
Copy Mode	14.4	5.56	14.4	5.56

PART V

Wow! CopyMode gives us more than *four times better performance* over Modulated mode texture mapping (with shading options turned on). An obvious conclusion is that making an effort to use pre-lit textures will definitely reap significant performance benefits. You could even use texture mapping with flat-shaded textures to get high-performance flat shading.

16.2.3 Adding a Z-Buffer to the Recipe

There was one other option that we looked at in the previous chapter: Z-Buffering. Without Z-Buffers, your application must send triangles to the renderer sorted in back-to-front order, and your application must also subdivide intersecting triangles.

With Z-Buffers, the driver correctly renders both unsorted and intersecting triangles, saving your application the cost of sorting and subdividing. So how much does Z-Buffered rendering cost?

TABLE 16-6 Rendering Cost of Z-Buffering (Direct3D RGB Driver)

Rendering Option	Without Z-Buffer	With Z-Buffer
Gouraud	55.3 milliseconds	60.8 milliseconds
Gouraud and Specular	60.3 milliseconds	66.6 milliseconds
Texture Map and Gouraud	62.5 milliseconds	69.5 milliseconds
Texture Map CopyMode	14.4 milliseconds	30.1 milliseconds

Table 16-6 compares the cost of rendering our triangle with and without Z-Buffering. And the verdicts are in:

■ Rendering with Z-Buffering *is* more expensive than rendering without. No surprises here, since Z-Buffering increases memory traffic.

■ The cost of Z-Buffering is only in the 10 percent range for the expensive rendering options, suggesting that Z-Buffering is a viable option in cases where performance isn't supercritical.

■ Rendering with Z-Buffering *severely impacts* CopyMode. This is unfortunate, since CopyMode is our fastest mode. Therefore, for high-performance 3D, you really need to measure the cost of sorting and segmenting triangles and compare this cost against the cost of Z-Buffering.

Our Timing Application gives you an opportunity to measure how much Z-Buffering will cost you. We hope that measurements (or measurement tools) like these will help you decide whether the performance of Z-Buffering is adequate or whether it's worth investing the effort on the non-Z-Buffered path.

In addition to rendering options, other factors also affect rendering performance. Both the size and the shape of a triangle can have effects on performance. Similarly, with texture-mapped rendering, the size and shape of textures also have an impact on rendering performance.

16.2.4 Getting Perspective: Comparing 3D (RGB Mode) to 2D

OK, we've bandied around numbers from 14 milliseconds to 70 milliseconds. But we've been comparing various options within the 3D realm. How do we know whether these numbers are acceptable? What if we compare our 3D rendering throughput against the 2D throughput we have seen when we worked with sprites in Part II?

Of course, 3D rendering will probably be slower. But how much slower—let's get some perspective. Table 16-7 compares Sprite render times from Part II to our measurements from this chapter. Note that the sprites in Part II were also about 5,000 pixels, and each was rendered sixteen times. In terms of speed, the comparison puts our best 3D render mode on an even par with spriting through GDI. Talk about backwards! We need to get better.

TABLE 16-7 Comparing 3D Throughput to 2D Sprite Throughput

Rendering Path	Time	Megapixels/Second
GDI	14.2 milliseconds	5.96[*]
CSpriteCCode	11.9 milliseconds	7.12[*]
CSpriteP5	~1.5 milliseconds	56.5[*]
CSpriteGrfx	~1.5 milliseconds	56.5[*]
CTriangle3D (Gouraud)	55.3 milliseconds[†]	1.45
CTriangleTex(Copy mode)	14.4 milliseconds[†]	5.56

[*] Some pixels are transparent, and throughput is somewhat less than what these figures indicate.
[†] Measurements will take longer when CTriangleTex is rendered directly to a triple-buffered video memory surface.

Why is it so important to get better performance? Let's assume

■ that we'd like a real-time feel with a frame rate of around 30 fps. At this frame rate we get 33 milliseconds per frame to work with; typically about half this time is consumed on peripheral activities such as responding to the user and carrying out geometry and lighting computations and audio and 2D graphics activities;

- a best-case scenario where the graphics device has enough memory to support triple buffering, and screen refreshes are occurring at no cost; and

- that we'd like our application to occupy a screen resolution of about 640 × 480; a 640 × 480 background gets drawn to the triple-buffered video surface at a cost of 5 milliseconds.

We're left with about 12 milliseconds for 3D rendering. Our best performance mode will render in that time about 65,000 pixels to a system memory buffer. Even if no pixel was rendered more than once, we would be painting an area of about 320 × 200 with 3D pixels—less than one quarter of the screen area. With more realistic assumptions that pixels are touched about 1.5 times on average, our 3D coverage reduces to about 240 × 180—a postage-stamp-sized field of action.

Better performance means covering more of the screen area with 3D pixels or alternately it means being able to run richer multimedia applications with, for example, full-motion video being used as texture map sources. So let's look at Direct3D's high-performance option—the Ramp (Mono) color model driver—to see if we can get better 3D rendering performance on a PC.

16.3 Improving Performance Using the Ramp Driver

We've mentioned before that the DirectX SDK ships with two implementations: an RGB color model driver and a Ramp (Mono) color model driver. The RGB driver offers truer color quality but runs more slowly. The Ramp (Mono) driver makes color approximations that degrade overall quality, but it offers higher performance. Let's start using the Ramp color model driver.

16.3.1 Loading the Ramp Color Model Driver

Right after we started using Direct3D in Section 14.4.2, we looked at code to enumerate available device drivers. With the code listed there we selected a driver based on a selection criteria that we passed down. Among the possible selection criteria was USE_RAMP. At the initialization level, loading the Ramp driver is simple, as shown in the code.

```
// init shared hardware device
CSharedHardware *pGrfx = new CSharedHardware();
// init direct draw
if (!pGrfx->InitDirectDraw()) return FALSE;

// init d3d
if (!pGrfx->InitDirect3D(USE_RAMP)) return FALSE ;


// set up cooperative level
if (!pGrfx->SetCoopLevel(hWnd, DDSCL_NORMAL)) return FALSE;
```

Initialize Direct3D with Ramp driver.

Do revisit the code in Section 14.4.2 if you need to refresh your memory on how to enumerate and select a driver.

16.3.2 Using the Ramp Driver—The First Try

Once we've loaded the new driver, can't we just go ahead and create objects CSurface3D and CTriangle3D or CTriangleTex as usual and run them using the Ramp driver, instead of the RGB driver? The answer is no.

When we first tried running our simple triangle with the Ramp driver, we saw our background being painted correctly, but our CTriangle3D (shaded triangle) was drawn as a black triangle. When we tried using CTriangleTex (texture mapped triangle), our application *crashed,* right in the middle of the Ramp driver rendering module, with no clue as to what was wrong.

The key lies in remembering how the *Ramp model* operates—through lookup tables (see section 15.3.4). The Ramp driver uses only the Blue component of a color specification and then accesses "a lookup table" to interpret the final result. The Ramp driver builds lookup tables from material definitions. If no lookup table has been built (because, say, no material was created), then the rendering module crashes. Solution: create materials.

16.3.3 Creating Materials for the Ramp Driver

We have repeated the definition of the D3DMATERIAL structure here for easy reference:

```
typedef struct _D3DMATERIAL {
    DWORD               dwSize;
    D3DCOLORVALUE       dcvDiffuse;
    D3DCOLORVALUE       dcvAmbient ;      Four different color components.
    D3DCOLORVALUE       dcvSpecular;
    D3DCOLORVALUE       dcvEmissive;
    D3DVALUE            dvPower ;         ◊ Specify sharpness of specular reflections.
    D3DTEXTUREHANDLE    hTexture;         ◊ Combine a texture with specified coloring.
    DWORD               dwRampSize;       ◊ Shading gradient of colors in Ramp/Mono model.
} D3DMATERIAL, *LPD3DMATERIAL;
```

The Ramp driver builds lookup tables based on the specifications in a material structure:

- For materials with no specularity, the driver builds a linear "color ramp" ranging from the ambient color to the maximum diffuse color.

- For materials with specularity, the driver builds a two-stage color ramp; the first stage ranges from the ambient color to the maximum diffuse color, and the second stage ranges from maximum diffuse color light to the maximum specular color. The gradient of the specular ramp is not linear, and it is controlled by the dvPower field.

- For materials with textures, the Ramp driver builds a color ramp for each color in the texture.

- The Ramp driver references the dwRampSize field to determine the size of the ramp built for each color.

For example, the following code sequence builds a color ramp with sixteen shades of red:

```
mMaterialDesc.dcvDiffuse.dvR = D3DVALUE(1.00);
mMaterialDesc.dcvDiffuse.dvG = D3DVALUE(0.00);
mMaterialDesc.dcvDiffuse.dvB = D3DVALUE(0.00);
m_MaterialDesc.hTexture = NULL;
m_MaterialDesc.dwRampSize = 16;
```

In this next example, the Ramp driver builds a color ramp with eight shades for each color in the associated texture:

```
mMaterialDesc.dcvDiffuse.dvR = D3DVALUE(1.00);
mMaterialDesc.dcvDiffuse.dvG = D3DVALUE(1.00);
mMaterialDesc.dcvDiffuse.dvB = D3DVALUE(1.00);
mMaterialDesc.hTexture = hTexture;
mMaterialDesc.dwRampSize = 8
```

16.3.4 Rendering a Triangle with the Ramp Driver

Now that we've taken a look at how the Ramp driver builds its lookup tables, let's create a CTriangleRamp to render a triangle with a shaded Ramp driver.

```
BOOL CTriangleRamp::Init(LPDIRECT3D pD3D, LPDIRECTDRAWPALETTE pPalette, UINT nRes)
{
```

Create material to "set" palette entries for color.

```
pD3D->CreateMaterial(&m_pMaterialFns, NULL);
m_MaterialDesc.dcvDiffuse.dvR = D3DVALUE(1.00);
m_MaterialDesc.dcvDiffuse.dvG = D3DVALUE(1.00);
m_MaterialDesc.dcvDiffuse.dvB = D3DVALUE(1.00);
m_MaterialDesc.hTexture = NULL;
m_MaterialDesc.dwRampSize = 16;
m_pMaterialFns->SetMaterial(&m_MaterialDesc);
m_pMaterialFns->GetHandle(p3dFns, &m_hMaterial);
```

The texture handle is NULL, the MaxDiffuse color is WHITE, and the RampSize is 16. The Ramp driver will create fourteen shades of gray between BLACK and WHITE.

Standard code to allocate system memory space for an Execute Buffer

```
#define nTRIS   1
#define nVERTS nTRIS*3
m_sztEx = sizeof(D3DTLVERTEX) * nVERTS;
m_sztEx += sizeof(D3DINSTRUCTION) * 5;
m_sztEx += sizeof(D3DSTATE) * 2;
m_sztEx += sizeof(D3DPROCESSVERTICES);
m_sztEx += sizeof(D3DTRIANGLE) * nTRIS;
m_pSysExBuffer = new BYTE [m_sztEx];
memset(m_pSysExBuffer, 0, m_sztEx);
```

Use standard code to initialize vertices and then override the colors.

```
D3DTLVERTEX *aVerts = (D3DTLVERTEX *)m_pSysExBuffer;
setupVertices(nTRIS, aVerts);
int    i;
for (i=0; i<nTRIS; i++) {
    aVerts[0].color = RGBA_MAKE(000, 000, 255, 255);
    aVerts[1].color = RGBA_MAKE(000, 000, 128, 255);
    aVerts[2].color = RGBA_MAKE(000, 000, 000, 255);
    aVerts += 3;
}
```

The Ramp driver uses only the blue component and ignores the red and green components.

The notable addition when setting up instructions for a triangle with the ramp model is the D3DOP_STATELIGHT opcode with its D3DLIGHTSTATE_MATERIAL operand. (We're using the OP_STATE_LIGHT macro.) Any materials that we've created have merely instructed the Ramp driver on how we want our lookup tables built. We use the D3DOP_STATELIGHT instruction in an Execute Buffer to instruct the Ramp driver to use a specific material for all future rendering.

The D3DOP_STATELIGHT instruction seems to turn off the render state. The default state is inoperative, and triangles will not be rendered unless you reset the render state. The D3DOP_STATERENDER specification must *follow* the D3DOP_STATELIGHT instruction, as render states set before the Light state become inoperative. You may want to set all render states that concern you and not assume the value of any state.

Set up instructions in Execute Buffer.

```
DWORD dwStart = sizeof(D3DTLVERTEX) * nVERTS;
LPVOID lpTmp = (LPVOID)(m_pSysExBuffer + dwStart);
OP_STATE_LIGHT(1, lpTmp);
    STATE_DATA(D3DLIGHTSTATE_MATERIAL, m_hMaterial, lpTmp);
OP_STATE_RENDER(1, lpTmp);
    STATE_DATA(D3DRENDERSTATE_SHADEMODE, D3DSHADE_GOURAUD, lpTmp);
OP_PROCESS_VERTICES(1, lpTmp);
    PROCESSVERTICES_DATA(D3DPROCESSVERTICES_COPY, 0, nVERTS, lpTmp);
OP_TRIANGLE_LIST(nTRIS, lpTmp);
for (i=0; i<nTRIS; i++) {
    ((LPD3DTRIANGLE)lpTmp)->v1 = i*3+0;
    ((LPD3DTRIANGLE)lpTmp)->v2 = i*3+1;
    ((LPD3DTRIANGLE)lpTmp)->v3 = i*3+2;
    ((LPD3DTRIANGLE)lpTmp)->wFlags = 0;
    lpTmp = ((char*)lpTmp) + sizeof(D3DTRIANGLE);
}
OP_EXIT(lpTmp);
DWORD dwLth = (LPBYTE)lpTmp - m_pSysExBuffer - dwStart;
```

Tell the renderer that we want it to use our material to render all future triangles. Note that we reset the render state to Gouraud, even though this is the default state.

We are now ready to render our triangle with the model. The Ramp model only seems to set palette colors once an instruction stream has been executed. Our code currently sets the palette on every End Scene. You may want to execute an instruction stream with just the D3DOP_STATELIGHT instruction to update the palette during an initialization stage.

PART 1

16.3.5   How Does the Ramp Driver Perform?

Table 16-8 compares the performance of the RGB and the Ramp color model drivers. We've shown results for various rendering options using Scene 2 (16×5000) from our previous tests.

TABLE 16-8 Comparing the Direct3D RGB and Ramp Color Model Drivers

Rendering Option	RGB Model	Ramp Model
Gouraud	55.3 milliseconds	4.3 milliseconds
Flat Shaded	55.3 milliseconds	1.8 milliseconds
Gouraud and Specular	60.3 milliseconds	4.3 milliseconds
Gouraud and Dither	55.3 milliseconds	20.6 milliseconds
Texture Map and Gouraud	62.5 milliseconds	16.7 milliseconds
Texture Map Copy Mode	14.4 milliseconds	14.9 milliseconds

Wow!

- *Look at the speed of the Flat Shaded, Gouraud, and Gouraud and Specular options. Now we're really screaming along!*

- The performance of Gouraud and Dither is not too shabby either. You may not want to use it on all your triangles, but at this performance level, you could use it on some.

- The only "disappointment" is that the performance of texture mapping in Copy mode has not improved. It would have been great if we could use texture mapping widely, but at this performance level you probably would want to limit its use.

EXTRA CREDIT

We did not measure the cost of state changes midstream in an Execute Buffer. We also did not study the impact of texture size on texture mapping. These are excellent extra credit opportunities.

16.4 Optimizing Texture Mapping

Before we close, we'd like to include some advice from the Direct3D documentation on optimizing texture mapping:

- Texture mapping performance is heavily influenced by cache behavior. Keep textures small; the smaller the textures are, the better chance they have of being maintained in the main CPU's secondary cache.

- Do not change the textures on a per primitive basis. Try to keep polygons grouped in order of the textures they use.

- Use square textures whenever possible. Textures whose dimensions are 256 × 256 are the fastest. If your application uses four 128 × 128 textures, for example, try to ensure that all the textures use the same palette, and place them all into one 256 × 256 texture. This technique also reduces the amount of texture swapping required. Of course, you should not use 256 × 256 textures unless your application requires that much texturing, because, as already mentioned, textures should be kept as small as possible.

Well, we've come to the end of this road. Cheers, and may all your 3D applications really sizzle.

WHAT HAVE YOU LEARNED?

We measured the performance of our simple RGB color model triangle, both its inner workings and its various rendering options. We tried some optimizations and found that the returns were decent for long Execute Buffers, but overall performance was still far from stellar.

Next we learned how to use the Ramp color model driver, including using materials and `D3DOP_STATELIGHT` to direct the driver to create its lookup tables. And we were rewarded with a dramatic improvement in performance.

We've spent sufficient time on Direct3D's Immediate mode. In the next chapter we will cover mixing our 3D results with 2D and video.

CHAPTER 17

Mixing 3D with Sprites, Backgrounds, and Videos

WHY READ THIS CHAPTER?

You might as well ask, "Why would I need to mix other graphics media types with 3D?" Well, here are some scenarios that might prompt mixing:

- You could create your application to be entirely 3D based. But 3D modeling and rendering is performance intensive. Drawing some objects with faster 2D mechanisms may bring an improvement in performance.

- You have your own object types, with their own rendering codes, and you want to intermingle these objects in a 3D model.

- Say you have designed 3D exploratorium within which you have real-life characters communicating with the Explorer. You have motion video footage of these characters, and you'd like to transparently overlay the video in your 3D world.

In short, you may want to mix media types because of performance advantages and/or because you want to add richness. In this chapter first you'll learn how to mix a 3D object within a 2D world, and then you'll learn how to use a video as a texture map within a 3D world.

17.1 Mixing a 3D Object on a 2D Background

We've already seen how mixing works in Part II, where we mixed a sprite on top of a background. In fact, over the course of Part II, we looked at a variety of options for mixing—using GDI, DirectDraw, and RDX.

In Part II we mixed a sprite on top of a background by:

- creating a CSurface from among the various options;

PART V

- creating a CBackground from among any options suitable to the CSurface and attaching the CBackground to the CSurface;

- creating a CSprite from among any options suitable to the CSurface and attaching the CSprite to the CSurface; and

- Blting the CBackground first, Blting the CSprite on top of the CBackground, and then refreshing the screen with the mixed image.

17.1.1 Our 3D Surface Is Also a 2D Surface

But wait! Let's think about where we are. We got access to a 3D surface in the first place by "querying" for 3D capabilities. As long as we retained access to the original 2D surface—that is, as long as we did not call *IDirectDrawSurface::Release()*—we can still use its innate 2D-ness.

So to mix a 3D object on top of a 2D background, we could

- create a CSurface suitable to be "extended" for 3D capabilities and then "extend" the 2D surface to a 3D surface while retaining access to the original 2D surface.

- create a 2D background from options suited to the 2D surface and then attach this background to the dual 2D-3D surface.

- create a 3D triangle from available render styles and then attach the 3D triangle to the dual CSurface.

- Blt the background first as usual, Blt the 3D sprite on top of the background, and then refresh the screen with the mixed image.

Here's the 3D version of the *FollowMouse()* method that handles dual surfaces:

```
long CSurface3d::FollowMouse(CPoint &point, int nTime)
{
```

> Pre Scene Init: Set up to use 3D driver and clear Z-Buffer (if any).

```
    m_p3dFns->BeginScene();
    if (m_bIsZEnabled) {
        D3DRECT    drDst;
        drDst.x1 = 0;
        drDst.y1 = 0;
        drDst.x2 = m_dwWidth;
        drDst.y2 = m_dwHeight;
        #define nRECTS 1
        m_p3dViewport->Clear(nRECTS, &drDst, D3DCLEAR_ZBUFFER);
    }
```

Set up BLTPARAMS structure for dual-surface usage.

```
BLTPARAMS xDst;
xDst.pddsDesc = &m_SurfDesc;
xDst.pddsFns = m_p2dFns;
xDst.p3dFns = m_p3dFns;
xDst.p3dViewport = m_p3dViewport;
```

Blt background to dual surface. Blt either 2D or 3D background based on Init.

```
if (m_nNeedLock & BKGLOCK)
    m_p2dFns->Lock(NULL, &m_SurfDesc, DDLOCK_WAIT, NULL);
if (m_pBackground != NULL) {
    RECT rSrc = {0, 0, m_dwWidth, m_dwHeight};
    POINT ptDst = {0,0};
    m_pBackground->Blt(&xDst, &ptDst, &rSrc);
}
if (m_nNeedLock & BKGLOCK)
    m_p2dFns->Unlock(NULL);
```

2D background may need surface to be locked.

Blt attached 3D Triangle.

```
if (m_pTriangle != NULL)
    m_pTriangle->Blt(&xDst, &point);
```

Scene End Stage: End Scene, refresh screen, and return.

```
m_p3dFns->EndScene();
// offset dst rect accounting for client area
long lRight = m_ptZeroZero.x + m_dwWidth;
long lBottom = m_ptZeroZero.y + m_dwHeight;
RECT rDst = {m_ptZeroZero.x, m_ptZeroZero.y, lRight, lBottom};
RECT rSrc = {0, 0, m_dwWidth, m_dwHeight};
// set palette and refresh screen
gpPrimary->SetPalette(gpPalette);
gpPrimary->Blt(&rDst, m_p2dFns, &rSrc, DDBLT_WAIT, NULL);
// return
return TRUE;
}
```

Notice the code added to pass both the 2D and the 3D descriptor to the object renderers in the BLTPARAMS structure. Also notice the code added to lock and unlock the 2D surface for most 2D background rendering (a hardware-accelerated 2D background would not need a Lock/Unlock).

Some hardware 3D devices may not allow 2D functions to be invoked between *BeginScene()* and *EndScene()*. These devices will set the DDCAPS2_NO2DDURING3DSCENE flag in the 2D caps structure (hwCaps.dwCaps2). If this flag is set, you will need to modify the FollowMouse code to render a 2D background *before BeginScene()*, but render a 3D Background *after BeginScene()*. We found that the HEL drivers do not impose this restriction, so we have not built this check into our current example.

PART V

17.1.2   Measuring Background Performance

Table 17-1 compares the performance of Bltting a sprite with both 2D and 3D rendering paths.

TABLE 17-1 Comparing 2D and 3D Backgrounds

Rendering Path	Time
CBackgroundCCode	7.1 milliseconds
CBackgroundP5	6.8 milliseconds
CBackgroundTex	46.5 milliseconds
CBackground3D	3.8 milliseconds[*]

[*] CBackground3D fills the background with a constant color; whereas all other options transfer an image to the screen. Therefore the comparison of CBackground3D with the other options is not a true apples-to-apples comparison. The figure is shown for reference.

CBackgroundTex is an implementation of a texture-mapped 3D background object. You implement a texture-mapped 3D background by loading a texture object and setting its handle in the background material structure. Check the source code for the Timing Application on our Internet site. (Note that unlike triangle textures, a background texture need not be sized using powers of two.)

A CBackgroundTex is texture mapped to the surface and is not merely Bltted to the surface. The implication is that if the source and destination sizes differ, the source is stretched (or shrunk) to fit the destination rectangle. Texture mapping is much costlier, as the results of our measurements demonstrate.

If all you need is a simple Blt of a background image, then as the performance results indicate, using 2D backgrounds behind 3D objects offers significant performance boosts over using texture mapping.

17.2 Mixing in Sprites

Hey, can't we add sprites to our dual surface just like we did with backgrounds? Technically, yes. But our code lets us have only one active sprite at a time. If we wanted to have more than one sprite, we would need to maintain some form of list (or array) of sprites and draw all the active sprites within our Refresh functions.

Since the Intel RDX library provides code to manage lists of sprites and draw them in back-to-front order, let's just use RDX to mix sprites in. If you've forgotten, or haven't had a chance to play with RDX yet, do take a quick trip through Chapter 8.

17.2.1 Using RDX to Mix in Sprites

The RDX programming model allows us to

- create a surface of a specified size and pixel depth;
- create mixable objects (such as sprites, backgrounds, grids, and AV objects) and connect them to the surface;
- manipulate attributes of the objects (such as draw order, position, transparency, and visibility); and
- mix and render all visible objects attached to a surface by invoking a single *srfDraw()* function provided by the surface object.

Typically you attach the surface to a window using *srfSetDestWindow()*, and the window is automatically refreshed by *srfDraw()*. RDX also has a *srfSetDestMemory()* function that we can use to specify that the output of *srfDraw()* be sent to a memory buffer that we provide. Let's use *srfSetDestMemory()* to have RDX output its data into our dual surface:

```
long CSurface3d::FollowMouse(CPoint &point, int nTime)
{
    // pre-scene init
    m_p3dFns->BeginScene();
    if (m_bIsZEnabled) {
        D3DRECTdrDst;
        drDst.x1 = 0; drDst.y1 = 0;
        drDst.x2 = m_dwWidth; drDst.y2 = m_dwHeight;
        m_p3dViewport->Clear(1, &drDst, D3DCLEAR_ZBUFFER);
    }

    // setup BLTPARAMS struct for dual-surface usage
    BLTPARAMS xDst;
    xDst.pddsDesc = &m_SurfDesc;
    xDst.pddsFns = m_p2dFns;
    xDst.p3dFns = m_p3dFns;
    xDst.p3dViewport = m_p3dViewport;

    // Blt either 2D or 3D background to Dual-Surface
    if (m_nNeedLock & BKGLOCK)
        m_p2dFns->Lock(NULL, &m_SurfDesc, DDLOCK_WAIT, NULL);
    if (m_pBackground != NULL) {
        RECT rSrc = {0, 0, m_dwWidth, m_dwHeight};
        POINT ptDst = {0,0};
        m_pBackground->Blt(&xDst, &ptDst, &rSrc);
    }
    if (m_nNeedLock & BKGLOCK) m_p2dFns->Unlock(NULL);
```

Draw RDX objects by invoking srfDraw on the Dual Surface's m_hSurfmember.

```
if (m_bIsRdx) {
    m_p2dFns->Lock(NULL, &m_SurfDesc, DDLOCK_WAIT, NULL);
    srfSetDestMemory(m_hSurf, m_SurfDesc.lpSurface, m_SurfDesc.lPitch);
    srfDraw(m_hSurf);
    m_p2dFns->Unlock(NULL);
}
```

Lock DirectDraw Surface and pass its data pointer to RDX using *srfSetDetMemory()*. Then draw all objects using *srfDraw()*. RDX draws its objects directly onto the surface with or without transparency.

```
// Blt 3D triangle
if (m_pTriangle != NULL)
    m_pTriangle->Blt(&xDst, &point);

// SceneEnd
m_p3dFns->EndScene();
// offset dst rect accounting for client area
long lRight = m_ptZeroZero.x + m_dwWidth;
long lBottom = m_ptZeroZero.y + m_dwHeight;
RECT rDst = {m_ptZeroZero.x, m_ptZeroZero.y, lRight, lBottom};
RECT rSrc = {0, 0, m_dwWidth, m_dwHeight};
// set palette and refresh screen
gpPrimary->SetPalette(gpPalette);
gpPrimary->Blt(&rDst, m_p2dFns, &rSrc, DDBLT_WAIT, NULL);
return TRUE;
}
```

In the new *FollowMouse()* method that we have outlined above we are drawing our background first and then mixing in the RDX output (a composite of all the RDX objects). Finally we add in our 3D object on top of the RDX and background combo.

GENERIC OBJECT RENDERING

Our *FollowMouse()* method is becoming fairly long. We are starting to invoke multiple object renderers of various types. Wouldn't it be nice to have a long generic list of objects that you could invoke within a loop using a generic object render function?

You could redesign our classes, so that all objects such as backgrounds, Sprites, and RDX objects derive from a generic object. Next you could define the generic object to have a Blt function that takes an enhanced BLTPARAMS structure. You would then find yourself set up to invoke a generic Blt function within a loop, and the objects will take care of all the object-specific details. In fact, you would find yourself set up to the point that the various CSurfaceXXX-derived objects were only doing initialization and tear down.

Pretty neat, huh! We didn't do this, because then we would have had to spend time explaining *our* architecture, which is not the point of the book! By the way, this is pretty much how RDX works. In fact, take a look at the Render Callback effect (FX_RENDER_CALLBACK) if you want to tie in 3D objects into the RDX generic object architecture.

You'll probably point out that if we're using RDX, we can have our background be an RDX background (CBackgroundRDX) and not have to worry about any CBackground code either. That is true. Very astute of you! In fact, Table 17-2 has measurements of mixing the various 2D and 3D objects (the sprite measurements were for sixteen sprites of about 5,000 pixels each, and the background measurements were for a background of 734×475 pixels).

TABLE 17-2 Measuring Mixed 2D and 3D Objects

Backgrounds		Sprites/Triangles	
Rendering Path	**Time**	**Rendering Path**	**Time**
CBackgroundCCode	7.1 milliseconds		
CBackgroundP5	6.8 milliseconds		
CBackgroundRDX	4.0 milliseconds	CSpriteRDX	1.1 milliseconds
CBackgroundTex	46.5 milliseconds	CTriangleTex (Ramp/CopyMode)	16.2 milliseconds
CBackground3D	3.8 milliseconds	CTriangle3D (Ramp/Flat)	2.2 milliseconds

Following are some observations based on the results:

- The MMX technology optimizations that RDX has used for background drawing make CBackgroundRDX run at the speed of color filling. Wow! There is a clear benefit to mixing 2D and 3D.

- With Ramp mode triangles being rendered in the low-millisecond speeds, our Execute Buffer overhead starts becoming important again. These tests were performed with only sixteen triangles. It becomes worthwhile to invest in code for long Execute Buffers, when you are rendering many small triangles with the Ramp mode driver.

- Flat-shaded Ramp mode triangles compare well with spriting. However, texture mapping at 16 milliseconds (half the 30 fps budget) still takes quite a bit of time. A judicious mix of shaded and texture-mapped triangles would be the way to go. And, of course, using 2D sprites wherever possible is also a good way to go.

17.2.2 Adding RDX Objects at Front and Back

What if you want to add RDX objects behind and ahead of the 3D object? Well, RDX lets you create multiple surfaces. So you can solve this issue by creating two RDX surfaces and retaining one as the "behind" surface and the other as the "ahead" surface. All objects attached to the behind surface, using *objSetDestination( )* will get drawn behind the 3D object. And all objects attached to the ahead surface will get drawn on top of the 3D object. This is a simple extra credit exercise. Go on! Try it for yourself.

17.3 Mixing in Video

Mixing in video is a little more complex than mixing sprites or backgrounds. The following factors need to be considered:

- Video files are actually a series of images that need to be displayed sequentially. To mix 3D on top of video, we would need to mix our 3D image whenever a new video frame is drawn—lest we "lose" sight of our 3D object.

- A video file is recorded at a specific frame rate. Playback of frames in the video must be synchronized to a timer, so that they can be displayed at the recorded frame rate.

- Video files are usually recorded in high-color resolutions to capture the broad range of colors in natural situations. Video codecs prefer to choose their own palettes, since they reduce the color range for palletized displays. They typically produce very poor quality if they are forced to use a specified palette.

The issues of synchronized drawing and timed playback are dealt with in detail in Chapter 10. We will use the same code to mix our 3D sprite on top of a video object.

17.3.1 Handling Palettes

We do need to add some code to handle palettes. Our 2D objects use colors only from the system palette, and there is no palette conflict between 2D and video objects. But Direct3D uses more than the system palette. Let's look at the code needed to manage palettes among these media.

There is no fast and high-quality solution to sharing palettes. Our code shows you how to communicate palettes amongst video and 3D objects. Since video codecs don't like palettes to be forced on them, we have written our code to tell Direct3D to use the video object's palette.

Following is the code that takes a palette from a video object file and uses this palette with Direct3D surfaces. Note that Direct3D expects the palette to be set on the 2D surface before *any* 3D functionality is requested.

Create a palette object

```
LOGPALETTE *plogPalette;
PBYTE pTmp = new BYTE [sizeof (LOGPALETTE) + sizeof (PALETTEENTRY)*256];
plogPalette = (LOGPALETTE *)pTmp;
plogPalette->palVersion = 0x0300;
plogPalette->palNumEntries = 256;
if (!rdxGetVideoPalette(plogPalette)) return FALSE;
```

Use RDX to talk to a video object and get its palette

Change palette entry flags to not allow D3D to change any of them

```
PALETTEENTRY *pPal = (PALETTEENTRY *) (pTmp + sizeof(LOGPALETTE));
for (int i = 0; i < 256; j++) pPal[i] .peFlags = D3DPAL_READONLY;
```

Querying for a palette from a video file takes a lot of steps. RDX simplifies these steps. So our code uses RDX to talk to the video codec. Refer back to Section 10.2 for an explanation of how to manage video with RDX. For quick reference, we've included here the essential code to query a palette from an AVI file using RDX:

```
BOOL rdxGetVideoPalette::GetPalette(LOGPALETTE *plogPalette, LPSTR *pFile)
{
    // first create a hFile object and load our AVI file
    err = hfilCreate(&m_hFil);
    macExitIfRdxError(err, FALSE);
    err = hfilLoad (m_hFil, pFile);
    macExitIfRdxError(err, FALSE);

    // create the AV object and initialize it with the video file
    err = avCreate(&m_hAV);
    macExitIfRdxError(err, FALSE);
    err = avAddVideoTrack(m_hav, m_hFil, 0, &m_hVid);
    macExitIfRdxError(err, FALSE);

    // get the palette from the video object
    DINORVAL err = vidGetPalette(m_hVid, pLogPalette);
    macExitIfRdxError(err, FALSE);
    return TRUE;
}
```

17.3.2   Using Video as a Texture Map

After seeing how to mix 3D and video on a DirectDraw surface, it is a fairly simple extrapolation to use video as a texture map. We merely modify our previous code to provide the Texture Map Address when we call *srfSetDestinationMemory()*.

Run the demo for this chapter on the CD and check the Texture Mapped Video option.

WHAT HAVE YOU LEARNED?

By the end of the chapter, you should have learned how to

- mix a 3D object on a 2D background using Direct3D and DirectDraw;
- mix a 3D object with RDX sprites and a background (Direct3D, DirectDraw, or RDX);
- mix a 3D object on top of a video file where the video file is played through RDX and can be either VFW or ActiveMovie based; and

- make the simple modification needed to use video as a texture map source (that is, if you perused the source code on the CD).

You've reached the end of our 3D coverage. We hope you have learned a lot.

PART VI

Processors and
Performance Optimization

WE'D LIKE TO EXTEND AN ACKNOWLEDGEMENT TO FRANK BINNS, SHUKY ERLICH, BRUCE BARTTLET, JULIE A BRAJENOVICH, K. SRIDHARAN, RICK MANGOLD, BOB FABER, BEV BACKMAYER, DEBBIE MARR, BOB REESE, TOM WALSH, MICKEY GUTTMAN, BENNY EITAN, KOBY GOTTLIEB, ODED LEMPEL, AND DAVID BISTRY

Chapter 21   VTune and Other Performance Optimization Tools

- VTune's coverage of pairing and scheduling rules
- Static and dynamic analysis
- Hot-spot monitor and time-based and event-based sampling
- VTune usage hints
- ReadTime StampCounter—RDTSC
- Using the PMonitor library

Chapter 22   The Pentium II Processor

- Architectural overview and new features
- Pentium II performance counters
- MMX pairing rules
- Detailed component description including event counters for each unit
- Write Combining memory type to speed graphics performance
- Branch mispredictions, partial stalls, and the 4:1:1 decoder template

Chapter 23   Knowing Your Data and Optimizing Memory

- Overview of memory subsystem
- Differences between Pentium and Pentium Pro member processors
- Cache differences, DCU splits, partial memory stalls
- MMX stack alignment
- Accessing cached memory
- Writing to video memory

When it comes to developing multimedia applications, you'll quickly realize that you're dealing with a huge amount of data—most of which is typically used once or twice and then thrown away. Unlike database, word processing, or transaction-based applications, multimedia applications must quickly display a sequence of pictures to give the illusion of motion; they must pump audio data in real time to play uninterrupted sound sequences; or they must render a 3D model to give the illusion of a 3D world. There are lots of calculations to make, lots of data to move around. In order to get smooth motion video, audio, and 3D, you still have to fine-tune your applications for the platform they are running on.

We decided to include this section because we believe that multimedia applications and processor optimization go hand in hand—at least for now. Some developers think optimization is an art; some think it's a science. We think it's a mix of both.

First we cover the Pentium family processors, their architecture, and how they work with code and data. We optimize our sprite sample for each of the processors we cover—the Pentium processor, the Pentium processor with MMX technology, and the Pentium II.

When you think about optimizing multimedia applications, don't just think about applying the optimization rules of the processor (pairing, AGIs, register contentions, and so forth);[1] you should first think about your data access pattern. Optimizing for the processor is most useful when you access the data in the L1 cache. From our experience, you should not try to squeeze every cycle out of your code; you need only focus on the code segments that are called very often and those that consume most of the CPU cycles.

Rather than telling you how to optimize your code, we'll tell you how we go about optimizing ours. Once the code is written, we typically use Intel's VTune to figure out how to schedule instructions for optimal pairing and how the code behaves when it runs on the PC—that's the science part. Since VTune does not know how to fix the code for us, we use our knowledge of the processor scheduling rules and rearrange the code for optimal pairing—that's the art part.

We typically start with VTune's static analyzer, which helps us figure out how to schedule the instructions for the specific processor we're optimizing for. Once the code is operational, we run it with VTune's hot-spot system monitor. It tells us how much of the CPU the application is using and which pieces of code are consuming most of the time. We then zoom in on these segments and try to optimize them even more—if possible.

To learn more about the behavior of a particular section of code, we run VTune's dynamic analyzer. With the dynamic analyzer we can collect an exact execution trace of certain sections of code and then analyze the traced instructions. It gives us information about branching, L1, L2, and cache hit rate, unaligned accesses, and many other things. With dynamic analysis, we get a better understanding of the behavior of our code.

As a general rule, we pay special attention to memory accesses when we write our code. We always try to guarantee that data that we want to use is already in the L1 cache when it is time to access it. We do this by fetching data ahead of time, by operating on a smaller subset of data at one time, or by changing our data access pattern.

We also pay special attention to branches—especially with the Pentium Pro and Pentium II processors. If we can avoid a branch instruction, we do. If not, we use the dynamic analyzer or the processor event counters to figure out how often we miss branches—then we see if we can do better by rearranging the branch logic.

---

1. The terms *pairing, AGI,* and *L1, L2 caches* are defined in Chapter 18.

CHAPTER 18

The Pentium Processor Family

WHY READ THIS CHAPTER?
You must be familiar with the Intel Inside® logo. But do you really know what's inside? Do you really know how the Pentium processors work? The real question is, "Do you want to know?" Come along, we'll take you on the grand Pentium processor tour.

In this chapter, you will

- be introduced to terms and concepts used throughout this part of the book;
- get an overview of the four Intel processors: the Pentium, Pentium with MMX technology, Pentium Pro, and Pentium II; and
- learn how to identify the different processors and detect their model-specific features using *CPUID.*

As of today, there are four major Pentium processors: the Pentium, Pentium Pro, Pentium processor with MMX technology, and, just recently, the Pentium II processor. Although the internal architecture of each processor differs from the others, all the processors are 100 percent compatible with the Intel 486 instruction set. As a law of evolution, newer processors offer new architectural features and new instructions to enhance the performance of existing applications, and to enable new classes of applications.

In this chapter we'll give you a brief overview of each of the processors without going into too many details. If some of the terms or concepts are not clear, refer to the chapter that covers that specific processor. Chapters 19,

20, and 22 give detailed information about the architecture of the internal components of each of the Pentium processors: one chapter for the Pentium processor, one for MMX technology, and one for the Pentium II processor. We don't cover the Pentium Pro because its features are a subset of the Pentium II processor.

We also devote one chapter to VTune and other performance optimization tools that make it easier for you to optimize your code, and, finally, in the last chapter of the book we discuss memory optimization issues and techniques related to memory, the caches, and the system bus.

18.1 Basic Concepts and Terms

Before we delve into too much detail, let's review some concepts and terms relevant to processors in general and to Intel Architecture (IA) processors in particular.

- *L1 Cache.* First level cache. The L1 cache is on-chip static memory that can provide data in 1 clock cycle on a cache hit. A cache hit occurs when the requested data is already in the cache; otherwise you get a cache miss, and the data is brought in from main memory or the second level cache (L2).

- *L2 Cache.* Second level cache. Typically the L2 cache is off-chip static memory that runs more slowly than L1 cache. Some Pentium Pro processor models have the L2 cache on the chip running at the speed of the processor core. The L2 is typically much larger than the L1 cache (256K–1 MB). The L2 cache has a cache miss/hit behavior similar to that of the L1 cache.

- *Cache line.* A cache line describes the smallest unit of storage that can be allocated in the processor's L1 cache; that is, when you read a byte or more from main memory, the entire cache line is burst into the L1 cache from the memory location where the bytes are read from. Cache lines are typically aligned on a byte boundary equal to their width. For example, all four Pentium processors have a 32-byte cache line aligned on a 32-byte boundary. If a read crosses the cache line boundary, the processor brings in both cache lines (64 bytes) from the memory location where the bytes are read from.

- *Fetch.* The process of loading raw opcodes from the cache or memory into one of two prefetch buffers inside the processor.

- *Decode.* The process of parsing and interpreting the raw opcodes. In the Pentium Pro processors, the IA instructions are decoded into micro-opcodes.

- *Writeback.* The process of committing the final results to IA registers, the cache, or main memory.

- *Micro-op.* The decoder in the Pentium Pro and the Pentium II processors breaks the IA instructions into micro-instructions (*micro-op codes*). These micro-ops are necessary for the *out-of-order execution* model used in these processors.

- *Out-of-order execution.* Pentium Pro processors execute micro-ops based on the readiness of their data rather than the order in which they entered the execution unit. This is out-of-order execution.

- *Branch Target Buffer (BTB).* The Branch Target Buffer holds a history of branches that were mispredicted during the execution of an application. It stores the address of the mispredicted branch instruction, the branch target address, and the result of the misprediction. When the same instructions show up again (in a loop for example), the branch prediction unit uses this information to predict the outcome of the branch.

- *Return Stack Buffer (RSB).* The Return Stack Buffer can correctly predict return addresses for procedures that are called from different locations in succession. The RSB is useful for unrolling loops that contain function calls, and it removes the need to in-line procedures called inside the loop.

- *U and V pipes.* The Pentium processor has two execution pipelines that operate in parallel and can sustain an execution rate of up to two instructions every clock cycle. These two pipes are known as the U and V pipes.

- *Pipelining.* The process of overlapping operations in the processor pipeline is called pipelining. As a result of breaking the instruction execution into multiple stages (fetch, decode, execution, and writeback), the processor can execute multiple instructions at the same time—each in a different execution stage. For example, one instruction could be in the prefetch stage, one in decode, one in execution, and one in writeback. This process is very similar to the assembly line at automobile plants, where one person installs a front door, another person installs the back door, and someone else installs the headlight, and so on. All of them are working at the same time but on different cars. Analogously, in the processor, all units are working at the same time but on different instructions.

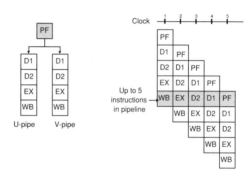

FIGURE 18-1 The Pentium processor pipeline can execute up to five instructions at any one time.

- *Superpipelining.* This is the same thing as pipelining except that the pipeline is deeper. For example, the Pentium processor is pipelined since it has five stages; the Pentium Pro and Pentium II are superpipelined because they have twelve execution stages.

- *Pairing.* Two instructions pair if and only if the first instruction can execute in the U pipe and the second instruction can execute in the V pipe. The pairing rules exist because only the U pipe can execute complex instructions, therefore, we need to ensure that a complex instruction is followed by a simple instruction. In the Pentium processor, you can have both the U and V pipes executing instructions as long as they adhere to the Pentium pairing rules. You can find the Pentium pairing rules in later chapters or in the *Intel Architecture Optimization Manual* found on the companion CD.

- *Address Generation Interlock* (AGI). An AGI occurs when you calculate an address in one instruction and use it in a following instruction. On the Pentium processor, this typically causes a 2-clock stall in both pipelines. You can remedy the problem by adding other useful instructions between the instruction that calculates the address and the instruction that uses the address.

  In the Pentium Pro and Pentium II processors, even though AGIs can theoretically happen, they are not as obvious or obstructive because of the out-of-order execution model that these processors use. So, basically, you don't have to worry about AGIs occurring in these two processors.

- *Partial stalls.* Partial stalls occur when you load a small register *(al)* and follow it with an access (read/write) to the larger register *(ax or eax)*. These occur only with Pentium Pro and Pentium II processors. Depending on the status of the pipeline, partial stalls can be extremely taxing on application performance. Removing partial stalls is typically one of the major optimizations that you can get from the Pentium Pro processors. More about this in a later chapter.

18.2 The Pentium Processors

Let's look at an overview of the Pentium and Pentium Pro processors and their MMX technology counterparts (see Figure 18-2).

18.2.1 The Pentium Processor

The Pentium processor marked a significant step over its predecessor, the Intel 486. It uses two parallel execution pipelines—U and V—which make it possible for the processor to execute up to two instructions in parallel. Each pipeline is divided into five execution stages, so the execution of up to five instructions can be pipelined (or overlapped) at any given cycle (see Figure 18-3).

The Pentium processor has also improved the performance of floating-point operations drastically and separated the instruction and data L1 caches, so the processor can fetch instructions and access data all within the

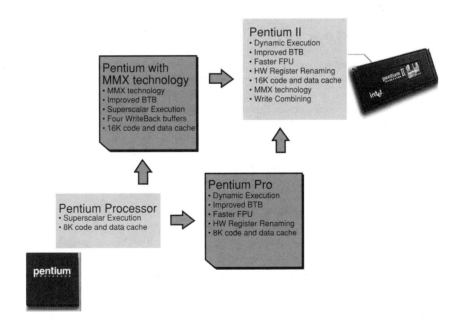

FIGURE 18-2 Evolution of the Pentium processor family.

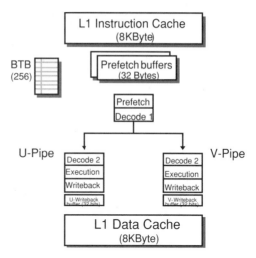

FIGURE 18-3 An architectural view of the Pentium processor.

same clock cycle. It includes two dedicated[2] 32-bit Write buffers, which make it possible for the processor to queue memory writes without stalling the execution of instructions within the processor.

Finally, the Pentium processor includes two prefetch buffers of 32 bytes each (one cache line each). With these prefetch buffers the processor can prefetch instructions from two different execution paths: one fetches from the next consecutive instruction address, and one fetches speculatively from a branch target address. The prefetch buffers, in conjunction with the Branch Target Buffer (BTB), help the prediction unit to speculate on the outcome of previously encountered branches.

18.2.2 The Pentium Pro Processor

Intel then introduced the Pentium Pro processor. Instead of a five-stage pipeline, the processor moved to a decoupled twelve-stage superpipelined architecture with in-order execution at both ends of the pipeline, and out-of-order execution in the middle. With the out-of-order execution capability, the processor can speculatively process instructions out of sequence. This capability is extremely useful when an instruction stalls while the processor waits for data to be read from memory or waits for the result of an earlier operation to be available. (See Figure 18-4.) The in-order units, in the front

---

2. The U pipe can only queue data in the U Write buffer, and the V pipe can only queue data in the V Write buffer.

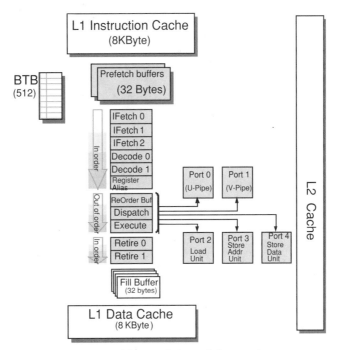

FIGURE 18-4 An architectural view of the Pentium Pro processor.

end and the back end, guarantee that instructions maintain the same sequence when they enter and when they exit the execution unit.

In addition to the two execution U and V pipelines (Port 0 and Port 1), the Pentium Pro processor added three more units: Port 2 loads data from the cache or memory, Port 3 calculates store addresses, and Port 4 stores data to the cache or memory.

Similar to the Pentium processor, the Pentium Pro maintains separate L1 data and instruction caches of 8K each. But the L2 cache has been moved inside the chip to provide faster access to data in the L2 cache. The processor also doubles the size of the BTB to 512 entries in order to improve the branch prediction rate. With a bigger BTB, more mispredicted branch instructions can be remembered just in case they get encountered later.

18.2.3   The Pentium Processor with MMX Technology

In 1997 Intel introduced the Pentium processor with MMX technology, which adds fifty-seven new instructions to the Pentium instruction set. MMX technology is geared to multimedia applications. The size of the L1 caches is doubled, and the number of Write buffers is increased to four.

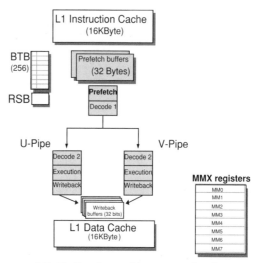

FIGURE 18-5 Pentium with MMX technology processor.

Since this processor is based on the Pentium processor, the internal architecture is identical except for a few changes. The size of the L1 caches is doubled to 16K each, and the number of 32-bit Write buffers is increased to four. A Return Stack Buffer (RSB) has been added; it can correctly predict return addresses for procedures that are called from different locations in succession (see Figure 18-5).

Finally, the number of 32-bit Write buffers is doubled to four undedicated buffers in this processor. Unlike the Pentium processor, which had a dedicated Write buffer for each pipe, in this processor the U and V pipes can write to any of the four Write buffers. This setup is beneficial when there are many writes to uncached memory.

18.2.4   The Pentium II Processor

The Pentium II processor was just released in the middle of 1997. It is basically a Pentium Pro processor with MMX technology. Similar to the Pentium with MMX technology, the Pentium II processor contains fifty-seven MMX instructions and eight MMX registers. The capacity of the L1 data and instruction caches has been doubled to 16K each, and the Return Stack Buffer (RSB) has been added. (See Figure 18-6.)

Unlike the Pentium Pro processor, the Pentium II moved the L2 cache off the chip. Notice that in the Pentium Pro processor, the L2 cache runs at the same speed as the core; however, in the Pentium II processor, the external L2 cache runs at half or one third the speed of the processor core. You'll find out more about this facet of the processor in the Pentium II chapter.

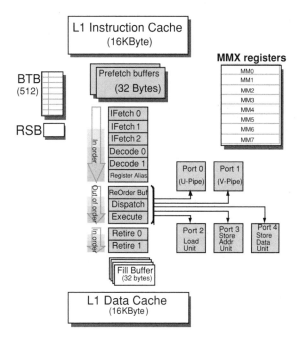

FIGURE 18-6 Architectural view of the Pentium II processor.

18.3 Identifying Processor Models

As the Intel architecture evolved with new features, Intel realized that it was essential to provide a simple way for software to identify the availability of such features. Starting from the Intel 386 processor, Intel provided a signature at processor reset. Later Intel added a special instruction, *CPUID,* so that applications could identify features related to a specific processor model.

The signature of the processor includes the vendor ID, model, and stepping. It also specifies whether certain features of the processor are supported; for example, MMX technology, CMOVxx, and FMOVxx instructions. In the Pentium Pro processor, *CPUID* also returns information about the organization of instructions and data caches.

Let's see how you can use *CPUID* to figure out whether or not MMX technology is supported on a certain processor. First you need to check whether the processor supports the *CPUID* instruction. An Intel processor supports the *CPUID* instruction if you can change bit 21 of the *eflags* register. The following code snippet checks whether *CPUID* is supported.

```
BOOL CpuIdSupported()
{
    BOOL fSupported;

    _asm {
        // Try to change bit 21.. save a copy of it in ecx.
        pushfd                              // Push EFLAGS to stack
        pop     eax                         // EAX=EFLAGS
        mov     ecx, eax                    // save it for later comparison
        and     ecx, 200000h                // isolate bit21
        xor     eax, 200000h                // change bit21
        push    eax                         // push it on stack
        popfd                               // pop it to EFLAGS

        // Now see if it changed
        pushfd                              // Push new value of EFLAGS
        pop     eax                         // EAX=new EFLAGS
        and     eax, 200000h                // isolate bit21
        xor     eax, ecx                    // compare it to last value
        mov     fSupported, eax             // EAX==0 if did not change
    }

    return (fSupported != 0);
}
```

After you have determined whether or not the *CPUID* instruction is available, you can use it to figure out if MMX technology is supported. MMX technology is supported only if bit 23 of the feature flag is set. You can obtain the feature flag by calling *CPUID* with the *eax* register set to 1.

```
BOOL MMXSupported()
{
    BOOL fSupported;

    _asm    {
        mov     eax, 1                      ; CPUID level 1
        CPUID                               ; EDX = feature flag
        and     edx, 0x800000               ; test bit 23 of feature flag
        mov     fSupported, edx             ; 0: not supported, !0: supported
    }

    return (fSupported != 0);
}
```

To give you a head start, we included a simple Dynamic Link Library on the CD that performs these operations for you. It returns information about the processor model, starting from the Intel 386, and enumerates all the information supported by the *CPUID*. You can find all the sources, binaries, and documentation on the companion CD.

WHAT HAVE YOU LEARNED?

Here is a recap of the points you will need to remember from this chapter as you read the following chapters:

- The Pentium processor implements a five-stage pipeline capable of decoding two instructions per clock.
- The Pentium Pro processor implements a twelve-stage, three-way superpipeline.
- Intel added the MMX technology to both processors, which are targeted toward multimedia applications.
- The Pentium processor has two dedicated Write buffers, the Pentium with MMX technology processor has four shared Write buffers, and the Pentium Pro processor has four 32-byte Fill buffers.
- The Pentium processor suffers AGI stalls, and the Pentium Pro does not.

CHAPTER 19

The Pentium Processor

WHY READ THIS CHAPTER?

In the previous chapter, we gave you an overview of the Pentium processor family. In this chapter, we'll peel the top off the Pentium processor and have a peek inside at the components. Then we'll delve into getting better performance from the components.

In this chapter you'll

- get a better understanding of the components of the Pentium processor, including the L1 cache, prefetch buffers, branch prediction unit, BTB, the U and V pipelines, and the Write buffers;
- learn the benefit of instruction pipelining and how to burst empty bubbles in the pipeline;
- learn the Pentium integer pairing and scheduling rules;
- see how to avoid Address Generation Interlock (AGI) stalls;
- look at the importance of branch prediction and the problems that come with misprediction;
- get an analysis of our earlier sprite sample and see how you can rearrange instructions to reduce the amount of cycles it takes to execute the sprite with this processor.

The goal of this chapter is to show you how to optimize your code to achieve optimal performance on the Pentium processor. To do that, you first need to learn about the internal components of the processor and how to extract the most out of them. For each component we'll give you a brief operational overview and then provide a few suggestions for gaining optimal operation of that component.

VTune can easily analyze your code and show you how well your instructions pair.

In this chapter, you'll learn about the L1 data and instruction caches, the prefetch unit, the BTB, the U and V execution pipelines, and the Write buffers. You'll also be introduced to the Pentium pairing rules that must be followed to achieve high application performance. Finally, you'll learn about AGIs and how to resolve them.

At the end of the chapter, we rewrite the sprite sample, from Part II, "Sprites, Backgrounds, and Primary Surfaces," in assembly language. We then show you how to use the Pentium pairing and scheduling rules to improve the performance of the sample.

19.1 Architectural Overview

The Pentium processor includes a set of features that enables it to sustain an execution rate of up to two instructions every clock cycle. These features include a five-stage pipelined architecture, dual execution pipelines (U and V), separate instruction and data L1 caches, two Write buffers, instruction prefetching, and branch prediction (see Figure 19-1).

In order to sustain a high execution rate, you must first understand how these components work and how to mold your code to satisfy their constraints. For example, you cannot assume that you have an unlimited instruction cache, so it would be best to fit your inner loops into an 8K block.

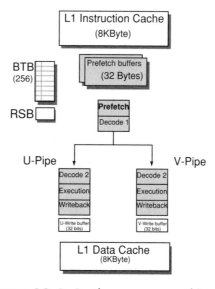

FIGURE 19-1 Pentium processor architectural diagram.

In the following sections, you'll get a detailed look into each of the Pentium processor features and understand what you can do to make them work more efficiently.

19.2 Instruction and Data L1 Caches

19.2.1 Operational Overview

The L1 cache is on-chip static memory that satisfies internal read/write requests more quickly than an external bus cycle to memory can. In addition, the L1 cache reduces the processor usage of the external bus, thus allowing other devices—DMA, bus maters, and so forth—to move data on the bus.

The Pentium processor has two independent L1 caches; one satisfies data accesses, and the other satisfies instruction fetches. The two caches exist on two separate internal buses (each bus is 64 bits wide), so the processor can load instruction and data in the same clock cycle. The Intel 486 can only load data or instructions at any given moment because its instruction and data share one L1 cache.

Both the instruction and the data L1 caches are divided into 32-byte cache lines—this is the minimum granularity of the L1 cache. When the processor transfers data between the L1 cache and the external bus (main memory or the L2 cache), it transfers a minimum of one cache line at a time.

The Pentium Pro exhibits different behavior on cache write misses.

On a read or write hit, the L1 cache satisfies the request in 1 clock cycle. On a read miss, the processor bursts an entire cache line into the L1 cache. If a multi-byte read crosses a cache line boundary, the next consecutive cache line is also brought into the L1 cache. On a write miss, the Pentium writes the data directly to the L2 cache or to main memory.

19.2.2 Performance Considerations

To put it simply, "Reuse it while it's in the L1 cache." If you have already brought in code or data from main memory to the L1 cache, make sure that you use it while it's still there—before it gets flushed out. Following are a few suggestions to accomplish this task.

■ *Keep the size of your inner loops below 8K.* If your most executed loop does not fit in the L1 code cache, the L1 cache will thrash continuously. To fix this problem, you can break the task at hand into smaller tasks with smaller loops that fit within the L1 cache. To find out the size of your loop, you can either look into the map file generated by the linker or use VTune's static analyzer (see Chapter 21).

You should also watch out for in-line macros and functions that, if used often, could bloat the size of your code.

- *Reuse data while it's in the L1 cache.* If possible, operate on the data while it's in the L1 cache. Since multimedia data does not typically fit in the L1 cache, you can operate on part of the data at one time rather than the full set. For example, instead of decoding the entire video frame in one loop, you can decode the top half of the frame from start to finish and then the bottom half—or whatever size fits in the L1 cache.

- *Allocate data ahead of time.* As we mentioned earlier, on a read miss, the Pentium processor brings in an entire cache line to the L1 cache. Once the requested data is available, it is forwarded immediately to the requesting instruction for processing. The processor then reads the remainder of the cache line.

Now, while the cache line is being brought in, if another instruction accesses uncached memory or causes another read miss (from another line), the second instruction will stall until the entire cache line is completely brought in. But if the second instruction accesses data that's already in the L1 cache, the instruction executes normally.

Accordingly, you could possibly achieve better performance if you could bring in data into the L1 cache before you're ready to use it—allocating data ahead of time.

For example, assume you're processing two buffers, A and B, sequentially and that you're processing one cache line every iteration of the loop as shown below:

```
ToOfLoop:
  Read cache line A[i]        Waits for A[i] to be completely brought in.
  Read cache line B[j]  ◄────
  Process cache lines A[i] and B[j]
  Increment i and j by one cache line
Goto TopOfLoop
```

So before you can process the two cache lines, you have to wait for the entire A cache line and some of the B cache line to be brought in—and the same thing happens for every iteration of the code. You can rearrange the code in such a way that you can interleave bringing in the data to the L1 cache with some useful operations.

In the following code we read the first two cache lines outside the loop and then we wait for both of them to finish. At the top of the loop, rather than processing the two cache lines, we allocate the A cache line for the next iteration ahead of time. While the cache line is being brought in, we do some processing on the first two cache lines—they're already in the L1 cache. We then read the B cache line for the next iteration and then finish processing the first two cache lines. By the time we get back to the top of the loop, we should have the next A and B cache lines waiting in the L1 cache—so we accomplish the same operations without the wait.

```
Read cache line A[i]
Read cache line B[j]

TopOfLoop:
  Read cache line A[I+32]          ◊ Pre-allocate for next iteration.
  Process some of A[i] and B[j]    ◊ Process them from L1 cache.
  Read cache line B[j+32]          ◊ Pre-allocate for next iteration.
  Process remainder of A[i] and B[j]  ◊ Process them from L1 cache.
  Increment i and j by one cache line
GoTo TopOfLoop
```

One of the major enhancements in the Pentium Pro processor is the Nonblocking Read feature. The Pentium processor stalls completely when two back-to-back read misses occur. The Pentium Pro, on the other hand, allows other instructions to execute while it's waiting for data to be brought into the L1 cache.

19.3 Instruction Prefetch

19.3.1 Operational Overview

The Pentium processor includes a prefetch unit that is capable of fetching unaligned instructions and instructions split between two cache lines without any penalty. It features two 32-byte prefetch buffers that operate in conjunction with the Branch Target Buffer (BTB) to fetch raw opcodes from the cache or main memory (see the discussion on BTB below). One prefetch buffer fetches instructions sequentially; the other fetches instructions speculatively, according to the branch history in the BTB. Notice, however, that only one of the prefetch buffers is active at any given time.

Prefetches are requested sequentially until a branch instruction is fetched. When a branch instruction is fetched, the address of the instruction is looked up in the BTB, and if it is found, the behavior history of the instruction is used to determine its outcome—taken or not taken. If the branch is predicted as not taken, prefetches continue with the next sequential instruction; otherwise the other prefetch buffer is directed to start fetching from the branch target address—as if the branch will be taken.

The actual outcome of the branch is only determined when the branch instruction is executed. If the branch was mispredicted, both the U and V instruction pipelines are flushed, and prefetching activity starts all over.

19.3.2 Performance Considerations

In reality, there are no special considerations for the prefetch unit in the Pentium processor. The following general guidelines are helpful, although they will be of more use for the Pentium Pro processor.

- Align loops, branch, and function labels on 16-byte boundary.
- Keep infrequently executed code separate from inner loops, such as initialization code and error handlers, so that it will not be prefetched and decoded unnecessarily.
- Do not interleave data with code, such as jump tables, because you don't want the data to be prefetched and decoded unnecessarily.

(We'll discuss improving the performance of the prefetch unit in more detail in the Pentium II chapter.)

19.4 Branch Prediction and the Branch Target Buffer

19.4.1 Operational Overview

The Pentium processor includes a branch prediction unit (BPU), which predicts the outcome of branch instructions when they are first decoded. What's important here is that the processor take the prediction seriously and start executing instructions from the predicted address—until it finds otherwise when the actual branch result is determined. When a branch instruction is mispredicted, the processor saves the address of the instruction and the correct path (taken or not taken) in the Branch Target Buffer (BTB), which is simply a lookup table with 256 entries.

How does the BTB work? When the BPU encounters a branch instruction, it looks up the address of the instruction in the BTB. If it finds the address, the BPU looks at the history of this instruction and determines whether or not the branch should be taken. If the instruction was taken before, the BPU assumes that it will be taken again, and if not, the branch won't be taken. This is called *dynamic prediction.* If the branch is predicted taken, the BPU directs the prefetch unit to fetch raw opcodes, from the predicted branch address, into the second prefetch buffer.

The Pentium Pro's static predictions are slightly different from those of the Pentium processor.

If the BPU does not find the branch instruction in the BTB, the Pentium processor assumes that the branch will not be taken and that execution will continue sequentially with the next instruction. This is called the *static prediction.*

19.4.2   A Closer Look at the BTB

If you're as unlucky as I am, you probably get a ticket when you're caught speeding. The next time you get caught speeding, the officer can easily look up your record and will probably give you a bigger fine. Now, if you're a good citizen—or you just never get caught—you won't have such a record.

The BTB works in a similar fashion; it only keeps a record of mispredicted branch instructions. When an instruction is mispredicted, the instruction is "ticketed" and a record of it is kept in the BTB. The address of the instruction, the target branch address, and the result of the branch are recorded in the BTB (Figure 19-2). The next time any instruction comes through, its address is matched against the instruction address in the BTB. If the address is found, the outcome of the instruction is predicted based on the "taken/not taken" flag in the BTB. If the instruction is predicted as taken, the prefetch unit is directed to fetch instructions from the target address in the BTB (see Figure 19-2).

	Instruction Address	Target Address	Taken or Not
1	80001000	80001D00	Taken
2	80003001	None	Not
3	8000D000	80002C00	Taken
	⋮ ⋮ ⋮	⋮ ⋮ ⋮	⋮ ⋮ ⋮
	⋮ ⋮ ⋮	⋮ ⋮ ⋮	⋮ ⋮ ⋮
256			

FIGURE 19-2 BTB structure.

PART VI

19.4.3 Performance Considerations

As we mentioned earlier, the actual outcome of a branch is only determined when the instruction is executed—in the execute stage. If the branch instruction was predicted correctly, the processor continues on its merry way. If the branch instruction was mispredicted, the processor flushes both pipelines and starts fetching from the correct address. As a result, the processor is stalled until the correct sequence of instructions is fetched and fed to the decoder unit.

You can determine how long it will take the processor to execute branch instructions, assuming that instruction opcodes are already in the L1 cache. Here's how the process works.

Pentium Pros exhibit a different behavior for backward branches not found in the BTB.

Branch instructions not found in the BTB are assumed not taken. Notice that this includes unconditional branches: if they're not in the BTB, they're assumed not taken. Why? As you recall, the BPU makes its prediction in the first decode stage of the pipeline. At that stage, the BPU does not know the branch target address of the instruction if the unconditional branch instruction is not in the BTB—because the instruction has not been fully decoded yet. This case is highlighted in Table 19-1.

Use Table 19-1 to determine how many clocks it takes to execute a branch instruction. Notice that the table assumes that the instructions of the correct branch address are already in the L1 code cache. If the instructions aren't in L1, it takes much longer to fetch the instructions from the L2 cache or main memory.

TABLE 19-1 Pentium Processor Branch Behavior

	Predicted	Unconditional	Conditional
Direct	Correctly	1	1
	Incorrectly	3	3U/4V
Indirect	Correctly	2	2
	Incorrectly	4	4U/5V

Now that you know how the branch prediction unit and the BTB operate, we'll leave you with a few suggestions that could help you minimize branch mispredictions in your code:

- *Minimize branch misprediction.* You can use VTune dynamic analyzer or the internal Pentium performance counters to determine if you have a high rate of branch mispredictions and to pinpoint the guilty routines. Armed with this information you can rearrange your code for better branch prediction.

- *Try to fit code with high branch misprediction in the L1 cache.* As we mentioned earlier, it only takes 3–4 cycles to recover from a branch misprediction if the correct target address is in the L1 cache. But if the mispredicted branch address is in the L2 cache or main memory, the penalty for branch misprediction is much higher. Refer to the "L1 cache" section for more information about the L1 cache.

- *Avoid loops with a huge amount of mispredicted branches.* A huge number of mispredicted branches will thrash the BTB, since it can hold only the last 256 mispredicted distinct instruction addresses. As a result, the next time the loop comes around, no history of the mispredicted instructions will exist, and as a result you could have a high branch misprediction rate.

19.5 Dual Pipelined Execution

19.5.1 Operational Overview

The Pentium processor includes two execution pipelines (U and V), which can execute two instructions in parallel (Figure 19-3a). Each pipeline is divided into five execution stages, which allow for overlapped execution of different instructions at any given time (Figure 19-3b).

At its maximum capacity, each pipeline can operate on up to five instructions at any given time, or a total of up to ten instructions in both pipelines (Figure 19-3c). Notice that although the two pipelines can operate on that many instructions at any given time, they can sustain only up to two instructions per clock cycle. The fact is, without pipelining, each instruction would require at least 5 clocks to complete. Because of pipelining, the Pentium processor can operate on five instructions at any given time and sustain an execution rate of up to two instructions per clock cycle.

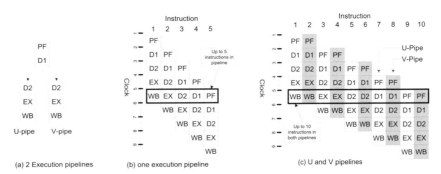

FIGURE 19-3 The Pentium processor's dual execution pipelines.

PART VI

19.5.2 Performance Considerations

Typically the pipeline is not maintained at its maximum capacity because of data dependency, register contention, or other restrictions imposed by the processor. These restrictions are known as the Pentium pairing rules (we discuss these in more detail in the following section).

Figure 19-4 shows a couple of stalls caused by data dependency and instruction prefetch. In the first case (inside bold box), the processor is waiting for data or the result of an address calculation. In the second case, the fetch unit is fetching instructions from the L2 cache or main memory, which causes bubbles to propagate in the pipeline.

Similar bubbles could fill up the V pipeline if your instructions don't adhere to the Pentium pairing rules. The Pentium processor issues two consecutive instructions in both pipelines only if the first instruction is pairable in the U pipeline and the second instruction is pairable in the V pipeline. If the two instructions don't pair, both will execute in the U pipeline in 2 clock cycles, and the V pipeline will be empty—bubbly.

19.5.3 Pentium Integer Pairing Rules

The Pentium processor pairs two instructions only if they satisfy *all* the pairing rules listed in Figure 19-5. In the figure, three examples are listed for each of the rules illustrating the usage of the rule.

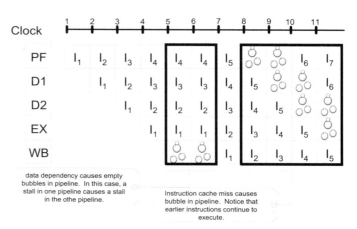

FIGURE 19-4 Data dependency and instruction fetch bubbles in the pipeline.

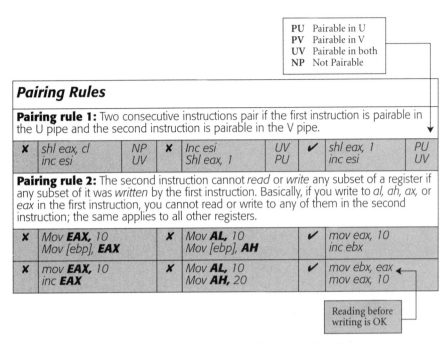

	PU	Pairable in U
	PV	Pairable in V
	UV	Pairable in both
	NP	Not Pairable

Pairing Rules

Pairing rule 1: Two consecutive instructions pair if the first instruction is pairable in the U pipe and the second instruction is pairable in the V pipe.

| ✗ | shl eax, cl | NP | ✗ | Inc esi | UV | ✔ | shl eax, 1 | PU |
| | inc esi | UV | | Shl eax, 1 | PU | | inc esi | UV |

Pairing rule 2: The second instruction cannot *read* or *write* any subset of a register if any subset of it was *written* by the first instruction. Basically, if you write to *al, ah, ax,* or *eax* in the first instruction, you cannot read or write to any of them in the second instruction; the same applies to all other registers.

✗	Mov **EAX,** 10		✗	Mov **AL,** 10		✔	mov eax, 10
	Mov [ebp], **EAX**			Mov [ebp], **AH**			inc ebx
✗	mov **EAX,** 10		✗	Mov **AL,** 10		✔	mov ebx, eax
	inc **EAX**			Mov **AH,** 20			mov eax, 10

Reading before writing is OK

FIGURE 19-5 Pentium integer pairing rules.

For optimal pairing, always use simple instructions such as memory moves, ALU operations, and logical operations. You can use VTune's static analyzer to easily determine the pairability of your instructions.[1]

19.5.4 Address Generation Interlock (AGI)

The Pentium Pro processor does not suffer from AGI stalls.

As an extension to pairing rule 2, the Pentium processor suffers a 1-clock penalty because of Address Generation Interlock (AGI). AGI stalls occur when an instruction writes to a register that is then used as a base or an index in the following clock cycle. For example, consider the following two instructions:

```
Mov esi, eax
Mov ebx, [esi]
```

The second instruction suffers from an AGI stall since it uses the *esi* register as a base register, and *esi* was just updated in the first instruction (see Figure 19-6). As a result, both processor pipelines stall for 1 clock cycle as below.

---

1. You can find a list of instruction pairability in the *Intel Architecture Optimization Manual* found on the companion CD.

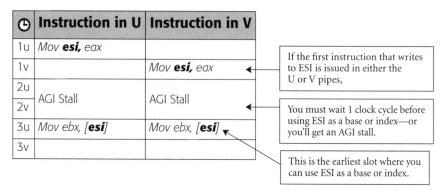

🕐	**Instruction in U**	**Instruction in V**
1u	*Mov **esi**, eax*	
1v		*Mov **esi**, eax* ◄
2u	AGI Stall	AGI Stall
2v		◄
3u	*Mov ebx, [**esi**]*	*Mov ebx, [**esi**]*
3v		

If the first instruction that writes to ESI is issued in either the U or V pipes,

You must wait 1 clock cycle before using ESI as a base or index—or you'll get an AGI stall.

This is the earliest slot where you can use ESI as a base or index.

FIGURE 19-6 AGI stall in the Pentium processor.

To avoid AGI stalls, you can insert other useful instructions between the two instructions—as long as the inserted instructions don't use *esi* as a base or an index.

19.6 Write Buffers

19.6.1   **Operational Overview**

The Pentium with MMX technology processor has four Write buffers that can be accessed by either pipe.

The Pentium processor features two 32-bit Write buffers that queue data on its way to the external bus—the L2 cache or main memory. One buffer is dedicated to the U pipe and one to the V pipe. The main purpose of the Write buffers is to enhance the performance of consecutive writes to memory. Note that the Write buffers are not used when you write to memory addresses that are already in the L1 cache; only writes to the external bus are queued in the Write buffers.

So why are the Write buffers useful? Without the Write buffers, when you write data to memory that is not part of the L1 cache—uncached memory

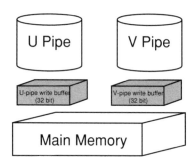

FIGURE 19-7 The Pentium processor's Write buffers.

or elsewhere—the processor has to wait until the data is completely transferred before it can move on to the next instruction. Depending on where the data has to go—main memory, the L2 cache, and so forth, the write can take a long time to complete compared to when you're writing to the L1 cache. The Write buffers can hold the data until it has a chance to write it to memory. Meanwhile the processor is allowed to continue execution at the next instruction.

Now, if the processor is asked to write another piece of data to memory—from the same pipe—while the first bit of data is still being written to memory, the processor stalls until the original data in the Write buffer is written to memory. The Write buffer is also flushed out if you read from a memory location that is not in the L1 cache or from uncached memory—and the processor stalls until the Write buffers are flushed before it executes the read.

19.6.2 Performance Considerations

You typically don't have to worry about the Write buffers unless you're writing data to video memory or some other uncached memory location. Multimedia video applications that write directly to video memory—uncached memory—could benefit greatly if developers paid special attention to the pattern in which video is written to video memory.

Since it takes time to write data to video memory, you could space out the writes and do some processing in between. The time it takes to write to video memory depends on many factors, such as the type of memory used on the graphics adapter. For the sake of simplicity, assume that on a 100-MHz processor it takes 10 CPU cycles to write a 32-bit word to video memory. If you continuously write from a register to video memory, you'll write 32 bits every 10 clock cycles—of course, you're stalling for 9 of them.[2] Now, if you have some other processing to do, you can fill the 9 cycles getting some useful work accomplished—as long as you access your data from the L1 cache. For example, in a color conversion routine, rather than converting the whole image in system memory and then writing it out to the video card, you can perform the color conversion calculations in between writes to video memory—as long as you only access registers or the L1 cache.

At this point, you might have the impression that you only need to assure that instructions pair correctly in order to gain performance. Ideally, this is

---

2. For a faster processor, you wait the same physical time, but you wait more processor clocks. That means you can squeeze in even more instructions between writes to memory.

true as long as your code and data are waiting in the L1 cache. Unfortunately, with multimedia applications, you cannot make such an assumption, since you typically deal with a huge amount of data, and not all of it will fit in the L1 cache at once.

Because the L2 cache and memory run much more slowly than the internal components, the processor has to wait for them to deliver code or data. Even though the L2 cache and memory can get faster, they can't have the same speed ramp as the processor. As a result, the situation gets even worse with faster processors, since they have to wait more clocks for the same response time from the L2 cache or main memory.

As a multimedia developer, you must pay special attention to how you access your data. Multimedia applications are memory intensive in nature and exert a huge demand on the memory subsystem. Depending on the nature of the data, certain access patterns are more efficient than others. For example, you can preload the data to make sure that it is in the L1 cache before you use it. You can also space out your writes to video memory and do some useful operations in between.

We could spend a whole chapter on memory optimization issues, and that is exactly what we did. We devoted the chapter at the end of this part to discussing memory optimization techniques.

19.7 Revisiting Our Sprite Sample

Great! You've made it this far. Now you can take a deep breath. But are your hands still itching to optimize something? Let's use the assembly version[3] of the sprite sample from Part II and try to figure out how we can optimize its performance on the Pentium processor.

19.7.1 Overview of the Assembly Version of CSprite

First let's see how the sprite sample works. As you know, a sprite is a regular bitmap where one of the colors is designated to be transparent. A sprite is typically overlaid on top of a background, and only the nontransparent pixels of the sprite show up against the background. Of course, there are many ways to overlay a sprite on top of a background. For example, you can read pixels from both images and merge them in memory and then write out the

---

 3. The assembly version of the sprite was only mentioned in Part II. You can find the sources on the companion CD.

merged result to the video screen. But if the background is already in video memory, this might be an expensive solution—video memory takes a long time to write and even longer to read.

In our implementation, we assume that the background is already in video memory. We first read 4 bytes (a DWORD) from the sprite and only write out the nontransparent pixels to the screen. To do that, you could look at each pixel in the sprite to determine if it is transparent or not, and only write out the nontransparent ones. But this strategy causes a huge branch misprediction problem since you don't really know yet what's in the sprite.

Since we're dealing with a static sprite, we decided to preprocess the sprite to figure out which pixels we really need to write. The outcome of the pre-processing is a command list indicating which pixels we should care about and which we shouldn't even examine. Another advantage of the command list is that we avoid using compare instructions while we're displaying the sprite, so we are saved all the branch mispredictions that otherwise would occur.

Consider the sprite bitmap in Figure 19-8. When we preprocess the sprite, we handle one DWORD at a time and decide what we're supposed to do for that DWORD. For example, the first DWORD in line 0 says: "only draw the third pixel." The next one says, "Draw all four pixels," and so on. These are basically the commands in the command list. Table 19-2 shows us the command list we would generate for this sprite.

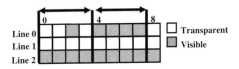

FIGURE 19-8 Simple sprite.

TABLE 19-2 Command List for a Sprite

Line	Command
0	*WriteByte3, WriteDWord, EndOfLine*
1	*SkipLine*
2	*SolidLine, EndOfSprite*

When it's time to display the sprite, we first read the command list and then do whatever the command says. Notice that we never have to deal with transparent pixels at all; we know exactly which pixels we need to write. This allows us to process the sprite in less time and reduces the bandwidth on the system bus.

To avoid branch mispredictions, we designed the commands in such a way that they could be used as an index to a jump table (Figure 19-9). The *JumpTable[]* array holds the address of the label that handles that task. You'll see what we're getting at soon.

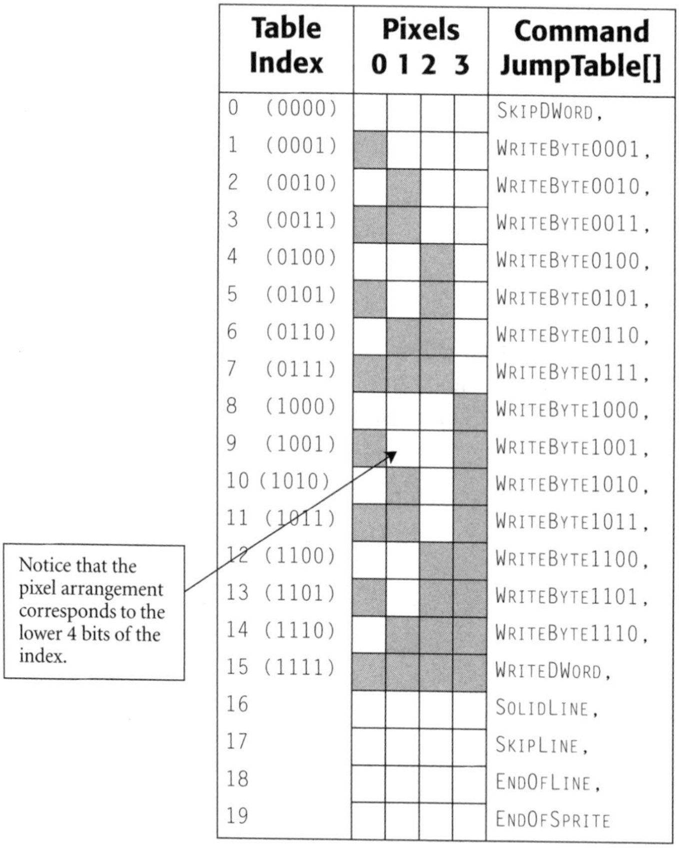

Table Index	Pixels 0 1 2 3	Command JumpTable[]
0 (0000)		SKIPDWORD,
1 (0001)		WRITEBYTE0001,
2 (0010)		WRITEBYTE0010,
3 (0011)		WRITEBYTE0011,
4 (0100)		WRITEBYTE0100,
5 (0101)		WRITEBYTE0101,
6 (0110)		WRITEBYTE0110,
7 (0111)		WRITEBYTE0111,
8 (1000)		WRITEBYTE1000,
9 (1001)		WRITEBYTE1001,
10 (1010)		WRITEBYTE1010,
11 (1011)		WRITEBYTE1011,
12 (1100)		WRITEBYTE1100,
13 (1101)		WRITEBYTE1101,
14 (1110)		WRITEBYTE1110,
15 (1111)		WRITEDWORD,
16		SOLIDLINE,
17		SKIPLINE,
18		ENDOFLINE,
19		ENDOFSPRITE

Notice that the pixel arrangement corresponds to the lower 4 bits of the index.

FIGURE 19-9 Sprite command jump table.

Now, if you apply this jump table to the sprite in Figure 19-8, you'll end up with the command list shown in Table 19-3.

TABLE 19-3 Command List for the Simple Sprite

Line	Command	CommandList[]
0	WriteByte0100,	4
	WriteDWord,	15
	EndOfLine	18
1	SkipLine	17
2	SolidLine,	16
	EndOfSprite	19

When the *BltSprite()* function is first called, it performs an unconditional jump to the first command in the command list. After a command is executed, a similar jump transfers control to the next command in the list. This process is repeated until the *EndOfSprite* is reached, which returns control to the caller routine. Notice in Figure 19-9 that each command processes at least one DWORD of the sprite.

```
// This is a pseudo code that demonstrates how the jump table works.
// The pCommandList points to the first command into the JumpTable.
BltSprite(PBYTE *pSrc, PBYTE *pDst, PBYTE *pCommandList)
{
    // Execute the first command in the list.
    goto JumpTable[*pCommandList++];

WriteByte0001:                          // Only write first byte of DWORD
    pDst[0] = pSrc[0];
    pSrc+=4, pDst+=4;                    // go to next DWORD
    goto JumpTable[*pCommandList++];

WriteByte0010:                          // Only write second byte of DWORD
    pDst[1] = pSrc[1];
    pSrc+=4, pDst+=4;
    goto JumpTable[*pCommandList ++];

WriteDWord:                             // Write entire DWORD
    ((DWORD*)pDst)[0] = ((DWORD*)pSrc)[0];
    pSrc+=4, pDst+=4;
    goto JumpTable[*pCommandList ++];

    // The rest of the operations are similar…

EndOfSprite:                            // Done…
    return;
}
```

19.7.2 Analyzing the Performance of Our Sprite Sample

Before we go into some analysis, you should be aware that you can easily use VTune to figure out if an instruction sequence pair will work. But in order to figure out how to optimize your code, you'll still need to have knowledge of the Pentium pairing rules.

In the following illustration, we'll show you our thinking process when we hand-optimize our code. For the purpose of our analysis, let's try to optimize the assembly version of the WriteDWord command shown below.

```
WriteDWord:
    mov ecx, [esi]          ; Read DWORD from sprite
    mov [edi], ecx          ; Write DWORD to background
    inc ebx                 ; increment index pointer
    mov dl, [ebx]           ; read jump table index
    add esi, 4              ; next DWORD to sprite
    add edi, 4              ; next DWORD in background
    jmp JumpTable[edx*4]    ; Jump to next macro based on index.
```

Typically, when you schedule instructions, you start the analysis from the first instruction in a block and try to pair it with the next sequential instruction according to the Pentium pairing rules. If the first two instructions do not pair, you would skip the first instruction and try to pair the second one with the third, and so on.

In Table 19-4, you can find the nonoptimized sequence of the WriteDWord command. In the first column we see the instruction sequence where paired instructions are separated by a blank line. The second column has the num-

TABLE 19-4 The Nonoptimized Version of the *WriteDWord* Command

Before (7 clocks)	🕐	Analysis Steps
1. mov ecx, [esi+1]	1	• (1,2) do not pair because (2) uses a register written by 1(**Pairing Rule 2**)
2. mov [edi+1], ecx 3. inc ebx	1	• (2,3) pair; both instructions are UV pairable, and there is no dependency
4. mov dl, [ebx] 5. add esi, 4	2	• (4,5) pair; however, there is an additional clock because of an AGI stall—EBX was just incremented.
6. add edi, 4	1	• (6,7) do not pair because (7) is not pairable (**Pairing Rule 1**).
7. jmp jumptable[edx*4]	2	• Indirect register jumps are not pairable; they also take 2 clocks to execute when the jump address is in BTB (**PR1 & Branch Timing**).

ber of clocks it takes to execute each pair of instructions, and the last column illustrates the step-by-step thinking process that we used to figure out if two instructions could be paired.

Based on the analysis, you can see that there are a few pairing and scheduling problems in the code. For example, instruction 4 has an AGI because the *ebx* register was just incremented in instruction 3. To avoid an AGI stall, you could switch the two instructions and use `mov dl, [ebx+1]` to reference the correct byte. See Table 19-5 for an optimized version of the WriteDWord command.

TABLE 19-5 Optimized Version of the *WriteDWord* Command from the Sprite Sample

Before (5 clocks)	🕒	Analysis Steps
1. mov ecx, [esi+1] 2. mov dl, [ebx+1]	1	• *(1,2) pair*
3. inc ebx 4. add esi, 4	1	• *(3,4) pair*
5. mov [edi+1], ecx 6. add edi, 4	1	• *(5,6) pair*
7. jmp JumpTable[edx*4]	2	• *Indirect register jumps are not pairable. Take 2 clocks when jump address is in BTB.*

This simple optimization resulted in a gain of 2 clocks. In reality, it would be great if either of the above samples executed in 5 or 7 cycles. Unfortunately, both sequences take much longer to execute than indicated because we are writing the results directly to video memory, and this process, as we mentioned earlier, is very slow compared to how fast the processor can run.

Also note that the same instruction performs unaligned memory writes depending on the position of the sprite on the screen. Misaligned memory writes take more cycles to execute because the processor splits the write into smaller writes.

In Table 19-6, you can see the actual measurements for both the nonoptimized and the optimized versions of the WriteDWord command. In our measurement, we used the worst-case sprite for the WriteDWord command, where all pixels are visible and the sprite width is a multiple of 4.

TABLE 19-6 Measured Cycle Timing for Nonoptimized and Optimized Versions of the *WriteDWord* Command

Output Buffer Alignment	Nonoptimized		Optimized	
	Clocks/ Sprite	Clocks/ 4 Pixels	Clocks/ Sprite	Clocks/ 4 Pixels
0	14550	11	14480	11
1	53600	40.5	53300	40
2	53700	40.5	53400	40
3	53600	40.5	53400	40

Notice that the 2-clock gain in performance is not even noticeable. As we mentioned before, this is because the slow video memory access chews up the 2-clock gain we saw in the optimized version.

You can use VTune to detect misaligned accesses.

Take a closer look at the measurements again. Notice that all misaligned writes to video memory result in a huge penalty compared to the aligned writes (~30 clocks/DWORD). As a result, we rewrote the WriteDWord command to perform only aligned memory writes with some shifting and masking. And, as we expected, we received a huge performance boost (~13 clocks/DWORD). You can find a copy of the aligned write implementation of the sprite on the companion CD.

19.7.3 Do I Really Need to Schedule My Code?

Absolutely! We deliberately selected this example for two reasons. First, to show you how to optimize your code from the processor's point of view. Second, to point out that other components in the system, such as video memory, can adversely affect your application performance. You will definitely benefit from scheduling instructions, especially if the data is close to the processor (basically, in registers or L1 or L2 cache). For example, sprites written into system memory execute at 8 clocks/DWORD, and sprites written into video memory execute at 38 clocks/DWORD. We have found that most multimedia algorithms, such as those for compression, decompression, image filtration, and 3D benefit from instruction scheduling.

WHAT HAVE YOU LEARNED?

At this stage, you should be familiar with the internal components of the Pentium processor, and you should have an idea of what you can do to achieve optimal performance on this processor. Here is a recap of the tips you should have picked up by reading this chapter:

- Know your data: what does it look like, where does it come from, and where is it going to? (See Chapter 23 for more.)
- Align loops, unconditional branches, and function labels to 8-byte cache boundary.
- Keep infrequently executed code and data separate from the inner loops.
- Use simple instructions for optimal pairing.
- Avoid branch mispredictions and AGI stalls.
- Measure the performance of your code, because this is the best way to get a sense of how well it is executing.

CHAPTER 20

The Pentium with MMX Technology Processor

WHY READ THIS CHAPTER?

In this chapter you'll learn about the Pentium with MMX technology processor and its own pairing and scheduling rules (the Pentium II processor is discussed in a later chapter).

In this chapter, you will

- get an architectural overview of MMX technology,
- learn about the MMX data types, instructions, and register set,
- learn the MMX pairing and scheduling rules,
- see how to mix floating-point and MMX instructions using the EMMS guideline,
- rewrite the sprite sample using MMX instructions, and
- optimize the sprite for MMX technology using the scheduling rules.

20.1 A Look at MMX Technology

With the Pentium processor, Intel implemented parallel processing with dual execution pipelines. MMX technology is the latest major addition to the Intel Architecture, including fifty-seven new instructions, and eight new 64-bit registers. With MMX technology, Intel took parallel processing to the level where a single instruction operates on multiple elements of data—this is known as Single Instruction Multiple Data (SIMD).

Although the name *MMX* might imply a specific set of applications, *multimedia*, the new instruction set is a general-purpose implementation of the

SIMD concept. It benefits all applications that perform the same operation repetitively on contiguous blocks of data.

MMX technology introduces a new set of instructions and registers. The instructions operate in parallel on BYTE, WORD, DWORD, and QWORD data types packed into 64-bit registers. They perform signed and unsigned arithmetic, logical, packing, and unpacking operations on the previously mentioned data types' boundaries. They allow for saturation or wrap-around to handle overflow and under-flow conditions.

In this chapter, you will first get an overview of MMX technology and a brief description of the instruction and register sets. You will then learn the MMX scheduling rules and how to apply them to the sprite sample.

20.2 SIMD

Typically, integer instructions operate on individual integer data elements $(A + B)$ (see Figure 20-1a). SIMD instructions, on the other hand, operate on integer data arrays $(A[1..n]+B[1..n])$, where n is the number of elements in the array, for example, $n = 4$ in (see Figure 20-1b).

In Figure 20-1, note that the SIMD processor duplicates the same execution unit four times. Consequently, the SIMD processor can process four data elements in the same clock cycle (Figure 20-1b) while the scalar single instruction, single data (SISD) processor takes four clock cycles to process the same data (Figure 20-1a).

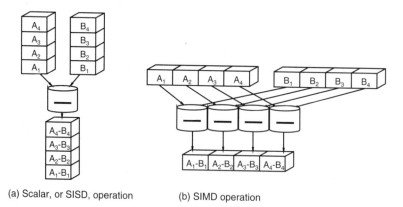

(a) Scalar, or SISD, operation   (b) SIMD operation

FIGURE 20-1 Scalar versus SIMD operations.

20.3 Architectural Overview

The Pentium with MMX technology is the first implementation of the MMX technology, based on the Pentium processor. Recently Intel added MMX technology to the Pentium Pro to create the Pentium II processor. In this chapter we'll discuss only the extension of MMX technology to the Pentium processor. The Pentium II processor is discussed in Chapter 22.

Figure 20-2 shows an architectural overview of the Pentium with MMX technology processor. The processor includes eight new MMX registers and fifty-seven new MMX instructions. In addition, the processor doubles the size of the L1 code and data caches to 16K each and adds a Return Stack Buffer, which reduces the overhead of function returns. Finally, the two dedicated Pentium Write buffers are replaced with four shared Write buffers—32 bits each.

20.3.1 The Pool of Four Write Buffers

In the previous chapter, we mentioned that the Pentium processor has two dedicated Write buffers, which are used to queue data writes that do not hit the L1 cache, write through cache, or write to uncached memory. In the Pentium processor without MMX technology, one buffer is dedicated to the U pipe and one is dedicated to the V pipe. As a result of this constraint, each pipeline is allowed to queue only one memory write before the pipeline gets stalled.

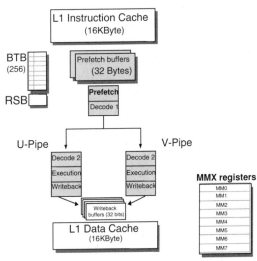

FIGURE 20-2 Architectural view of the Pentium with MMX technology processor.

PART VI

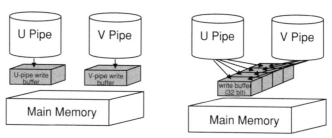

FIGURE 20-3 Write buffers for Pentium and Pentium with MMX technology processors.

To enhance write performance, the Pentium with MMX technology processor doubled the number of Write buffers—to four 32-bit Write buffers. It also removed the constraint that buffers are dedicated to a specific pipeline. Any of the four buffers can be accessed from either pipeline allowing up to four back-to-back 32-bit memory writes or two 64-bit writes regardless of which pipeline the writes came from. As a result, each pipeline can write up to four 32-bit writes before stalling the pipeline (see Figure 20-3).

20.3.2   MMX Uses Floating-Point Registers

To maintain operating system compatibility, MMX technology maps the MMX registers on top of the IA floating-point (FP) registers. Figure 20-4 shows a diagram of the MMX registers mapped one-to-one to the mantissa part of the floating-point registers. As a result, when you read or write to an MMX register, you read and write to one of the floating-point registers and vice versa. The only difference is how the data is interpreted in the register—after all, it's only bits. MMX instructions interpret the data as packed bytes, words, or double words; floating-point instructions interpret the same data as the mantissa part of a floating-point number.

REASONING FOR ALIASING THE MMX REGISTER

Why are the MMX registers aliased? Current operating systems save and restore the contents of the integer and floating-point registers between task switches. If a new set of registers is added to the processor, the operating system would have to be modified in order to save and restore the new MMX registers between task switches. By mapping the MMX registers onto the floating-point registers, the contents of the MMX registers are saved and restored automatically between task switches. After all, they are the same bits. As a result, you can run MMX instructions under the current operating system without encountering any problems between task switches.

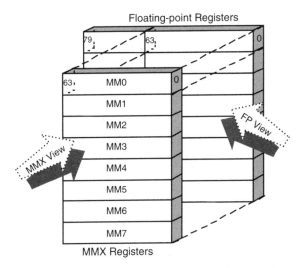

FIGURE 20-4 Aliasing of MMX registers on top of the floating-point registers.

So what's the catch? First, it's obvious that you cannot rely on the contents of the floating-point registers after you execute an MMX piece of code, or vice versa. What's not readily obvious is that the processor could generate floating-point errors when you execute a floating-point instruction after an MMX instruction. Why? Since an MMX instruction treats the entire 64 register bits as packed integers, it can write any sequence of bits in the MMX register. But from the floating-point of view, certain bit combinations in the mantissa combined with certain bits in the exponent generate floating-point errors such as NAN,[1] stack overflow or under-flow. Refer to the Pentium processor programmer's manual on the CD for more details.

20.3.3 EMMS to the Rescue: How to Mix MMX and FP Instructions

That is not to say that you can never mix MMX and floating-point code fragments in the same application. Rather, you can mix the two types of instructions if and only if you can guarantee that no floating-point errors will occur when you switch from MMX to floating-point. To do so, you must use the new MMX instruction *EMMS* (Empty MMX Technology State), which marks all the floating-point registers as *Empty*. To the floating-point unit, an empty register indicates that it does not have any data in the register and, therefore, does not generate stack overflow errors.

---

1. NAN: "Not a Number" in floating-point terminology.

EMMS takes 0–11 cycles on the Pentium II processor.

Notice that you should use the EMMS instructions wisely since the EMMS instruction can take up to 53 clock cycles to execute on the Pentium with MMX technology.[2] Ouch! Keeping that in mind, you should use the EMMS instructions only in the following situations:

- If you plan on mixing MMX and floating-point code in the same application, insert the EMMS instruction at the end of each MMX block.
- If your DLL exports an MMX function that could be called by an application that uses floating-point operations, insert the EMMS instruction before you return from the routine.

To use the EMMS instruction properly, just remember these simple rules:

- Minimize switching between MMX and floating-point instructions because the switch can be expensive (costing up to 53 cycles).
- Never mix MMX and floating-point instructions at the instruction level—separate the MMX and floating-point calculations into separate routines and use EMMS at the end of MMX routines.
- Never assume that the state of the registers is valid across transitions because both MMX and floating-point instructions write and read from the same physical register file.
- Always insert an EMMS instruction at the end of an MMX block unless you are absolutely sure that no floating-point instruction will be used.

20.4 MMX Technology Data Types

You can interpret the 64-bit data format in an MMX register according to the instruction that you use. Notice that with the exception of EMMS and the 32-bit memory transfer instruction (MOVD), all MMX technology instructions operate on one of the data formats shown in Figure 20-5.

The MOVD instruction operates on the lower 32 bits of an MMX register, where it transfers the register's contents to memory or to an integer register (*eax, ebx,* and so forth). The MOVD instruction also transfers 32 bits of data from memory or an integer register to the lower 32 bits of the MMX register; in this case, the high 32 bits are set to zero.

---

2. The actual EMMS instruction takes only 1 clock cycle to execute, but when the first floating-point instruction executes, it takes up to 53 cycles to completely switch to the floating-point mode.

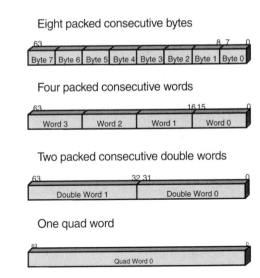

Eight packed consecutive bytes

Four packed consecutive words

Two packed consecutive double words

One quad word

FIGURE 20-5 Data formats for MMX technology instructions.

The EMMS instruction only affects the tag bits of the floating-point registers. It sets all the tag bits to 1, indicating that the floating-point registers are empty.

20.5 The MMX Instruction Set

With the introduction of MMX technology, Intel added fifty-seven new instructions to the IA architecture. These instructions consist of arithmetic, comparison, conversion, logical, shift, and data transfer instructions.

With the exception of EMMS and data transfer instructions (MOVQ and MOVD), all MMX instructions follow the format shown in Figure 20-6.

 In Table 20-1, you can find a list of the MMX instructions with a brief description of each. For a detailed description, please refer to the *Intel Architecture MMX Technology: Programmer's Reference Manual* found on the companion CD.

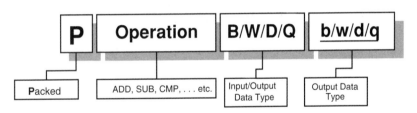

FIGURE 20-6 The MMX instruction format.

PART VI

TABLE 20-1 Summary of MMX Instruction Set

Instruction Type	Instruction	Description
Arithmetic	PADD[**B|W|D**]	Add with Wraparound
	PADDS[**B|W**]	Add signed with saturation
	PADDUS[**B|W**]	Add unsigned with saturation
	PSUB [**B|W|D**]	Subtract with Wraparound
	PSUBS[**B|W**]	Subtract signed with saturation
	PSUBUS[**B|W**]	Subtract unsigned with saturation
	PMULH**W**/ PMULL**W**	Multiply four words and store high/low 32-bit result in register
	PMADD**Wd**	Packed multiply and add
Comparison	PCMPEQ[**B|W|D**]	Compare if equal
	PCMPGT[**B|W|D**]	Compare if greater than
Conversion	PACKSS**Wb** PACKSS**Dw**	Convert signed WORD/DWORD to signed byte/word using signed saturation
	PACKUS**Wb**	Convert signed word to signed byte using signed saturation.
	PUNPCKH**Bw** PUNPCKH**Wd** PUNPCKH**Dq**	Interleave the high order 32-bit data elements of the source and destination operands across data type boundary.
	PUNPCKL**Bw** PUNPCKL**Wd** PUNPCKL**Dq**	Interleave the low order 32-bit data elements of the source and destination operands across data type boundary.
Logical	PAND	Bitwise logical AND
	PANDN	Bitwise logical AND NOT
	POR	Bitwise logical OR
	PXOR	Bitwise logical XOR
Shift	PSLL[**W|D|Q**] PSRL[**W|D|Q**]	Shift left/right logical without carry across data type boundary
	PSRA[**W|D**]	Shift right arithmetic where the sign is the most significant bit (MSB) for the specific data-type.
Data Transfer	MOVD	Transfers 32 bits between MMX register and integer register or memory
	MOVQ	Transfers 64 bits between MMX register and MMX register or memory
EMMS	EMMS	Empty MMX technology state. Clears FP tag word.

paddus **B**: Add 8 bytes using unsigned arithmetic with saturation.

FF	00	01	FF	FE	80	FF	FF

+

04	03	02	01	00	99	99	01

FF	03	03	FF	FE	FF	FF	FF

paddus **W**: Add 4 words using unsigned arithmetic with saturation.

FF	00	01	FF	FE	80	FF	FF

+

04	03	02	01	00	99	99	01

FF	FF	04	00	FF	19	FF	FF

Notice that some of the instructions have few formats for signed versus unsigned and wraparound versus saturation calculations. You already know about signed versus unsigned calculations, so let's make sure you understand the wraparound versus saturation modes.

Assume that you have 2 bytes, and you want to add them together using unsigned arithmetic. Since both are unsigned, their values can only range from 0 to 255. But when you add them together, the results could range from 0 to 510, which does not fit in 1 byte. So what do you do? Well, one option is to saturate the result to 255, and the other option is to keep only the lowest 8 bits of the result (the wraparound). Let's see how that works.

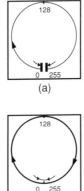

FIGURE 20-7 Unsigned case (a) and wraparound mode (b).

When you use *saturate* instructions, results greater than the maximum possible value are clamped to the maximum value. Results less than the minimum value are clamped to the minimum value. In the unsigned case, the final result would be clamped to 0 and 255, and in the signed case, they would be clamped to −127 and 127. It is just like trying to go around in a broken circle.

On the other hand, when you use *wraparound* mode, you would calculate the result to whatever precision possible and only keep the lowest significant 8 bits. It is just like going around in a circle.

20.6 Using MMX Technology to Render Our Sprite Sample

It's time to revisit our spite again. This time, let's use the new MMX instructions to implement our favorite sprite. When we worked with the sprite sample in the previous chapter, we used integer instructions to selectively write only the visible pixels of the sprite using byte writes (for example, mov [mem], al). Since MMX technology does not offer byte write operations, we cannot selectively write the visible pixels (1 byte at a time); rather we have to merge the sprite and the background in an MMX register and write the merged bytes to video memory. To do that, we use a Read/Modify/Write algorithm.

DEBUGGING MMX TECHNOLOGY INSTRUCTIONS

MSVC 4.1+ Support

Microsoft added support to the MMX technology instruction set starting from MSVC 4.1 in the form of in-line assembly using the _asm directive. Unfortunately, this support is not enabled by default, and there is no selection in the compiler settings to enable it. Microsoft added the compiler switch /G5M to allow the compiler to recognize and process MMX instructions.

The sprite sample makefile (project file) has the /G5M switch set. This is done in the compiler setting dialog box.

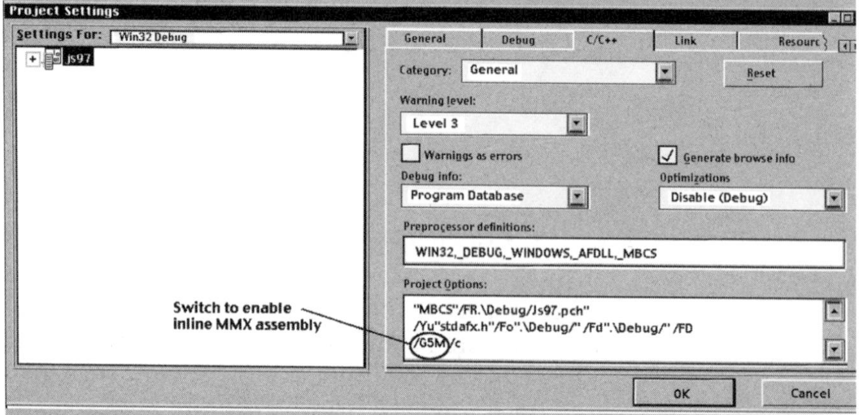

FIGURE 20-8 MSVC in-line MMX assembly support.

NuMega WinIce

NuMega WinIce also supports the new MMX instructions and registers. To view the MMX registers, use the command

WF | B, W, D where (assume an MMX register has the value 0×8877665544332211)

WFB displays MMX registers in BYTE format:

88	77	66	55	44	33	22	11

WFD displays MMX registers in DWORD format:

8877	6655	4433	2211

WFW displays MMX registers in WORD format:

88776655	4432211

With this method, first we read 8 bytes from the background image into one of the MMX registers, and then we apply the *visible* pixels to the background using some logical masking techniques. Finally, we write out the modified background to its original location.

In this sample, we'll simply re-implement the sprite sample we worked with in the previous chapter, but this time we will use MMX instructions. We start out by redefining the transparency color member variable to a 64-bit entity and duplicating the 8-bit transparency color byte to all 8 bytes.

```
class CSprite {
public:
    __int64 m_qwTransp;  // Allow space for 64 bit for MMX transparency
};

CSprite::CSprite(CBitmap &bitmap, BYTE byKeyColor)
{
    // Duplicate the transparency color accross the 8 bytes.
    memset (&m_qwTransp, byKeyColor, 8);
}
```

Next we replace the contents of the *Blt()* routine with our MMX technology sprite *Blt()* routine. This implementation of the sprite using MMX instructions is not yet optimized.

Before we start, notice that we're assuming an 8 bpp RGB color format and that the sprite is at least 8 pixels wide. The *Blt()* routine processes each scan line in two stages: The first stage handles the left side of the scan line 8 pixels at a time; the second stage handles the situations when the sprite width is not a multiple of 8 and handles the remaining pixels at the end of the scan line. Since both stages use the same technique for overlaying the sprite on top of a background, we'll discuss only the first stage, shown in the code that follows.

```
void CSprite::Blt(LPBYTE lpSurface, long lPitch, CPoint &point)
{
    PBYTE     pDst;
    DWORD     row, col;
    DWORD     dwHeight = m_dwHeight;
    __int64   qwTransp = m_qwTrasnp;
    PBYTE     pSprite = m_pData;
```

> Since the inline **_asm** cannot access class members, we have to copy it to a local variable first and then use the local within the **_asm** block.

```
    // compute address dst and src pixels.   note pitch can be negative
    pDst = (PBYTE)((long)lpSurface + point.x + point.y * lPitch);

    int n8ByteBlocks = m_dwWidth >> 3;  // number of 8-byte blocks
```

```
_asm {
    mov     edi, pDst
    mov     esi, pSprite
    movq    mm3, qwTransp

DoOneLine:
    // Check if sprite has more than 8 bytes in width.
    mov     ecx, n8ByteBlocks
    cmp     ecx, 0
    je      LessThan8BytesLeft

DoQWord:
    // This loop processes 8 pixels at a time
    movq    mm0, [esi]      // Sprite
    movq    mm1, [edi]      // BkGnd

    movq    mm2, mm3        // Transparency Color
    pcmpeqb mm2, mm0        // Transparency Mask
    pand    mm1, mm2        // keep bkgnd pixels
    pandn   mm2, mm0        // keep sprite pixels
    por     mm1, mm2        // merge them
    movq    [edi], mm1      // write out

    add     edi, 8          // advance pointers
    add     esi, 8
    dec     ecx
    jnz     DoQWord
    }
}
```

T = transparent pixel

The routine processes 8 contiguous pixels at a time starting from the left-most pixel of a sprite scan line. For each quad word (8 pixels), the routine uses the PCMPEQB instruction to create a transparency mask from the sprite pixels and the transparency color. The PCMPEQB instruction compares the 8 bytes of the sprite with the 8 bytes of the transparency color. For each byte, the result of the comparison is "FF" if the bytes match (these are the transparent pixels) and "0" if they don't match (these are the opaque pixels).

Next the PAND instruction is applied to the newly created mask and the background allowing the background pixels to occupy the space of the transparent pixels in the sprite (the ones that resulted in FF); the other pixels are zero. The PANDN instruction is then used to create a similar pattern for the opaque pixels in the sprite. In this step, the mask is first inverted and then ANDed with the original sprite pixels—this basically clears out the bytes corresponding to the transparent pixels in the sprite. Finally, the last two results are combined together with the POR instruction in order to form the image—the sprite on top of the background.

20.7 MMX Technology Optimization Rules and Penalties

Before we start the analysis of the sample, it would be helpful to go through some of the essential optimization rules and penalties for Pentium processors with MMX technology.

All the general rules that apply to the Pentium and the Pentium Pro processors apply to their counterparts with MMX technology. There are also new rules that only apply to MMX instruction scheduling, as well as associated penalties that go with them. In the following paragraphs, we will discuss MMX instruction pairing and scheduling rules as well as variations from the general Pentium scheduling rules.

Note that although the rules are listed here with minimal explanations of how to apply them, most of the rules will be demonstrated in the section where we apply MMX technology to optimizing the sprite sample. For a complete explanation, refer to the *Intel Architecture Optimization Manual* found on the companion CD.

20.7.1 MMX Exceptions to General Pentium Rules

The Pentium processor with MMX technology relaxed some of the penalties we had to endure with the Pentium processor. The MMX-related rules allow for better performance on both MMX technology and integer applications. See Table 20-2 for a summary of the new rules.

TABLE 20-2 Comparison of Pentium Processor versus Pentium Processor with MMX Technology

On the Pentium Processor	On Pentium with MMX Technology
Two instructions do not pair if either of them is longer than 7 bytes	MMX instructions do not pair if the U pipe instruction is longer than 11 bytes or the V pipe instruction is longer than 7 bytes; note that prefixes are not counted here.
Prefixed instructions are only pairable in the U pipe	Instructions with 0Fh, 66H, or 67H* prefixes are pairable in either pipe. The relaxation of this restriction helps integer, floating-point, and MMX instructions. *All MMX instructions are prefixed with 0Fh.*

* 0Fh: first byte of a 2-byte opcode; 66H: operand size prefix; 67H: address size prefix.

20.7.2 MMX Instruction Pairing Rules

The pairing rules are the internal processor guidelines that must be followed in order to execute two instructions in the same clock: one instruction executes in the U pipe, and the next one executes in the V pipe.

In the previous chapter we examined the general Pentium pairing rules that are used with integer and memory operations. In this chapter, we'll examine the MMX specific pairing rules. You can find a list of the MMX instruction pairing rules in Table 20-3. Each rule is followed by three samples illustrating the application of that rule. Notice that when the pairing rules are violated, the reason for the violation is highlighted in bold for better readability.

TABLE 20-3 MMX Pairing Rules for Pentium with MMX Technology

Pair Rule 1: Two MMX instructions do not pair if they both use the MMX shifter, *(Pack Unpack, Shift instructions)*.						
✗	**Pshlld** mm0, 2 **Packuswb** mm1, mm2	✓	pshlld mm0, 2 pmulhw, mm0, mm2	✓	Pshlld mm0, 2 Movq mm1, mm2	
Pair Rule 2: Two MMX instructions do not pair if they both use the multiplier unit *(pmull, pmulh, pmadd)*.						
✗	**Pmulhw** mm0, mm1 **Pmaddwd** mm2, mm3	✓	pmulhw mm0, mm1 pand mm1, mm2	✓	Pmulhw mm0, mm1 movq mm1, mm2	
Pair Rule 3: An MMX instruction accessing memory or an integer register can only be issued in the U pipe.						
✗	Movq mm0, Mem1 Paddsb mm1, **Mem2**	✗	movq mm1, Mem1 movd mm2, **eax**	✓	movq Mem1, mm0 movq mm2, mm0	
Pair Rule 4: If the U pipe MMX instruction is accessing memory or an integer register, the V pipe instruction must be an MMX instruction in order for the two to pair.						
✗	Movq mm0, Mem1 **inc esi**	✗	movd mm0, Mem1 **add eax, 1**	✓	Movq Mem1, mm0 Pand mm2, mm0	
Pair Rule 5: The MMX destination register of the U pipe should not match the source or destination register of the V pipe *(dependency check)*.						
✗	movq **mm0,** Mem1 movq mm1, **mm0**	✗	pand **mm0,** mm1 movq **mm0,** mm2	✓	Movq mm1, mm2 Pand mm2, mm0	
Pair Rule 6: EMMS is not pairable.						

✓ Pairable
✗ Not Pairable

20.7.3 MMX Instruction Scheduling Rules

The scheduling rules are the internal processor guidelines that indicate the number of clocks it takes to execute certain instructions or when you can perform certain operations. Basically, these rules indicate when the data is ready after certain operations.

You can find a list of MMX instruction scheduling rules in Table 20-4. Study the example at the bottom of each rule to understand the restrictions imposed by the rule. We highlighted the two instructions affected by the

TABLE 20-4 MMX Scheduling Rules

Scheduling Rule 1: MMX instructions take a single clock to execute except for MMX multiply instructions, which take 3 clocks to execute. In other words, multiply instructions require 3 clocks before their data is ready for use. (See the Note on "One Clock MMX Multiply.")

Original Sequence	🕐	Actual Behavior	🕐	Optimized Sequence
Pmulhw mm0, mm1	*1u*	*Pmulhw mm0, mm1*	*1u*	*Pmulhw mm0, mm1*
*Movq mm2, **mm0***	*1v*	*Stall*	*1v*	*Inc esi*
Inc esi	*2u*	*Stall*	*2u*	*Movq mm4, mm1*
Inc edi	*2v*	*Stall*	*2v*	*Inc edi*
Pand mm3, mm1	*3u*	*Stall*	*3u*	*Pand mm3, mm1*
Movq mm4, mm1	*3v*	*Stall*	*3v*	*Dec ecx*
Dec ecx	*4u*	*Movq **mm2, mm0***	*4u*	***Pmulhw mm2,** mm3*
Jnz again	*4v*	*Inc esi, and so forth*	*4v*	*Jnz again*

The second instruction movq mm2, mm0 stalls for 3 clocks before it enters the execution stage because it needs the result of the multiply "mm0". With proper instruction scheduling, you could fill the empty slots with useful instructions.

Scheduling Rule 2: When an MMX register is updated, 1 extra cycle is needed before you can store it to memory or to an integer register; no extra clock is needed if data is moved to an MMX register.

Original Sequence	🕐	Actual Behavior	🕐	Optimized Sequence
Pand mm0, mm1	*1u*	*Pand mm0, mm1*	*1u*	*Pand mm0, mm1*
*movq [esi], **mm0***	*1v*	*Stall*	*1v*	*Add esi, 8*
Movq mm2, mm0	*2u*	*Stall*	*2u*	*Movq mm2, mm0*
Add esi, 8	*2v*	*Stall*	*2v*	*Dec ecx*
Dec ecx	*3u*	*Movq [esi], **mm0***	*3u*	*Movq [esi-8], **mm0***
Pxor mm2, mm1	*3v*	*Movq mm2, mm0*	*3v*	*Pxor mm2, mm1*

Since mm0 was just updated, the memory write instruction MOVQ [ESI], MM0 stalls for 1 extra clock. Notice that, In the optimized sequence, it takes only 1 clock to copy mm0 to another MMX register after the update. This rule applies only to memory or integer register writes.

(Continued)

TABLE 20-4 MMX Scheduling Rules (Continued)

Scheduling Rule 3: No penalty for 0Fh prefix. There's a 2-clock penalty for 66h and *67h* prefixes.
Scheduling Rule 4: The Pentium processor suffers a 1-clock penalty for address resolution (AGI). (Refer to Chapter 19 for a detailed discussion of AGI stalls.)
Scheduling Rule 5: Switching between MMX technology and FP is an expensive task. (Refer to the beginning of this chapter for more information about register aliasing and EMMS.)

rule. In the first column of the table, we show the original sequence of the two instructions (back to back). In the second column we show the actual behavior of the processor when it encounters these two instructions, followed by the number of wasted clocks that result from that arrangement. In the last column, we show an optimized version of the code sequence, in which we rearranged the instructions to fill up the wasted slots.

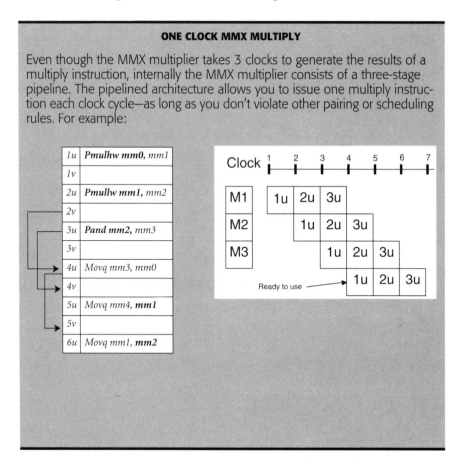

ONE CLOCK MMX MULTIPLY

Even though the MMX multiplier takes 3 clocks to generate the results of a multiply instruction, internally the MMX multiplier consists of a three-stage pipeline. The pipelined architecture allows you to issue one multiply instruction each clock cycle—as long as you don't violate other pairing or scheduling rules. For example:

20.8 Performance Analysis of Our Sprite

Now that you know the essential optimization rules for MMX technology coding, let's have a look at the inner loop of our sprite sample (Table 20-5). As you can see, there are lots of problems here; let's see how to fix them.

Typically, we start the analysis from the first instruction in the loop and try to pair it with another instruction in the sequence according to the pairing and scheduling rules above. If we cannot find an instruction that pairs with the first instruction, we skip it and try to pair the second instruction with the third, and so on, as we saw in the previous chapter.

The original instruction sequence is listed in the first column. The second column shows the number of clock cycles it takes to execute an instruction or an instruction pair. The last column shows our step-by-step analysis of this code sequence.

TABLE 20-5 Nonoptimized MMX Technology Sprite Loop Analysis

Before (9 clocks)	⏱	Analysis Steps
`DoQWord:` `1. MOVQ MM0, [ESI]`	1	• *(1,2) do not pair because they both access memory (PR 3)**
`2. MOVQ MM1, [EDI]` `3. MOVQ MM2, MM3`	1	• *(2,3) pair, since (2) is issued in the U pipe, and (3) is an MMX instruction*
`4. PCMPEQB MM2, MM0`	1	• *(4,5) do not pair because* mm2 *is the destination register and it is used in (5) as a source operand (PR 5)**
`5. PAND MM1, MM2` `6. PANDN MM2, MM0`	1	• *(5,6) pair*
`7. POR MM1, MM2`	1	• *(7,8) do not pair. (8) is an MMX instruction accessing memory (doesn't go in V pipe [PR 3]).*
`8. MOVQ [EDI], MM1`	2	• *(8) has a pipeline stall for one more cycle, since it is writing* mm1 *to memory, and* mm1 *was just updated. (SR 2)**
`9. ADD EDI, 8` `10. ADD ESI, 8`	1	• *pair*
`11. DEC ECX` `12. JNZ DoQWord`	1	• *pair*

* PR stands for "pairing rule"; SR stands for "sheduling rule."

In the second table, Table 20-6, we show an optimized version of the instruction sequence above, where we reordered some of the instructions to fill in the empty slots.

TABLE 20-6 Optimized MMX Technology Sprite Loop Analysis

After (7 clocks)	🕐	Analysis Steps
DoQWord: 1. MOVQ MM0, [ESI] 2. MOVQ MM2, MM3	1	• *pair*
3. MOVQ MM1, [EDI] 4. PCMPEQB MM2, MM0	1	• *pair*
5. PAND MM1, MM2 6. PANDN MM2, MM0	1	• *pair*
7. POR MM1, MM2 8. ADD EDI, 8	1	• *pair*
9. ADD ESI, 8 10. DEC ECX	1	• *pair*
11. MOVQ [EDI-8], MM1	1	• *(11 & 12) don't pair because 11 is writing to memory and 12 is not an MMX instruction (PR 4)**
12. JNZ DoQWord	1	

*PR stands for "pairing rule."

Note that the optimization resulted in a gain of 2 clocks. Pay special attention to the memory transfer instructions (1, 3, and 9 in the optimized loop). The table indicates that these instructions take only 1 or 2 clock cycles to execute. This is true if the address being accessed is in the L1 cache.[3] But if this is not the case, then it would take extra cycles to execute the instructions depending on where the data actually resides (L2 cache, uncached memory, video memory, and so forth).

Let's assume that the background image, pointed to by pDst, resides in video memory. Video memory is typically uncached and has a *very slow access pattern* relative to that of the fast processor. As a result, all reads and writes from/to video memory consume much longer than 1 clock. The 2-clock gain in the optimized sprite loop is very small compared to the time it takes to access video memory. In this case, the sprite sample is said to be I/O bound; that is, the CPU is just waiting for the memory to respond to its requests.

---

3. L1 cache is a small but very fast memory that resides on the processor itself. In contrast, the L2 cache is typically bigger, slower, and resides outside the processor.

Table 20-7 shows measurements of both loops using the internal CPU clock cycle counter. We collected the measurement in eight buckets corresponding to the alignment of the sprite's top-left pixel on the screen. Please note that regardless of the alignment, the optimized version gave a small performance advantage over the nonoptimized version, which is the contribution of the gain of 2 clocks.

TABLE 20-7 Measured Cycle Timing of Both Nonoptimized and Optimized MMX Technology Sprite Loops

Alignment	Nonoptimized		Optimized	
	Clocks/ Sprite	Clocks/ 8 Pixels	Clocks/ Sprite	Clocks/ 8 Pixels
0	110407	159	109732	158
1	180585	260	179676	259
2	180425	260	179558	259
3	180546	260	179487	259
4	150358	217	149725	216
5	185099	267	184392	266
6	185399	267	184364	266
7	185398	267	184277	266

Nonetheless, each loop is consuming more cycles (158–267 clocks) than we expected from the static analysis (7–9 clocks). Again, this increase is attributed to the video memory access time being slow as compared with the processor access time.

Similar to the integer sprite we worked on in the previous chapter, unaligned memory accesses have a dramatic effect on the performance of the sprite. Note that we achieve the best performance when memory accesses are 8-byte aligned. Performance drops significantly when memory accesses are not aligned.

 When we reimplemented the sprite sample to perform aligned memory writes, we received a huge performance gain—the sprite now executes at an average of 160 clocks/8 pixels. You can find the aligned sprite implementation on the companion CD.

20.8.1 MMX versus Integer Implementation of the Sprite

So how does this MMX implementation of the sprite compare to the integer implementation in the previous chapter? Not good! If you recall from the previous chapter, the WriteDWord command of the integer sprite could attain an average of 3 clocks/pixel for a full sprite.[4] This is about seven times faster than the sprite implementation we achieved using MMX technology! Let's have a closer look at the two sprite samples to understand why the difference is so marked and to figure out how to fix it.

The MMX sprite uses a Read/Modify/Write algorithm, which requires two accesses to uncached video memory: one for reading the initial bitmap, and one for writing the final result. The sprite in the previous chapter only accessed video memory once—when it wrote the visible pixels to the screen. The additional read from video memory degrades performance significantly for the MMX sprite.

Apparently, we made the wrong assumption about the location of the background image—it was fine for the integer sprite, but it's not appropriate for the MMX sprite. To speed up access to the background image with MMX, we decided to build the mixed sprite/background in video memory first and then send the mixed result to the screen. The only drawback here is that we have to allocate additional system memory to hold the mixed background.

The result of the new implementation is shown in Table 20-9. WOW, the MMX sprite is now faster than Speedy Gonzales, with an average of *1.7–1.8 clocks/pixel*. By moving the background to system memory, the read and write of the background image worked much faster than it did with the integer sprite—even when the integer sprite uses system memory. You can find a copy of this sample on the companion CD.

TABLE 20-8 Integer versus MMX Sprites Both Overlaid Either in Video or System Memory

Alignment	Integer (clocks/pixel)		MMX (clocks/pixel)	
	Video	**System**	**Video**	**System**
0	2.75	2	20	1.7
1–3	3.25	2.375	32	1.8
4	2.75	2	32	1.8
5–8	3.25	2.375	33	1.8

---

4. *Full Sprite* refers to a sprite that does not have any transparent pixels.

WHAT HAVE YOU LEARNED?

At this point you should have a good idea about the MMX technology, its instruction set, registers, pairing and scheduling rules, and EMMS. You should be able to manually optimize an MMX technology code fragment to obtain best performance.

Another important point to take from this chapter is that it is vital that you know your data. Know where it comes from, and where it goes to. We will talk more about this in the last chapter of this part.

REFERENCES

Intel Corporation. *The Complete Guide to MMX Technology.*

————. *Intel Architecture MMX Technology: Programmer's Reference Manual.*

————. *Intel Architecture MMX Technology: Developer's Manual.*

————. *Intel Architecture Optimization Manual.*

CHAPTER 21

VTune and Other Performance Optimization Tools

Your head must be steaming after reading the last couple of chapters. You're thinking: Boy! I wish there were a better way to optimize my code than this manual, tedious process! You are in luck. This chapter introduces some useful tools you can use to optimize your code for the Pentium processors. In this chapter you will

- become familiar with Intel's Visual Tuning Environment (VTune), which contains a few tools including static and dynamic code analysis, the hot-spot system monitor, and processor event counters;
- analyze the sprite in the MMX example using VTune and compare it to the previous results;
- learn how to count cycles using the internal Time Stamp Counter; and
- learn how to use the PMonitor event counter library to monitor internal processor events such as cache hits, misaligned accesses, and so forth.

You can find an evaluation copy of Intel VTune on the companion CD.

In addition to the scheduling rules discussed earlier, Intel added three programmable performance counters to provide an accurate method for measuring application performance on the Pentium processors. One counter measures the number of clock cycles executed by the processor, and the other two counters measure various internal events such as the number of data reads or writes, L1 cache hit rate, and so forth.

To program events into counters, the processor must be running in privileged level 0 (also known as ring 0). Therefore, you must write a ring 0 driver in order to be able to access these counters from a ring 3 application.

You might be thinking, "It's not enough that I have to remember all of these scheduling rules. Now I have to write a ring 0 driver." But you don't. That's why you're reading this chapter.

In this chapter you will learn about VTune—Intel's Visual Tuning Environment for Windows. With VTune you don't have to memorize the scheduling rules or write a ring 0 driver to access the performance counters. VTune remembers all the pairing and scheduling rules and provides you with a detailed analysis of your code. It can also provide you with a systemwide view of your application using either time-based sampling (TBS) or event-based sampling (EBS). You can accomplish all of this without any modification to your code.

At the end of the chapter we will show you an alternate way of using the Time Stamp Counter and event counter. Unlike VTune, which monitors the entire application, this method allows you to monitor a specific portion of your code.

21.1 Overview of Performance Counters

Before we start with the actual tools, let's have a brief overview of the performance counters. The Pentium performance counters are the best means of getting accurate feedback about your application's performance. They give you insight into how the processor behaves when you run your application.

On a 200 MHz processor, it takes the TSC counter 2,924 years to roll over!

The Pentium processors include a 64-bit Time Stamp Counter (TSC), which counts the number of clocks executed by the processor. When the processor is reset, the TSC starts counting at zero. You can also program an initial value into the counter using the WRMSR instruction, which executes only in ring 0. Once the counter is started, you can sample its value using the RDTSC instruction at all processor privilege levels.

The Pentium processors also include two 40-bit counters (T0 and T1) that can be programmed to monitor various internal processor events that affect application performance. These events can be either *duration* events or *frequency* events. When monitoring duration events, the performance counters measure the *number of cycles while the event was active*. When monitoring frequency events, the event counters measure the *number of times the event occurred*. For a list of the types of events, refer to the *Intel Architecture Optimization Manual* found on the companion CD.

As with the TSC, you can program the event counters with the WRSMR instruction, which executes in ring 0. On the Pentium Pro and Pentium processors with MMX technology, you can read the event counters using the new RDPMC instruction at any privilege level. But on the Pentium processor without MMX technology, you can only use the privileged level instruction RDMSR to sample the event counters at ring 0.

21.2 Introducing VTune

VTune offers an easy-to-use Windows interface that simplifies optimization for the Intel Architecture. It is a collection of both simple and complex optimization methodologies that greatly help developers optimize their code for the Pentium, Pentium Pro, and Pentium with MMX technology processors.

In our discussion we will focus on the various VTune features without going into the details of how to use them. You can find more detail in VTune's online help files.

Let's start with a summary of VTune features and what they are used for. In Table 21-1, we list VTune features with a brief description of each. We also highlight the purposes of the features and how you can benefit from them. You can find out more details about these features later in the chapter.

TABLE 21-1 VTune Feature List

Feature	Description
Static analysis	Analyzes application (.obj, .exe, or .dll) and shows instruction pairing, warnings, and penalties for the selected processor.
	You can use static analysis in the first stage of instruction scheduling. Once you write your application, load the object file into VTune and examine scheduling issues.
Dynamic analysis	You can collect an execution trace of a range of instructions in your application. The execution trace is collected using the dynamic analyzer, and it represents the actual instructions executed. VTune analyzes the execution trace and presents you with a view that shows any potential problems with your application. The dynamic view includes details about BTB prediction, L1 code, and data cache hits, and other dynamic properties.
	You can use dynamic analysis to understand the branch and cache behavior of your application.

(Continued)

TABLE 21-1 VTune Feature List (Continued)

Systemwide monitoring	VTune can monitor all applications, drivers, and operating system components executing in the system. VTune gets control periodically from a timer interrupt (TBS) or from one of the internal event counters (EBS) and saves the instruction pointer where the interrupt occurred. It then displays a graphical view of the modules and their system usage. With systemwide monitoring you can determine which applications are consuming the most processor time or if the processor is idle.
Hot-spot analysis	This tool shows the percentage of CPU time spent executing each hot spot or active function relative to the execute time for the entire application or relative to the entire system. The analysis is based on the samples collected in *systemwide monitoring*. With hot-spot analysis you can zoom in on functions and instructions that take a long time to execute.

21.2.1 VTune Static Analysis

VTune's static analyzer is a smart tool that understands all the timing and scheduling rules of the Pentium processors. Basically, when you use static analysis, VTune analyzes the instructions in your code for pairing information and presents you with a simple view illustrating the results. We went through the tedious process of analyzing code in the last couple of chapters. With VTune you don't have to remember any of the pairing and scheduling rules, AGIs, or the number of micro-op codes per instruction. VTune does it for you.

It is much faster to use *.obj files for static analysis

The static analyzer accepts executable (*.*exe*), object (*.*obj*), and Dynamic Link Library (*.*dll*) files. When you load one of these files, VTune disassembles the instructions in the file and applies the pairing rules to them.

You can see the static analysis view of the nonoptimized MMX sprite from the previous chapter in Figure 21-1. From the static analysis view, you can select the *Source View, Assembly View,* or a mix of both. You can also select which processor to consider for the analysis (Pentium, Pentium Pro, Pentium processor with MMX technology, or Pentium II). In addition, VTune provides an option for *Blended processor* analysis mode; that is where it displays any scheduling issues that affect any of the supported processors.

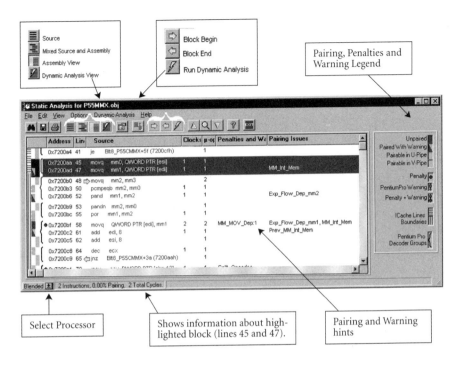

FIGURE 21-1 VTune static analysis view of the MMX sprite.

VTune presents information about each instruction in column format using either symbols, numbers, or descriptive pairing hints. Let's see what each of these columns or symbols mean. In the following table you can find a brief description of the symbols and columns of VTune's analysis view.

TABLE 21-2 VTune Symbols and Column Description

	The instruction is issued in the U pipe, and it did not pair with the next instruction. The reason for not pairing is listed in the *Pairing Issues* column either on this line or the next line.
	This instruction is issued in the U pipe, and it paired with the next instruction. It also has a warning, which is listed in the Penalties and *Warnings* column.
	This instruction is issued in the U pipe and could pair with the next instruction. Note: That this does not mean that it paired with the next instruction; it only means that it is pairable.
	This instruction is issued in the V pipe and pairs with the previous instruction.
	There is a penalty associated with this instruction. The penalty is listed in the *Penalties and Warnings* column

(Continued)

TABLE 21-2 VTune Symbols and Column Description (Continued)

	The warning listed in the *Penalties and Warnings* column affects only the Pentium Pro processors.
	There is a penalty and a warning associated with this instruction. It is listed in the *Penalties and Warnings* column.
	This indicates Instruction Cache Line boundaries. The instruction cache line size is 16 bytes for the Intel 486 and 32 bytes for the Pentium and Pentium Pro processors.
	The instructions included by these braces represent a Pentium Pro decoder group. The Pentium Pro decodes the instructions in a decoder group in 1 clock cycle. A decoder group can include up to three consecutive instructions where the first one is decoded to four or less micro-op codes, and the other two are decoded to one micro-op. This is the "4:1:1" sequence described in the Pentium II processor chapter (Chapter 22).
Address	This column shows the relative address of this instruction.
Line	This column shows the line number of the instruction in the source file.
Source	This column shows the assembly format of the instruction. In the mixed mode, the column shows the source line followed by the assembly instruction.
Clocks	For the Pentium processor, this column indicates the number of clocks it would take to execute this instruction. This, of course, assumes perfect L1 cache.
UOps	For the Pentium Pro processor, this column lists the number of micro-ops this instruction represents.
Penalties and Warnings	This column lists the shorthand explanation of a penalty or a warning. When you double-click the left mouse button on the line, you get more information about the warning.
Pairing Issues	This column lists the shorthand explanation of pairing issues related to this instruction. When you double-click on the line, you get more information about the pairing issue.

Notice that when you highlight a sequence of instructions, VTune displays the total number of cycles and instructions at the bottom status bar. For example, the highlighted instructions at lines (45–47) take 2 cycles to execute, and they have 0 percent pairing rate.

In Figure 21-1, to get more information about the warnings and penalties, you can double-click with the left mouse button on the problematic instruction. VTune pops up another window with more information about the problem (Figure 21-2). You can get even more explanations by selecting the help button ⌗Help⌗ associated with the problem.

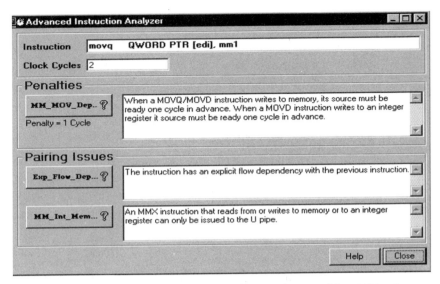

FIGURE 21-2 Explanation of problems on line 58 of the MMX sprite.

Now, let's compare the results of VTune's static analysis of the MMX sprite with our manual analysis in the previous chapter. For your convenience, we have duplicated the table from the previous chapter (Table 20-6). Notice that both methods yield the same number of clocks for each instruction and both reach the same conclusions about scheduling problems. But although it took us half an hour to figure this out, it took VTune less than half a minute to do the same.

TABLE 21-3 Nonoptimized MMX Sprite Manual Analysis

Before (9 clocks)	⏱	Analysis Steps
DoQWord: 1. MOVQ MM0, [ESI]	1	• (1,2) do not pair because they both access memory
2. MOVQ MM1, [EDI] 3. MOVQ MM2, MM3	1	• (2,3) pair, since (2) is issued in the U-Pipe, and (3) is an MMX instruction
4. PCMPEQB MM2, MM0	1	• (4,5) do not pair because mm2 is the destination register and it is used in (5) as a source operand
5. PAND MM1, MM2 6. PANDN MM2, MM0	1	• (5,6) pair
7. POR MM1, MM2	1	• (7,8) do not pair. (8) is MMX instruction accessing memory (doesn't go in V-Pipe).
8. MOVQ [EDI], MM1	2	• (8) has a pipeline stall for one more cycle, since it is writing mm1 to memory, and mm1 was just updated.
9. ADD EDI, 8 10. ADD ESI, 8	1	• pair
11. DEC ECX 12. JNZ DoQWord	1	• pair

PART VI

Let's have another look at the *clocks* column of the static analysis view in Figure 21-1. Notice that VTune assumes that all memory accesses take 1 clock cycle to execute. It also assumes that branch instructions take 1 clock regardless of whether the branch is taken or not. Since these assumptions are not always valid, VTune implements the dynamic analysis feature discussed below.

21.2.2 VTune Dynamic Analysis

Dynamic analysis provides more realistic timing information about your code. With dynamic analysis VTune collects an actual trace of instructions executed in your program and uses this trace for dynamic analysis. Since VTune knows exactly which instructions actually executed, it can provide better information about L1 cache hits, branch timing, and BTB hits.

To use dynamic analysis, you must select a block of instructions to analyze from the static analysis view (lines 48–65 in Figure 21-1). When you run the dynamic analyzer, VTune launches the application and collects a trace of the actual instructions executed within the selected block. When you terminate the application, VTune analyzes the collected trace and displays the result in the dynamic analysis view.

We are not showing the dynamic analysis view since it looks exactly the same as the static analysis view in Figure 21-1. The only difference is that the dynamic view displays the actual instruction pairing and a more realistic clock count. It also displays BTB hits, L1 code and data cache hits, and branch behavior.

In Windows 95, your system might hang if you use VTune dynamic analyzer in the middle of a *DirectDraw Lock* section. DirectDraw holds the *Win16Lock* between DirectDraw Lock and UnLock operations, which prevents VTune from running properly. The *Win16Lock* is a Windows 95 critical section that serializes access to GDI and USER system DLLs. As a result, the *Win16Lock* prevents Windows from running and blocks applications from using GDI or USER DLLs.

21.2.3 Systemwide Monitoring—Time- and Event-Based Sampling

So far, you've optimized your application and salvaged every wasted cycle in it. But do you know how your application behaves from the point of view of the entire system? What if your application calls an operating system or third-party function, do you know how long it takes to execute? Do you know where the CPU spends most of its time? *Simple.* Use VTune.

VTune includes a systemwide *time-* or *event-based sampling* (TBS or EBS) feature, which monitors every running component in the system. This includes operating system drivers (ring 0 and ring 3), DLLs, and other executables. VTune analyzes the time or event samples and presents a *percentage usage summary* for each module in a bar graph format (Figure 21-3).

When TBS monitoring is active, VTune gains control from a *periodic timer interrupt* where it records the instruction pointer (CS:EIP), *process ID,* and *module name* where the interrupt occurred. At the end of the monitoring session, VTune associates the collected pointers with their corresponding module and presents a *percentage usage summary* bar graph. The *y* axis of the bar graph represents the module name, and the *x* axis represents the percentage CPU usage of each module relative to the entire system.

When EBS monitoring is active, VTune gains control from a *performance counter event interrupt* where it records the instruction pointer (CS:EIP), *process ID,* and *module name* where the interrupt occurred. As with TBS, VTune associates the collected addresses with their corresponding module and generates a *percentage occurrence summary* bar graph. The *y*-axis of the bar graph represents the module name, and the *x*-axis represents the percentage of occurrence of that event within modules relative to the entire system.

We have compiled a few hints that are worth knowing about the systemwide monitoring feature in VTune:

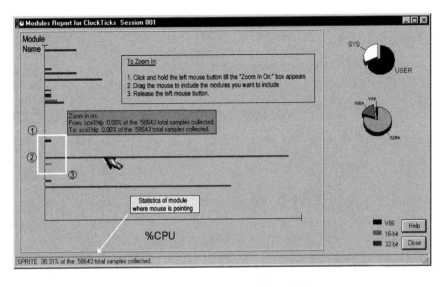

FIGURE 21-3 Systemwide monitoring module usage summary.

- For Pentium processors, you need a special processor socket to use event-based sampling (EBS) with VTune. But you don't require a special socket for the Pentium Pro processors. (Note: For Pentium processors, you can use PMonitor for event monitoring, and no special socket is needed.)

- When the mouse points to a module in the bar graph, VTune displays statistics about that module at the bottom status bar.

- You can pinpoint the amount of time that the operating system is *idle* (not executing any threads or tasks including yours). The VMM module reflects the idle CPU time in Windows 95, and the NTOSKRNL module reflects the idle CPU time in Windows NT.

When you zoom in on a function in one of the modules, VTune displays a time-based analysis view that shows the statistics for each instruction of the MMX sprite (Figure 21-4). When TBS is used, the Time column shows the hit rate of each of the instructions relative to the entire application. A high hit rate indicates that the instruction took a long time to execute.

Pay attention to the highlighted instruction on line 50 Figure 21-4. The Time column indicates that this instruction was executing 71 percent of the time when the timer interrupt occurred. But this is a simple instruction that uses only register operands and should execute in only 1 clock cycle. OK, let's look at the instruction in the previous cycle, specifically on line 47. If you remember from the previous chapter, this instruction reads data from

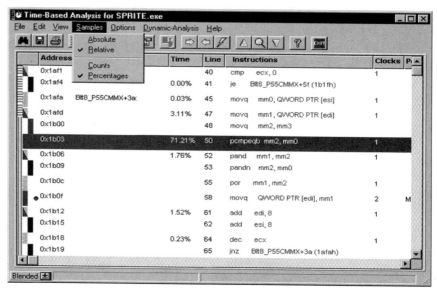

FIGURE 21-4 Time-based analysis view for the MMX sprite.

uncached video memory and takes a long time to execute. So it is likely that this instruction is the culprit spending 71 percent of the time! And it is.

Remember that VTune records the current instruction pointer when the timer interrupt occurs. When the interrupt occurs on line 47, the processor has to finish executing this instruction before it acknowledges the interrupt. But after the processor executes the instructions in lines 47 and 48 (they pair), it advances the instruction pointer to line 50 and then generates the interrupt. As a result, VTune records that line 50 was executing 71 percent of the time when the timer interrupt occurred.

You're thinking, Why doesn't VTune just adjust the instruction pointers to point to the previous instruction (or previous cycle)? VTune does not always know what the previous cycle was. For example, if the timer interrupt occurs in the middle of a branch instruction (CALL, JMP, JCC), the interrupt will occur at the branch target instruction (after it jumps). When VTune gets control, it has no idea that this is a branch target instruction, and if it is, VTune has no idea from where it was called.

USEFUL HINTS WHEN USING VTUNE

- VTune takes a long time to load an executable or a DLL because it analyzes the entire file, and that is a time-consuming process. So during the static analysis phase, you can load just the object file.

- When you run TBS, you need to stop it or set up the timer to stop after a certain time.

21.3 Read Time Stamp Counter

Now, let's see how we can use the Time Stamp Counter to measure a small or large portion of code using the RDTSC instruction. Since MSVC inline assembly does not recognize the RDTSC instruction, we implemented the instruction as an in-line function:

```
// Value returned in EDX:EAX which is the 64bit counter value.
1.    __inline __int64 ReadTimeStampCounter() {
2.    _asm xor eax, eax    // prevent compiler from optimizing around RDTSC.
3.    _asm xor edx, edx
4.    _asm _emit 0x0f
5.    _asm _emit 0x31
6.    }
```

Now you can use the inline *ReadTimeStampCounter()* function to execute the RDTSC instruction. Notice that the RDTSC instruction returns its values in the *eax* and *edx* registers.

```
1.  Function()
2.  {
3.   __int64 qwStart;
4.   __int64 qwElapsedTime = qwStart;      // Force qwStart into L1 Cache
5.
6.   qwStart = ReadTimeStampCounter();
....  Code you want to measure
1.   qwElapsedTime = ReadTimeStampCounter() - qwStart;
2.  }
```

Notice that we read the qwStart variable in line 4 in order to eliminate a cache miss when we fill it with the initial value of the counter. In this case, qwStart was *preallocated* into the L1 cache. We intentionally preallocated qwStart so that we can minimize the side effects of the profiling code and achieve the most accurate results.

Depending on the amount of time it takes for your code to execute, you might want to calibrate the overhead of the RDTSC instruction (found on the CD) and subtract it from the measured time. This is necessary for measuring code fragments that take a small number of cycles to execute. In the following code we show how to calibrate the RDTSC instruction overhead using *CalibrateTimer()*:

```
main() {
    int nOverhead;
    // Invoke it once to bring in the code for the function into the
    // L1 code cache.  Then invoke it with a high counter value so it
    // would calibrate the RDTSC instruction.
    CalibrateTimer(1);
    CalibrateTimer(10000000);
    printf ("Overhead of RDTSC: %d\n", nOverhead);
}

int CalibrateTimer(int nIterations)
{
    __int64 iCounter;
    __int64 iOverhead = iCounter; // Force iCounter into the L1 cache

    // Run a counter loop executing only the RDTSC instruction
    // Figure out how much time that takes.
    iCounter = ReadTimeStampCounter();
```

```
    _asm {
        mov ecx, nIterations
LoopAgain:
        _emit 0x0f
        _emit 0x31
        dec ecx
        jnzLoopAgain
    }

    // Overhead of RDTSC loop
    iOverhead = ReadTimeStampCounter() - iCounter;
    // Now, figure out the loop overhead without the RDTSC instruction
    iCounter = ReadTimeStampCounter();

    _asm {
        mov ecx, nIterations
LoopAgain1:
        dec ecx
        jnzLoopAgain1
    }

    // Overhead of empty loop
    iCounter = ReadTimeStampCounter() - iCounter;

    // Overhead of one RDTSC instruction
    return (int)(iOverhead- iCounter)/ nIterations;
}
```

Again, notice that we called the function twice to avoid any cache misses—once to make sure the function code is loaded into the L1 code cache, and the other time to perform the actual calibration.

21.4 The PMonitor Event Counter Library

With the PMonitor library you can access the event counters from a ring 3 application. Unlike with VTune, you do not need a special socket on your Pentium processor to use PMonitor's event counters. Instead the PMonitor library implements a Windows 95 Virtual Device Driver (VxD), which executes in privileged level 0 to read the event counters.

To use the counters, first you need to program one or both counters with the events that you want to monitor. Once you start the counters, you can sample their values before and after the section of code that you want to measure.

For example, let's use counter 0 to measure the *total number of instructions executed,* and counter 1 to measure the *number of instructions executed* in the V pipe. First let's initialize and start the counters as follows:

```
#include "Dll_If.h"        // PMonitor interface file
main()
{
    struct Pmon32Version Version;

    // Load and initialize the Pmon library
    DWORD dwPmon32Status = Pmon32Init(&Version);

    // Now program the two counters with the required events.
    if (dwPmon32Status == Pmon32_OK) {
        Pmon32Start(
            INST_EXECUTED,          Ring3,   // Counter 0 settings
            INST_EXECUTED_VPIPE,    Ring3    // Counter 1 settings
        );
    }
}
```

First we use *Pmon32Init()* to initialize the PMonitor library and make sure that it loads the VxD successfully. We then request that PMonitor program counter 0 to count the total instructions executed in the user level (ring 3) and counter 1 to count only the instructions executed in the V pipe (also in ring 3). Once the counters are started, we can use them to measure the two events as follows :

```
#include "dll_if.h"       // PMonitor Interface file
#define Get64bit(x) ((__int64 *)&x)[0]

SomeFunction()
{
    struct Pmon32Reply Start, End;

    Pmon32ReadCounters(&Start);
    **** Code To Profile
    Pmon32ReadCounters(&End);

    // Calculate the number of instructions executed.
    __int64 qwTotalInst = Get64bit(End.T0_l) - Get64bit(Start.T0_l);
    __int64 qwPipeInst = Get64bit(End.T1_l) - Get64bit(Start.T1_l);
}
```

Struct PMON32REPLY:
DWORD T0_l; // Counter 0 low
DWORD T0_h; // Counter 0 high
DWORD T1_l; // Counter 1 low
DWORD T1_h; // Counter 1 high
....

Notice that the *Pmon32ReadCounters()* function has a big overhead because it requires two ring transitions[1] to read the event counters—and that work consumes a lot of precious time. On the Pentium Pro and Pentium processors with MMX technology, you can eliminate such overhead by sampling

---

1. *Ring transition* refers to the switch between two privilege levels.

the counters with the new RDPMC instruction. So the above sequence of code can be changed as follows:

```
// Value returned in EDX:EAX which is the 64bit counter value.
__inline __int64 ReadPerformanceMonitorCounter(int nCounter) {
    _asm xor eax, eax          // Prevent compiler from optimizing -
    _asm xor edx, edx          // around RDPMC.
    _asm mov ecx, nCounter     // 0: Counter0, 1:Counter1
    _asm _emit 0x0f            // RDPMC
    _asm _emit 0x33
}

CSprite::Blt()
{
    __int64 qwTotalInst;
    __int64 qwVPipeInst = qwTotalInst;  // force qwTotalInst in L1 Cache.

    qwTotalInst = ReadPerformanceMonitorCounter(0);     // Counter 0
    qwVPipeInst = ReadPerformanceMonitorCounter(1);     // Counter 1

    **** Code To Profile

    // Calculate the number of instructions executed.
    qwTotalInst = ReadPerformanceMonitorCounter(0) - qwTotalInst;
    qwVPipeInst = ReadPerformanceMonitorCounter(1) - qwTotalInst;
}
```

WHAT HAVE YOU LEARNED?

We're positive that you would prefer to remember this chapter over the previous couple of chapters. Here are a few points to carry with you:

- VTune simplifies optimizing applications on the Pentium processors, but it does not do all the work for you.
- Start with static analysis for looking at the initial scheduling of your instructions.
- Use dynamic analysis to verify your scheduling assumptions and to understand branch and L1 cache behavior.
- Use systemwide monitoring and hot-spot view to zoom in on sections of time-consuming functions so you could optimize them if possible.
- To get more control over which pieces of code to profile, add timing code inside your application with TSC and event counters.
- Use PMonitor counters to gauge performance.

CHAPTER 22

The Pentium II Processor

WHY READ THIS CHAPTER?

Are you ready for the latest Intel processor, the Pentium II processor? Do your applications run at their best on this new processor?

By reading this chapter, you will

- learn about the new features of the Pentium II processor and how to optimize your application for them;
- learn how to use Pentium II performance counters to measure various events that affect performance on the processor;
- understand how to properly use the Write Combining memory type to substantially speed up accesses to the video frame buffer and reduce the utilization of the system bus; and
- in the process of optimizing for the Pentium II processor, take a closer look at branch mispredictions, partial register stalls, and the 4:1:1 decoder template.

Simply put, the Pentium II processor is a Pentium Pro processor with MMX technology. In 1996 Intel introduced the Pentium with MMX technology processor, which adds MMX technology to the Pentium family of processors. In the middle of 1997 Intel extended the same technology to the Pentium Pro processor family with the introduction of the Pentium II processor. The Pentium II processor is well suited for both business and multimedia applications.

You may have noticed that we did not discuss the architecture of the Pentium Pro processor. As a matter of fact, since the Pentium II processor is derived from the Pentium Pro processor, any discussion of the Pentium II processor already incorporates the Pentium Pro processor—except for the MMX technology, of course. We'll point out the differences between the two processors early in the chapter.

We start the chapter with an architectural overview of the Pentium II processor, including a brief discussion of the internal operations of the components of the processor. We follow that with a more detailed explanation of each of the processor units and what's important for them to deliver optimal performance. For each unit we will give you a few guidelines or tips that could help you attain optimal performance on the Pentium II processor. If appropriate, we'll also include a list of useful internal event counters and an explanation of how you can use them to gauge the performance of that unit.

Finally, we'll show you how to use the *Write Combining* (WC) memory type[1] to speed up your graphics performance. WC is a new memory type that was first introduced in the Pentium Pro processor and will be widely available on systems using the Pentium II processor.

Wherever appropriate, we advise you to use VTune if we feel that it can help you with performance measurement and analysis. The latest release of Intel's VTune[2] includes support for the Pentium II processor.

22.1 Architectural Overview

As we mentioned earlier, the Pentium II is basically a Pentium Pro processor with MMX technology. The Pentium II processor moved to a twelve-stage pipelined architecture with an out-of-order execution core—as compared to the five-stage pipeline of the Pentium. In addition, the Pentium II processor includes three parallel decoders, five execution ports, a branch target buffer (BTB) with 512 entries, and four 32-byte Write buffers (see Figure 22-1).

---

1. Memory types include cached, uncached, Write Combining, and so forth.

2. We've included a three-month fully functional evaluation copy of VTune on the companion CD.

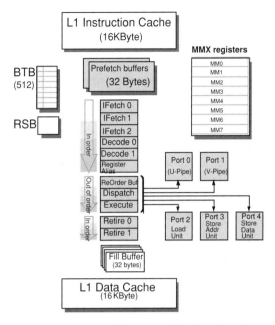

FIGURE 22-1 Architecture of the Pentium II processor.

Similar to the Pentium with MMX technology processor, the Pentium II processor doubled the size of the L1 instruction and data caches to 16K each and added eight MMX registers and a Return Stack Buffer (RSB).

22.1.1 The Life Cycle of an Instruction on the Pentium II

The Pentium II processor fetches instructions in a fashion similar to that of the Pentium processor. It uses the Branch Target Buffer (BTB) to predict branch behavior and prefetches instructions to one of the two 32-byte prefetch buffers.

The Pentium II processor includes three parallel decoders capable of processing up to three instructions in 1 clock cycle. The first one decodes instructions up to four micro-op codes long, and the other two can only decode instructions that are one micro-op long. In addition, the Pentium II processor includes a microcode sequencer that decodes complex instructions that are five or more micro-ops long.

4:1:1 is the preferred decoder sequence.

The Register Allocation Table (RAT) accepts up to six micro-ops from the decoder and posts up to three micro-ops to the Reorder Buffer (ROB; a.k.a. the Reservation Station). For each micro-op, the RAT renames the logical IA-based registers to one of forty internal Pentium Pro registers and inserts them into the ROB. This is where the "out-of-order" processing begins.

PART VI

The Reorder Buffer is the heart of the "out-of-order" execution. The ROB consists of forty "seats" where the micro-ops "hang out" waiting for one of the units to take care of them (they'll be dispatched, executed, or retired).

The dispatch unit determines when a micro-op is ready to execute based on the *readiness* of its data, not on the *order* in which it came in (since this is an out-of-order system). The dispatch unit marks a micro-op as "ready for execution" only when all of its operands are available.

The execution unit looks around the ROB for micro-ops that are ready to execute. Depending on the type of micro-op, one of the five execution ports executes it, marks it as "ready for retirement," and then places it back into the ROB. Note that the execution unit can execute up to five micro-ops in 1 clock cycle.

At this stage, the results of a micro-op are forwarded to other dependent micro-ops in the ROB. Also the results of branch instructions are determined, and if a branch was previously mispredicted, the fetch unit is directed to fetch instructions from the correct address, and all those mispredicted instructions are flushed out of the ROB, RAT, decoder, and fetch unit. In addition, the mispredicted instruction is logged into the BTB for better future branch prediction.

The retirement unit waits for micro-ops that are ready to retire. When a micro-op retires, its result is forwarded to the Memory Order Buffer (MOB), where it gets committed to the IA registers (*eax, ebx,* and so forth), the cache or main memory. The MOB guarantees that the results are committed in the order of the instructions as they came in. The retirement unit can retire up to three micro-ops every clock cycle.

22.1.2 Comparing the Pentium II with the Pentium Pro Processor

Following are the differences between the Pentium II and the Pentium Pro processors:

■ The Pentium II processor adds fifty-seven new MMX instructions and eight MMX registers.

■ The Pentium II doubles the size of the L1 caches to 16K each.

■ The Pentium Pro processor has an on-chip L2 cache, which runs at the speed of the processor core. The Pentium II processor has the L2 cache off the chip, and it runs at one half to one third the speed of the core—the fraction depends on the frequency of the processor.

- Systems with the Pentium II processor have better support for the Write Combining (WC) memory type and thus better access to video frame buffers.

22.1.3 Comparing the Pentium II with the Pentium with MMX Technology Processor

The Pentium II processor has the same support for MMX technology as the Pentium with MMX technology processor. Fortunately, owing to architectural differences in its processor core, the Pentium II processor relaxes some of the scheduling constraints imposed by the Pentium with MMX technology processor. In Table 22-1 the left column lists the MMX scheduling rules of the Pentium with MMX technology scheduling, and the right column specifies whether such a rule applies to the Pentium II processor.

TABLE 22-1 Comparison of the MMX Instruction Scheduling Rules

Pentium with MMX Technology	Pentium II
Two MMX shift or two MMX Multiply instructions cannot execute in the same cycle.	
MMX instructions accessing memory or an integer register can only execute in the U pipe.	Both these rules don't apply to the Pentium II. You need only worry about the 4:1:1 decoder sequence discussed later in this chapter.
If the U pipe MMX instruction accesses memory or an integer register, the V pipe must hold an MMX instruction to pair.	
The destination register of the U pipe instruction should not be accessed from the V pipe instruction.	This rule does not apply here because of the Pentium II's out-of-order execution.

22.2 Instruction and Data Caches

It is important to note the differences in cache architecture between the Pentium II processor and previous processors. As we mentioned earlier, the Pentium II processor doubled the size of the L1 caches (to 16K each) and moved the L2 cache off the chip (running at one half or one third the speed of the core). You might expect that moving the cache off the chip at a fraction of the speed could have a huge negative impact on application performance. Fortunately, doubling the size of the L1 cache positively outweighs the negative effect of moving the L2 cache off the chip.

Except for write misses, the cache behavior of the Pentium II processor is similar to that of the Pentium processor. On a write miss, the Pentium II processor first loads the cache line where the write miss occurred into the

L1 cache, and then it writes the data to the L1 cache. The Pentium processor, in contrast, writes the data through to the L2 cache or main memory without preallocation into the L1 cache.

One of the major enhancements of the Pentium II processor, over the Pentium processor, is that the read operations are nonblocking. As we mentioned in the Pentium chapter, the Pentium processor stalls completely when two back-to-back read misses occur—that is, it stalls until an entire cache line is brought into the L1 cache. The Pentium II processor, on the other hand, allows other micro-ops to execute while it's waiting for data to be brought in to the L1 cache—this improvement is made possible by the out-of-order execution model.

22.2.1 Operational Overview

The L1 cache is on-chip static memory that satisfies internal read/write requests more quickly than an external bus cycle to memory can. In addition, the L1 cache reduces the processor usage of the external bus, thus allowing other devices to move data on the bus—the DMA, bus maters, and so forth.

Similar to the Pentium with MMX technology processor, the Pentium II processor has two independent L1 caches (16K each): one satisfies data accesses, and the other satisfies instruction fetches. The two caches exist on two separate internal buses (each bus is 64 bits wide), which allows the processor to load instructions and data, simultaneously, in the same clock cycle. In contrast, the Intel 486 can only load either data or instructions, not both, at any given moment because both instructions and data have to share the L1 cache.

Both the instruction and data L1 caches are divided into 32-byte cache lines; this is the minimum granularity of the L1 cache. When the processor transfers any amount of data between the L1 cache and the external bus (main memory or the L2 cache), it transfers a minimum of one cache line at a time.

The read behavior of the Pentium II processor is identical to that of the Pentium processor. On a read or write hit, the L1 cache satisfies the request in 1 clock cycle. On a read miss, the processor transfers an entire cache line into the L1 cache. If a multi-byte read crosses a cache line boundary, the next consecutive cache line is also brought into the L1 cache.

But the write miss behavior of the Pentium II processor is different from that of the Pentium processor. On a write miss, the Pentium II processor first loads the entire cache line where the write miss occurred into the L1 cache and then writes the data to the L1 cache. This behavior is useful for applications that exhibit spatial data locality and access more than one element in a cache line—such as applications that involve sequential access of an array or access of local function variables.

22.2.2 Performance Considerations

To put it simply, "Reuse it while it's in the L1 cache." If you have already brought in code or data from main memory to the L1 cache, make sure that you use it while it's still there—before it gets flushed out. Here are a few suggestions on how to get good performance on the Pentium II processor.

- *Keep the size of your inner loops below 16K.* If your most executed loop does not fit in the L1 code cache, the L1 cache will thrash continuously. To fix this problem, you can break the task at hand into smaller tasks with smaller loops that fit within the L1 cache. To find out the size of your loop, you can either look into the map file generated by the linker or use VTune's static analyzer. You should also watch out for in-line macros and functions that, if used often, could bloat your code.

- *Reuse data while it's in the L1 cache.* If possible, operate on the data while it's in the L1 cache—before it gets flushed out. Since multimedia data does not typically fit in the L1 cache, you can operate on some part of the data at one time rather than the full set. For example, instead of decoding the entire video frame in one loop, you can decode the top half of the frame from start to finish and then the bottom half—or whatever part of the frame fits in the L1 cache.

22.3 Instruction Fetch Unit

22.3.1 Operational Overview

The Pentium II processor (Figure 22-2) has an aggressive prefetcher with two 32-byte prefetch buffers that operate in conjunction with the branch target buffer (BTB) to fetch raw opcodes from the L1 cache, L2 cache, or main memory (see section 19.4 for more information about the operation of the BTB).

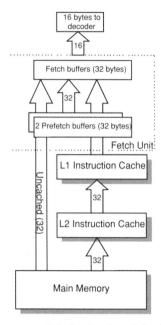

FIGURE 22-2 Pentium II fetch unit.

22.3.2 Performance Considerations

Typically, you do not have to worry about the performance of the fetch unit because the Pentium II processor uses an aggressive prefetcher, deep branch prediction, and has a large L1 instruction cache. The combination of prefetching and branch prediction allows the processor to determine the correct execution path and have instructions ready for execution ahead of time. The larger L1 cache improves the chance of a cache hit when the processor fetches raw opcodes from the L1 cache, which can deliver 32 bytes in 1 clock cycle.

Nonetheless, we've listed a few guidelines that could help you attain optimal performance from the fetch unit point of view:

- *Keep the size of inner loops less than 16K.* If the size of inner loops does not fit in the L1 cache, the cache will thrash. As a result, fetches are satisfied from the L2 cache or main memory, both of which are much slower than the L1 cache. To fix the problem, you can break the task at hand into smaller tasks with smaller loops that fit within the L1 cache. To find out the size of your inner loop, you can either look into the map file generated by the linker or use VTune's static analyzer.

- *Align heavily executed loops and branch and function labels on the 16-byte boundary.* By labels we're referring to the address of the branch when the branch instruction is taken. The idea here is to fill up the execution pipeline quickly after a branch is taken. By aligning the beginning of an execution block on 16-byte boundaries, you guarantee that there will be enough opcodes to feed the three parallel decoders and, hence, quickly fill up the ROB with micro-ops for the execution unit to work on.

- *Avoid interleaving code with data such as jump tables.* Because of aggressive prefetching, the processor could end up decoding data unnecessarily if it is mixed with code.

- *Reduce the number of mispredicted branches.* Mispredicted branches can have a drastic effect on the Pentium II processor because of the deep pipelining architecture: it will take more clocks to propagate new micro-ops to the execution unit. The delay is even worse if the branch target is *not* in the L1 cache—since it takes longer to fetch raw opcodes and thus takes longer to feed the pipeline.

Depending on the state of the processor, the effect of mispredicted branches on the fetch unit could be hidden if the branch target is in the L1 cache. On a mispredicted branch, the entire processor core becomes busy trying to recover from the false branch prediction. If the branch target is in the L1 cache, the fetch unit typically has enough time to fetch the branch target instructions while the rest of the units are busy recovering. But if the target branch is out of the L1 cache, the fetch unit cannot fetch the correct instructions in time to satisfy the other stages of the pipeline, so they just stall.

22.3.3   Fetch Performance with Event Counters

You can use the processor's internal event counters[3] to measure the efficiency of the fetch unit as shown in Table 22-2 and Figure 22-3. In the figure you can see where each of the counters is sampled by the processor. Notice that all instruction fetches or misses represent a 32-byte quantity. For example, the IFU_Fetch counter increments by one every time the fetch unit loads 32 bytes of instructions from anywhere.

You can use these counters to determine how well your critical loops fit in the L1 and L2 caches. The following equations may give you some insight into where the fetch unit is getting its instructions.

$$\text{\% External Fetches (L2 and uncached)} = \frac{\text{IFU\_IFetchMiss}}{\text{IFU\_IFetch}}$$

This percentage gives you an indication of the actual instruction fetches that missed the prefetch buffer and the L1 cache. These unexpected fetches are probably caused by a branch misprediction or an interrupt.

---

3. See Chapter 21 for more about using VTune or PMonitor for event counter measurement.

TABLE 22-2 Pentium II Instruction Fetch Unit Performance Event Counters

Event Counter	Usage
IFU_Fetch	Number of all fetches including cached and uncached fetches.
IFU_Ifetch_Miss	Number of fetch misses that miss the prefetch buffer and the L1 cache. This number also includes uncached fetches.
L2_Ifetch	Number of cached fetches that miss the L1 cache. So this is the number of L2 cache fetches.
BUS_Tran_IFetch	Number of cached fetches that miss the L2 cache. It does not include uncached fetches that always go to the bus.
IFU_Mem_Stall	Number of cycles that the instruction fetch unit is stalled for any reason.

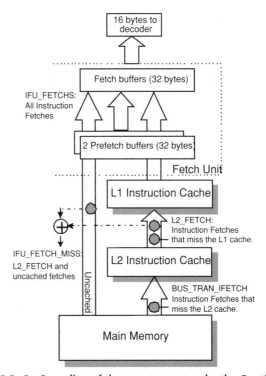

FIGURE 22-3 Sampling of the event counters by the Pentium II processor.

$$\% \text{ External Fetches from L2} = \frac{L2\_IFetch}{IFU\_IFetch}$$

This percentage gives you an indication of the number of "demand fetches" that could not be satisfied from the prefetch buffers or the L1 cache. Notice that this number does not indicate all fetches from L2, only the demand fetches. The fetch unit has a stream buffer that continuously fetches instructions from the L2 cache or main memory to keep the IFU fed properly; this happens during normal operations. Since these fetches do not hinder application performance (they are actually good fetches), they are not counted by the L2_IFetch event counter. This counter only counts instruction fetches that miss the prefetch buffer and the L1 cache, because these fetches affect application performance.

$$\text{\% External Fetches from System Memory} = \frac{\text{BUS\_TranIFetch}}{\text{IFU\_IFetch}}$$

This equation indicates the percentage of fetches that came from the system bus. In this situation the instructions could not be found in either cache or the prefetch buffer. This typically happens with applications executing from uncached memory.

22.4 Branch Prediction and the Branch Target Buffer

22.4.1 Operational Overview

The Pentium II processor features a deep branch prediction mechanism that enables the processor to better predict the outcome of branch instructions. This mechanism employs a Branch Target Buffer (BTB) that can hold up to 512 branch addresses of previously mispredicted branch instructions. (You can find a detailed discussion about branch prediction and the BTB in section 19.4.)

The Pentium II processor has a static prediction algorithm similar to the Pentium processor's with one exception: backward branch instructions that are not in the BTB are predicted as taken in the Pentium II processor; the Pentium processor assumes that all branch instructions not in the BTB are not taken.

22.4.2 Performance Considerations

Branch misprediction is one of the first issues that you should consider when you are optimizing for the Pentium II processor. When a branch is mispredicted, the Pentium II processor has to flush the entire pipeline and start fetching the correct instructions. With a deep pipelining architecture, twelve stages, the new instructions take more clock cycles to propagate from the fetch unit to the execution unit, making branch misprediction more costly than with the Pentium processor, a five-stage processor.

You can determine how long it takes the processor to execute branch instructions, assuming that instruction opcodes are already in the L1 cache. With the exception of backward branches, all branch instructions that are not in the BTB are predicted not taken, *including unconditional branch instructions.*[4] However, backward branch instructions that are not in the BTB are predicted taken. Use Table 22-3 to determine, on average, how many clocks it takes to execute a branch instruction. Notice that the table assumes that the instructions of the correct branch address are already in the L1 code cache. If they aren't, it takes much longer to fetch the instructions from the L2 cache or main memory.

The Pentium exhibits a different behavior for backward branches not found in BTB.

TABLE 22-3 Pentium II Processor Branch Behavior

Predicted	Unconditional (clock cycles)	Conditional (clock cycles)
Correctly	1	1
Incorrectly	6	9–15

Now that you know how the branch prediction unit and the BTB operate, we'll leave you with a few suggestions that could help you minimize branch mispredictions in your code:

■ *Minimize branch misprediction in your code.* You can either use VTune's dynamic analyzer or the performance event counters to pinpoint portions of your code that are highly affected by branch mispredictions. You can then rearrange your code to achieve better branch prediction behavior.

■ *Use Conditional Move* CMOVXX, FCMOVXX *instructions.* If possible, use these instructions to eliminate some of the branches in your application. For example, you can use CMOVZ to eliminate a branch as follows:

```
mov eax, 0           mov eax, 0
dec ecx              dec ecx
jnz  Continue        CMOVZ eax, 1
mov eax, 1
Continue:
```

■ *Try to fit code with high branch misprediction within the L1 cache.* If the correct target branch instructions reside in the L1 cache, the fetch, decode, and RAT units can typically recover from the branch misprediction while the execution unit is still recovering from the misprediction.

---

4. Refer to section 19.4 for more details about branches.

22.4.3 Branch Performance with Event Counters

You can use the Pentium II event counters to determine the behavior of branch instructions within your code. Table 22-4 lists the important event counters for branch prediction.

TABLE 22-4 Event Counters for Fetch Unit Instructions on the Pentium Pro

Event Counter	Usage
BR_Inst_Decoded	Number of branch instruction decoded.
BR_Inst_Retired	Number of branch instructions retired.
BR_BTB_Misses	Number of branch instructions encountered with no history of the branch target address in the BTB.
BR_MissPred_Retired:	Number of branch mispredicted branch instructions that eventually executed and retired.

You can measure the percentage of mispredicted branches in your code as follows:

$$\text{mispredicted branches} = \text{BR\_MissPred\_Retired} / \text{BR\_Inst\_Retired}$$

You will also want to measure the percentage of branch instructions within your code as follows:

$$\text{branch instructions} = \text{BR\_Inst\_Retired} / \text{Inst\_Retired}$$

To get an accurate assessment of your branch misprediction, you must have both values. If the percentage of branch instructions within the code is very small, then the percentage of mispredicted branches is insignificant regardless of how high it is.

22.5 Instruction Decoders

22.5.1 Operational Overview

The Pentium II processor features three parallel instruction decoders that can decode up to three instructions generating up to six micro-ops in 1 clock cycle. The complex decoder processes instructions of four or less micro-ops, and the simple decoders process only instructions of one micro-op (4:1:1 decoder template described below). The micro-code sequencer handles instructions greater than four micro-ops in length. The generated micro-ops are forwarded to the Register Alias Table (RAT) for further processing.

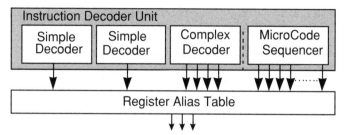

FIGURE 22-4 Instruction decoder.

22.5.2 Performance Considerations

The only thing that you have to worry about, as far as the decoders are concerned, is to apply the 4:1:1 template as often as you can. With the 4:1:1 template, when you schedule your instructions, you need to arrange them such that the first instruction breaks down to four or less micro-ops, and the following two instructions break down to one micro-op each. By repeating this template, you guarantee maximum decoder efficiency. You can easily apply the template with the help of VTune's static analyzer described in the previous chapter. Ideally, the Pentium II processor can decode three instructions every clock cycle. However, in reality, you never sustain this throughput because you cannot always apply the 4:1:1 template or because the decoder stalls from branch misprediction or RAT stalls.

Use the event counters to measure the efficiency of the instruction decoder as follows:

$$\text{Instructions Decoder per clock} = \text{Inst\_Decoded} / \text{Clock Cycles}$$

22.6 Register Alias Table Unit

22.6.1 Operational Overview

Internally, the Pentium II processor has forty virtual registers, which are used to hold the intermediate calculation results. When a new micro-op is decoded, the Register Alias Table (RAT) unit renames the IA register (*eax, ebx,* and so forth) to one of the virtual registers. At any given instance an IA register could be mapped to one or more virtual registers.

How does it work? Consider the following sequence of instructions and their related micro-ops. (Notice that the listed micro-ops are just mnemonics that we made up to illustrate the point.)

The RAT aliases each of the IA registers, *eax* and *edx,* to one of forty internal virtual register *vr1, vr2,* and so forth. Notice that the RAT assigns a new virtual

TABLE 22-5 IA Instructions and Their Related Micro-ops

IA Instruction	IA Instruction Decoded to Micro-op
mov eax, Mem	uLoad vr0:eax, Mem
add edx, eax	uAdd vr1:edx, vr0:eax
mov eax, 12	uLoad vr2:eax, 12
add eax, ecx	uAdd vr2:eax, vr3:ecx
add ecx, edx	uAdd vr3:ecx, vr1:edx

register for the same IA register *only* when the IA instruction is loaded with a new value. If the register is only read from, the last virtual register is used. In our example, the *eax* register is assigned a new virtual register in both instructions 1 and 3 since both instructions load a new value into *eax*. But in instruction 5 the RAT uses the same virtual *vr1:edx* register since the instruction does not load a new value into *edx*; it is a source operand.

Now, let's see what happens to the micro-ops from Table 22-5 once they're handed to the execution unit:

■ In clock 1 the execution unit executes micro-ops 1 and 3—in two different execution ports. Even though both micro-ops write to the same IA register, *eax*, the processor executes the opcodes at the same time since they write to two different virtual registers.

■ In clock 2 the execution unit stalls on micro-ops 2 because of the dependency on the *vr0:eax* register from micro-op 1. But micro-op 4 is ready to execute, so it does—assuming that *vr3:ecx* is ready.

■ Since micro-op 5 depends on the result of micro-op 2, it can only execute after micro-op 2 executes. Micro-op 2 executes whenever the value of *vr0:eax* gets its value from memory. Meanwhile, the execution unit processes other micro-ops that are ready and waiting in the ROB.

So why is register renaming useful? Consider the third micro-op `uLOad vr2:eax, 12`. Without register renaming, the micro-op has to wait for the first two micro-ops to execute before it can execute; of course, micro-op 4 has to wait as well. With register renaming, micro-ops 3 and 4 were able to execute while the processor was loading data from memory.

22.6.2   Performance Considerations

The RAT is affected by one of the major performance bottlenecks in the Pentium II processor—*partial register stalls.* You'll typically notice such stalls when you run Pentium optimized code on the Pentium II processor. Eliminating partial register stalls is one of the *most obvious* and *most rewarding optimizations* you can achieve on the Pentium II processor.

Partial stalls occur when an instruction that writes to an 8- or 16-bit register (*al, ah, ax*) is followed by an instruction that reads a larger set of that same register (*eax*). For example, the Pentium Pro will suffer a partial stall if you write to the *al* or *ah* register and then read the *ax* or *eax* register.

Notice that partial stalls can still occur even if the second instruction does not immediately follow the first instruction. Since partial register stalls could last for more than 7 cycles, on average, you can avoid partial stalls if you separate the two instructions in question by a minimum of 7 cycles. Or you can fix them.

The Pentium II processor implements special cases to eliminate partial stalls in order to simplify the blending of code across processors. In order to eliminate partial stalls, you must insert the SUB or XOR instructions *in front of* the original instruction and clear out the larger register. Figure 22-5 shows all the possibile partial register stalls and which flavor of the XOR or SUB instructions you can use to eliminate such stalls.

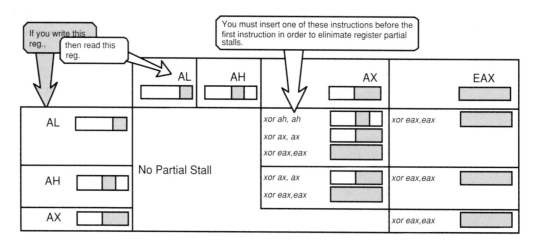

FIGURE 22-5 How to eliminate partial register stalls in the Pentium II processor.

In the three examples we've added the XOR or SUB instructions in front of the original code in order to eliminate partial register stalls.

```
xor ah, ah        sub ax, ax        xor eax, eax
mov al, mem8      mov al, mem8      mov ax, mem16
read ax           read ax           read eax
```

You can use VTune's static analyzer to easily detect partial register stalls in your code. You can also use the Partial_Rat_Stalls event counter to measure the amount of cycles wasted by register partial stalls.

22.7 Reorder Buffer and Execution Units

22.7.1 Operational Overview

The Reorder Buffer (ROB, a.k.a. Reservation Station) is at the heart of the out-of-order execution of the Pentium II processor. The ROB can receive up to three micro-ops from the RAT and can retire up to three micro-ops in one clock cycle. It can hold a maximum of forty micro-ops at any given time. (See Figure 22-6.)

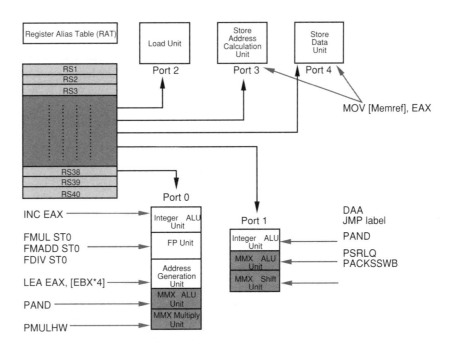

FIGURE 22-6 Pentium II processor Reorder Buffer and the execution unit (port 0–4).

The Pentium II processor implements a data flow machine, which leads to the out-of-order execution. In a data flow machine, the order of execution of micro-ops is determined solely by the readiness of their data, not by the order in which it entered the ROB. Let's see how this model works.

Consider the coined pseudo-code fragment to the left. Assume that only one instruction can execute, and it takes the number of cycles to the right to execute. In a sequential (in-order) processor, it takes the code fragment 8 clocks to execute.

```
                    🕓
1. load    R4, [R1] 4
2. shiftL  R4, 2    1
3. move    R2, R3   1
4. shiftL  R2, 2    1
5. add     R2, R3   1
```

Now, consider a data flow machine where instructions execute based on the availability of their data not on the order in which they appeared. Let's examine what happens every clock cycle:

1. The first instruction starts to execute immediately.
2. The second instruction stalls for the next 3 clocks in the ROB because it needs the value of R4 to execute. Instead, instruction 3 executes (no data dependency).
3. Instruction 4 executes.
4. Instruction 5 executes. Also, R4 value becomes valid.
5. Instruction 2 is now ready to execute, so it does.

As you can see, with out-of-order execution, it only takes 5 clocks to execute compared to 8 clocks for the sequential execution model. Even though the micro-ops were executed out-of-order, the final results are exactly the same because they are written out in the order they came in.

22.7.2   Performance Considerations

As a programmer, you do not have direct control over the operation of the ROB and the execution unit. But you can affect its behavior indirectly based on your understanding of the internal architecture. Here are a few guidelines that could help you maximize the number of executed micro-ops every clock cycle.

- **Blend your instruction types.** The execution unit has five execution ports that can execute up to five micro-ops in 1 clock cycle. To maximize this number, you should use a mix of instructions as much as possible. Avoid clumping the same kind of operations together (back-to-back loads, stores, ALUs).

- **Minimize mispredicted branches and partial stalls.** Both of these are detrimental to the performance of the ROB and the execution units.

■ **Keep your data in the L1 cache.** This allows the load port (2) to bring in the data as fast as possible and in turn avoids data dependency stalls among micro-ops.

22.8 Retirement Unit

The retirement unit accepts up to three micro-ops in 1 clock cycle. It commits the final results to the IA registers or to memory. The retirement unit guarantees that the micro-ops are retired in the order in which they came into the ROB. There is almost nothing that you can do to affect the performance of the retirement unit.

22.9 Rendering Our Sprite on the Pentium II

Now that we know what's important to the Pentium II processor, let's see if our favorite sprite has any problems when it runs on it. This time, however, we'll use VTune to do the analysis.

Figure 22-7 shows the MMX sprite code analyzed for the Pentium II processor using VTune. Notice that, rather than showing the U/V pairing

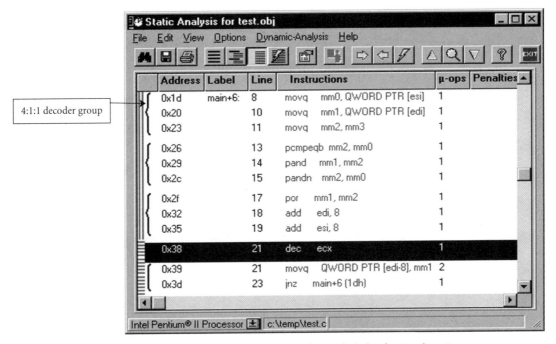

FIGURE 22-7 MMX sprite analysis for the Pentium II processor.

PART VI

columns, VTune shows a "decoder group" column and a micro-op count column. The decoder group column, indicated by the curly bracket "{," indicates when two or three instructions are decoded simultaneously because they adhere to the 4:1:1 decoder template (refer to section 22.5 for more details). In the "μ-ops" column, VTune shows the number of micro-ops that are generated when the instruction is decoded.

In the figure, notice that the highlighted instruction dec ecx was decoded by itself because the instruction sequence does not adhere to the 4:1:1 decoder template. The problem is caused because the movq [edi-8],mm1 consists of two micro-ops and, thus, has to be the first instruction in a decoder group sequence.

You can easily optimize the code for the Pentium II processor by switching the two instructions. In this case, the movq [edi-8], mm1 will be decoded by the complex decoder, and the following two instructions are decoded by the two simple decoders. Figure 22-8 shows the results of optimizing our sprite. Note the differences in Line 21 of the number of micro-ops and the improvement gained.

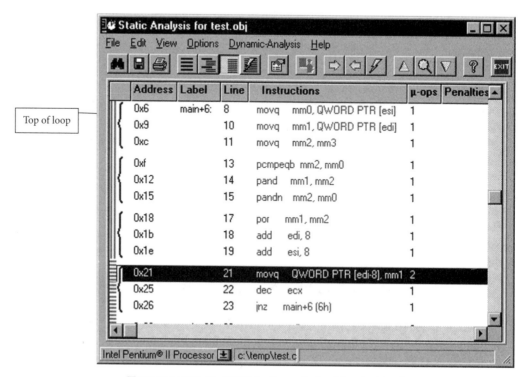

FIGURE 22-8 MMX Sprite optimized for the Pentium II processor.

VTune also warns you about partial register stalls, which are very useful to remove. Typically, you can remove partial register stalls with little or no impact on performance on the Pentium processor.

In the fetch unit section, we recommended that you align loops on a 16-byte boundary. Notice, however, in Figure 22-8, we did not bother to apply our own recommendation: the top of our loop, "main+6:," is not aligned on a 16-byte boundary. Why not? The purpose of that rule was to assure that the decoder would have three instructions to decode when it jumps to the top of the loop; with luck, the three instructions follow the 4:1:1 rule. If you examine the first three instructions in the loop, you'll notice that they fit within a 16-byte block 0x00 to 0x0F. And since the fetch unit forwards 16 bytes at a time to the decoder, the decoder will have three instructions to decode in these 16 bytes.

22.10 Speed Up Graphics Writes with Write Combining

22.10.1   Operational Overview

By the time the Pentium II processor is in the mainstream market, software-only 3D games and high-resolution MPEG2 video will be widely available. Unfortunately, one of the greatest bottlenecks for these applications is the access speed to graphics memory. A typical software only MPEG2 player consumes up to 30 percent of the CPU writing to video memory.

The Pentium II processor implements the Write Combining (WC) memory type[5] in order to accelerate CPU writes to the video frame buffer. The 32-byte buffer *delays* writes on their way to a WC memory region, so applications can write 32 bytes of data to the WC buffer before it bursts them to their final destination. The 32-byte burst writes are faster than individual byte or DWORD writes, and they consume less bandwidth from the system bus.

Typically, the video driver or the BIOS sets up the frame buffer to be WC (similar to the way it is set up now as uncached memory). As usual, you can use DirectDraw to retrieve the address of the frame buffer. Therefore, there is no change required from an application point of view (well, you might want to read on).

---

5. Memory type: These include cached, uncached, WC, and other memory types.

Let's have a closer look at WC and determine how it enhances graphics application performance.

Assume that you are writing a 320×240 image to a WC frame buffer as shown in Figure 22-9. Typically, you would write the pixels from left to right, sequentially, one pixel at a time. For the sake of simplicity, also assume that the address of the frame buffer is aligned on a 32-byte boundary.

When you write the first 32 bytes of line 1 to the frame buffer, those 32 bytes actually end up in the WC buffer rather than in video memory. Once you write byte 33 to the frame buffer, the WC buffer bursts its contents (the first 32 bytes) to video memory and captures the thirty-third byte instead. Similarly, the next 31 bytes are held in the WC buffer until the sixty-fifth byte is written out. The same process repeats for every package of 32 bytes of data aligned on a 32 byte boundary.

So what about the last 32 bytes in the image. How are they flushed out? They are eventually flushed out when you write somewhere else in the video buffer (for example, when your write out the next frame) or when a task switch occurs. Actually, there are plenty of circumstances that cause the WC buffer to be flushed out:

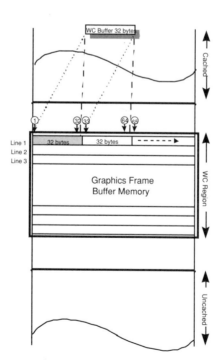

FIGURE 22-9 WC frame buffer.

- Any L1 uncached memory loads or stores (L1 cached loads and stores do not flush the WC buffer).
- Any WC memory loads or WC stores to an address that does not map into the current WC buffer.
- I/O reads or writes.
- Context switches, interrupts, IRET, CPUID, Locked instructions and WBINVD instructions.

Notice that the Pentium II processor generates a 32-byte burst write only if the WC buffer is completely full. Otherwise, it performs multiple smaller writes to the WC region. These multiple writes are still faster than writing to an uncached frame buffer.

22.10.2 Performance Considerations

In short, your WC could enhance your graphics performance if you write your data sequentially to the frame buffer. We have listed the following guidelines to remind you of what you should consider when you optimize for a WC frame buffer.

- Always write sequentially to the frame buffer in order to gain performance from 32-byte WC bursts.
- Avoid writing to the frame buffer vertically. For example, if you write to the first pixel in line 1 then line 2, since the second write does not map to the current WC buffer, the WC buffer (holding only 1 byte) will be flushed out. The same thing happens when you write to line 3, 4, and so forth.

WHAT HAVE YOU LEARNED?

Now you know about the internal units of the Pentium II processor. More importantly, you know what matters to these units so you can get the best performance for your application. As a last reminder:

- Maximize your code execution from the L1 cache,
- Use the new instructions to minimize branches and mispredicted branches.
- Avoid partial stalls. They are deadly.
- Use VTune to analyze performance.
- Use a mix of instructions (loads, stores, ALUs, MMX, and so forth) and apply the 4:1:1 decoder template.
- Use Write Combining to blast your video images to the screen.
- Read the next chapter to familiarize yourself with memory optimization issues.

PART VI

CHAPTER 23

Memory Optimization: Know Your Data

WHY READ THIS CHAPTER?

Throughout this section, we've stressed again and again that you should "know your data," know where it is coming from and know where it is going. We've also stressed that the optimizations for the internal components of the processor are mostly useful if the code or data is already in the L1 cache. It's a nice premise, but that's not always the case.

In this chapter we'll talk about

- how the data behaves away from home: in the L2 cache or main memory;
- how the data moves between the L1, L2, and main memory and what affects the movement of data;
- how to bring the data into the L1 cache and keep it there as long as it's needed; and
- as an added bonus, accesses to video memory, so you can understand how to write effectively to video memory.

As you know, multimedia applications deal with a huge amount of data that changes continuously from one second to the next. For example, a typical MPEG2[1] clip has 30 fps with a frame size of 704 × 480 pixels per frame at an average of 12 bits per pixel. Moreover, since MPEG2 uses bidirectional frame prediction, the size of the working data set[2] is typically three to four

---

1. *MPEG2 is a High Resolution Motion Video Compression Algorithm.*
2. The working data set refers to the maximum size of data that is used by the application at any given moment.

times the size of one frame. Taking all of this into account, you can calculate the size of the working data set for an MPEG2 decoder as follows:

$$\text{Data Set Size} = \frac{4 \text{ frames} * \left(704 * 408 \text{ pixels}\right) * 12 \text{ bits/pixel}}{8 \text{ bits/byte}} = 1.9 \text{ MB}$$

All of these bits definitely do not fit in the L1 cache or even in the L2 cache—the L1 cache is 8 or 16K, and the L2 cache ranges between 256 and 512K. Therefore, at any given moment, the majority of the data resides in main memory rather than in the caches.

The main purpose of this chapter is to emphasize that memory access can be very costly, in terms of clock cycles, and to highlight certain access patterns that are more efficient than others. We'll also point out the differences between the various flavors of the Pentium and Pentium Pro processors with regards to cache and memory behavior. We'll top the chapter off with a brief discussion about accessing video memory.

23.1 Overview of the Memory Subsystem

23.1.1 Architectural Overview

Figure 23-1 shows a simplistic diagram of the memory subsystem for computers with the Pentium II processor. Notice that the L1 code and data caches are internal to the processor and run at the same speed as the core engine. The L2 cache resides on a dedicated L2 bus, external to the processor, and runs at one half to one third the speed of the processor.[3] The memory subsystem is connected to the PCI chip set, which connects the processor to main memory, PCI bus, and other peripheral devices.

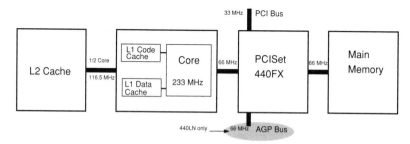

FIGURE 23-1 Memory architecture of a system with the Pentium II processor.

---

3. The fraction of the bus speed depends on the type of L2 cache used and the speed of the processor.

The PCI chip set is the glue logic between the processor, memory, DMA, and the PCI and AGP[4] buses. It manages and controls the traffic between the processor and all of these devices. A dedicated bus connects the system memory to the PCISet. The PCI bus connects the PCISet to I/O adapters, such as graphics, sound, and network cards. The AGP bus is a specialized graphics bus that was designed with 3D acceleration in mind; notice that the 440LX PCISet is the first chip set with the AGP bus.

23.1.2 Memory Pages and Memory Access Patterns

We've mentioned, throughout this section, that the L1 and L2 caches are divided into 32-byte cache lines, which represent the least amount of data that can be transferred between the L1 cache and main memory. For the curious only: you can find out more about the internal architecture of the caches from the Intel manuals (things like two-way and four-way set associate, and so forth).

Internally, the system memory is divided into smaller units called *memory pages*. Memory pages are typically 2K in size and are aligned on a 2K boundary. The only reason we're talking about memory pages here is that because of the design of DRAM chips, certain memory access patterns are more efficient than others. In the discussion that follows, you need to come out with one thing: *consecutive accesses within the same memory page are more efficient than consecutive accesses that cross multiple memory pages.*

In this discussion, we're assuming that the processor missed both the L1 and L2 caches and that it is now fetching data from main memory. As we mentioned earlier, the processor fetches an entire cache at a time from main memory and writes it out to the cache. Since the processor has a 64-bit data bus, it can fetch an entire cache line with *four* bus transactions.

Now, when the processor requests data from main memory, the memory page where the data exists is first "opened"—this is done in the hardware—and then the data is retrieved. Once the page is open, it takes less time to read or write other data to the same page. Typically, the data sheet for the memory chip specifies how long it takes to open the page and perform the first read, and how long it takes to perform subsequent reads once the page is open.

---

4. The Accelerated Graphics Port (AGP) is a specialized graphics bus designed with 3D rendering in mind.

For example, the data sheet of an Enhanced Data Out (EDO) memory chip specifies the sequence {10-2-2-2}{3-2-2-2} where the numbers represent clock cycles. Each curly bracket indicates four bus cycles of 64 bits each—that's one cache line. The first sequence, {10-2-2-2}, specifies the timing if the page is first opened and accessed four times. The second sequence, {3-2-2-2}, specifies the timing if the page was already open and accessed four additional times—that means you did not access any other memory page in between. The last sequence repeats as long as you access memory within the same page. One last thing: only one memory page can be open at any given moment.

The data sheet we have been discussing relates to a memory bus running at 66 MHz. Now, if we look at another processing speed, say a 233-MHz processor, the timing becomes {35-7-7-7}{11-7-7-7} in processor clocks.

Whenever your application jumps to another memory page, the current open page is first closed before opening the new page. As a result, it takes an additional 24 processor clocks to switch between memory pages—that's a lot of processor clocks to waste. So what can you do about it? Maybe nothing! Maybe a lot! The whole point is that you should try to organize your memory footprint in such a way that you bring the data from main memory to the L1 cache in the most efficient manner. For example, if you know that most of your data resides in main memory, for example, MPEG2, you might try to arrange the data in a smarter fashion such that you can burst it to the L1 cache faster.

In MPEG2's motion compensation,[5] for example, you typically access three reference frame buffers and write the output to a fourth buffer or directly to the screen. Typically, when the buffers are allocated, they are allocated in a contiguous fashion, separately, as shown in Figure 23-2.With the allocation scheme shown in Figure 23-2a, when you access the three frames, you'll definitely cross memory page boundaries and thus reduce the overall application performance. Now, if you interleave the frames on a line-by-line boundary, as shown in Figure 23-2b, you'll have a better chance of accessing the three frames from the same memory page, and thus increasing memory access efficiency.

---

5. Motion Compensation is used when inter-frame decoding is used.

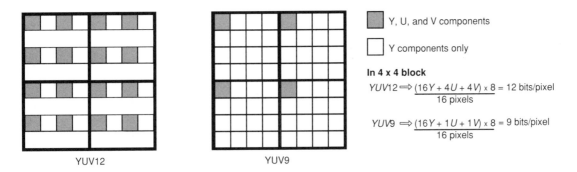

FIGURE 23-2 MPEG2 frame buffer allocation strategy.

23.1.3 Memory Timing

To complete the picture, let's look at a comparison of the L1 and L2 caches and system memory.

TABLE 23-1 Memory Architecture and Timing for a System Using the Pentium II Processor and EDO Memory

Bus	Bus Clocks	CPU Clocks at 233 MHz	Total CPU Clocks (Bandwidth)
L1 cache	{1-1-1-1}	{1-1-1-1}	4 (1864 MB/Second)
L2 cache	{5-1-1-1}	{10-2-2-2}	16 (466 MB/Second)
EDO memory	{10-2-2-2} {3-2-2-2}	{35-7-7-7} {11-7-7-7}	56 (133 MB/Second) 32 (233 MB/Second)
SDRAM	{11-1-1-1} {2-1-1-1}	{39-4-4-4} {7-4-4-4}	51 (146 MB/Second) 19 (392 MB/Second)

Access timing for main memory depends on the type of PCISet and memory used in the system (available types include EDO, FPRAM, SDRAM[6]). SDRAM offers the best access timing because it has a lower repetition[7] rate {11-1-1-1}{2-1-1-1} relative to EDO {10-2-2-2}{3-2-2-2}. But SDRAMs are only supported on systems with the PCISet 440/LX chip set or later.

---

6. EDO: Enhanced Data Out; FPRAM: FastPage RAM; SDRAM: Synchronous DRAM.
7. Repetition rate: the timing for fetching the last 3 quad words in a cache line.

From the CPU point of view, notice that the total number of clocks spent accessing main memory depends on the speed of the processor. Faster processors actually wait more clocks for memory than do slower processors. For example, if a memory chip takes one nanosecond to respond, a processor running at 233 MHz waits 233 clocks before it receives the data, and a 200 MHz processor waits 200 clocks before it gets the same data. Even though both processors waited the same physical time, 1 nanosecond, the faster processor ticked more clocks in that time—and thus it is losing more clocks that could be spent doing something more useful.

23.1.4 Performance Considerations

The Pentium II processor includes event counters that can help you understand the memory footprints of your application. Notice that even though some of these counters are not 100 percent accurate, they can give you a good indication of your application cache and memory behavior.

TABLE 23-2 Pentium II Processor Cache and Bus Performance Event Counters

Event Counter	Usage
DATA_MemRef	All memory accesses including reads and writes to any memory type
L2_LD, L2_ST	Number of data load/store that miss in the L1 data cache and are issued to the L2 cache
L2_LD_Ifetch	All instruction and data load requests that miss the L1 cache and are issued to the L2 cache
L2_Rqsts	All L2 requests including data loads/stores, instruction fetches, and locked accesses
BUS_TranAny	Number of all transactions on the bus
BUS_Tran_BRD	Number of data cache line reads from the bus
BUS_Trans_WB	Number of cache lines evicted from the L2 cache because of conflict with another cache line
BUS_BrdyClocks	Number of clocks when the bus is not idle

Assuming that you can quantify the amount of data that you read and write in a portion of your application, you can derive the following formulas:

$$\text{L1 Data Miss Ratio} = \frac{\text{L2\_LD} + \text{L2\_ST}}{\text{Total Mem Ref}}$$

Since L1 cache misses generate L2 cache accesses, we are using the L2 event counters to quantify the L1 data miss ratio rather than using the DCU (L1) event counters.

$$\text{L2 Data Read Miss Ratio} = \frac{\text{BUS\_TranBRD} - \text{BUS\_TranIFetch}}{\text{Total Mem Ref}}$$

$$\% \text{ L2 Data Requests} = \frac{\text{L2\_LD} + \text{L2\_ST}}{\text{L2\_Rqsts}}$$

The L2 data read miss ratio represents the number of cache line reads or writes that missed the L2 cache and caused a line to be brought in from memory. L2 holds both instruction and data. The *%L2* data requests represent the percentage of data accesses only from L2.

$$\text{Bus Utilization} = \frac{\text{BUS\_BrdyClocks}}{\text{Total Clocks}}$$

$$\% \text{ Bus Data Reads} = \frac{\text{BUS\_TranBRD} - \text{BUS\_TranIFetch}}{\text{BUS\_TranAny}}$$

The Bus Utilization indicates how often the bus is busy moving data around (not idle). This includes all bus transactions whether it's from the CPU or from another bus master, DMA, or another processor.

The *%Bus Data Reads* represents the percentage of the bus used for data reads.

23.2 Architectural Differences among the Pentium and Pentium Pro Processors

To optimize your application for multiple IA processors, you need to pay attention to some of the architectural differences between the Pentium and Pentium Pro processors. For example, there are differences in the behavior of the cache subsystem and the organization of the Write buffers. These architectural differences affect the way you should proceed in optimizing your memory.

23.2.1 Architectural Cache Differences

On Pentium processors, when you write to an address in memory that does not exist in the L1 cache, the data is written directly to the L2 cache without touching the L1 cache. If the data does not exist in the L2 cache, the data is written directly to system memory without touching the L2 cache. This is known as a *Read Allocate Cache.*

Watch out if

■ Only small portion of cache line is touched or

■ Write stride is greater than 32 bytes cache line.

On Pentium Pro processors, if the processor encounters a cache write miss, it first bursts the entire cache line to the L1 cache from main memory or the L2 cache, and then writes the data to the L1. This is known as a *Write Allocate on a Write Cache Miss.* This behavior is typically advantageous since sequential stores in the same cache line are faster because they hit the L1 cache—unlike the Pentium processor where they'll be written through. In addition, when the stores are committed to main memory or the L2 cache, they are committed in one 32-byte burst write, which is faster than individual memory writes—thus reducing overall bus utilization.

The Pentium Pro processor implements a nonblocking cache compared to the Pentium processor, which implements a blocking cache. When the Pentium processor encountered a read miss, first the processor has to satisfy the read before it continues execution at the next instruction. When the Pentium Pro processor encounters a read miss in the L1 cache, it blocks the execution of that specific micro-op and all future micro-ops depending on its results; but it allows other micro-ops to execute and even access data off the L1 cache.

Processors with MMX technology double the size of the L1 cache relative to their non-MMX counterparts. The Pentium and Pentium pro processors include two independent instruction and data L1 caches of 8K each. Processors with MMX technology include two independent instruction and data L1 caches of 16K each.

23.2.2 Write Buffer Differences

Write buffers allow the processor to go on to the next instruction while it is writing data to uncached memory, writing through memory, or when the write misses the L1 cache. Instead of waiting for the write to go all the way to memory, the processor places the data in one of the Write buffers and goes to the next instruction. The Write buffers are flushed out to memory when the data bus is available or on the next write to a full Write buffer.

As we mentioned in the Pentium processor chapter, the Pentium processor has two dedicated 32-bit Write buffers: one for the U pipe and the other for the V pipe. The Pentium processor with MMX technology has four independent 32-bit Write buffers, all of which can be accessed from either pipe.

```
Sequence 1
1.  mov [esi], eax      <- U
2.      inc esi         <- v
3.  mov [edi], ebx      <- U
4.      inc edi         <- v

Sequence 2
1.  mov [esi], eax      <- U
2.      mov [edi], ebx  <- v
3.  inc esi             <- U
4.      inc edi         <- v
```

For higher write performance on the Pentium processor, you should arrange your memory writes through both pipelines, rather than through just one. Consider the first code sequence to the right where instructions 1 and 3 are both issued in the U pipe. When instruction 1 executes, it writes its data into the dedicated U pipe Write buffer, allowing the processor to execute the next instruction. But when instruction 3 executes in the U pipe, the processor stalls until the contents of the U pipe Write buffer are flushed out to memory. Now, if you rearrange the code as shown in Sequence 2 the second write will be issued in the V pipe and will end up in the V pipe's dedicated Write buffer—and the processor can go on to the next instruction in both pipes.

On the Pentium processor with MMX technology, both sequences execute the same since both pipelines can write to any of the four Write buffers.

The Pentium Pro and Pentium II processors implement four independent *32-byte* Write buffers. The Write buffers temporarily hold memory writes until the bus is available. They combine multiple data writes into larger memory writes—up to 32 bytes each—which can be burst to main memory. Typically, you don't have to worry about scheduling instructions for the Write buffers since you cannot easily affect their behavior.

PART VI

23.2.3 Data Controlled Unit Splits on the Pentium Pro Processor

DCU splits happen on Pentium Pro processors *without* MMX technology, when an unaligned access crosses a cache line boundary. On average, the processor takes 9–12 cycles to recover from a DCU split—that is a huge amount of time compared to the 1 cycle that it takes for aligned access.

In addition, Pentium Pro processors *without* MMX technology encounter a similar problem when an unaligned cache access crosses an 8-byte boundary. Such a split imposes a 5–7 clock penalty on the processor.

You can minimize DCU splits by minimizing misaligned memory accesses. You can use the Misalign_MemRef event counter to quantify the amount of DCU splits in your application. Notice that this counter only counts the number of misaligned data memory references that cross an 8-byte boundary rather than all misaligned accesses. Since the other misaligned accesses, DWORDs, for example, do not affect performance, there is no need to count them.

23.2.4 Partial Memory Stalls

The Pentium Pro and Pentium II processors stall when a memory store is followed by a memory load of a different data size or alignment. Notice that this problem is different from but similar to the *partial register stall* problem. When a partial memory stall occurs, the micro-op that wants to load memory has to wait until the micro-op that stored the data retires—and that could take a long time depending on the state of the machine. You can easily avoid such stalls by rewriting the code to avoid the penalty. Even though you might end up with more instructions to execute, the extra instructions can reduce stall time considerably.

In Figure 23-3, you see a list of all the situations in which a partial memory stall can crop up. The highlighted text is a modified sequence of code that will accomplish the same exact thing as the original code, only without the partial memory stall.

👎	`mov      [esi], cx`	16 bit store
	`mov eax, [esi]`	32 bit load
	`mov    eax,      [esi]`	No Partial Memory Stall
👍	`mov      [esi], cx`	
	`mov ax, cx`	
👎	`mov      [esi], ecx`	32 bit store
	`mov eax, [esi+2]`	32 bit load
	`mov eax, [esi+2]`	No Partial Memory Stall
👍	`mov [esi], ecx`	
	`shr ecx, 16`	
	`mov ax, cx`	
👍	`mov [esi], eax`	32 bit store
	`add ebx,[esi]`	32 bit load

`mov      [esi], cx`	16 bit store
`mov eax, [esi+1]`	32 bit load
`mov    eax,      [esi+1]`	No Partial Memory Stall
`mov      [esi], cx`	
`mov al, ch`	
`mov      [esi],eax`	32 bit store
`movq mm0,[esi]`	64 bit load
`mov [esi], eax`	No Partial Memory Stall
`movd mm0, [esi+4]`	
`movd mm1, eax`	
`psllq mm0, 32`	
`por mm0, mm1`	
`movq [esi],mm0`	64 bit store
`pand mm1, [esi]`	64 bit load

FIGURE 23-4 Restarting your code to avoid partial stalls.

23.3 Maximizing Aligned Data and MMX Stack Accesses

You recall, from Chapter 20, that MMX instructions that perform unaligned accesses to video memory execute more slowly than do instructions that perform aligned accesses. Actually, the same concept applies to all types of memory accesses including integer, floating point, and MMX. On an unaligned memory access, the Pentium and Pentium Pro processors split the unaligned memory accesses into 2 bus cycles, causing a slowdown by more than 50 percent.

The Pentium processor takes 3 cycles to execute an unaligned cache access. The Pentium Pro processor wastes 5–7 cycles on unaligned cache accesses that cross a 64-bit boundary and 9–12 cycles on unaligned cache accesses that cross a cache-line boundary (DCU splits).

Unaligned accesses to *uncached* memory are split into two accesses, and the result is degradation of application performance. It's bad enough that uncached memory accesses take a long time to execute; unaligned memory accesses to uncached memory could take double the time to execute and can drastically degrade application performance.

23.3.1 The Pitfalls of Unaligned MMX Stack Access

MMX = __int64:
Compilers align local and global variables according to their types.

Declare MMX variables with the __INT64 TYPE.

One of the common pitfalls in MMX programming is accepting the default compiler alignment for function parameters' variables. When a function is called, the compiler ensures that the function parameters are aligned on a 4-byte boundary, which is not ideal for MMX instruction performance. To remedy this problem, copy any MMX function parameters to local variables and use the local variables instead, as follows:

```
void MMXFunction (
    int iWidth,
    __int64 iColor)                 ◊ Parameter __int64 aligned on 4 byte.
{
    __int64 iColorCopy = iColor;    ◊ Local __int64 aligned on 8 byte.
    -> Use iColorCopy in function
}
```

23.4 Accessing Cached Memory

So what's the moral of the story? Well, there are two: (1) maximize your "good" accesses from the L1 cache; and (2) bring in the data to the L1 cache as fast as possible.

You've already seen what a good cache access can accomplish in the above discussions about aligned accesses, DCU splits, and so forth. You can reap the best benefits of such accesses if you maximize your L1 data accesses.

What do we mean? Let's assume that you want to access a 32-K buffer multiple times within a loop, and you have obeyed all the good access rules above (assuring proper alignment, avoiding DCU splits, and so forth). First, notice that the buffer size is larger than the L1 cache. In this case, if you access the entire buffer on every pass of the loop, when you access the second half of the buffer, the first half will be evicted from the L1 cache. As you restart at the top of the buffer, the first half of the buffer will be brought into the L1 cache, again, and the second half will be evicted. Now, depending on your application, you might be able to avoid thrashing in the L1 cache by breaking the processing of your loop into multiple parts and accessing half of the data at a time.

What about the issue of bursting data from main memory to the L1 cache on the Pentium processor family? As we mentioned in the Pentium processor chapter, it is advantageous to pre-allocate the data specially if you expect back-to-back L1 cache misses or if you will be performing multiple writes to uncached memory (refer to Chapter 19 for more details). But keep in mind that preallocation is useful only if (1) the size of the data set does not fit in the L2 cache (if it does, pre-allocation might actually take more cycles); or (2) you use the majority of the data that you pre-allocate into the L1 cache.

23.5 Writing to Video Memory

23.5.1 Using Aligned Accesses to Video Memory

In Chapter 20, you've seen that unaligned writes to video memory take much longer to execute than do aligned writes. We've repeated the table from that chapter below for your convenience (see Table 23-3).

TABLE 23-3 Measured Cycle Timing of Both Nonoptimized and Optimized MMX Technology Sprite Loops

Alignment	Nonoptimized		Optimized	
	Clocks/ Sprite	Clocks/ 8 pixels	Clocks/ Sprite	Clocks/ 8 pixels
0	**110407**	**159**	**109732**	**158**
1	180585	260	179676	259
2	180425	260	179558	259
3	180546	260	179487	259
4	150358	217	149725	216
5	185099	267	184392	266
6	185399	267	184364	266
7	185398	267	184277	266

Here are the rules: processors with MMX technology achieve the best write bandwidth to video memory if they perform *aligned quad word* write. Processors without MMX technology achieve their best write bandwidth to video memory if they perform *aligned double word* writes. In either case, unaligned memory writes to video memory have a detrimental effect on the bandwidth of writes to video memory.

With the sprite example, we had a choice between making an unaligned access to read the original sprite from system memory or making an unaligned access to write the final result to video memory. Since unaligned accesses to video memory are more costly than unaligned accesses to system memory, we decided to go with the first alternative—ensure that all accesses to video memory are aligned on an 8-byte boundary. With this implementation, we achieved an average time of 160 clocks per quad word, regardless of the location or alignment of the sprite on the screen.

23.5.2 Spacing Out Writes to Video Memory with Write Buffers

The Pentium processor has two Write buffers and the Pentium processor with MMX technology has four Write buffers. Write buffers queue uncached memory writes on their way to memory and allow the processor to continue execution at the next instruction. For more details about these Write buffers, refer to section 23.2.2.

Since there is a limited number of Write buffers, you can easily fill up these buffers if you perform back-to-back writes to video memory, in a bitmap copy, for example. Once the Write buffers are full, the processor stalls on the next video memory write until one of the Write buffers is flushed out. The series of stalls will be repeated for the entire bitmap. As a result, valuable processor cycles are wasted between video memory writes.

Notice that the processor stalls only if you access uncached memory (read or write) or if you encounter an L1 cache miss (read or write). If you can guarantee that all accesses are in the L1 cache or a register, however, you can spare those dead cycles and perform some useful operations in between writes to video memory.

Consider a situation where you manipulate an image in system memory and then copy the result to video memory—for example, a color space conversion routine.[8] In this case, the back-to-back copy of the final image will

---

8. Color space converters are used in video decoders where they convert from the YUV color space preferred by video compression algorithms to the RGB color space.

stall the processor once the Write buffers are full. You can spare those dead cycles if you rearrange the code in such a way that you would perform color conversion in between writes to video memory. From our experience, you actually get the color conversion for free.

Upon a closer analysis of our MMX sprite sample, we found that we are getting the calculations for merging the sprite with the background for free. Moreover, we actually have a few more dead cycles in the loop that we could use to do more, so we did. We decided to add a new effect to the sprite—a bias would be added to the visible pixels of the sprite every time the sprite is updated on the screen.

Notice in the following code that since an MMX register can hold up to 8 packed pixels, we needed to duplicate the bias value in each of the 8 bytes—for example, to add 7 to each pixel, we need to use the value 0×0707070707070707. Even though it is not necessary, we decided to build this packed bias using a few shift and OR operations inside the inner loop rather than using a lookup table, for example. Once the packed bias is ready, we would add it to the sprite before we merge it with the background, as shown in the highlighted code below.

```
DoQWord:
        // build the packed bias...   Assume it is 0x07
        movq    mm5, qwBias          // 0x00000000 00000007

        movq    mm6, mm5
        Psllq   mm5, 8               // 0x00000000 00000700
        por     mm5, mm6             // 0x00000000 00000707

        Movq    mm6, mm5
        Psllq   mm5, 16              // 0x00000000 07070000
        Por     mm5, mm6             // 0x00000000 07070707

        Movq    mm6, mm5
        Psllq   mm5, 32              // 0x07070707 00000000
        Por     mm5, mm6             // 0x07070707 07070707

        movq    mm0, [esi]
        paddb   mm0, mm5             // add it to the sprite

        movq    mm2, mm3
        movq    mm1, [edi]
        pcmpeqb mm2, mm0
        pand    mm1, mm2
        pandn   mm2, mm0
        por     mm1, mm2
        add     edi, 8
        add esi, 8
        dec ecx

        movq    [edi-8], mm1
        jnz     DoQWord
```

When we measured the performance of the code with the new calculations, we got little or no difference in the time it would take to execute this loop.

WHAT HAVE YOU LEARNED?

In this chapter, we examined the issues surrounding the system components, other than the processor, that affect the overall performance of your application. At this stage you should

- have a good understanding of the architecture of the memory subsystem on the PC;
- understand the timing and the internal structure of memory;
- have an idea of the architectural differences between the Pentium and Pentium Pro processor families;
- know how to access both cached and uncached memory types; and
- be able to figure out how to write data to video memory in the most efficient way.

EPILOGUE

The Finale

We've reached the end of the book. We've covered several multimedia architectures including DirectDraw, Direct3D, DirectSound, DirectShow, RDX, RSX, and RealMedia. We've also talked about some of the most recent Intel Architecture processors for the PC. But this is far from the end. Welcome to the treadmill.

In these closing pages, we'd like to touch upon some upcoming areas of development, such as

- the spiral continues: faster processors, tighter multimedia architectures;
- multimedia amidst the Internet explosion;
- cheaper, faster, better 3D;
- multimedia in the home;
- and multimedia conferencing.

We hope you find the years ahead as exciting as we think they will be.

E.1 The Spiral Continues

E.1.1 The Hardware Spiral

Processors have gotten faster and continue to get even faster. It seems that barely a year after the introduction of a processor, it becomes the baseline processor, and a newer, faster processor is introduced. Of late we've begun

RANDY (THE KID) KWONG, A GRESHAM HIGH SCHOOL STUDENT, SURPRISED US WITH HIS SAVOIR-FAIRE.

PART VI

to see multiprocessor systems become popular as server platforms. Before we know it, we may find multiprocessor systems becoming commonplace on our desktops.

Similarly, the entire PC subsystem continues to evolve. It needs to, in order to keep up with the data transfer demands forced by speedier processors and more complex peripherals. In the near future you can expect both a whole slew of new AGP-based multimedia peripherals and other advances in memory architectures.

With new processors, evolved subsystems, and possibly multiprocessor platforms, you will once again be faced with the issues you face today, namely, more power and scalability. We hope that tools like Intel's VTune and NuMega's SoftIce will continue to support optimizing for the new system architectures.

E.1.2   The Software Spiral

Just as the hardware will evolve, so too will the software architectures. Today's architectures for 2D and 3D graphics, video, audio, and spatial audio were developed as individual entities. The DirectX SDK packages these technologies together as a single offering.

Look for future generations of DirectX to improve the integration of the individual components. Also, look for continued merging of other architectures. Take, for example, the recent announcement by Microsoft of its incorporation of Real Networks' Real Media Architecture.

With luck continued advances in these multimedia architectures will support scalability across system architectures.

E.2 Remote Multimedia (a.k.a. Internet Multimedia)

The Internet is everywhere! Everyone is talking about it! Just about everyone wants to get onboard. Yet the Internet hasn't been with us for very long. There's a lot more in store for us. For those who can remember that far back, the Internet's development is probably as exciting as the birth of the PC itself.

E.2.1   Internet Languages

Internet Web pages today are based on static description languages such as HTML or VRML. These languages respond to user interactions with a simple hypertext interface. More sophisticated languages are needed to allow richer responses. Enter Java and VRML 2.0.

Created by Sun Microsystems, the Java programming language is becoming widely accepted as the de facto Internet interactive language. VRML 2.0, based on the Moving Worlds proposal from Silicon Graphics, adds audio and video sources and time and user responses to the static 3D worlds of VRML 1.0. But the cross-platform capabilities and security features of these languages may impose significant performance overhead.

If performance becomes a bottleneck, keep an eye out for alternative Internet programming languages that are tuned to the PC platform. Microsoft's Dynamic HTML, to be released as part of Internet Explorer 4.0, is one such candidate.

The standard Java programming language does not inherently contain rich multimedia constructs. Intel, Sun, and Silicon Graphics have jointly specified Java Media Framework (JMF) for multimedia extensions to Java. Intel will deliver JMF optimized for Intel Architecture platforms; Sun and Silicon Graphics will deliver JMF versions optimized for their respective platforms. In addition, the MPEG committee is working on expanding the scope of the MPEG standard in upcoming versions (MPEG4, MPEG7) to define a multimedia programming language that can be implemented on top of Java.

E.2.2 Multimedia on the Internet

Bringing multimedia to the Internet is not a trivial problem. Bandwidth constraints on today's Internet connections do not allow for rich multimedia. So companies are inventing multimedia technologies tailored for the Internet. For example, Progressive Downloads try to maintain user interest by allowing users to preview partial multimedia data while entire files are being downloaded. Similarly, Progressive 3D Meshes and Multi-Layered video codecs allow data to be authored with many levels of detail: the higher bandwidth the connection, the richer the picture.

Delivering real-time audio and video data across the Internet requires architectures to support streaming data types, to support synchronizing the streams, and to address end-to-end delays for continuous timely delivery. RealNetworks' RealMedia Architecture and Bamba from IBM AlphaWorks are two such architectures. IPIX technology from Interactive Pictures Corporation is another Internet audio/video architecture that provides surround video capabilities. Look for upcoming Internet multimedia architectures to integrate the progressive download solutions with the streaming architectures.

E.2.3 Evolving Hardware for the Internet

Just as software architectures will evolve, so too will the hardware. Hardware providers are aggressively pursuing increased bandwidth channels. Cable, satellite, and 56K modems are technologies targeted to the home and small businesses. Other technologies such as DSL and ADSL are being tested to improve bandwidth to the home over regular phone lines.

This increasing variation of bandwidth capabilities will require Internet content providers to author scalable multimedia content. Similarly, application developers will look for scalability constructs (hardware mechanisms and software APIs) to tailor applications to available bandwidth and effective throughput.

E.2.4 Multimedia Conferencing

Today we have primitive video and audio conferencing over the Internet and over POTS[1] lines. With the better bandwidth capabilities of ISDN, companies like Intel and PictureTel have developed teleconferencing products that deliver better picture quality and a reasonably acceptable user experience. As the Internet pipes to the home get bigger, we'll see similarly improved teleconferencing quality over the Internet.

Teleconferencing applications need teleconferencing APIs, and today's products are based on in-house interfaces. Microsoft has recently introduced NetShow, a conferencing API for Windows 9x, but it is still in its early stages. Look for more comprehensive APIs to support echo cancelation, initiating and responding to calls, packaging and parsing multiple data streams, data sharing, recording a conference, and sharing documents among multiple remote sites.

E.3 Better, Faster, Cheaper 3D

We've seen the first few generations of 3D on the PC, with the initial 3D games, followed by several general-purpose libraries and most recently the first revisions of Microsoft's Direct3D. 3D on the PC has been born, and now for its growth.

---

1. POTS: Plain Old Telephone System.

E.3.1   3D Hardware Spiral

The birth of 3D has fueled the demand for richer, faster 3D through hardware accelerators. A whole slew of 3D hardware products has been introduced recently, including, among others, products based on the Virge family of 3D chips from S3, the 3D RAGE family of 3D chips from ATI, the Vérité family from Rendition, and the Voodoo product line from 3Dfx Interactive.

Early revisions had difficulties with Direct3D support. Look for drivers to deliver improved performance and stability with the upcoming DirectX5 release from Microsoft.

In addition, some second-generation 3D hardware products have been announced. Two announcements of particular interest are the Talisman effort from Microsoft and the Intel740 effort from Intel.

The Talisman effort, spearheaded by Microsoft, is aimed at developing high-performance, high-quality 3D with approximations tailored for the PC environment. Microsoft is developing a full-featured Talisman reference card in conjunction with Philips, Cirrus, SEI, and Fujitsu. De-featured Talisman cards at lower price points will also become available.

The Intel740 effort is a codevelopment of Intel, Lockheed Martin, and Chips and Technologies. The three companies are developing a graphics chip that combines Real 3D technology from Lockheed Martin with 2D and video technology from Chips and Technologies and AGP technology from Intel. Lockheed Martin's Real 3D is also featured in Sega Enterprise's Model 2 and Model 3 arcade platforms.

E.3.2   3D Software Spiral

Once again, just as the hardware evolves, so will the software. DirectX5 offers 3D advances such as the Draw Primitives API to simplify base 3D. Similarly, in response to customer demand, expect improvements in the performance and feature set of Direct3D's Hardware Emulation Layers.

3D APIs and objects have grown based on 3D application needs. With faster computers, the demands will grow, and we will see newer 3D concepts and APIs. For example, traditional polygonal modeling is not well suited for rendering streaky objects like hair. Developers will experiment with software modeling techniques. Techniques that win favor with the development community will probably be implemented in hardware.

E.3.3   3D Scalability

Once again, the hardware and software spiral presents us, developers, with the power-spectrum/scalability problem. In the 3D area, special features are being introduced to control scalability, such as Procedural Textures, Levels of Detail, and Progressive Meshes.

Procedural Textures define textures as parameterized images. The parameters can be varied based on the capabilities of the platform. The more powerful the computer, the richer the textured image. Representations of fire, water, and clouds are examples of some parameterized textures.

Levels of Detail and Progressive Meshes allow a 3D scene to be authored with elaborate detail. On less powerful platforms, details are dropped in order to provide real-time response, although at reduced richness.

E.3.4   Emerging Application Areas

As 3D technologies have progressed, more research is being invested in the application of 3D into emerging areas. One such emerging area is information visualization, which attempts to deal with the problem of parsing through the large quantities of information unleashed upon us by the computer age.

Spotfire, a Data Mining product from the Swedish IVEE Development AB, and various Information Visualization projects in the Civiscape project at MIT's Media Lab are examples of efforts in this field.

Based on visualization research at Xerox PARC, InXight, a Xerox New Enterprise Company, was launched to convert research efforts into usable products. InXight markets an SDK with advanced UI controls such as Hyperbolic Tree, Cone Tree, Table Lens, and Perspective Wall to manipulate large quantities of data.

Look for more advances in 3D user interfaces and 3D controls. From there, it won't take long until 3D creeps into commonplace business and home applications.

E.4 Multimedia in the Home

Electronic mail and browsing for information (surfing the Web) are the primary activities on the Internet today. WebTV seems to be providing a continuation of this model by making it easier to Web-surf in comfort.

Much like the Sega and Nintendo entertainment machines, WebTV uses the TV as a display device for Web-surfing computers. As digital TVs enter the marketplace, we will see more devices using the TV for display purposes. And we will herald a new class of applications to take advantage of the computing power in the home. We will also see applications being developed for electronic commerce, as soon as adequate security mechanisms and APIs are developed.

For the PC to be used as the central compute facility in the home, it will have to be powered on for use by remote devices. Answer: Instant On, a new feature in Windows98, will allow the PC to be "awoken" by peripheral devices even though the PC may seem to be off. For example, an Internet call from the outside can awaken your PC to receive a mail message, or your PC can wake up to act as an Internet answering machine.

Instant On can offer "compute-power" to any smart device. Expect, therefore, a slew of new "peripherals" to control home devices—the VCR, air-conditioning, or the sprinkler. Imagine, calling in on your vacation to turn off that iron!

Obviously all these advances will require new APIs and new communication protocols. More excitement for us programmers.

E.5 Some Web Sites for Further Reading

This Book

http://www.awl.com/cseng/titles/0-201-30944-0

Multimedia Architectures

rdx, rsx, directx, rma, apple

Upcoming 3D Graphics Hardware

http://www.microsoft.com/hwdev/devdes/talis1.HTM
http://www.research.microsoft.com/SIGGRAPH96/Talisman
http://www.intel.com/pressroom/archive/releases/lock.htm
http://www.real3d.com

Current 3D Graphics Hardware

http://www.3dfx.com
http://www.atitech.ca
http://www.diamondmm.com
http://www.s3.com

PART VI

Internet Multimedia

http://www.sdsc.edu/vrml
http://www.alphaworks.ibm.com/formula/bamba
http://www.ipix.com

3D User Interfaces

http://civiscape.media.mit.edu/civiscape
http://www.inxight.com/index.shtml
http://www.ivee.com

Index